D0217620

The Christian College

RenewedMinds

The Christian College

A HISTORY OF PROTESTANT HIGHER EDUCATION IN AMERICA

Second Edition

WILLIAM C. RINGENBERG

Introduction by Mark A. Noll

A RenewedMinds Book

Baker Academic

A Division of Baker Book House Co
Grand Rapids, Michigan 49516

Published by Baker Academic
a division of Baker Book House Company
P.O. Box 6287, Grand Rapids, MI 49516-6287
www.bakeracademic.com

Printed in the United States of America

Library of Congress Cataloging-in-Publication Data
Ringenberg, William C., 1939–
    The Christian college : a history of Protestant higher education in
America / William C. Ringenberg.—2nd ed.
        p.   cm.
    Includes bibliographical references and index.
    ISBN 10: 0-8010-3145-1 (pbk.)
    ISBN 978-0-8010-3145-8 (pbk.)
    1. Church colleges—United States—History. 2. Protestant churches—
United States—History. I. Title.
LC621.R56 2006
378´.0710973—dc22   2005055586

Dedicated to

Those church-related colleges who are earnestly exploring how they might more clearly explain the Christian worldview to their students;

Those Christian college leaders who have worked so faithfully to aid in the recovery of the quality of Christian higher education in the recent past and who wish to assist in finding ways to increase the quantity of students who can experience such an education in the near future; and

Those graduate students who are considering or have already begun careers in Christian higher education.

CONTENTS

PREFACE TO THE SECOND EDITION

The last two decades have been a very good period for the intentionally Christian college. One will recall that the lowest point for Christian higher education had been the 1920 to 1960 era when many of the church-related institutions followed the state universities and elite private institutions in the movement toward secularization (chapter 4). Then after World War II the continuing Christian colleges—most often the least affluent institutions—began to recover slowly. This process of recovery, described in chapter 6 of the original edition, has not only continued since 1984, but it has done so at an accelerated rate, as measured by institutional resources, commitment to a broad learning informed by Christian insights, and general recognition in society. Today the Christian college is the strongest that it has been since at least 1930. Of no less significance is the growing disillusionment within the general academy in the intellectual framework of a rational scientific humanism and the parallel growing interest by college-age youth in seriously exploring the spiritual dimension of human existence.

Even more than was the case in 1984, the book title calls for some explanation. The choice of title is meant to provide definition rather than to suggest exclusion. The Roman Catholic colleges almost invariably refer to themselves as Catholic institutions.[1] Many of the mainline Protestant colleges prefer to be known as church-related or historically church-related; this study gladly wishes to include the latter to the extent that they also wish to be identified with the Christian worldview. This book then is a history of those Christian colleges of the Protestant variety that at any given time have operated with the educational philosophy that the key to understanding the human condition is the idea that God has come to us in Christ.

This 2006 edition is more of an update than a revision of the 1984 edition. The primary changes are an updated introduction; a new preface, chapter, and epilogue; and a set of appendices. This is the second time I have written an update of a historical survey nearly twenty-five years after the original edition.[2] Writing very recent history is quite different from writing the history of the more distant past. An author must place greater reliance upon oral history, normally there are fewer mature historical studies to draw upon,[3] and many of one's conclusions are necessarily more tentative in nature. Of course, one unique advantage in conducting research in the twenty-first century is the efficient assistance of the Internet in locating data and sources.

In the writing of a book as in the living of a life, one receives much help from many people and institutions. The Lilly Endowment and the Council for Christian Colleges & Universities (CCCU) have both played significant roles in the encouragement and support of this present project and in the promotion of Christian higher education in general in recent decades. Many thanks to Chris Coble and Craig Dykstra at Lilly and Bob Andringa, Rich Gathro, Ron Mahurin, Nita Stemmler, and Kimberly Spragg at the CCCU. I am also grateful for the contributions of Robert Hosack and Brian Bolger of Baker Academic in guiding the book through the editorial process. Many people at my home institution of the past generation, Taylor University, have contributed meaningful ideas and resources; they include David Gyertson, Steve Bedi, Jay Kesler, Dwight Jessup, Tom Jones, Dan Bowell, Roger Phillips, JoAnn Cosgrove, Steve Dayton, Gary Friesen, Deb Kim, Skip Trudeau, and Alan Winquist. Among the other scholars who generously shared their knowledge and bibliographical suggestions are Bob Agee, Erich Baumgartner, By Bayliss, Tim Beach-Verhey, Mike Beaty, Bob Benne, Larry Braskamp, Marcia Bunge, Jerry Cain, Joel Carpenter, Michael Cartwright, Kathleen Cummings, Bryant Cureton, Phil Dearborn, David Eller, Tom Englund, Carl Esbeck, Jesse Esbeck, Larry Eskridge, Peg Falls-Corbitt, Jason Ferenzi, Bobby Fong, Jason Fowler, Margaret Franson, Ed Gaffney, Zenas Gerig, Ken Gill, Philip Goff, Mike Hamilton, Jim Heidinger, Richard Hughes, Kota Kath, Tom Kennedy, Stein LaBianca, Gary Land, Tom Lehman, George Marsden, James Earl Massey, Bruce McCracken, Hugh McGuigan, Larry J. McKinney, Steve Moore, Mary Muchiri, Mark Noll, David Osielski, Mel Piehl, Paul Rader, Bernard Richardson, Gordon Ringenberg, John Schmalzbauer, Don Schmeltekopf, Mark Schwehn, Dennis Sheridan, Bob Shuster, Mark Smith, Harvey Stalwick, Russell Staples, Timothy Thyreen, Charles Tidwell, Mary Todd, Mark Tranvik, Will Willimon, Greg Wills, Karen Wood, and David Woodyard. Also, Mark Noll revised his earlier interpretive introduction, Christopher Burns and David Tripple provided research assistance and Tripple wrote the appendix on the international colleges, Neal Friesen transferred the original edition into modern format, and Darlene Jordan typed the manuscript in its many advanced drafts. Finally, I am thankful for the contributions of my wife, Becky Ringenberg, who not only gladly accompanied me on the research trips but also willingly provided countless hours of copyediting and preliminary typing services.

The first edition of the book was published in 1984 by the Christian College Consortium with William B. Eerdmans Publishing Company. I am grateful to Consortium president Thomas Englund as well as the presidents of the member institutions of the Consortium who, in their collective role as the organization's board of directors, have surrendered the original copyright to the Council of Christian Colleges and Universities for the publication of this second edition with Baker Academic. Parts of chapter 7 appeared previously as a review essay in the *Christian Scholar's Review* and are used here by permission. Also, Robert Andringa (appendix A) and Robert Benne together with the William B. Eerdmans Publishing Company[4] (appendix B) have consented to the reproduction here of their helpful summary diagrams.

PREFACE TO THE FIRST EDITION

This work seeks to trace the history of the Protestant college in the United States from its beginning at seventeenth-century Harvard to the present day. Before deciding to undertake this study, I consulted a variety of scholars, asking among other things their judgment on the need for it. Frederick Rudolph, who generally is considered the dean of historians of American higher education, advised: "The idea is a good one. In working on my recent book, *Curriculum: A History of the American Undergraduate Course of Study since 1636,* I ran into nothing that came near being what you have in mind." Additionally, Charles R. Bruning, a Lutheran scholar who has studied extensively the literature in the field of Protestant higher education, observed in his book *Relationships between Church Related Colleges and Their Constituencies* (1975) that "there is no comprehensive history of church-related higher education in the United States."[1]

Lacking a history of the American Protestant college, the continuing Christian colleges are limited in their ability to appreciate fully their own tradition. As Carl Henry wrote, "The problems faced by evangelical colleges . . . increasingly include [that of] the presence of faculty who though competently trained, are not deeply informed in the evangelical heritage because their training was secular."[2] The purposes, then, of this book are both to assist Protestant colleges in increasing their understanding and appreciation of their educational and spiritual heritage and to help fill a void in the historiography of American higher education.

One could use many themes in tracing the history of American higher education (e.g., the increase in the number of colleges and the size of their enrollments as the country expanded westward, the growing democratization of the student bodies, the evolution of the curricula, the growth of the extracurricular, and the increasing role of the state and federal governments). The most significant theme, however, is the changing influence of the Christian worldview in the intellectual life of the colleges.

The founding of private colleges in America has been primarily a Christian endeavor. Religiously motivated individuals and church organizations led in the creation and early operation of nearly all colleges — private and public — before the Civil War and in the great majority of private institutions since 1865. Yet only a minority of these colleges remain avowedly Christian today. Most state universities became largely secularized by 1900; however, not until the twentieth century did the Christian religion lose its dominant intellectual position in those institutions which began as private Protestant colleges. The degree of secularization in the liberal arts colleges has increased steadily since 1900, so that by 1966 the authors of a major study on the small private colleges in America could conclude that "the intellectual presuppositions which actually guide the activities of most church colleges are heavily weighted in the secular direction."[3]

In the 1980s several types of colleges operate as church-related institutions. They include the type which was once in the Protestant camp but is now becoming — or has become — a secular college. The other two major models still wish to be called Protestant; however, theologically one is liberal and the other conservative.

While my attempt in this book is to be as fair as possible in presenting the history of the several varieties of Protestant institutions of higher education, my greatest sympathy is with those institutions which promote an open search for truth (i.e., every question may be asked and every perspective may be analyzed) and which require of the faculties both intellectual competence and Christian commitment. Whether he recognizes it or not, every historian starts from a set of assumptions or values, and from these he tells his story. My assumption is that of the several approaches to Protestant higher education during the last 350 years in America, the orthodox/evangelical model represents the best approach in the search for truth.

Books which are general surveys of a broad topic usually depend heavily upon the work of other scholars, and such is the case with this study. Although I have used college catalogs and other types of primary source material, I have relied for my information primarily upon books and scholarly articles, especially those which discuss in detail a single aspect of the history of Protestant higher education (e.g., curricula, student activities, financial support, religious activities, admission procedures, and academic freedom); studies of higher education among specific groups (e.g., denominations, Bible colleges, women, blacks, fundamentalists); and contemporary studies in the philosophy and practice of higher education. I used histories of specific institutions primarily for the purpose of locating appropriate illustrations of broad trends. The most useful of the many journals and magazines contributing to this study were the *History of Education Quarterly*, the *Harvard Educational Review*, the *Teachers College Record*, the *Journal of Higher Education*, the *College and University Journal*, *Religious*

Education, Liberal Education, School and Society, Christianity Today, and the *Christian Century.*

The majority of the material for this book was obtained through the highly effective Taylor University Inter-library Loan Service. In addition I have worked in the Fort Wayne Public Library, the Library of Congress, and the libraries of Ball State University, Michigan State University, and Wheaton College.

I am indebted to many people for their contributions to this book. David Dickey, Timothy Sutherland, and Lois Weed were unusually generous with their time in bringing books and articles from libraries across the country to Upland where they could be studied conveniently. Gregg Holloway, Jill Lawrence, Deborah Minnick, Alane Messersmith, Alberta Miller, Jo Ellen Nelson, Ruth Osenga, Sherri VanBelkum, and Doris Wallace typed the manuscript. Gregg Holloway prepared the index. Robert C. Andringa, Thomas A. Askew, Randall E. Bell, Lawrence Cremin, John R. Dellenback, Edward E. Dinse, Edward E. Ericson Jr., Gary Greinke, Arthur F. Holmes, Roger L. Jenkinson, Carl Lundquist, Robert W. Lynn, David O. Moberg, Tom Mullen, Edward M. Panosian, Charles Ramsay, Milo A. Rediger, Loyal R. Ringenberg, Douglas Sloan, Richard Solberg, John W. Snyder, W. Richard Stephens, Kenneth D. Swan, Gerald C. Tiffin, D. Elton Trueblood, Arthur L. Walker, and Alan H. Winquist shared helpful insights, bibliographical suggestions, and encouragement. Also, much earlier, Robert H. Ferrell and Harry J. Brown provided instruction and inspiration in historical inquiry and literary expression for which I will be forever grateful. Harold Z. Snyder, who in many ways is a wise steward in support of Christian higher education, provided financial assistance for much of the research expenses; and a grant from the Institute for Advanced Christian Studies and a Taylor University sabbatical leave allowed time to devote to the project.

I owe a special word of appreciation to Mark A. Noll, author of the introductory essay. To an unusual degree he possesses an informed and sympathetic understanding of the history of Christian higher education and a willingness to help promote such understanding. His is no ordinary introduction. He correctly identifies this work as a general history of the Protestant college; then, after he calls for scholars to use it as a foundation for preparing more specialized studies, he responds to his own call by presenting a concise intellectual history of the Christian college. His introduction, therefore, provides both a conceptual framework for the general institutional history which follows and an exemplary model for the specialized studies he encourages.

Parts of the book appeared previously in article form in *Christianity*

Today, the *Mennonite Quarterly Review, Michigan History,* and the *Taylor Magazine,* and are reprinted here by permission.

Finally, let me add a technical explanation. Many colleges currently carry different names from those with which they began. My usual practice, unless noted otherwise, has been to identify an institution by its present name.

INTRODUCTION

The Christian Colleges and American Intellectual Traditions

Mark A. Noll

When in 1984 William Ringenberg published *The Christian College: A History of Protestant Higher Education in America*, I was pleased to offer an introductory intellectual history to complement his extensive and well-researched institutional and social history. Now that Professor Ringenberg has prepared a thoroughly updated edition of his valuable book, I am glad for the chance to prepare a revised version of my earlier introduction.

In preparing this revision, I have made some abridgments and quite a few minor changes of wording and emphasis. Yet since my general conclusions about the subject remain pretty much as they were, I have not introduced major changes. Footnotes have been omitted. But readers who wish full attention to the matters discussed here may find such discussion in a number of outstanding books that have appeared since 1984. As a very abbreviated list, they include Louise L. Stevenson, *Scholarly Means to Evangelical Ends: The New Haven Scholars and the Transformation of Higher Learning in America, 1830–1890* (Johns Hopkins University Press, 1986); Michael James Lacey, ed., *Religion and Twentieth-Century American Intellectual Life* (Cambridge University Press, 1989); George M. Marsden and Bradley J. Longfield, eds., *The Secularization of the Academy* (Oxford University Press, 1992); George M. Marsden, *The Soul of the American University: From Protestant Establishment to Established Nonbelief* (Oxford University Press, 1994); William M. Shea and Peter A. Huff, eds., *Knowledge and Belief in America: Enlightenment Traditions and Modern Religious Thought* (Cambridge University Press, 1995); Bruce Kuklick, *A History of Philosophy in America, 1720–2000* (Oxford University Press, 2001); J. David Hoeveler, *Creating the American Mind: Intellect and Politics in the Colonial Colleges* (Rowman & Littlefield, 2002); and Elizabeth Fox-Genovese and Eugene D.

Genovese, *The Mind of the Master Class* (Cambridge University Press, 2005).

For the very curious who would like even more of my opinions on these subjects, a précis of much that appeared in the original introduction was published as "Christian Thinking and the Rise of the American University," *Christian Scholar's Review* 9 (1979): 3–16. I have expanded some of the themes taken up by this introduction in later books, including *Princeton and the Republic, 1768–1822* (Princeton University Press, 1989); *The Scandal of the Evangelical Mind* (Eerdmans, 1994); and *America's God, from Jonathan Edwards to Abraham Lincoln* (Oxford University Press, 2002). In the last of these books appears a much better accounting of "The Second Great Awakening" than I provide in this introduction.

The most important thing to stress about this new edition, however, is the same that needed to be stressed in 1984. Whatever one may think of my appetizer, William Ringenberg has prepared the hearty main course that will provide readers with their primary intellectual nourishment.

Christian higher education in America has passed through several distinct stages, with alternating periods of stability and change. These stages have reflected the developing nature of America's religious and intellectual culture. To understand especially how Christian colleges have promoted Christian worldviews, it is helpful to have a sketch of the historical terrain. Before roughly 1925, it is clear that American Christian thinking experienced two long and relatively stable periods of synthesis and two great and tumultuous periods of transition. Since 1925 the picture is not as clear, but even in more recent times it is possible to note some general tendencies.

The Puritan worldview provided the first relatively stable period of American Christian higher education. For the sake of convenience, we can date the prominence of this perspective from the founding of Harvard College in 1636 to the death of Jonathan Edwards in 1758. Then from about the mid-eighteenth century to the period of the Second Great Awakening (roughly 1795–1820), great changes took place in American society, affecting not least the nature of Christian thought. This transitional period was succeeded by another relatively stable time stretching from the Second Great Awakening to the beginning of the academic revolution that created the modern American university (1869 and 1876 are both useful chronological pegs at the end of this stable period, the first being the year when Charles Eliot began his momentous tenure as president of Harvard, the second being the year in which Johns Hopkins University began operation as a graduate school based on the German model). From that time until early in the twentieth century (the Scopes Trial over evolution in 1925 is another convenient date), there was once again a great tumult in American thought and religion that profoundly affected the shape of education generally and Christian higher education particularly. Since 1925 several forces have been at work within the thinking of theologically conservative Protestants. One effort seeks to roll back the clock to the early nineteenth century (i.e., to deny or repudiate the great changes at the end of the century). We might call that effort "fundamentalism." Another effort attempts to incorporate some of the ideas set in motion during the late nineteenth century into a Christian picture of the world. We might call that effort "evangelicalism."

These very general chronological divisions beg to be clarified. Each of the stages in American Christian thinking witnessed the development of complex intellectual problems. Each of these developments, in turn, had major implications for the shape of Christian higher education. And each contributed significantly to the present issues facing those who desire to develop Christian higher education appropriate for both modern culture and the students at Christian colleges.

Puritanism

The Puritans remain an object of discomfort for modern Americans, Christians no less than secularists. Some of this discomfort is warranted, for these energetic and sober Englishmen who set out to tame "the howling wilderness" could be an intimidating group. They would tolerate few concessions to human weakness and precious few alternatives when considering the path to the "city on a hill."

At least for modern believers concerned about the life of the mind, however, the Puritans deserve considerable praise. They remain, more than two centuries after the passing of their communities, still the only significant group of theologically conservative Protestants in American history who attempted both a Christian and an academic reconstruction of formal thought. Their colleges, of which seventeenth-century Harvard was most representative, were the most self-conscious practitioners of the integration of faith, life, and learning in the history of Christian higher education in America.

The magnitude of the Puritans' accomplishment is suggested by the breadth of their reforming interest. This included not only the spiritual renovation of individuals and the systematic renewal of church and society, but also the reconstruction of the mind. Drawing upon ideas of covenant, which they traced back to Scripture but which also reflected the creative jurisprudence of Elizabethan England, the Puritans formulated relatively sophisticated theories of political and social cohesion. More than simple piety knit the Puritans together who ventured into the New World during the 1630s. Their covenantal theology, extrapolated into theories of church, state, and society, provided a potent intellectual balance to what Oliver Cromwell once called "the heart of the matter," the soul's personal attachment to God. To be sure, Puritan theories of social order were not overly successful: England's "Puritan Revolution" lasted less than two decades and came to an end conclusively with the restoration of the monarchy in 1660; America's "Holy Commonwealths" in Massachusetts and Connecticut exchanged Puritan piety for Yankee profitability before a century had gone by in the New World. Yet the very presence of these experiments, not to speak of the lingering impact that so many Puritan ideas have exerted in America, distinguishes Puritan educational effort as a rare commodity in American history.

Puritan thought was also notable for its explorations in psychology and rhetoric. Its emphasis on conversion, witnessed in diaries, sermons, and formal treatises, went much further than either Luther or Calvin had gone in charting the migration of a soul from darkness to light. So careful could this reflection become, as illustrated in the diaries of Thomas Shepard or the sermons of Thomas Hooker and John Cotton, that later revivalistic and evangelistic thinking since the seventeenth century has amounted to little more than abridgments, popularizations, or simplifications of the Puritan standard. Puritans reflected with similar seriousness on the style of public speech appropriate to their messages. The development of the "plain style" sermon and the other forms of direct public address that the Puritan sermon encouraged was a result of self-conscious strategy. Rhetorical analysis, in this rare case, preceded argumentative speech. Even more rare was the fact that Puritans designed this rhetorical style to meet the needs of their larger commitments, rather than letting instances of rhetorical success dictate the shape of the larger commitments.

The Puritan intellectual tradition reached its culmination in Jonathan Edwards (1703–58), who faced a more difficult task than had Puritans a century before. By the early eighteenth century, a new form of ethics had emerged in the Western world that grounded virtue in the state of the inner being much as Puritan ethics had also done. This "new moral philosophy" differed from Puritanism, however, in its assertion that people possessed by nature the capacity to nurture goodness. For the Cambridge Platonist Henry More (1614–87), the British sentimentalist Lord Shaftesbury (1671–1713), and the Scottish moral philosopher Francis Hutcheson (1694–1746) there was no need for the specific activity of God's grace to prepare the heart for virtuous behavior. Edwards, consequently, was faced with the task of defending a volitional and affectional ethics against the older Aristotelian legacy and a Reformed and Augustinian theology against his era's new moral philosophy.

Edwards's treatise, *The Nature of True Virtue* (published posthumously in 1765), was his major attempt at performing this task. In this book Edwards praised the new moral philosophers for certain aspects of their work. On the basis of a belief in common grace, Edwards held that natural conscience did possess a prudential value for regulating conduct, that sentiments of beauty provided insights into the nature of morality, that pity and familial affection helped stabilize society, and that the natural "moral sense" revealed some truths about the world. Edwards went on to assert, however, that these useful products of natural virtue fell far short of true virtue, which had its basis only in the saving grace of God. "Nothing is of the nature of true virtue," Edwards wrote, "in which God is not the first and the last."

Edwards's work did not convince everyone who read it in his day, nor has it ever enjoyed widespread approbation in American intellectual history. Nevertheless, modern evangelicals should be impressed with Edwards's effort, even if they may not approve its specific details. Modern Christian academics especially ought to be able to learn valuable lessons from Edwards as they plan their own strategies for effective use of learning. The importance of Edwards lies in the example he set by carefully dissecting and analyzing the intellectual discoveries, assumptions, and reflexes of his age. Edwards not only possessed a strong belief in God's particular grace, he also respected the wisdom that God had given to believers and nonbelievers alike. He thus studied very carefully not just the spokesmen for his own basically Puritan positions, but also Locke, Newton, the philosophers Samuel Clarke, Shaftesbury, and Hutcheson, and many more beside. In fact, Edwards's ability to mount effective counterarguments against the "new moral philosophy" depended upon his capacity to take the best thinkers of his day with utter seriousness. For Edwards, total dependence upon the Holy Spirit pushed him toward contemporary intellectuals, not away from them.

Edwards was virtually the last of his breed. After his time, even the best American Christian thinkers gave in readily to the idea that people possessed by nature the mental capacities necessary to understand the deepest secrets of the world and the moral ability required to act in accordance with conscience or the demands of the gospel. Yet even though Edwards had few heirs, his efforts deserve attention from those in our day who labor in Christian higher education. They hold up the vision of a Christian education at once open to the world's finest wisdom and fully consistent with biblical orthodoxy.

Before the changes of the mid-eighteenth century, the earliest American colleges had done their part in promoting the Puritan intellectual synthesis. College authorities assumed that students would matriculate with a full knowledge of Scripture, which then would mark the conceptual boundaries of collegiate instruction. At least until the tumults of the colonial Great Awakening in the 1740s made officials skeptical about "enthusiastic" religion, they encouraged students to seek conversion. In addition, they provided instructional materials from the Reformed communities of England and the continent that depicted education as a practical service to God. They encouraged students to master the classical European curriculum (especially the grammar, rhetoric, and dialectic of the traditional university) because they regarded this curriculum as the distillation of the common grace that God had given to the ancients. But college authorities also taught the students that the classics could not provide the essential orientation to the world that came by God's grace alone. A student, in the words of Harvard's earliest set of "Rules, and Precepts," was to "be plainly instructed, and earnestly pressed to consider well, the main end of his life and studies is, to know God and Jesus Christ which is eternal life . . . and therefore to lay Christ in the bottom, as the only foundation of all sound knowledge and Learning." The result was wholistic education that gave nature its due while reserving the essential framework, in both personal lives and academic instruction, for grace.

The Revolutionary Generation

From the end of the French and Indian War in 1763 to well beyond the start of the next century, America's cultural values were in flux. Within the space of a half century, Americans threw over the rule of the world's most powerful nation. They dallied with several forms of the European Enlightenment before coming to embrace a conservative expression of that great movement. They embarked on a love affair with the idea of liberty that had both bracing and unsettling consequences. And they reestablished Christian thinking and the churches on new foundations. It is hardly surprising that in this rapid realignment of values, the nature of instruction at the country's colleges, and the colleges themselves, also changed dramatically.

The ideology that lay behind the War for Independence certainly played an important part in the change. Stress on the corruption of the Old World, insistence upon "natural rights" in the face of Parliament's "tyranny," and a vision of history as a never-ending struggle between forces of oppression and freedom shaped perceptions not only for politics but for every sphere of American life. Thus, upstart religious bodies broke from the settled traditions of established denominations, the older denominations themselves were forced to reconstitute on American principles, formerly respected professions like the law came under attack as unjustly privileged sanctums, and politicians began to make much of "the people." In general, the forces that led both to "the age of the common man" and to the Civil War were set in motion.

A Christian-Cultural Synthesis

In the years between America's War for Independence (1776–83) and the American Civil War (1861–65), Protestant values and the values of American public life joined in a powerful cultural synthesis. The Revolution had brought the United States into existence; its ideology of liberty provided a powerful impetus for constructing a new nation. Similarly, the Second Great Awakening witnessed the conversion of many people; its twin engines of evangelism and reform also offered means to reconstruct society. When these two influences came together—as they did so clearly for the great revivalists such as Charles G. Finney, the great reformers such as abolitionist Theodore Dwight Weld, the great organizers such as Lyman Beecher, the great educators such as Noah Webster, and the great politicians such as Abraham Lincoln—the result was a singularly powerful set of cultural values that decisively shaped the character of America's Christian higher education.

Three central beliefs governed the synthesis. Antebellum America believed in America itself, it believed in individual freedom, and it believed in what could be called Protestant Newtonian philosophy. The belief in America is evident most clearly from a northern perspective during the years immediately before the Civil War. For many in both North and South, this struggle brought together reform, millennialism, and the sense of America's unique destiny under God. For northerners the preservation of the union meant no less than breathing life into Manifest Destiny, overcoming slavery (the greatest evil remaining in America), and perhaps even bringing in the millennium. "Stand up, stand up for Jesus, the strife will not be long," wrote George Duffield in 1858. The words of the New School Presbyterians at their General Assembly of 1861 spoke for many others: "Rebellion against such a government as ours . . . can find no parallel, except in the first two great rebellions, that which assailed the throne of heaven directly [Satan], and that which peopled our world with miserable apostates [Adam and Eve]. . . . We here, in deep humiliation for our sins and the sins of the nation, and in heartfelt devotion, lay ourselves, with all that we are and have, on the altar of God and our country." For their part, southerners often looked at Yankees as lawless aggressors destroying the precious Christian heritage of the United States.

Christian America believed not only in itself as a nation, but in the individual freedom of its citizens. This second belief was compounded of much that was vital in America's young history: the stirring words of the Declaration of Independence, the convictions of Presidents Thomas Jefferson and Andrew Jackson, the philosophical individualism of John Locke and the Scottish Realists, the accelerating influence of the Methodists, and even the newer theories of some Calvinists. In its extreme form the belief in individual freedom resulted in visions of human perfection—some arising out of the Unitarian departure from Calvinism, others from the more advanced forms of Methodism. In its usual forms, American individualism foresaw great social benefits arising from individuals organized against social evils — slavery, drunkenness, dueling, prostitution, the theater, and frivolous amusements. Although America's infatuation with the individual was not confined to Christian circles, Christians no less than non-Christians gave their whole-hearted commitment to the individual as the hope of the future.

Finally, the educated elite of nineteenth-century America were committed to a worldview in which first principles were God-ordained laws and motivating forces were innate human capacities. This was the philosophy of Protestant Newtonianism. Americans were Protestant in their convictions about Scripture, their commitment to the priesthood of believers, and their primitivistic allegiance to first-century Christianity. They were Newtonian, and hence of the Enlightenment, in their commitment to simplicity in ideas and in a corresponding distaste for intellectual ambiguity. They reflected this Newtonianism even more in their commitment to a concept of static law. It was, for example, as axiomatic as the law of gravity that national prosperity was a sign of God's blessing or that the exercise of correct stimuli in a revival would bring the correct results. Protestant Newtonians held that externally fixed laws governed the "facts" of national life and morality as surely as they did the "facts" of nature.

Intellectual life in America's colleges before 1870 bears little resemblance to what we know today. The curriculum of the old college consisted of a little mathematics; a great deal of praise for empirical science with, however, only meager opportunities to carry out actual experiments; much drill in the classics; and an exposure to systematic arguments for morality, civic virtue, and the existence of God. Modern languages and literature had no place in the curriculum, and history as a discipline was just beginning to be recognized. Instruction proceeded by recitation. The professor, acting more as scorekeeper than teacher, called upon the students to translate, parse, recapitulate, or summarize. Close discipline, extending well beyond the classroom, was the rule. Teachers were regarded as keepers of the peace. At Harvard in 1827 a financial crisis forced the college to increase teaching loads, consolidate positions, and also extend the responsibilities of the faculty to nightly bed checks of the undergraduates. Not surprisingly, the tedium of the classroom, the rigor of extracurricular discipline, and the natural feistiness of late adolescence led to student unrest. One of the less destructive ways in which students protested their lot was to disrupt morning prayers by herding a compliant cow into the chapel. Student unrest often led to violence as well, including once or twice the murder of professors who had offended students.

By 1870 it was clear that the old college was barely keeping pace with the intellectual needs of the country. In that year the nation's colleges enrolled about 52,000 out of a general population of 40 million (the equivalent of 350,000 students in our present population). Furthermore, the rate of growth in the number of college students was falling behind the rate of growth in the country as a whole.

For all of its weaknesses, however, the old-style American college had one important advantage: with very rare exceptions, it was founded and operated as an avowedly Christian institution. In the great westward expansion of the country before the Civil War, Protestant denominations exceeded one another in founding educational institutions. Many denominational schools were founded through the efforts of a single clergyman. Most struggled along with pitifully few students and a rapidly changing faculty. Most suffered from a surplus of competition and a deficit in financing. All sought to answer the Protestant need for a literate laity and a learned clergy and the democratic American need for informed citizens.

The capstone of the college experience during this period was a year-long course, often taught by the college president, in "moral philosophy" or "mental science." It was a course with vast horizons, including everything having to do with human beings and their social relations (the subjects studied under this rubric would later become the separate disciplines of psychology, philosophy, religion, political science, sociology, anthropology, economics, and jurisprudence). The course almost always included an investigation of epistemology in general and the epistemological foundations of Christianity in particular. The purpose of the course was to provide final Christian integration for the college career and final exhortations concerning the kind of citizenship good Christians should practice.

The Rise of the Seminary

A number of different factors led, in the early nineteenth century, to the founding of schools devoted specifically to the training of candidates for the ministry. Before this time ministerial education had been a random process. Among the older denominations like Congregationalists and Presbyterians, college graduates regularly studied as apprentices with older ministers for a year or two before seeking their own charges. The newer denominations such as the Baptists and the Methodists did not require formal training in college or elsewhere but relied rather upon native intellectual ability and the more direct calling of the Holy Spirit. This varied approach to ministerial training changed first for Congregationalists and Presbyterians, but by the time of the Civil War, formal seminary education was standard for most of the major Protestant bodies. The effects on the Christian colleges, and on the effort to formulate Christian perspectives on the world, were considerable.

Andover Seminary in Massachusetts was the first of the new institutions. It came into existence in 1808 specifically as a trinitarian and evangelical protest against the appointment of a Unitarian to the professorship of divinity at Harvard College. Soon there were other seminaries. Princeton, established in 1812, was the first of many such schools founded by Presbyterians. Yale created its own Divinity School shortly thereafter to serve primarily Congregationalists. Soon almost all of the major Protestant bodies possessed their own specialized institutions for training clergymen.

More than anything else, the cultural crisis of the Revolutionary period was responsible for the rise of the seminary. The Revolutionary picture of the past as a sink of corruption and its great stress on the rights of individuals created a situation in which authority had to be a function of individual ability and accomplishment. In addition, the rapid growth and spread of the population led to a desperate need for clergymen to minister in the new centers of population. As an indication of the dimensions of this problem, annual reports of the Presbyterian General Assembly during the 1790s and the first decade of the nineteenth century regularly showed more vacant "preaching stations" than churches with regularly settled ministers. In addition, secularization (or "infidelity," in the terms of the day) seemed to be spreading much more rapidly than the gospel. At least until the full effects of the Second Great Awakening were felt in the 1820s, church leaders wondered if a Christian witness could be preserved in the country. In response to all of these needs, the theological seminary seemed to be an idea whose time had come. It offered a respectable certification for candidates against the threat of egalitarianism, single-minded attention to training for ministry against the threat of unreached people, and specialized study in the Bible and theology against the threat of infidelity.

The seminaries did meet these needs. In the process they went on to become the prototype for graduate education in the country and, into the twentieth century, remained the nation's most successful institutions for advanced study. By the time Princeton Seminary celebrated its centennial in 1912, for example, it had trained more than six thousand students, far more than any other institution of graduate education in any field in the United States. The only competitors at that time were Andover Seminary, which had educated already nearly 3,600 students, and the Southern Baptist Seminary in Louisville, with 4,500 alumni. The seminaries also served as effective training grounds for Christian workers and were one of the reasons why American missions, home and abroad, possessed the personnel to accomplish its great tasks in the nineteenth century. In addition, the seminaries provided a setting conducive to serious academic work. Until the Civil War, journals from the Protestant seminaries were probably the most sophisticated general publications in America, and they retained some of their intellectual weight and cultural breadth into the twentieth century. The autonomous seminary, separate from college or university and often under the direct control of a denomination, was a singularly American creation. It has exerted a profound influence on the shape of the Christian faith in America.

Its existence, however, also created problems for Christian liberal arts education. If seminaries specialized in theology and encouraged systematic reflection on Christian interaction with the world, what theological role remained for the Christian colleges? This question did not loom as large in the antebellum years before the rise of academic specialization and professionalization, but it was still a difficulty. Should the colleges become miniature seminaries in focusing their curriculum on biblical and theological subjects? Are theological reflection, and the consideration of how revelation affects other areas of thought, to be left with the professors at the seminaries? Such questions took on increased importance when it became clear that the most influential, and perhaps also the most intelligent, Christian commentary on science, and eventually the social sciences, on public ethics, and on the religious destiny of the United States came from the seminaries instead of the Christian colleges. To this day, professors at evangelical seminaries are the best trained of all professional academics identified with evangelical institutions, and their work is read far more widely in evangelical circles than work from professors in the Christian colleges.

The rise of the seminary was a phenomenon of the early nineteenth century that continues to have an influence on American Christian thinking to this day. Even more, the educational changes of the late nineteenth century still shape the intellectual world in which the Christian colleges attempt to accomplish their tasks.

The Emergence of Modern Higher Education

No historical event has been more important for contemporary Christian higher education than the reorganization of the colleges at the end of the nineteenth century. We must not forget, however, that it was but one aspect of another broad crisis in cultural values comparable to that of the Revolutionary era. The issues constituting this crisis, however, were broader than those of the previous century. Would America be able to offer her freedoms not only to Northern European Protestants, but to Southern European Catholics, to Jews, to Asians, and to the African Americans who began to insist on civil liberties? How would the reconstruction of economic life in an industrial society affect perspectives on consumption, social status, and personal worth? How would America's emergence as a world power change its image of itself? Perhaps above all, how would American culture react to the momentous ideas of nineteenth-century Europe promoted by seminal minds like Marx, Freud, Nietzsche, and Darwin? The educational story, as it affects the Christian colleges today, is the story of changes so striking as to deserve the overworked term "revolution."

The years from 1865 to 1900 constituted the great period of transition for American higher education. When Charles Eliot became president of Harvard in 1869, he set that influential institution on a course of innovation and expansion. The Johns Hopkins University, founded in 1876, exercised leadership in the establishment of graduate education. Other major changes were also under way: new universities were founded such as Cornell, Chicago, Stanford, and Clark; older private colleges such as Yale, Princeton, and Columbia were transformed into universities with the addition of graduate and professional schools; major state universities such as Michigan and Wisconsin grew up almost overnight in the Midwest and West.

It is of the greatest significance that the money for this academic explosion did not come from the Christian communities that had hitherto been the financial bellwether for American education. Rather, the federal government began to provide land and money for the practical arts through the Morrill Act of 1862. Even more important were the large sums coming from the new industrialists — that is, from those who had best exploited the expansion of the American economy after the Civil War. Before citing names and numbers, it would be helpful to establish a standard of comparison from the old-time college. Harvard enjoyed a $10,000 annual grant from the Massachusetts legislature for the ten years following 1814 and was the envy of struggling academicians everywhere. When Princeton a decade later audaciously sought $100,000 from its alumni, it created a sensation.

The sums contributed to establish the new universities, however, were on a different level entirely. Ezra Cornell, who made his money in telegraph construction and banking, donated $500,000 to the school that bears his name and managed a Morrill grant for $2,500,000 more. Johns Hopkins, a banker and investor in the Baltimore & Ohio Railroad, left $3,500,000 to the university and an equal sum to establish a teaching hospital. Cornelius Vanderbilt (steamships and railroads) gave an initial gift of $1,000,000 to establish Vanderbilt University in Tennessee and later followed up with other generous bequests. Leland Stanford, who parlayed political office into control of the Central and Southern Pacific Railroads, left $20,000,000 to establish a university in honor of his son. James Duke, of the American Tobacco Company, assigned the largest part of the income from a $100,000,000 trust fund to the university that bears his name. John D. Rockefeller's gifts to establish a great Baptist university in Chicago eventually totaled $45,000,000. From a different but still dizzying perspective, private donors in the twenty years from 1878 to 1898 gave $140,000,000 to American colleges and universities. What this could do for an individual institution can be seen from the jump in Harvard's permanent endowment from $2,500,000 in 1869 to $20,000,000 in 1909.

The number of students attending colleges and universities grew almost as rapidly as the number of dollars going into education. While the country's population nearly doubled (40 million to 76 million) from 1870 to 1900, the number of college students leaped nearly fivefold (from 52,000 to 238,000). In 1870, 1.7 percent of the eighteen- to twenty-one-year-old population was in college. By 1930, the figure had reached 12.4 percent. To cite again the example of Harvard, it grew from 1,000 students in 1869 to 4,000 in 1909; during the same period its faculty grew even more rapidly, from 60 to 600. The surge in attendance was fueled by the growth in public high schools, by the growing numbers of women seeking higher education, and by an increasing desire for higher education by individuals outside of the traditional Anglo-Saxon Protestant sources.

Almost unnoticed in the great influx of dollars and students was the decline of the Christian characteristics that had earlier marked higher education. Neither the new donors nor the new breed of administrators were overly concerned about the orthodoxy of their faculties. Visible signs of this change abounded. At Harvard, compulsory chapel ceased in 1886. The opening ceremonies at Johns Hopkins in 1876 contained no prayer but did feature an address by British evolutionary theorist Thomas Huxley. As money from businessmen increased, so did their concern that boards of trustees and college administrators function in a businesslike way. Thus it was that businessmen replaced clergymen as trustees, and laymen replaced ministers as college presidents. In 1839, fifty-one of the fifty-four presidents of America's largest colleges were clergymen (forty of these being Presbyterians or Congregationalists). By the end of the century the number was greatly reduced. Princeton, always conservative, waited until 1902 to name its first lay president, Woodrow Wilson.

If the German example was the source of the university's professionalization, the new science was the source of its pride. This new science was popularly, if inaccurately, associated with the name of Charles Darwin, whose *Origin of Species by Means of Natural Selection* had been published in 1859. Darwinism, which one scholar has neatly summarized as "a scientifically credible theory of random and purposeless change," stood for an intellectual perspective that went well beyond questions in biology. It is in fact possible to see three levels of Darwinism: a scientific method, a scientific result, and a philosophical system. At each level, Darwinism both undercut the antebellum scientific world of American higher education and offered the glowing prospect of unprecedented scientific progress.

A whole new idea of the faculty member was also coming into existence. The new professional enjoyed certifiable training and coveted standing in an academic specialty. He, and gradually she as well, normally went through a probation period as teacher-researcher-scholar. Scholars sought employment at institutions offering specialized instruction. They were committed to publishing the results of their research for scholars outside their own institutions. Their scholarly functions and professional reputation became at least as important as their teaching responsibilities or their institutional loyalty. Befitting this new status, faculty members were spared some of the responsibilities they had traditionally exercised. One of the first of their traditional tasks to go was disciplinary responsibility for the students during their non-class hours.

The new professors also adopted a different role in society and in the world at large. Old-time college leaders had spoken to society as a whole, but mostly as moral cheerleaders or defenders of a public faith. The new academicians achieved their recognition as experts, individuals with extraordinary competence in one or another of the new disciplines cultivated at the new university. The public pronouncements of Oliver Wendell Holmes on the law, Thorsten Veblen on economics, or William James and John Dewey on philosophy were not always followed, but they were heard. Worldviews were now coming from the university.

In sum, more than just thirty-five years separated the new university at the start of the twentieth century from the old college at the close of the Civil War. The new university was professional; it offered technical training in a wide variety of separate fields; it was funded by large gifts from America's industrial giants; it had laid aside the external marks of Christianity; its professors sought to become well known in their specific disciplines and to speak expertly to society as a whole; its new science purported to illuminate a better way to truth, progress, and perhaps even happiness; and it was offering its wares to an ever-growing part of the American population.

In almost every way imaginable the new university undercut the traditional values of Christian higher education in America. Excess capital generated by the industrialists after the Civil War arose from a widespread exploitation of new scientific technology. This excess wealth was generated, furthermore, by individuals who had largely laid aside the constraints of Christian altruism that moral philosophy, for which the new capitalists had no time, sought to inculcate in college graduates. American industrialists, to one degree or another, seemed to have favored the kind of social Darwinism popularized by Herbert Spencer. One of the reasons this new class of wealthy Americans funded education was to encourage more of the practical science and managerial theory coming from the new universities and less of the moralism coming from the old colleges. Whether through the direct influence of the industrialists or not, clergymen were replaced by businessmen on college boards of trustees and ministers were replaced as college presidents by educators alert to management ideas and the demands of the new science. These new presidents, in turn, focused much more attention on scholarship than on orthodoxy. Furthermore, the new scholarship that these presidents encouraged had been supposedly "liberated" from the old orthodoxies of moral philosophy. It was frankly naturalistic in science and pragmatic in philosophy. In turn — and this brings the circle full — the new naturalistic science and the new pragmatic philosophy encouraged industrial giantism by providing training and technique to the capitalists while at the same time offering few criticisms of the new industrial wealth.

Against this combination of new money, social Darwinism, and naturalistic science, the old Christian moral philosophy and the old Christian college stood almost no chance. Its reductionistic Christianity had little guidance to offer industrialists or the new urban masses. Its individualistic ethics could not comprehend the magnitude of new economic and social developments. Its empiricism had been turned against the traditional orthodoxy.

The collapse of moral philosophy signaled the collapse of the effort to preserve a unified Christian worldview in America. From the point of view of the new university, the effort to view knowledge whole was abandoned under the assumption that discrete parts of truth, discovered through empirical science, could stand on their own. The effort to integrate religious faith with learning was abandoned under the assumption that the pursuit of science carried with it no antecedent commitments to a worldview.

This transitional period in American higher education marked the demise of the nineteenth-century Christian-cultural synthesis as the dominant American worldview. The earlier alliance between Christian and Enlightenment values experienced notable strain. For many scholars in the new universities, an enlightened pursuit of learning led to the abandonment of historic Christianity. The crisis, however, did not lead conservative Protestants to break with the Enlightenment. American evangelical educators tended rather to insist upon the Enlightenment-Christian synthesis even as it slipped from dominance in the colleges and universities. Theologically conservative Protestants, in other words, were not returning to the model of Edwards or the Puritans, nor attempting to reconstruct the life of the mind on the basis of a new perspective on the categories of special revelation and common grace. They were rather digging in their heels and insisting upon the continuing validity of the earlier synthesis.

The fundamentalist-modernist controversy certainly exacerbated problems for Christian thinking in this transitional era. So thoroughly had evangelicals internalized the values of the Enlightenment into their Christian worldview that they reacted to both modernistic theology and new proposals in science, philosophy, and the arts as equally heretical. Fundamentalists, committed both to historic Christianity and to the thought forms of the early nineteenth century, were naturally suspicious of proposals that called either into question, especially when the new ideas were allied with assaults upon traditional theology or morality.

Many modern evangelical colleges are heirs of the rearguard action that preserved a Christian dimension in American higher education at the turn of the century. Much has happened since then to force rethinking of the distinctions that fundamentalists drew between historic Christianity and the new learning. By their continued adherence to Christian norms, evangelical colleges today testify to their debt to the fundamentalist nay-sayers of the late nineteenth and early twentieth centuries. Just as surely, however, by their selective reengagement with modern forms of thought they testify to their implicit judgment that the reductionistic faith, the Baconian science, and the individualistic ethics of the nineteenth-century Enlightenment-Christian synthesis had become a burden as much as a blessing in the pursuit of Christian higher education.

The Twentieth Century

Since the academic revolution at the turn of the century and the fundamentalist-modernist controversies of roughly the same period, the evangelical colleges have returned at least part way to the educational mainstream. At the same time, they have also maintained many of the theological and ethical convictions of the nineteenth-century Christian colleges. Living between two worlds as they are, committed both to Christian values and to modern learning, the evangelical colleges have singular opportunities and singular difficulties as they attempt to encourage Christian perspectives on the world.

As demonstrated extensively by Professor Ringenberg's research, the most obvious characteristic of the evangelical colleges in recent American history is their institutional vigor. A form of higher learning that seemed doomed by the educational revolution of the late nineteenth century has not only survived, but prospered. As an indication of strength, there are now more than one hundred colleges and universities associated with the Council for Christian Colleges and Universities; many of these institutions are doing at least fairly well in terms of students, finances, and intellectual vitality.

Several distinct elements have contributed to that prosperity. One is the colleges' ability to provide students with the necessary educational certification for entering the major vocations and the leading professional schools. Another is their success in cultivating the support of Christian communities that had come to distrust modern higher education but that expressed confidence in those institutions which retained Christian professions and traditional behavioral standards. A third is the capacity of faculties at the evangelical colleges to articulate to themselves, to college administrators, and to wider Christian constituencies the theoretical and practical necessity for distinctly Christian views of the world.

Merely to note these factors, however, does not take us very far into the many different histories represented by the various Christian liberal arts colleges. Although the evangelical colleges do share much in common, they also are products of many different strands in Protestant history. As such, the relationship between colleges and the constituencies which they serve can be very different in spite of the fact that they advertise nearly identical educational goals. Some of the colleges, founded by more recent immigrants, have never had to overcome the distrust of higher education that characterized the American fundamentalists. Others, however, wage a constant battle to convince their supporters of the values of the liberal arts and the virtues of an acquaintance with modern thought. Just to note that Baptists, Presbyterians, Reformed, Independents, Pentecostals, Nazarenes, Brethren, Mennonites, Lutherans, and still others work together in the Council of Christian Colleges and Universities is enough to indicate the varied traditions that participate in evangelical higher education. The most that can be said now is that distinctly different patterns do appear. Some evangelical colleges are the lengthened shadow of one person or one family. Others rest securely within a particular denomination, and still others serve complex interdenominational networks. These patterns, and wide variations within each, call for explication of the sort that follows in this book.

Something of the same may be said for the question of faculty professionalization. Quite clearly the modern evangelical college expects its faculty to possess standard graduate training and to take some part in the ongoing professional activities of their academic disciplines. While the Christian colleges employ only a few professors who have become prominent in their disciplines, they are home to many scholars who regularly read papers at academic conferences, review books for professional journals, and engage in some kind of continuing research. This pattern, however, is fairly recent; it developed only after World War II. A number of factors contributed to this professionalization, among them a growing distance from the fundamentalist-modernist controversies and wider exposure to European forms of orthodox Christianity. Yet this is a subject needing more serious investigation. Faculty professionalization touches upon the recent history of the evangelical colleges at many points. One of the most interesting of these pertains to the renewed relationships that these colleges have established in wider worlds of American higher education. Especially at a time of increasing competition for government funds, Christian colleges are finding common cause with other private institutions. Relations established here, within the accrediting associations and among administrators and faculty at many levels, beg for insightful research and clarification.

Faculty professionalization also raises larger questions of self-identity. Do the evangelical colleges desire the presence of faculty with Ph.D.s only to be respectably certified? Do they mean their professors to affect the actual shape of the academic disciplines by encouraging faculty publication? Do they want students to have models of caring teachers who occasionally do a little research, or do they themselves want to make a contribution to knowledge?

Also important in the recent past are those developments that relate especially to the promotion of a Christian view of the world. Commitment to a Christian worldview is the academic raison d'être for the evangelical colleges. Yet much in the heritage of the colleges and in their present operation militates against either the creation of Christian perspectives or their application to modern intellectual life.

A series of conundrums can show the difficulties that the evangelical colleges face in this regard. In an age when the thinking that shapes worldviews comes regularly from research universities, there is only one evangelical institution that is trying to function as a full-scale research university. Baylor University in Texas has made great strides in reaching that goal, but whether it will succeed fully is still an open question. In an age when secularism tugs at Christian thinking from one side and long-entrenched denominational shibboleths tug at it from the other, evangelical higher education retains the distinct college and seminary tiers of its heritage and the barriers to cohesive Christian thinking that this structure perpetuates. In an age when scholars (sometimes even Christian scholars) have called into question almost every settled intellectual tradition in the West, evangelicals remain surprisingly content with the intellectual synthesis of the early nineteenth century. In an age when sophisticated secular intellectuals set the tone for considerations of politics, economics, and secular values, evangelicals continue to set their course by popular preachers who are not reluctant to pronounce judgment on every facet of modern learning. In an age, finally, demanding forceful Christian responses to powerful secular ideologies, careful Christian probing of complex intellectual issues, and creative Christian initiatives for pressing contemporary problems, much of evangelicalism still retains a stultifying nineteenth-century suspicion of all thinking that does not rest on mythic views of America's past, egalitarian common sense, or popular interpretations of the Bible.

These conundrums speak as much to the broader evangelical culture as to the liberal arts colleges themselves. They are nonetheless the pressing problems that evangelical colleges face in attempting to articulate Christian views of the world. They are problems, moreover, rooted in the history of the colleges and their constituencies.

The Path Ahead

The Puritans who established the colonial colleges had a vision. The intrepid ministers who created a vast network of higher education in the opened frontier, the energetic theological conservatives who founded Bible colleges or who maintained Christian distinctives during the academic revolution of the late nineteenth century, the hard-pressed immigrants who scraped together the means to preserve both Christian and Old World commitments, and the evangelical trustees, administrators, and faculties who guide Christian higher education through the perils of contemporary life have all shared this vision. Their vision, however inarticulate at times, has been to capture thinking for Christ, and by so doing to contribute also to good citizenship, the spread of the gospel, social harmony, and the general well-being of students and constituencies alike.

At the same time there remain challenges for the future. Most obviously, evangelical colleges face many of the problems that confront all private colleges in the early twenty-first century. Financial pressure, the changing nature of governmental support, and uncertainties concerning the number of available students are difficulties as urgent on the campuses of the Christian colleges as elsewhere in private higher education. Yet these may be the least serious issues facing the Christian colleges.

Far more germane to the purposes for which these institutions exist are questions related to overall academic purpose and to relationships that the college sustains with their wider constituencies. The history of Christianity in America, not to speak of its worldwide history, testifies to the precariousness of Christian thinking. The tendency has ever been present for Christian academics to drift into the secularism of the wider culture or to relapse into the obscurantism of cultic sectarianism. Only an unambiguous loyalty to the priority of special revelation can check the propensity to secularism; only an unswerving commitment to the values of common grace can restrain the sectarian impulse. Against the children of the world, Christian colleges must stand for grace; against the children of grace, Christian colleges must stand for the world.

More particularly, Christian institutions of higher education are poised between the demands of free academic inquiry and of committed theological loyalty. Without the first, it is hard to see the Christian colleges preserving intellectual viability, but without the second they will not retain their Christian character. Again, the evangelical tradition in America has had difficulty finding a place for intellectual freedom within the general framework of orthodoxy. The challenge for the future is to broaden expectations for creativity while at the same time heightening the value of theological commitment.

Finally, social and political factors pose a growing dilemma for evangelical higher education. The Christian Right has strong convictions about social and political questions and (often) the money to promote those ideas in the colleges. The Christian Left has less money, but its positions are argued with equal moral fervor. The challenge to evangelical higher education is to open doors wide to any political or social position that claims to rest on Christian foundations, but then to go on to rigorous scrutiny of the position and its supposed Christian base, never allowing the gospel to be equated with any changeable form of human conviction.

In the pages that follow, William Ringenberg provides a well-connected and up-to-date history of many of the developments that I have sketched in this introduction. His history, rather than my speculations, is the proper place to begin serious consideration of today's Christian colleges in relationship to their past. But because his history is done so well, it too will illuminate some of the questions that I have attempted to address.

1

The Colonial Period

The average American living in the late twentieth century finds it difficult to identify with the colonial period, for that era differs sharply from the present in many ways. The colonial population, even at its peak, never equaled 2 percent of today's census; those few million colonists lived in only that small section of North America between the Atlantic Ocean and the Appalachian Mountains; they found it very difficult to travel even moderate distances except by water; and nearly everyone was a farmer, while almost no one worked in an industrial or service occupation.

Higher education, then and now, also offers a study in contrasts. Only a very small percentage of colonial young men enrolled in college (the colleges awarded only nine thousand baccalaureate degrees between 1642 and 1800);[1] the professors had acquired little training beyond their own undergraduate courses of study and they usually cultivated additional professional interests such as the ministry or medicine; the curriculum placed primary emphasis upon the study of Latin, Greek, and mathematics; and the colleges were more, rather than less, religious than was society in general (by 1800 only 7 percent of the population had joined a church, although approximately twice as many attended without formal membership).[2]

The Pervading Christian Purpose of Colonial Education

The Christian worldview, more than any other system of thought, dominated American intellectual development during the colonial period. As clergymen were the leading representatives of the intellectual class, it is not surprising that they, and the denominations that they represented, took the lead in founding colleges and instructing the students. While religious leaders founded institutions of higher learning primarily to educate future ministers, these colleges never operated solely as ministerial training seminaries. They also sought to provide culture and breadth of thought for the other leaders of society.

Regardless of the vocation for which a student was preparing, the colonial college sought to provide for him an education that was distinctly Christian. At Harvard the original goal of higher learning was "to know God and Jesus Christ which is eternal life (John 17:3), and therefore to lay Christ in the bottom as the only foundation of all sound knowledge and learning." Yale in the early 1700s stated as its primary goal that "every student shall consider the main end of his study to wit to know God in Jesus Christ and answerably to lead a Godly, sober life." Similarly, President Samuel Johnson of Columbia, in a 1754 advertisement, declared that the primary purpose of his college was "to teach and engage the children to know God in Jesus Christ and to love and serve him in all sobriety, godliness, and righteousness of life with a perfect heart and willing mind; and to train them up in all virtuous habits and useful knowledge as may render them creditable to their families and friends, ornaments to their country, and useful to the public Weal in their generations." The Calvinist-related colleges probably promoted their religious goals more intensely than did the Anglican ones. Only Pennsylvania maintained primarily secular goals; perhaps it would have been more religious if the dominant denomination in its state, the Quakers, had desired during this early period to educate their clergymen. Even Pennsylvania experienced some Christian influence, however. For example, the first president was the Rev. William Smith, an Anglican clergyman who "gave the students all the Anglicanism the traffic would bear."[3]

Although Massachusetts Bay was not the oldest colony in the new world, it was the first to establish a college. The unusually well-educated and spiritually earnest Puritans waited only six years to found Harvard primarily because they feared that if they delayed much longer they would risk leaving "an illiterate ministry to the churches when our present ministers shall lie in the dust." Thirty-five of the university men in early New England, including a large majority of the Harvard founders, had attended Emmanuel College of Cambridge University. As a result, that "hot bed" of Puritanism became the institution after which Harvard modeled itself.

During the early years of Harvard, such a large percentage of its graduates entered the ministry that many referred to the college as "the school of prophets" and the students as "the sons of prophets." By the eighteenth century, however, a growing number of New Englanders believed that Harvard was no longer the school where true prophets taught, but rather had become an institution which true prophets denounced. Among the leading denouncers were Increase Mather (Harvard president, 1685–1701) and his son Cotton Mather, who hoped to prevent Harvard from moving away from its original Calvinist orientation in an Arminian direction.

Even though Increase Mather was the most distinguished president to serve Harvard during the colonial period, he could not check the declining influence of the old faith. During the eighteenth century, Harvard not only moved away from Calvinism, but to and then beyond Arminianism toward a Unitarianism that became its most characteristic theological expression by the early nineteenth century.[4]

What the Calvinists could not maintain at Harvard they sought to establish at Yale. Although the citizens of Connecticut had long wished for a college of their own, the actual establishment of Yale in 1701 was considerably encouraged by the belief of many New England Calvinists that Harvard was slipping from the true path. Yale also experienced early challenges to its Calvinism; however, it dealt with these threats differently from Harvard. For example, in 1722 a rumor circulated that Rector (President) Timothy Cutler, Tutor Daniel Brown, and a handful of influential citizens in the New Haven community were beginning to accept Anglicanism. The trustees conducted an investigation which confirmed their worst fears. Subsequently, they dismissed both Cutler and Brown. Also, the board determined that the students should be taught Calvinist theology and none other, and that every officer of the college must publicly subscribe to the Westminster Confession of Faith and the Saybrook Platform of the Congregational churches in Connecticut before receiving an appointment. As a further effort to protect its students, Yale forbade them from attending Episcopal church services in New Haven. By contrast, a 1747 oath bill proposed at Harvard to impose Calvinism upon the members of that community failed to advance beyond the talking stage.[5]

While nine colonial colleges eventually appeared, to speak of them as a group is misleading because during most of the seventeenth century only Harvard existed, and until the generation before the American Revolution, only two more appeared (see table 1). Something must have happened, therefore, about the middle of the eighteenth century to stimulate the founding of six colleges during such a short period. More than any other factor, this active period of college founding is explained by the Great Awakening (or the First Great Awakening) of the 1730s and 1740s. This first major period of mass revivalism in American history swept through every colony and every denomination. As a result, several major religious groups which heretofore had not operated colleges quickly established such institutions in an effort to improve the quality of their increasing number of ministerial recruits. Therefore the Presbyterians founded Princeton; the Baptists, Brown; the Dutch Reformed, Rutgers; and the pro-revival Congregationalists, Dartmouth.[6]

Table 1. Colonial Colleges by Religious Affiliations[7]

College	Founding date	Religious orientation
Harvard (MA)	1636	Puritan/Congregationalist
William & Mary (VA)	1693	Anglican
Yale (CT)	1701	Congregationalist
Princeton (NJ)	1746	New Light Presbyterian
Columbia (NY)	1754	Essentially Anglican
Pennsylvania (PA)	1755	Primarily secular
Brown (RI)	1765	Baptist
Rutgers (NJ)	1766	Dutch Reformed
Dartmouth (NH)	1769	New Light Congregationalist

While the four new colleges understandably sympathized with the emotional faith which had helped give them birth, the two oldest colleges in the North reacted strongly against what they saw as the Awakening's irrational approach to religion. The Harvard and Yale faculties recoiled particularly at the direct charges made against them by the leading preacher of the Awakening, the youthful and sometimes excessively exuberant itinerant minister George Whitefield. He charged, "As for the Universities, I believe it may be said, their light is become Darkness, Darkness that may be felt, and is complained of by the most Godly ministers." Even worse, the Harvard and Yale students sometimes echoed the charges of Whitefield.[8]

The major theological controversy resulting from the Great Awakening was the question of whether experiential and emotional factors or rational factors should play the prominent role in religion. Many Presbyterians, particularly those in the South and West, accepted the New Light (e.g., pro-revival) position and consequently became increasingly dissatisfied with Harvard and Yale. A major related problem for them was that ministerial candidates who grew up in the East and attended colleges there hesitated to leave their native homes to assume ministerial responsibilities for the needy parishes in the Appalachian Mountain regions. Consequently, the need for ministers in the West was met by several Presbyterian academies, the most famous of which was Rev. William Tennent's "Log College" at Neshaminy in Bucks County, Pennsylvania.

The Log College—actually a simple cabin "about twenty feet long and nearly as many wide," as remembered by George Whitefield—and the

twenty or thirty other academies that were modeled after it were apprenticeship institutions that in level of instruction operated somewhere between a grammar school and a college. Groups of students, especially
ministerial candidates, would move in with a learned minister and study
divinity and related subjects with him. The ministers who conducted
these schools tended to be of the New Light persuasion and included such
able figures as Samuel Davies, Samuel Finley, Jonathan Dickinson, and
Aaron Burr. Gradually, however, William Tennent grew older and the
supply of preachers being furnished by the other academies became inadequate; as a result the New Light Presbyterians sought an alternate means
of training their future ministers. Thus by the mid-eighteenth century,
both the western log colleges and the older established eastern colleges,
for different reasons, were becoming increasingly unable to provide the
type of training desired by the New Light ministers. Consequently, they
founded Princeton.[9]

While Dartmouth developed into the school for New Light Congregationalists, it did not begin that way. It came into existence in 1754 as an institution for teaching American Indians. Its most famous early Indian students included Joseph Brant and Sampson Occum. Brant became a
Mohawk chief, a colonel in the British army, and a Christian missionary
who translated the Episcopal Prayer Book and part of the New Testament
into Mohawk. Occum was a Mohegan who could speak fluent English
and deliver stirring sermons. Eleazar Wheelock, the Dartmouth founder,
sent Occum to England to raise funds, and his appearance in that country
caused a major stir. Englishmen, who at this time were experiencing the
Wesleyan revivals, were moved by the sight of a devout and persuasive
Indian, seeking funds to convert and educate the members of his race in
England's leading colony. Consequently, when Occum and Nathaniel
Whitaker, who accompanied him, returned in 1766, they brought with
them more than £12,000 for the college. Although it was not the intention
of Wheelock, the college quickly began to train many more whites than Indians, with the latter studying primarily in the preparatory department.[10]

The fact that the colonial institutions were religious in nature does not
mean that they were private colleges in the modern sense of the term, for
the twentieth-century distinction between public and private institutions
did not exist in the colonial era. Although each of the three earliest colleges, Harvard, William and Mary, and Yale, was chartered by the established church in its colony, each also held a direct relationship to the state
and served as the center for training civic as well as clerical leaders for its
region. The governments in turn recognized the importance of the colleges and contributed significant amounts of financial aid to support
them. For the most part, the colleges welcomed students and instructors of

the several Protestant denominations, although usually they gave preference to members of the denomination sponsoring the college. Most of the
new colleges founded in the mid-eighteenth century wrote into their charters specific provisions prohibiting denial of admission on the basis of religion. As a further reflection of their public nature, most of the new colleges named public officials as ex-officio members of their boards.[11]

If colonial higher education operated from a Christian foundation, it
did so primarily because such an intellectual framework also characterized the European institutions that served as models for the colonial college founders. The essential characteristics of American church-related
higher education can be seen as early as the fifth century in the palace,
monastic, and cathedral schools, and during the Middle Ages in the continental universities and British universities and dissenting academies. In
each of these periods, there was something about Christianity which stimulated people to inquire deeply about the nature and meaning of the
universe.

The greatest influences on the colonial colleges, however, came from
the universities of Cambridge and Oxford in England. The colonial colleges imitated the pattern of these two English institutions in several
ways: religious groups largely controlled the institutions, the curriculum
was narrow, the students resided as well as studied on the campus, higher
education was primarily for the elite, and teaching youthful minds rather
than discovering new knowledge was the primary purpose.[12]

During the eighteenth century, many of the new colleges looked more
to the dissenting academies in Great Britain than to Cambridge and Oxford. Despite the vast emotional distance between the academies and the
universities, they were very similar in structure and program. The academies came into existence in the late seventeenth century when following
the period of Puritan rule the restored Parliament dismissed all non-
Anglican faculty members from the universities. Some of the released faculty members attracted a group of sympathetic students and founded dissenting academies for the primary purpose of providing training for the
ministers of such groups as the Congregationalists and the Presbyterians.
The academies were smaller but often better institutions than the universities; their quality was unpredictable, however, varying widely depending upon the ability of the master. Where young men were able to study
under an instructor like Philip Doddridge of Northampton, they probably
received as good an education as was available anywhere in Great Britain
at the time. The curriculum of the academies was broader than that of the
universities and supplemented the primary emphasis upon ancient languages, philosophy, and theology with substantial work in mathematics,
natural philosophy, and even English literature and public speaking. The

founders of Princeton as well as those of the other Presbyterian schools that began in the South shortly after the Revolution knew well the work and nature of the dissenting academies and were strongly affected by them.[13]

Beginning in the eighteenth century, influences from Scotland became increasingly significant in shaping American higher education. The increasing number of immigrant Presbyterian ministers who filled the pulpits in Scotch-Irish communities in the middle and southern colonies usually had graduated from Scottish universities or academies, and a number of them operated similar academies in their own manses. Also, some of the leaders of the American colleges had received their training in Scotland. The first president of William and Mary, James Blair, graduated from the University of Edinburgh, and the first provost of Pennsylvania was a graduate of the University of Aberdeen. John Witherspoon, who received his education at the University of Edinburgh, migrated directly from Scotland to become president of Princeton.[14]

Witherspoon was easily the most important force in bringing Scottish thinking into American higher education. Not only did his ideas dominate Princeton during the last third of the eighteenth century, but the Scottish system of philosophy called Common Sense Realism spread from Princeton to become the dominant mode of philosophical thought in American colleges for the next century. In essence the Scottish system replaced the abstract idealism of George Berkeley, the pessimism of David Hume, and the quasi-materialism of John Locke with a commonsense, easily understood verification of the Christian ideals.[15]

Instructors and the Instruction

Very few men served as college instructors during the colonial period. The typical college hired a president and two or three tutors, the latter being the approximate equivalent in status and function of today's graduate assistants. Such was the case at Harvard throughout the seventeenth century and at Princeton as late as the 1760s. The number of regular professorial appointees (to be distinguished from those who served only as tutors) in all colleges numbered only ten as late as 1750, but grew sharply to forty-one in the late 1760s and approximately one hundred in the 1790s. This sharp increase during the late eighteenth century reflected both the increasing size of the faculties of the older schools and the growing number of new colleges that came into existence shortly after the Revolution. Altogether, between 1750 and 1800, there were approximately two hundred different men listed in catalogs and college histories as holding professorial positions.[16]

The president was often the most distinguished instructor. When an institution was very small, especially in its beginning years, he sometimes did much of the teaching himself. One can even find examples of presidents — such as Samuel Johnson of Columbia and Jacob Hardenbergh of Rutgers — who taught every subject in the curriculum. Consequently, the president of a small developing college needed to know something about almost every area of learning; even such an unusually able scholar as Jonathan Edwards harbored serious doubts about his qualifications to be president of Princeton when he was called in 1757. (He thought himself deficient in certain parts of mathematics and Greek literature.) Usually, however, the president restricted his teaching activity to philosophy and theology instruction for the upper-division students. Once a college was established, the president was far too busy to teach more than this, for he also served as fund-raiser, secretary, treasurer, purchasing agent, librarian, student counselor, college spokesman, and Sunday preacher.

A college tended to select as its president a man who had achieved distinction in education, the ministry, and public life in general. Usually he was selected from among the most widely respected ministers of the denomination supporting the college, and usually he had achieved something of a reputation for intellectual ability and theological orthodoxy. These college leaders normally emphasized a rational approach to religion and the importance of order and stability in society. Among the more noteworthy colonial college presidents fitting this description were Samuel Johnson of Columbia, Jonathan Edwards of Princeton, and Thomas Clap and Ezra Stiles of Yale.[17]

All the professors, president or not, usually came from families of high or at least middle social status, received their training at the most widely recognized colonial colleges, limited their teaching careers to a single institution, and pursued professional interests other than teaching. Approximately two-thirds of the colonial professors came from families in which the father was a clergyman, a large planter, or a wholesale merchant. Another one-third of the instructors grew up in farm, artisan, or retail business families. Most of the colonial instructors received their college training at Harvard, Princeton, Yale, Pennsylvania, or Edinburgh. Almost invariably, professors limited their instructional careers to a single institution. Very few taught at two different colleges, and only three men taught in more than two institutions. No more than 20 percent of the late-eighteenth-century professors considered college teaching to be their major lifetime occupation, and less than one-half of them devoted all of their energies to teaching during the period of their college appointments. The great majority pursued a second vocation (usually the ministry or medicine) at some point during their working years.[18]

The role of the tutors in the early American colleges was an unenviable one. Most tutors had graduated recently from college and were selected because of exemplary records in piety and scholarship. Few thought of staying in the position more than a short time; frequently teaching offered the opportunity to pursue post-graduate work in divinity with the president prior to assuming a pastoral charge. The position offered neither financial reward nor great popularity with the students. The pay was sufficiently small that the tutors could not raise families on it. They roomed in dormitories with the students and served as first-line institutional disciplinary officials. Most of them found this disciplinary role very difficult; they lacked the experience and often the tact to perform it well. Consequently, the students resented — and sometimes hated — them, and, as one commentator noted, they "seldom lasted long enough to become experienced at anything but dodging stones thrown through their windows by unappreciative students." As instructors, the tutors each assumed responsibility for teaching all or nearly all of the subjects for one and in some cases two of the classes. The tutors tried, but the role demanded more experience and maturity than most of them possessed. The situation was unfair both to them and to the students they attempted to teach. This system of relying heavily upon the services of young, inexperienced tutors did cost very little, however, and perhaps the colonial economy could not yet support a more expensive system.[19]

If the tutors did not need to be experienced, both they and the regular professors did need to be religiously orthodox. For example, at Harvard the Massachusetts civilian authorities expected the college to hire as instructors only "upright Christians and not any that had shown themselves to be unsound in faith or scandalous in their lives." Even in the eighteenth century, the Harvard board of overseers insisted on examining on the subject of his religion every serious candidate for a teaching position.[20]

With some notable exceptions, the American instructors failed to acquire the authority to govern their own institutions. Only William and Mary followed the medieval practice of self-government after the manner of the guilds. Harvard adopted an intermediate position whereby the corporation of fellows (the internal group) and the board of overseers (the outside group) shared power. It was Yale that developed what was to become the typical pattern in America. At Yale, the Congregational clergymen who founded the college (in part because of their suspicion of Harvard) decided that it would be wise to keep the control of the institution in their own hands. In that way they hoped to protect the college's orthodoxy. By the early nineteenth century, even William and Mary and Harvard were joining the newer schools in adopting the Yale model.

Why did the instructors lose to the trustee boards in the contest to become the primary governing force in higher education? In addition to concerns about the college's orthodoxy, there was also the fact that during the colonial period many of the instructors were young men who held only temporary positions. Obviously, they were not in a strong position to seek increased authority. Also since the colleges then, as now, struggled to balance their budgets, the institutional leaders believed it financially advantageous to have wealthy businessmen and lawyers closely related to and responsible for the institution.[21]

As the single most important reason for founding the colleges was to provide ministerial training, it is not surprising that the early leaders designed a curriculum that would be broadly useful for aspiring clergymen. The New England churches expected a minister to be able to read the Scriptures in the original languages and to consult the large number of theological writings in Latin. They also expected him to be broadly learned, and, since the ancient classics were valued as a timeless source of wisdom and truth, it was important to have a sophisticated knowledge of Latin and Greek language and literature. It was also necessary for the minister to develop skill in public speaking and reasoning, thus the emphasis upon oral communication and philosophy. The early ministerial students met these goals better than did the divinity scholars of the eighteenth century.

The curriculum was also largely relevant for the aspiring lawyer and doctor. Law and medicine both assumed that their practitioners were familiar with Latin. Lawyers and other public officials needed the same public speaking skills that the clergymen sought to acquire, and societal leaders of all types found useful a careful study of the ancient classics.

The usefulness of the studies in divinity were obvious for the clergymen but also were considered important for the lay Christian leader. The extent to which the curriculum included studies in biblical content—in contrast to biblical languages—is not clear; however, at Princeton, at least, every student presumably "had to know his Bible from cover to cover." At Harvard, ministerial students often stayed beyond graduation for up to three years to pursue courses of independent study in divinity with the president, while perhaps teaching a course or two. As an optional program, Harvard ministerial students, following graduation, could live with practicing clergymen and read divinity with them as apprentices. Not until 1811 did Harvard organize classes in divinity for graduate students.[22]

One careful student of the colonial curriculum has attempted to translate the early Harvard courses into the modern system of granting an hour of credit for attendance at one class per week for a term. Under such a plan, he found that Harvard students in the 1640s would have earned 140 hours of credit in a three-year period with the curriculum divided as follows:

Logic and disputations (in Latin)	30 hours
Greek	24 hours
Hebrew, Aramaic, and Syriac	24 hours
Rhetoric and declamation	16 hours
Divinity	16 hours
Ethics and politics	8 hours
Arithmetic and geometry	6 hours
Physics	2 hours
Botany	2 hours
Astronomy	2 hours
History	2 hours

The most striking fact about this early colonial curriculum, in contrast with the pattern of the eighteenth and early nineteenth centuries, is its minimal emphasis upon science and mathematics. The eighteenth-century curriculum did not change dramatically from that of the earlier colonial period, but, in part as a result of Enlightenment thinking, there were some shifts of emphasis from ancient to modern languages, from divinity to the social sciences, and from metaphysics to the natural sciences.[23]

Although the seventeenth-century students and faculties appreciated science, they studied it only minimally. Before 1750, work in science included only tasks like memorizing the major commentaries on the physical world and performing simple arithmetic computations. By the middle of the eighteenth century, the colleges increased their emphasis upon science, and some institutions even appointed professors to chairs of science and mathematics. Other colleges, even as late as 1820, went through long periods of time without any science instructor. They delegated their meager science instruction to the tutors, who often operated without the help of any significant equipment for laboratory and demonstration purposes. William and Mary established the first professorship of natural philosophy (natural science) and mathematics in 1711; unfortunately, the first incumbent, a Mr. LeFevre, created controversy nearly the whole of his tenure because of the "idle hussy wife" who accompanied him from London and because of his own drunkenness, negligence of duties, and other irregularities which led to his dismissal in 1712. Of more lasting importance was the creation at Harvard in 1727 of the Hollis Professorship of Mathematics and Natural Philosophy, whose first important occupant was John Winthrop IV. Winthrop held the position for four decades after his 1738 appointment, and he became the most able science and mathematics instructor in the colonial period. He conducted research as well as taught, he was the first college instructor to lead an excursion for astronomical observations and, during the American Revolutionary War, he assisted the colonial government in the design and development of armaments.[24]

The most common teaching method in the colonial colleges was recitation, in which the professor or tutor quizzed students individually to see how well they had studied the lesson for the day — or whether they had studied at all. On the occasions when the seventeenth-century tutors varied the routine by lecturing to their classes, it usually involved nothing more exciting than reading aloud from a prescribed textbook in Latin with the students taking notes or following in texts of their own. Gradually the more knowledgeable professors began to depart from the recitation method to offer lectures of the twentieth-century variety. This type of lecturing appeared earliest in the eighteenth-century science classes. In such disciplines as physics and chemistry, an illustrated lecture using the new scientific equipment was the natural teaching method. Gradually the colleges began to compete with each other in acquiring expensive scientific apparatus, including such devices as globes, barometers, thermometers, microscopes, telescopes, prismatic glass, air pumps, mirrors, lens, levers, pulleys, electrical machines, and orreries. Especially popular were the latter machines, which served to show the relative sizes and positions of the planets and other bodies in the solar system. David Rittenhouse built the most acclaimed orrery in 1767 and placed it at Princeton. Thomas Jefferson believed that in constructing this device Rittenhouse "approached nearer his creator than any man who has lived from the creation to this day."[25]

In the mid-eighteenth century, Princeton and then Harvard departed from the traditional instructional system, under which a tutor taught all of the subjects to one or two classes, by having tutors specialize in subject matter rather than in classes. For example, one tutor might provide all of the instruction in Greek and Latin. This increased degree of specialization represented only one step in the direction of improved instruction. Another, and more important, step was the declining instructional role of the young and inexperienced tutors as the colleges hired a larger number of older, more mature, and more learned professors. These professors, who possessed more knowledge about which to lecture, made greater use of the newer instructional method than had the tutors.[26]

The college library, then as now, offered students one of the greatest

learning opportunities; however, it remained largely an untapped resource during the colonial period. The libraries were small; as late as 1775
Harvard owned only four thousand volumes; William and Mary, three
thousand; and Pennsylvania, Columbia, and Dartmouth, two thousand
each. Even more limiting was the narrow range of subject matter in the
collections. As clergymen donated most of the volumes, the libraries emphasized theology. The colleges bought very few books and generally did
not encourage the students to make use of their collections. Princeton
claimed as highly unusual its invitation to the senior class to browse in the
library.[27]

Students and Student Life

Most colonial college students came from the culturally and financially
elite class. Other groups usually possessed neither the interest nor the
time to send their sons to college or even to provide them with the necessary preparatory work to be able to gain admission. It was not impossible
for a student from a poor and obscure family to enter college, but it was
very difficult. An impoverished lad who showed unusual success in
grammar school and then classical school might find a wealthy sponsor or
some fund for assisting pious youths — especially if he wished to become a
minister. Such a student was most likely to be attracted to Princeton and
Brown, which had the lowest rates, or Dartmouth, which offered employment opportunities. Princeton and Brown represented denominations
whose constituencies contained members of the lower class; therefore the
institutions responded to pressure from their denominations to keep the
rates as low as possible. Often Presbyterian and Baptist ministerial students came from the artisan and farmer classes. By contrast, Columbia and
Pennsylvania were the most expensive institutions.[28]

Some correlation existed between the amount of fees charged by a college and the size of its student body. Costly Columbia and Pennsylvania
attracted the smallest enrollments, and the relatively inexpensive Princeton enrolled the largest number of students in any of the colleges founded
in the mid-eighteenth century. The 120 students who studied at Princeton
in 1766 placed that institution on nearly the same level with the older Harvard and Yale, which, by the end of the colonial period, were enrolling
about 150 students each. Most of the newer colleges other than Princeton
attracted no more than forty or fifty students; consequently, by the eve of
the Revolution the three oldest institutions still enrolled a majority of the
students.[29]

Colonial students gained admission to college at an earlier age than do
today's students. During the third quarter of the eighteenth century, the
median age for admission was sixteen or seventeen at Yale, sixteen at Penn-

sylvania, and fifteen at Columbia. In some cases especially bright lads of eleven to thirteen might gain admittance. For example, Timothy Dwight enrolled in Yale at the age of thirteen in 1752, after passing the entrance examination with ease. Most applicants, however, took the admissions examination with much less skill and more fear than did the able Dwight. To gain admittance, applicants sat before the instructors to demonstrate their ability to translate elementary Latin and Greek. Also, after about 1750, a student often needed to demonstrate proficiency in lower-level mathematics. The specific examination at Rutgers in the late colonial period required the entering student to be able to translate into English Caesar's *Commentaries,* the *Ecologues* of Virgil or one of the Aeneids, and one of the four Gospels. An especially able candidate might gain placement in the sophomore or junior class, while an inadequate performance did not necessarily mean that the student could not attend the school. In this period when the skills of the applicants varied widely, a student might be allowed to study on the pre-college level to make up his deficiencies. When a college admitted applicants liberally, it might do so more to assure its survival than to show generosity to the students. As President Johnson found at Columbia, often the choice was either to admit students "very raw" or to have no students at all.[30]

The colonial college officials administered their institutions with an orderliness that they hoped would create disciplined Christian gentlemen. Many would have concurred with the statement of acting president Charles Inglis of Columbia to his students: "The sacred law of Order [is] Heaven's first Law." The Harvard rules identified eighty-three separate student offenses, and to the students at Harvard and elsewhere it must have seemed that they were required to obtain permission for nearly every activity apart from the normal daily routine. There were regulations governing such things as hunting, sailing, spending money, and even lying down on one's bed during daytime. The laws called for showing respect for one's elders, including the lads in the classes ahead of yours. The infamous "freshman laws" required first-year students to run errands for all upperclassmen and to take off their hats when approaching an upperclassman or a tutor. Even the system of collegiate architecture, in which the major hall contained dormitory rooms and dining halls as well as classrooms, reflected the philosophy of total student control.

The detailed list of college rules carried specific penalties for those who chose to disregard them. For example, at Princeton a student who failed to attend Sunday church faced a fine of four pence, and if he left town without permission, he owed five shillings. Most colleges imposed a similar system of fines for such minor offenses, or perhaps confined the student to campus or his room or gave him extra lessons to translate. Those who committed more serious breaches of acceptable behavior (such as the Columbia student who challenged the president, Myles Cooper, to a duel with pistols in the middle of a recitation) faced expulsion with readmission sometimes possible only following a public confession.[31]

A sharp change in student behavior occurred at Harvard between the seventeenth and eighteenth centuries. In the earlier period, there were few cases of misconduct, and these usually involved individual students. The typical seventeenth-century Harvard student was serious about his relationship with his God and with his studies. The later group of young men, however, "came to be made gentlemen, not to study," and they were more likely to enjoy their sinfulness rather than to lament over it. The new students resulted from a new admissions policy at Harvard in which the college seemed willing to accept nearly everyone who applied, particularly the sons of the newly rich merchants. Perhaps the new students would have behaved better if the college had modified its program to accommodate their interests, but it did not.

The college began to witness an increase in wild parties, pranks, stealing, drunkenness, fighting, lying, swearing, and card playing. One favorite nighttime activity began with a foray to a neighboring farm to steal geese, continued with a feast of the roasted fowl, and ended with a drunken brawl.[32] Sometimes the more pious students — especially those preparing for the ministry — organized themselves into clubs (e.g., "The Association for the Suppression of Vice") to protect themselves as well as to effect spiritual reform in the lives of the wayward students.[33]

Harvard changed in the eighteenth century in large part because New England was changing. After 1689, Massachusetts no longer operated as an official Puritan commonwealth, and subsequently Calvinism no longer completely dominated the approach to religious instruction at Harvard. Also, with the growth of the colonial population and with its increasing interest in acquiring higher education, Harvard began admitting young men who were preparing for a much broader range of vocations. Perhaps it was too much to expect that either the Massachusetts colony or Harvard would remain as religiously orthodox as they were at their founding. The original Puritan founders were a highly selective, especially pious group, which the law of averages would suggest could not be reproduced indefinitely, yet the authorities at Yale thought that Harvard did not try hard enough to continue the earlier religious traditions. Yale did try to continue the old Puritan piety, and it was more successful in the effort; for this reason it, together with Princeton, served as the model for most American colleges founded before the Civil War.

The colonial colleges chose to feed and house their students for several reasons. The students were young, the college wanted to exert the maximum possible religious influence upon them, and alternate housing was minimal. In addition, the residential plan was the model then in vogue in English colleges. The typical colonial college student compared in age to today's high school student; for that reason alone he needed considerable supervision. Also the deeply religious college officials viewed the student as more than a mind to be trained. Most of them would have considered themselves remiss in their duties if they had not educated soul and spirit as well, and they thought that they best could realize this goal by influencing the student's total environment. Some students could have lived off campus, but because the colonial communities were small, such opportunities were limited. Even if they had wanted to do so, most colonial colleges could not have relied upon their communities to house all of their students.

Probably the single most significant factor in explaining why colonial colleges adopted the residential pattern, however, is that it characterized English colleges of that day. English institutions served as the primary model for the colonial colleges, and the English philosophy of the residential college included bringing professors and students together for social and intellectual exchange outside the classroom. Unfortunately, the colonial institutions rarely realized this idea. Still, the residential pattern in America at least allowed the colleges to exert a greater influence over the lives of their students than did the universities in continental Europe, where students generally lived in the community rather than on campus.[34]

Some students preferred to eat their meals off campus even though it cost them more to do so, because in that way they could obtain a more attractive diet. The college dining hall, usually located in the basement of the main building, typically featured bread and butter for breakfast; meat, potatoes, and beer for dinner; and leftovers for supper. Although college students have always tended to criticize even the best dining commons offerings, reports of very bad food appearing in the colonial refectories occur with sufficient frequency to suggest that there must have been some truth to them. Occasionally the students went beyond complaining to rebelling over the situation, as during the late-seventeenth-century "butter rebellion" at Harvard. On that occasion, some students reacted to their diet with "A Book of Harvard," a protest written in a biblical style, containing such passages as:

> Behold! Bad and unwholesome butter is served unto us daily; now therefore let us depute Asa the Scribe to go unto our rulers and seek redress. Then arose Asa the Scribe, and went unto Belcher, the Ruler, and said behold our butter stinketh, and we cannot eat thereof; now give us we pray the butter that stinketh not. . . . And Belcher the Ruler said, Trouble me not, but be gone unto thy own place. But Asa obeyed him not.[35]

The financing of colonial higher education depended more upon student fees and private philanthropy than is the case in the modern era, when most students attend publicly supported institutions. Yearly student expenses for room, board, and tuition in the late eighteenth century varied from £9 at Princeton to £18 at Columbia. Other expenses (e.g., firewood, candles, clothing, travel, and books) added significantly to the comprehensive costs. By the eve of the Revolution, even the cheapest institution cost £25–35, and Columbia charged its students £50–80. By comparison, the cost of a college year in England in this period was more than £100. One can better appreciate the significance of such figures by noting that the average annual income for a skilled carpenter in America at this time was £50; for a college instructor, £100; for an army captain, £136; and for an able lawyer, £500.[36]

Harvard in the seventeenth century charged its students much less than the full cost of their education, thus setting the precedent followed thereafter in America of balancing the books by supplementing student charges with income from other sources. Public financial support was a significant factor in the early financing of only William and Mary, which received about £2,300 per year from such sources as export taxes on skins, furs, and tobacco, and export taxes on liquor; however, Harvard, Yale, and, to a lesser extent, Columbia received a limited amount of aid from their colonial legislatures. Before 1726, Harvard received approximately £8,500 from the Massachusetts Assembly, but it raised nearly £20,000 from private donors.[37]

Not only did Harvard create the pattern of charging students much less than the total cost of educating them, it also developed many of the fund-raising methods used ever since by college agents to raise money from private benefactors. These methods included the following:

1. Preparing literature to state the case for giving to the college (Harvard's famous initial promotional piece was entitled "New England's First Fruits").
2. Convincing wealthy citizens — especially the merchants, who were the most affluent colonial group — that (*a*) they owed their fortunes to the blessings of God; (*b*) therefore they had an obligation to perform to society; and (*c*) aiding the education of Christian youth was one of the best ways to discharge this obligation.
3. Appealing to the pride of a donor by suggesting that his name be used for a college building or program, or perhaps for the institution itself.
4. Appealing to the longer established regions (in the colonial pe-

riod this usually meant England) for aid in furthering the promotion of the Gospel by training future Christian leaders.

English philanthropy constituted more than 30 percent of all private
gifts to Harvard before 1712. The greatest gift from England came after
this date when Thomas Hollis, a London merchant, contributed more
than £5,000 to establish endowed chairs in theology and science. The
Hollis Professorship of Divinity was the first endowed chair of any kind
established in the British colonies. Hollis was a Baptist, and his gift carried with it the condition that the chair thus endowed be open to
qualified applicants of all orthodox Christian denominations. Curi-
ously, however, the Board of Overseers initially restricted the holders
of the Hollis chair to those who subscribed to orthodox New England
Congregationalism.[38]

Other colleges quickly followed the Harvard example of sending
agents to Great Britain to raise funds. In 1753–54, Samuel Davies and
William Tennent raised £1,700 for Princeton. William Smith, provost of
Pennsylvania, and James Jay, a representative of Columbia, together collected more than £16,000 in the 1760s in what was probably the first cooperative college fund-raising effort. A year abroad by President Wheelock
of Dartmouth produced £5,000, but unfortunately he lost it all—and
nearly his life also—when the returning ship wrecked off Cape Cod. Anglican William and Mary met with the greatest success in England. Its
fund-raising efforts, beginning in the 1680s, provided the Virginia college
with an endowment that probably surpassed that held by the other eight
institutions combined. William and Mary, consequently, became the rich-
est of the colonial colleges by 1776.[39]

Another method of fund-raising used during the colonial period was to
locate or relocate the college in the town or city which was willing to make
the best financial offer. For example, Providence residents contributed
more than £4,000 in outbidding Newport, Rhode Island, to obtain Brown.
Princeton was nearly a ten-year institution when the city whose name it
now bears convinced the Presbyterian authorities to relocate it by offering
£1,000, ten acres of land for the campus, and two hundred additional acres
of woodland to heat the college buildings.

Perhaps the most controversial means of raising funds was to conduct a
lottery. Princeton officials solicited the services of Benjamin Franklin to
print eight thousand tickets, which they sold at a fair profit throughout the
colonies in 1750. A few years earlier, the New York State Assembly had
authorized a lottery to raise funds for Columbia, and within five years the
school received nearly £3,500 from the effort. Thus did the colleges use
even unusual means in the effort to remain solvent.[40]

The battle to remain solvent has been an ever-present one in Christian higher education. From the colonial period to the present, college officials have struggled to maintain balanced budgets, but if the struggle usually has been difficult, it also usually has been successful—at least for those colleges that survived the trauma of birth to become firmly established institutions.

2

The Old-Time College

The American Revolution marked the end of the first chapter in the history of higher education in the New World. Until then, imperial control had served to limit the founding of colleges, especially in the South. Between the war and the end of the eighteenth century, however, the number of new permanent colleges to appear was approximately twice the nine of the colonial period, and by the Civil War approximately 180 permanent institutions were in operation. Similarly, the college population in the 1800–1860 period grew four times as fast as did the overall population.[1]

Several factors contributed to this great boom in college founding. One major stimulus was the religious zeal stemming from the Second Great Awakening. Another was the growing tendency for local communities to want to have their own colleges. Finally, the growing spirit of democracy, which characterized American society during the administration of Andrew Jackson and beyond, resulted in a much higher percentage of middle-class and even lower-class students enrolling in college. Many of these common-class young people came from the rapidly growing Methodist and Baptist denominations, both of which began to lose their fear of higher education after about 1830 and to establish colleges in each of the southern and midwestern states into which they were spreading. Even the growing number of state universities operated almost without exception as Protestant institutions. This period thus became one of maximum influence for the Christian faith in America's system of higher education.

With the exception of its numerical growth, higher education did not change dramatically between the Revolution and the Civil War. Its dominant intellectual force continued to be the Christian faith, and the curriculum changed only modestly. Especially noteworthy, however, was the rise of the literary society as the primary extracurricular activity.

The Expansion of Christian Higher Education

The Second Great Awakening (approximately 1800–1835) brought the American college from what may have been its lowest point spiritually into its fastest growing era. A surprising number of students on the late-eighteenth-century campuses professed skepticism and even atheism while belittling orthodox Christian beliefs. At Dartmouth in 1798, only one member of the class of 1799 publicly professed the Christian faith; at Yale in 1796, only the senior class could claim more than one such believer. The new Williams College in western Massachusetts (founded by the Congregationalists in 1793) identified as Christians only five of its ninety-three graduates in the 1790s.[2]

Then came the awakening that swept through all of the country and all of the major denominations and their colleges! The state of religion in the eastern colleges changed sufficiently that some referred to the revival as the "Protestant Counter-Reformation."[3] Stimulated by the Second Great Awakening, the eastern denominations sought to convert the West. Accordingly, they sent home missionaries to the new developing regions. In order to guarantee that the changes wrought by the missionaries would become permanent, denominational representatives together with local officials established colleges to train future ministers and to indoctrinate the younger generation with the eternal verities.

Thus colleges sprang up rapidly throughout the frontier regions between 1780 and 1860, with the greatest proliferation occurring after 1830. The traditional authority on college founding in this era identifies only 29 permanent colleges as beginning before 1830, while 133 began in the 1830–1861 period. By the eve of the Civil War, the denominations with the most colleges were the Presbyterians, 49; the Methodists, 34; the Baptists, 25; and the Congregationalists, 21. The total college enrollment in 1860 equaled approximately 30,000.[4]

A major factor in the rapid growth of higher education was that the two denominations that experienced the greatest increases in membership because of the Awakening, the Methodists and the Baptists, at the same time came to accept the idea that a trained mind might help rather than hinder a minister's effectiveness in proclaiming the gospel. Consequently, in the generation after 1830 the Methodists founded such schools as Randolph-Macon (VA), McKendree (IL), Wesleyan (CT), Emory (GA), Wesleyan (GA), DePauw (IN), Emory and Henry (VA), Ohio Wesleyan, Centenary (LA), Baldwin-Wallace (OH), Lawrence (WI), Taylor (IN), Albion (MI), Northwestern (IL), College of the Pacific (CA), Wofford (SC), Duke (NC), Willamette (OR), Illinois Wesleyan, Cornell (IA), Hamline (MN), Iowa Wesleyan, Birmingham-Southern (AL), Mt. Union (OH), and Baker (KS).[5]

Also during the antebellum generation the Baptists organized Colby (ME), George Washington (Washington, DC), Georgetown (KY), Denison (OH), Shurtleff (IL), Franklin (IN), Mercer (GA), Samford (AL), Wake Forest (NC), Richmond (VA), Hillsdale (MI), Mississippi, Furman (SC), Rochester (NY), Carson-Newman (TN), and Kalamazoo (MI).[6]

Often graduates of the revived colleges led in the founding and developing of newer institutions in the West. Especially significant in this respect were the alumni of Yale, the stronghold of orthodox Congregationalism; Princeton, the stronghold of orthodox Presbyterianism; and Oberlin (OH), the stronghold of an evangelical and aggressive social reform emphasis. Oberlin's students and faculty helped establish a number of institutions including Olivet and Hillsdale in Michigan, Tabor and Iowa in Iowa, Drury in Missouri, Ripon in Wisconsin, and Carleton in Minnesota. Of the American college presidents in office before 1840, thirty-six had graduated from Yale—that "mother of colleges"—and twenty-two from Princeton. Yale and Princeton exerted much greater influence than can be identified by direct connections, however, for it was the largely conservative religious and curricular patterns of these Ivy League schools that set the tone for higher education in general during this period.[7]

As much as the Second Great Awakening influenced college founding in this era, many institutions came into existence because community leaders in the West were anxious to work with the ministers in founding colleges. While religious factors may have loomed large in the motives of the ministers, it was only one of several factors influencing community leaders to seek colleges.

Not unimportant was the element of prestige. A community with a college rated higher on the social and cultural scale than did its less sophisticated neighboring towns. Also important was the economic stimulus that a college could bring to a town. Population growth was a major criterion of success for a community, and the establishment of a successful college insured the influx of a significant number of residents. More residents, of course, meant a greater volume of business for the town merchants.

While the role of denominations in founding colleges has been exaggerated, that of individual ministers has not. Frequently, enthusiastic preachers, working somewhat ahead of their denominations, negotiated with community leaders in several potential areas to see where they could obtain the best local offer. For example, in Michigan, four frontier Methodist preachers cooperated with a local business group known as "The Albion Company" to begin Albion, and three aggressive pioneer farmers doubling as Free Will Baptist missionaries fought to overcome the reluctance of their denomination before opening Hillsdale.[8]

The typical old-time college, then, operated more as a Christian community college than as a denominational institution, and rarely did it reflect narrowly sectarian interests. It gained wide support from the members of the affiliated denomination and other denominations. The town and surrounding area supplied a high percentage of the students, many of whom boarded in the community. The college's public events made it a cultural center for the locality and the area citizens responded favorably to fund drives (college agents did much of their fund raising within a fifty-mile radius of the college).[9]

One of the reasons the colleges were popular in their communities was that often they provided the only secondary instruction in the area. The great majority of students studied on the secondary level. For example, at Oberlin, whose enrollment surpassed 1,300 during the 1850s, only one-eighth of the students were enrolled in a regular college course, and only one-third were pursuing college work of any type. Similarly, only 10 percent of Wheaton (IL) students in 1860 were studying at the college level, and when Colorado College opened shortly after the Civil War, only one-fourth of its enrollees were college-level scholars.[10] The Christian colleges devoted major attention to training secondary students in part to meet local needs, in part to generate sufficient total tuition to justify offering instruction to a limited number of college students, and in part to assure a supply of students with adequate training and interest to enroll in their college programs.

While most of the western colleges were local in nature, one can find examples of institutions that reflected the regional nature of the colonial colleges. For example, Transylvania (KY) became one of the leading colleges in America by instructing many of the future leaders of the Old South. By 1860 its medical school had taught with distinction more than six thousand students and had graduated nearly two thousand doctors. Perhaps the majority of trained physicians practicing in the South and Southwest in the antebellum period had studied at Transylvania. The graduates of the Transylvania Law School were fewer in number but more widely known. Among the alumni from this period are Stephen Austin, Albert Sidney Johnston, Cassius Clay, Jefferson Davis, John Breckenridge, John Marshall Harlan, and John Crittenden.[11]

The wide distribution of many new colleges meant that higher education was becoming increasingly accessible to the middle and lower classes. Many students of modest means lived at home while studying, and in a day when room and board charges rather than tuition comprised the principal part of college expenses, this was especially significant. The growing democratization of higher education did not characterize only the West, for even New England after 1800 witnessed a sharp increase in the number of students from poor families. Some of these went to Harvard and

Yale; however, they enrolled primarily at Brown, Dartmouth, and six new colleges: Williams, Middlebury (VT), Vermont, Bowdoin (ME), Colby (ME), and Amherst (MA).[12]

The overall increase in college enrollment over the colonial period occurred less from sharp growth in individual colleges than from the greater number of institutions that came into existence to serve modest numbers of students. In the mid-nineteenth century, a large eastern institution like Yale would enroll about five hundred students. As a typical school in the West, Beloit (WI) in 1860 enrolled only sixty college and 108 normal and preparatory students. Some institutions operated with even as small a student body as that of Franklin in 1847 with its twenty-five college and twenty-five preparatory students.[13]

The Continuing Mission

The old-time college leaders sought to create an environment in which the Christian faith and Christian morality influenced every aspect of the collegiate experience. Often founders located their institutions in remote, rural places in an effort to protect the students from undesirable recreational centers. For example, James McBride, an Ohio legislator who was influential in the founding of Presbyterian-oriented Miami, argued for a rural location for the school by stating, "I had rather send my son to a seminary of learning provided there were able professors even though it should be immersed in the gloom of the deep woods than to send him to an urban setting like Cincinnati where he would be exposed to the temptations and vices which are always prevalent in large cities."[14]

College officials made certain that students properly observed the Sabbath. Most required their students to attend Sunday worship in one of the neighborhood churches, and some added a second service on campus later in the day. Some colleges held classes on Tuesday through Saturday, using Monday as the second weekend holiday and thus reducing the need to spend Sunday preparing for classes. Other institutions that did hold Monday classes found means of discouraging study on the Sabbath. For example, Amherst professors arranged their assignments so that the students did not need to make specific preparation for Monday classes.[15]

The faculty members were often ministers and almost invariably dedicated Christians; therefore, they sought to promote the spiritual development as well as the intellectual growth of their students. The instructors watched for natural opportunities both inside and outside the classroom to lead an unconverted student to receive Christ as Savior. Many parents expected the college to serve as an evangelistic agent for their youths. The parents of one Wofford student sent the faculty a letter expressing great appreciation for the recent conversion of their son: "We felt that if we could obtain the means of sending him to Wofford, God would convert him."[16]

The old-time colleges played a larger role in evangelizing their students than do contemporary Christian colleges with equally strong evangelistic goals, because then a much smaller percentage of Protestant college students were professing Christians. The explanation is simple. In a day when nearly every college was a Christian college, the non-Christian student who aspired to a higher education had little choice but to enroll in a religious institution. The colleges, in turn, rarely imposed a religious test as a basis for admission.[17]

Probably fewer than one-half of the antebellum students were professing Christians. One comprehensive study by the American Education Society in 1831 considered it very encouraging to note that following the Second Great Awakening, 683 of 3,582 students in fifty-nine colleges were "hopefully pious." An 1856 study by the Amherst College Society of Inquiry showed little more than one-third of the students in eleven New England colleges as claiming to be Christian. The highest percentages were at Wesleyan (75 percent) and Amherst and Middlebury (60 percent each), while the lowest percentage was at Harvard (10 percent).[18]

The most effective method for bringing a large number of unsaved students into the fold was the periodic revival. College after college almost annually reported sweeping revivals that not only converted many students but led Christian youths to consider seriously careers as ministers and missionaries. Many students changed their manners of living, and often the changes were permanent. For example, Princeton witnessed an unusual awakening in the winter of 1814–15 when "in many a chamber where formerly mischievous youths plotted to burn an outhouse or to set off firecrackers in the lecture rooms, there was earnest prayer or anxious discussions over religious matters." Sometimes a revival upset the regular college routine, as at Randolph-Macon in 1852 where a student reported: "Lessons and text books are fast being supplanted by prayers and hymn books and Bibles. Study seems today as if it were entirely a secondary matter." Sometimes such enthusiasm combined with the natural adolescent desire to seek temporary escape from the academic routine. In the midst of a revival season at DePauw in 1842, a student burst into a classroom with an announcement to the scholars that "President Simpson preaches at the Campground at 1:00." The result was immediate confusion, and the students "without dismissal or leave gathered up their books and hastened away."[19]

Insightful revivalist leaders warned that emotional awakenings were not the ideal religious activity. President Jonathan Blanchard of Knox (IL) and Wheaton (IL) preferred no revivals at all if the work of the church could be realized without them. "When they are successful," he said, "they tend to make us vain and conceited because we do so much. Then they beget disrelish for ordinary labors in the church and make them seem tedious, and they also exalt religious activity above the grace of God. If unsuccessful, they produce discouragement, faintness of heart, and fretfulness in the church."[20]

While evangelism was one aim of the old-time colleges, it was not their primary purpose. After all, churches could evangelize, but they could not provide the necessary education for aspiring ministers; among clergymen and denominational officials, at least, the ministerial training function was cited regularly as the most important reason for founding a college. Contrary to popular opinion, very few colleges enrolled only or even mostly ministerial candidates (this was the case briefly at Mercer and Geneva in Pennsylvania). It is true, however, that colleges sometimes placed undue pressure on students to consider ministerial careers. For example, one Denison student just after the Civil War stated that "it would be probably impossible to exaggerate the prominence given to the duty of devoting one's life to the ministry or missions." He especially remembered how "old Professor John Stevens speaking in chapel on the Day of Prayer for Colleges would cast his eyes solemnly over the assembly and remark 'Let those who must study law.'"[21]

While the colleges eagerly welcomed ministerial candidates, they also were pleased to train students for a variety of other professions, especially law, medicine, and teaching. Usually no more than 25 percent of the graduates of a college were preparing for the ministry, but a great majority of them were planning to enter some profession. On the eve of the Civil War, approximately 16 percent of the students in eleven New England colleges were ministerial candidates. During the whole of the antebellum period, approximately 20 percent of the graduates of Randolph-Macon and between 20 and 25 percent of the graduates of the Michigan church colleges entered the ministry. By comparison 80 percent of the graduates of Randolph-Macon and 90 percent of the graduates of Amherst prepared to enter one of the four major professions.[22]

Of the campus activities officially designed to promote the Christian faith, the one most regularly scheduled—although probably not most popular—was the chapel. As had been the case in the colonial period, most colleges held a chapel service immediately following an early rising bell and again late in the afternoon. Frequently, these services took the name "prayers" because of their brevity—usually not longer than fifteen minutes—and because they often seemed more like family devotions than worship services. A typical service included singing, Scripture reading, prayer, and perhaps a brief homily. At some institutions, such as Episcopal Columbia about 1800, the service might be very formal. There, at a typical service, President Johnson alone or with the students recited or chanted the Ten Commandments, thirty verses of Psalms, the Gloria Patri, a collect, the One-Hundredth Psalm, the Nicene Creed, the Lord's Prayer, and other prayers.[23]

There is evidence that most colleges did not make their chapel services as attractive as they could have. A student at Amherst in the 1840s, William Hammond, probably expressed the sentiments of many students in other colleges when he noted, "I really think that these public prayers do more harm than good to the religious feeling of the majority of the students; they are regarded as an idle bore." Students did not seem to object to the required Sunday services as much as to the chapel services, perhaps because home habits had accustomed them to attend Sunday worship—but not religious exercises every morning and every afternoon. The students especially objected to the early morning services. At Yale, where morning prayers in the winter began at 5:30 in an unheated chapel, one student observed that it was "cold, cold, cold work to get up and march to chapel by moonlight in the early dawn of winter mornings." The timing of the afternoon chapel was scarcely better planned, for it was held at a time of day when the physiology of the body is more conducive to physical activity than to mental concentration.[24]

Some colleges, however, succeeded in planning effective chapels. The students seemed to accept more readily a service that included a dynamic sermon than one that did not. When a college had an especially eloquent president as a regular chapel speaker, the effect upon the students could be electric. This was the case, for example, at Yale under Timothy Dwight, Princeton under John McLean, Brown under Francis Wayland, and Oberlin under Charles Finney.[25]

Student religious societies began at least as early as 1719 when a group of pious students at Harvard organized the "Society of Young Students." They organized partly to promote their own spiritual welfare but also as a reaction to the significant number of irreligious students then in attendance. Student religious societies, however, became much more prominent in the first half of the nineteenth century, and most of these organizations took the name of "Theological Society," "Society of Inquiry," or "Society of Missionary Inquiry." One of the earliest theological societies was organized at Harvard. There, in the late eighteenth century, students debated questions such as "Whether the prevailing spirit of toleration proceeds more from an enlarged and liberal way of thinking than from an indifference to matters of religion?" and "Whether poverty be more injurious to religion than ignorance?" The societies of inquiry promoted academic discussion and debate on the problems of religion, and they also sought to stimulate the devotional and moral lives of their members. Usually the societies limited their membership to professing Christians, and some of them required additional commitments. To become a member of the "Yale Moral Society," for example, a student promised to regulate his conduct by the rules of morality contained in the Bible and to refrain from profane language, playing cards, and the intemperate use of alcoholic beverages.[26]

By far the most important type of college religious society in this period was the society of missionary inquiry, which was designed to study and promote foreign missionary activity. On college campuses and in churches alike, a sharp increase in foreign missionary interest developed from the Second Great Awakening. American historians usually date the beginning of the modern missionary movement from a group which met under a haystack at Williams in 1806. The group, led by Samuel J. Mills, retreated to the haystack for shelter during a thunderstorm and proceeded collectively to pledge to volunteer for foreign service wherever God called. The young men met regularly for the next two years and influenced others, including Luther Rice and Gordon Hall, also to dedicate their lives to foreign service. At almost exactly the same time, Andover Theological Seminary (MA) came into existence as an expression of protest by the evangelicals of New England against the increasing influence of Unitarianism, particularly at Harvard. When in 1810 one of the members of the Williams group transferred to Andover, he took with him the handwritten records of the missionary group and continued the organization on that campus. At Andover, the society quickly recruited new members including Adoniram Judson of Brown, Samuel Nott Jr. of Union (NY), and Samuel Newell of Harvard. Consequently, Andover became not only a bastion of defense for evangelical Christianity but also a center for the stimulation of interest in missionary activity abroad. In 1812, Hall, Rice, Judson, Nott, and Newell sailed for India as the first five modern American missionaries.[27]

Because Christian college leaders believed deeply in the importance of providing Christian higher education for as many qualified young people as possible, they charged very low tuition rates — so low, in fact, that they subsidized the cost of a student's education to a greater extent than do most contemporary colleges. In 1830, comprehensive annual costs to attend college totaled $180–200 at Pennsylvania, $170 at Harvard, $140 at Yale, and $120 at both Brown and Williams. On the eve of the Civil War, yearly costs were $100–120 at Richmond, $176 at Hampden-Sydney (VA), and $340 at the College of the Pacific. Unlike today, tuition charges comprised only a small part of the total yearly costs. Yale students in 1860 paid $39 annual tuition, while charges at western colleges usually ranged from $20 to $30.[28]

Many western and southern colleges in the 1830s and 1840s sought to reduce their already low tuition rates by providing work in "manual labor" programs for many or even all of their students. The plan was that many students would meet most of their expenses while improving their health and the overall college discipline at the same time. The colleges quickly lost enthusiasm for these programs, however, when they saw that they were running out of work and the students were having too little time to concentrate on their studies.[29] Only rarely (e.g., at Berea in Kentucky) did such a program survive longer than a few years.[30]

Some colleges, denominations, and other religious agencies provided financial aid, especially to ministerial candidates. Most of the scholarships at nineteenth-century Hobart (NY), for example, went to students preparing for the Episcopalian ministry. No agency aided students more generously than did the Congregationalist American Education Society. By the eve of the Civil War, that organization was granting an average of more than $60 per year to nearly four hundred ministerial students. Most of these were enrolled in orthodox Congregational colleges and seminaries like Amherst, where five hundred of the first 1,300 students received such aid. Elsewhere in New England, about 25 percent of the students in the early nineteenth century obtained funds from sources other than their families or colleges. College-based student loan funds were uncommon, perhaps nonexistent, in this period. Wake Forest claims that one of its students initiated the first such fund in America in the 1870s.[31]

Many of the same groups that aided students also gave support directly to the colleges. Again the Congregationalists provided the most generous support; through their Society for the Promotion of Collegiate and Theological Education of the West, they raised over $500,000 during the generation following 1843 to promote education and evangelism in the western states. Most of the society's aid went to Congregational schools such as Knox, Illinois, Heidelberg (OH), Western Reserve (OH), Marietta (OH), Wabash (IN), Beloit, and Ripon. By the time of the Civil War, Theron Baldwin, Yale graduate and long-time society leader, could boast that more than 10,000 students had experienced religious conversion in the thirteen colleges regularly supported by the society since 1844.[32]

One unfortunately widespread fund-raising method introduced in this period was the long-range tuition scholarship. A typical scholarship entitled an individual who paid a given amount, say $100 or $250, to send one student to school tuition-free each year for a long period — frequently twenty years — but sometimes for an unlimited period. These scholarship sales did succeed in bringing immediate revenue to college treasuries, but the long-term results were not good. Gradually, rejoicing over the scholarship sales faded to disillusionment. Often the scholarships had not been completely paid but rather given as promissory notes that were difficult to collect. The major problem, however, was that the institutional leaders had borrowed future tuition income to pay current expenses. When the scholarship funds were spent, many non-paying students remained, and the administrators found themselves in the embarrassing position of having to refuse to honor the perpetual scholarships or *else* having to buy them back.

Much more successful were the beginning efforts at raising endowment funds and using the interest from them to award scholarships to able students. For example, President McLean of Princeton raised $60,000 for this purpose just before the Civil War.[33]

A College Education

The 1864 Ripon catalog stated: "Instruction will be conducted on Christian principles, and it will be the aim of the instructors to pervade it with a strong and healthful moral and religious influence."[34] Most antebellum colleges shared this goal and regularly employed instructors who applied biblical principles to their disciplines.

At most colleges, students attended classes in the same large building in which they roomed and took their meals. They enrolled according to class, usually in three prescribed recitation or lecture sessions. The classes, interspersed with meals, study sessions, free periods, chapel exercises, and other special college activities, comprised a typical college day.

The curriculum during the first half of the nineteenth century remained much the same as that of the late colonial period except that science instruction became increasingly important — particularly in the eastern colleges — and some institutions broadened the range of their course offerings. Latin and Greek served as the primary subjects for freshmen and sophomores and even continued into the junior year with major emphasis being given to such authors as Livy, Herodotus, Horace, Cicero, Euripides, and Homer. Also important in the lower-division curriculum were such mathematical studies as algebra, geometry, trigonometry, and conic sections. During the junior and senior years, language and mathematical studies gave way to emphasis upon science, philosophy, religion, social science, and, in some cases, literature.[35]

American educators in general continued to believe that a classical curriculum provided the best intellectual framework for an educated person. Latin and Greek classics were studied because they contained eternal truths and values which every student should know. They were translated because the translation process was an excellent way of shaping the mind. Sometimes this emphasis upon disciplining the mind became so strong, however, that it prevented the students from giving serious consideration to the ideas of the writers. Mathematics also served to "train the mind"; therefore, it ranked next to the ancient languages in importance.

Frequently the most engaging courses were those in philosophy and re-

ligion. They were taught almost invariably by the president to the senior
class. The most common names for these courses included mental, moral,
and intellectual philosophy (described by some as "the science of what
ought to be"); evidences of Christianity; logic; and ethics. The exact content of the courses varied according to presidential discretion, but they
usually gave emphasis to the social sciences as well as to philosophy and
religion. As discussed in detail by Mark Noll in his introduction to this
book, these courses almost always sought to combine Enlightenment ra-
tionalism with the Christian faith, using the former to support the latter.[36]

Many senior class instructors, particularly in the early years of this period, used textbooks by English or Scottish authors such as William Paley,
the Anglican scholar. Yale students, for example, read the Paley texts for
over sixty years. His *Natural Philosophy* argued for the existence and goodness of God from nature; his *Evidences of Christianity* offered the data supporting Christianity as the true and supreme revelation of God; and his
Moral and Political Philosophy presented the personal and social obligations
of man that resulted from natural and revealed religion.

Not all students found Paley's prose to be exciting. For example, at
Haverford (PA) the sophomore class traditionally ended the school year
by burning in effigy the author of the most unpopular textbook. For years
the choice was Paley — because of his *Evidences* — until a school official decided it was bad publicity for a Christian college to "burn at the stake the
author of the book that was supposed to safeguard their faith," and he encouraged the students to redirect their aggressions to the author of the
trigonometry book then in use. After 1835 the Paley texts began to be replaced by those of such American moral philosophers as Francis Wayland
of Brown; Mark Hopkins of Williams; Joseph Haven of Amherst; John
Dagg of Mercer; Charles Finney, Asa Mahan, and James Fairchild of Oberlin; Archibald Alexander and James McCosh of Princeton; and Noah
Porter of Yale.[37]

After 1815 the northeastern colleges significantly improved their science
programs. The schools in this region — which as late as 1830 still provided
the majority of college graduates — broadened their science curricula, purchased expensive laboratory equipment (or philosophical apparatus, as it
was called), and hired well-trained and permanent professors to replace
the transitory tutors. Consequently, the number of science professors in
America grew from twenty-five in 1800 to sixty in 1828 to more than three
hundred by 1850. Unfortunately the status of science instruction did not
improve nearly as rapidly in the South and West, where most schools offered no more than a smattering of introductory work taught by a single
science instructor who often doubled as the mathematics professor.[38]

Although the quantity and quality of science instruction varied widely, the approach of the scientists toward the Christian religion did not. Representative of nearly all colleges and scientists were the views of Benjamin Silliman of Yale, Walter Minto of Princeton, and James Dwight Dana of Yale. Silliman, probably the leading scientist in the country, saw no difficulty in accepting both the findings of science and the record of Scripture, and viewed himself as "the honored interpreter of a portion of . . . [God's] works." Minto, a distinguished astronomer, believed deeply that

> The study of natural philosophy leads us in a satisfactory manner to the knowledge of one almighty, all wise, and all good Being who created, preserves, and governs the universe. . . . Indeed I consider a student of [natural philosophy] . . . as engaged in a continued act of devotion. . . . This immense, beautiful, and varied universe is a book written by the finger of omnipotence and raises the admiration of every attentive beholder.

Dana told the American Association for the Advancement of Science in 1856 that "we but study the method in which boundless wisdom has chosen to act in creation," and then he observed that "almost all works on science in our language endeavor to uphold the Sacred Word." Not only were American scientists in this period deeply religious; they also viewed their Christian beliefs as directly related to their scientific investigations, indeed, as providing the ultimate meaning for them.[39]

In the days before the elective system, students sometimes could supplement their required studies with work in other areas by giving extra money and time to such pursuits. For example, in the early nineteenth century Samuel Morse, the future artist and inventor, studied French privately with two recitations per day in addition to his regular work at Yale. Also, when the Yale tutors in the late eighteenth century wished to supplement the regular curriculum with English language and literature, the university approved only on the condition that the courses be taught to interested students outside the regular classroom schedule.[40] Only a few colleges officially introduced the teaching of written composition and literature before the Civil War, while many schools suspected that moral evil resulted from reading novels. Reflecting the concern of his college, one Oberlin student explained in verse what tends to happen when girls become addicted to novel reading:

> The live, long day does Laura read,
> In a cushioned easy chair,
> In slip shod shoes and dirty gown,
> And tangled, uncombed hair,
> For o the meals I'm very sure

> You ner' did see such feeding
> For the beef is burnt and the veal is raw,
> And all from novel reading.[41]

Only rarely did a literature course in the English Bible appear in the official curriculum. President Alexander Campbell of Bethany (in present-day West Virginia) claimed that his school opened in 1840 as the only literary college in America to maintain a Department of Sacred History and Biblical Literature as an integral part of the curriculum. Also, Geneva, from its start in 1848, offered a Bible curriculum as well as the proscribed classical curriculum. The religion courses at Geneva included Psalms, Bible history, and church history as well as the more traditional Greek New Testament and evidences of Christianity. Bethany and Geneva were exceptional, however. Biblical literature courses did not become common until the late nineteenth century, and then more because of the introduction of the elective system than because of a decision that Bible courses per se ought to be offered in the curriculum of a Christian college.[42]

While study of the Bible rarely appeared as part of the official course offerings, the colleges almost always offered it as a vital part of their unofficial curricula. In the early nineteenth century, Princeton students studied Bible lessons on Sunday after morning prayers and before breakfast. After morning church and dinner, they recited to the president on five chapters of the Bible. Oberlin in the 1860s required student participation in extracurricular Bible study courses which met one hour per week. During the typical four college years, an Oberlin student studied nearly the entire Scriptures. At Lafayette (PA) in the 1860s, faculty minutes note that the college "designed to make the Bible the central object of study in the whole college course." The Sunday requirements at Wake Forest included not only a Sunday morning worship service but also a Sunday evening Bible class for which all students prepared recitations. These nearly universal extracurricular Bible studies, when added to the regular senior-level religion courses and the frequent injection of biblical values into the entire curriculum, meant that students studied the Bible and the Christian faith nearly as much as do students in the seriously Christian liberal arts colleges today.[43]

Heretofore this discussion of curriculum has included only the college-level programs. As noted earlier, however, outside of the Northeast most colleges enrolled fewer—sometimes far fewer—college students than preparatory pupils. They had to operate their own preparatory departments in many cases because of the absence of public secondary institutions during most of the period. Ideally, secondary students were preparing for entrance into college, but often they never achieved this goal. The preparatory course included both advanced common school subjects and college preparatory courses, and many of the students were taking courses to aid them in their work as common school teachers. Some of the common school subjects taught were reading, grammar, geography, and arithmetic, while elementary courses in Latin, Greek, and higher mathematics prepared students for college entrance.[44]

A limited number of colleges offered graduate instruction before the Civil War. Andover Seminary, which opened in 1808, was probably the first autonomous graduate school. Also a few established institutions introduced programs in medicine, law, and theology. Harvard began schools in all three of these areas before 1829, and Yale achieved the same by 1843.[45]

With the increase in the number of middle-class students who brought to college their interest in agriculture and business, there gradually developed a demand for a less traditional curriculum. President Wayland of Brown led the movement for a program of study that would better meet the needs of the new type of student. He argued:

> That such a people should be satisfied with the teaching of Greek, Latin, and the elements of mathematics was plainly impossible. Lands were to be surveyed, roads to be constructed, ships to be built and navigated, soils of every kind under every variety of climate were to be cultivated, manufactures were to be established . . . all the means which science has provided to aid the progress of civilization must be employed if this youthful republic would place itself abreast of the empires of Europe.

In essence, Wayland was calling for the abandonment of the fixed, four-year course and the introduction of an elective system in which colleges would establish courses to meet newly developing societal needs, and students would choose from a variety of offerings those which would best meet their intellectual needs and educational goals.[46]

The response of the American colleges before the Civil War was not to discard the old curriculum but rather to create an alternate "scientific" or "literary" degree program. This alternate curriculum either reduced or replaced the classical studies and gave greater emphasis to modern languages, physical and biological sciences, history, literature, and the application of science to commerce. Students studying this alternate curriculum earned a Bachelor of Science degree.[47]

In one way or another, the American colleges have always offered master's degrees. The earliest of these followed the medieval tradition in which a student needed to study seven years to earn such a degree. Consequently, during the early period at Harvard when most students were studying for the ministry, they were encouraged to spend part or all of the three years following the receipt of the baccalaureate continuing their studies on campus "reading divinity" with the president and perhaps serving as tutors for the undergraduates as well. For example, during the 1649–56 period, fifty-three Harvard men earned an A.B. degree and thirty-five an M.A. degree; of the thirty-five earning graduate degrees, nearly all continued their studies in residence, although not all stayed the full three years.[48]

By the eighteenth century, one could earn a master's degree with less effort. Often a student needed to complete no assignment other than to deliver a thesis in public assembly and to serve usefully in some vocation for three years following his undergraduate studies. By the early nineteenth century, however, even this minimal requirement disappeared, and a common joke among undergraduates was that all it took to earn a master's degree was to "keep out of jail for three years and pay the five dollar fee." The modern type of master's degree involving significant graduate work began to appear in the 1850s, and by the 1870s it had largely replaced the essentially honorary degree of the early part of the century.[49]

By twentieth-century standards, most pre–Civil War professors possessed an inadequate academic background. In the best eastern schools the typical professor had completed nothing more than the classical course of undergraduate studies and some theological training. Only a few instructors held Ph.D. degrees before 1860, and they earned these in European universities. Most of the frontier colleges employed a mixture of professors with and without degrees; presumably the students on degree programs did most of their work with professors who held degrees.

An effective college program required a minimum of four instructors. This allowed for professors in moral philosophy (usually the president), the classics, mathematics, and one—frequently a person with some science training—for the rest of the curriculum. While many frontier colleges felt fortunate to have four such professors, the larger eastern institutions employed much larger staffs. For example, twenty-four professors taught at Harvard in 1860 and seventeen at Princeton in 1868. Few professors were specialists, at least by the modern definition of that word; yet, the early schools thought that many of their instructors were very learned. One early Olivet professor described even a retired minister who served as a substitute teacher as being very competent in every area: "It did not matter what the lesson was to be, for in every department he was a proficient scholar."[50]

Faculty salaries varied widely from reasonable levels in the better eastern colleges to bare subsistence wages in new, struggling institutions in the West. At Brown in 1827 the president earned $1,500 and professors $1,000 per year. Princeton in 1868 paid a professor $2,100 and the occupancy of a rent-free house. Bucknell in 1873 provided the president with $2,000 and the professors with $1,200 to $1,800. By contrast, on the Michigan frontier of the 1840s, Professor Oramal Hosford of Olivet received $36 for teaching six hours daily during the college's first year, and James Stone, president of Kalamazoo, earned approximately $200 per year at the same time. By the 1860s the Michigan salaries were better; Kalamazoo and Olivet paid their professors $600 to $700 per year, while the Kalamazoo president earned $1,500.[51]

Historically, college professors have been willing to work for moderate or low pay because of the deep sense of satisfaction inherent in their work. They are free to use their creative skills in dealing with the great issues of life, and they have opportunities to influence young people in a life-changing manner. Christian college instructors frequently view their vocation as a calling from God equally sacred as that of a call to the ministry; some even have seen the teaching profession as providing greater opportunities than the ministry. For example, Jonathan Blanchard resigned from his very satisfying pastorate at the Sixth Presbyterian Church in Cincinnati because "he saw in teaching the possibility of multiplying his efforts at the source through the inculcation of Christian . . . principles among young men who would go forth to spread them abroad."[52]

The Extracurriculum

The literary society was by far the most influential activity in American student life before the Civil War. The literary society movement began during the late colonial period and in some places continued well into the twentieth century; however, it reached its peak during the first two generations of the nineteenth century. Nearly every college maintained at least two societies that competed intensely against each other in a variety of activities. Each sought to recruit the most capable members of the freshman class, each sought to have a larger and better library collection than the other, each sought to outfit its society hall more lavishly than did the other, and each sought to win the intersociety contests in oration, debate, and written composition.[53]

In each college the societies worked to enroll both the best and also the largest number of freshmen each fall with vigor equal to that with which modern-day athletic coaches recruit athletes for their teams. Society scouts traveled to neighboring towns to board the trains bringing new students to the college town. They also visited preparatory schools and delivered highly passionate speeches extolling the virtues of their societies while denouncing the opposition. At Wake Forest the Euzelian Society so desired to enlist the son of a Chinese missionary that it promised to pay his tuition if he would join.[54]

One is amazed that the students were willing to pay large sums of money, which in some cases equaled their tuition charges, to decorate their societies' lavish halls and to build their impressive library collections. At DePauw the students of one society spent more than $8,000 on portraits to hang in their hall.[55]

The societies disciplined their members as rigorously—and more effectively—than did the colleges themselves. The Philomathesian Literary Society at Middlebury fined absent members twelve cents and tardy members eight cents. At Oberlin, where students also fined one another for irregular attendance, one society boasted in 1877 that not one member had missed a performance in eleven years. At Princeton the official society censor carefully watched the behavior of members even when away from society meetings and activities; any member who neglected his work, wasted his time at a tavern, or displayed other than exemplary behavior might be admonished or even suspended. On one occasion the society moderator himself received punishment when he became irritated at the levity of a member whom he was swearing into office and hit him over the head with a copy of the organization's constitution.[56]

The most important society activities occurred at the regular meetings, where students competed in debates, oratory, and oral criticism. This emphasis on developing articulate and persuasive speaking skills served a functional purpose, as the great majority of students were preparing for public careers in the ministry, politics, law, or teaching. Often students exerted greater intellectual effort in preparing for literary society activities than in studying for their regular classes. In the days before the rise of athletics, the debate hero was the college hero. To be recognized as such was more highly prized than to be acclaimed the classroom valedictorian. The most popular debate topics involved current events (e.g., "Have the United States justly acquired Texas?"), but the students also enjoyed debating historical issues (e.g., "Was the Reformation the Result of Natural Causes or the Special . . . [Intervention] of Divine Agency?"). Philosophical and religious topics received less attention from student debaters than they were given in the classroom. Probably the most popular debate topic during the decades before 1860 was that of slavery.[57]

The highlight of the year for student orators occurred during commencement week when the seniors or the star orators from each of the societies performed before large audiences. At Randolph-Macon, the faculty dismissed the seniors from all classes for four weeks prior to commencement to allow them to write, memorize, and polish their orations with one of the instructors. At Oberlin, as commencement week approached, "Strange sounds might have been heard at any time of day, and sometimes far into the evening, issuing from any of the groves in the vicinity. Every available stump was pre-empted, and the attention of quietly grazing herds was arrested by the scores of orators in training for those grand occasions." The student narrations served not only as the climax of the literary society activities for the year, but also as major public relations events for the colleges. The college presidents anxiously desired that the students perform ably and, above all, that they avoid any controversy that might embarrass college officials. Consequently, at Bucknell the president carefully monitored the orators during their preparation period. He required the students to submit their orations to him well in advance so that he might strike any objectionable passages. If the student chose to use forbidden material on the day of graduation, he forfeited his degree.

The students enjoyed the excitement of the oratory performances, but they displayed much less enthusiasm for another commencement week activity, namely the public examinations, when not only the faculty but also trustees and other educated gentlemen might quiz them on their recently completed courses. Sometimes the students resented the trustees for pretending to know more than they actually did. One such indignant Princeton student noted that "trustees are monstrous humbugs as well as arrant bores."[58]

The literary societies maintained significant libraries to provide resource material for students preparing for their public performances. In some cases, the society libraries exceeded in size the college library. For example, in 1839 the Yale society libraries numbered 15,000 books while the college library had only 10,500 volumes. In the same year at Union, the society libraries had 8,450 books, 300 more than the regular library collection. The two literary society libraries at Trinity (Duke) in 1866 contained 2,200 volumes each, while the college library had only 650 books. The societies developed such extensive library collections only because the college libraries were inadequate[59] and inaccessible. The typical college library held a disproportionately large number of old theological, legal, and medical books. The Dickinson library of 3,100 volumes in 1837 contained 700 works in theology, 600 in law and politics, and 400 in medicine and chemistry. Even worse, many of these studies were long outdated. For example, of the 400 volumes in medicine and chemistry, 35 had been printed in the sixteenth century, 244 in the seventeenth century, 53 in the eighteenth century, and only 4 in the nineteenth century. Furthermore, only 11 of the 400 volumes were in English.[60]

Even when students demonstrated a special interest in an area where the library was strong, they faced considerable difficulty in gaining access to the collection because few college libraries held regular hours for students. For example, at Columbia, "Freshmen and sophomores were allowed to visit the library only once a month to gaze at the back of books; the juniors were taken there once a week by a tutor who gave verbal information about the contents of the books, but only seniors were permitted to open the precious volumes which they could draw from the library during one hour on Wednesday afternoons." The society libraries, then, invariably exceeded the college libraries in the breadth of their collections and in the extent of their usefulness and availability to the students.[61]

It is difficult to exaggerate the extent to which the literary societies exerted a positive influence upon student life. They provided some of the best intellectual activities — often better than those found in the classroom — and served as the only major organized social activity at the schools. They broadened the students' scope of information by emphasizing areas of knowledge that complemented more than duplicated the classroom work. They forced the students to analyze current events and to develop skill in precise reasoning and oral persuasion. Also, as the one aspect of campus life that was not dominated by the faculty, they provided students with a sense of participation in campus government and the opportunity to develop leadership skills. Many if not most colleges in this period could have echoed the experience of Hillsdale, whose historian wrote of the societies that "nothing else ever exerted so profound an influence upon Hillsdale students." Many students could have identified with the comment of William Seward, secretary of state under Abraham Lincoln, who stated about his years at Union (NY) in the early nineteenth century: "If I were required now to say from what part of my college education I derived the greatest advantage, I should say the exercises of the Adelphic Society."[62]

After the Civil War, the literary societies in colleges in the Northeast and Southeast began to decline, while those in the newer schools in the West reached their peak in the period before 1900. The eastern societies declined in part because many of the newer middle-class students began to prepare for vocations in which oral persuasion was not of major importance, in part because other types of competitive extracurricular activities (musical organizations, athletic teams, and fraternities) began to appear, and in part because the new courses added in the late nineteenth century absorbed many of the areas of inquiry that the society students had found most exciting.[63]

After the Civil War, intercollegiate athletics were to offer the greatest challenge to the monopoly of the extra curriculum by the literary societies, but almost no such organized athletic activity existed before the war. Faculties generally frowned upon most sports contests as unbecoming of gentlemen and scholars and perhaps even dangerous to their health. At best the games were tolerated. One of the earliest athletic games was a very rough form of football known as "rushing," which was as much fighting as sport. After 1840, handball and cricket appeared at Princeton, and a few colleges began to construct gymnasiums. Boating was the first organized sport, with Yale forming the first club in 1843. Nine years later Yale and Harvard rowing crews competed on Lake Winnipesaukee (NH) in the first intercollegiate sports event in America.[64]

In the days before organized sports, many of the institutions that introduced manual labor systems also placed great emphasis upon the value of regular programs of physical labor. Dartmouth was an early leader in promoting the idea that manual labor should be part of the students' education. President John Shipherd of Oberlin viewed the manual labor system as part of his department of physiology. President George Junkin of Lafayette argued that "the healthful pursuits of mechanical and agricultural labor preserve the youthful constitution from the wasting effects of mental exertion and at the same time give to the mind that strength and independence which always results from the proud consciousness of self support."[65]

Few colleges encouraged or even allowed the existence of student government organizations until after the Civil War. Perhaps the first experiment with student government in America appeared at Amherst in 1888 when the president, Julius Seelye, established a college senate comprised of students and himself; he presided and also held veto power. The "Amherst system" gained wide recognition; however, Amherst students viewed it with mixed feelings, not being certain that the college was much different than it would have been without the system.[66]

A limited number of colleges and their students participated in social reform activity. Oberlin and several Midwestern colleges influenced by it were noteworthy centers for the promotion of a variety of causes, including temperance and especially abolitionism. When in 1833 Lane Seminary trustee Asa Mahan and his abolitionist students transferred from the Cincinnati school to Oberlin, the northern Ohio institution quickly organized the seven-thousand-member Oberlin Anti-Slavery Society. The southern students were less likely than their northern counterparts to establish organizations to promote their views on slavery; nevertheless, the southern church colleges, primarily through their faculty spokesmen, served as important centers of proslavery promotion. Presidents A. B. Longstreet of Emory, William A. Smith of Randolph-Macon, and Thomas R. Dew of William and Mary were influential writers of proslavery literature.[67]

If a college leader promoted one reform, he very likely might crusade for other causes as well. For example, when Knox president Blanchard — who once led the entire student body to a neighboring town to support him in a four-hour debate with Senator Stephen Douglas — saw his emancipation goals realized, he immediately transferred his energy into opposing secret societies. In the latter cause he found considerable support from other college leaders, probably because of their concern about the secret activities of many of the newly developing college fraternities.[68]

Discipline in the old-time college continued to be nearly as severe as that practiced during the colonial period. The colleges still specified the students' daily schedule for rising, studying, attending classes, playing, and retiring as well as the rules for them to follow. The rule books were usually explicit and often very detailed. For example, the laws of Union in 1802 consisted of eleven chapters, each of which contained from seven to twenty-three sections. Wheaton had a similarly long list including the usual forbidden activities of Sabbath breaking, foul language, games of chance, alcohol, tobacco, and disorderly conduct. Then, as if to make sure it had forgotten nothing, the catalog concluded with the comment that "everything is forbidden which will hinder and everything is required which we think will help students in the great object for which they assemble here which is the improvement of mind, morals, and heart." Sometimes the presidents assisted the tutors and residence hall supervisors in enforcing the rules. President McLean of Princeton frequently took evening walks to catch offenders and sometimes chased them to their rooms or up trees.[69]

The discipline enforced in the pre–Civil War colleges appears severe to the twentieth-century observer, but for several reasons it is not fair to judge these schools by modern standards. The students were younger; more than half were of high-school age and thus needed closer attention than do today's older college students. Furthermore, as mental discipline was one of the basic goals of the prevailing curriculum, it should not be surprising that social discipline was also strongly emphasized. Society in general approved of this type of control at the colleges. For example, in 1867 the Michigan legislature passed a law forbidding the sale of alcohol to students in public or private schools and prohibiting the students from playing cards, dice, billiards, or games of chance in buildings where liquor was sold.[70]

It is difficult to know the extent to which students violated the rules of their schools. College histories frequently describe the most celebrated student pranks, and many alumni delighted in recalling their youthful escapades (e.g., J. Sterling Morton, who became President Cleveland's secretary of agriculture and the founder of Arbor Day, recalled his student days at Albion: "I achieved the unenviable reputation of being so full of the devil that the very pores of my skin were said to exude the essence of diabolism"). People have generalized too much from these stories. The behavior of the students was probably no worse than that of similarly aged young people in other social settings then. Some student actions were harmless or merely annoying — such as scraping feet on the floor under

the dining hall or classroom tables to express disapproval of food preparation or teaching performance, making frequent loud noises such as the inappropriate use of college bells and horns, and placing animals in unex-
pected places (such as the ram that appeared suddenly in the Davidson
chapel and then proceeded to butt a professor out of the hall). College authorities worried more about the periodic smashing of doors and windows, the rolling of canon balls down the dormitory halls, the greeting of
patrolling tutors with showers of sticks and stones, and the relocation of
outhouses from neighboring properties to the college lawns. The Princeton lads thought it delightful to awake in the middle of the night to the cry
of "heads out, heads out" and then to look out the windows to the back
campus where a privy had been set on fire. On some campuses a limited
number of students would engage in "hazing" practices two or three
times a year. On such occasions they might victimize other (usually
younger) students by cutting off their hair, branding their bodies with in-
delible ink, smearing them with paint, or leaving them bound and gagged
in a cemetery all night. Still more rare were reports of students seriously
wounding or even killing faculty members.[71]

While the targets of aggression usually were other students or instructors, students sometimes engaged in small wars with town residents. Most
college communities witnessed at least some tension between the students
and the local citizenry. The townspeople often resented the social and educational privileges of the college students and the real or imagined arro-
gance that resulted. The likelihood of "town-versus-gown" riots was
greatest in those college communities where there resided unusually large
numbers of non-college young men, such as the lumberjacks near Bowdoin or the sailors near Yale. Even instructors were not free from attack by
town bullies. Such a mob once sent an arsenal of clubs and stones through
the windows of the house of Professor Silliman of Yale, an incident that
led him to carry two loaded pistols for the remainder of the summer. Fortunately, however, most town-and-gown conflicts were not physical
battles.[72]

The State University as a Protestant College

At least since 1754, when William Livingston, a New York state assem-
blyman, unsuccessfully sought to convince his legislative colleagues to establish a state college, interest had existed in the idea of publicly controlled universities. It was not until after the Revolution, however, that
such institutions began to appear, the first of these being the University of
Georgia in 1785. By 1849 state governments had founded thirty-six colleges of all types, and by the time of the Civil War there were twenty-two
major state universities in operation.[73]

Almost without exception, these institutions were Protestant in nature and emphasis even though theoretically under public control. The University of Michigan, for example, operated as a Christian college by virtually all standards of measurement. The faculty professed belief in the Christian faith, and most of them were members — and frequently clergymen — of the Methodist, Baptist, Presbyterian, or Episcopal denominations. The president and faculty frequently sought to instill Christian teachings in the minds of the students. President Henry Tappan delivered lectures entitled "Evidences of the Christian Religion," and Erastus Haven preached six hundred sermons during his six-year tenure as president. Despite the fact that the university admitted very few preparatory students, it still watched over the students' morals with rules as rigid as those in the denominational schools (the prohibited list included gambling, playing cards, intoxicating liquors, profanity, and violence and vice of all types). The University of Michigan regents also acted from a sense of religious duty. After 1860 they frequently opened their meetings with prayer, and when they discharged a professor in 1851 for expressing unacceptable views, the justification was that he "openly advocated a doctrine which is unauthorized by the Bible."[74]

By contrast, when Thomas Jefferson founded the University of Virginia in 1819, he intentionally avoided official religious influences, explaining his purpose as follows: "By bringing the rival sects together and mixing them with the mass of other students we shall soften their asperities, liberalize and neutralize their prejudices, and make the general religion the religion of peace, reason, and morality." Accordingly, there was no chapel at all at the University of Virginia until 1846, at which time both chapel and Sunday church attendance were voluntary.[75]

The University of Virginia's neutral approach toward religion did not, of course, characterize higher education in this period; its significance lies in its exceptionality. It was, rather, the University of Michigan's approach that typified the manner in which state institutions as well as private ones sought to promote both the Christian faith and learning in general.[76]

Almost invariably the leaders of early state institutions obtained their posts in part because of records of spiritual leadership. In 1840, 67 percent of the state universities — as well as 85 percent of the denominational colleges — had ministers as presidents. For a century after 1811, the University of Georgia hired only preachers as presidents. An admirer praised an early leader of a state agricultural college because "he could run a Methodist revival, an educational campaign, a domestic science class, or an agricultural and fine stock meeting with equal success." Colleges considered themselves very fortunate to have professors like James Thornwell of the University of South Carolina, who experienced notable success in leading students to Christian conversion.[77]

Like the church colleges, state universities almost invariably required students to attend chapel services and Sunday religious exercises. In many cases these requirements continued through the end of the century. As late as 1885, the faculty of the University of Illinois expelled a student for willfully missing compulsory chapel. Also, the faculty at Miami and the trustees at Ohio State voted against presidents whom they considered negligent in maintaining attendance at the daily compulsory chapel exercise.[78]

The state institutions also required study of religious courses and encouraged student participation in voluntary religious organizations. In the years before the introduction of the elective system, the state schools offered the same religion courses taught in the church colleges, namely moral philosophy, natural theology, and evidences of Christianity. Religious organizations at the University of Michigan included a missionary society, a Christian library association, weekly prayer meeting groups, and a student Christian association. At nearby Michigan State shortly after the Civil War, the college Christian union was the most active campus organization, with a majority of the student body participating in it.[79]

The state university rules governing behavior and amusements varied little from those found in church colleges. Some state institutions (such as Ohio University) simply adopted the regulations in effect at one of the church colleges. Despite the similarity of rules, however, there is some evidence, especially in the South, that students in the church colleges behaved better than did those in state universities. For example, in the southern institutions there was no record of dueling in the church colleges as there was in the state universities, and the student riots in the church colleges were not as severe as those in the universities where, on occasion, the militia was called in to bring order.[80]

If one cannot distinguish the state universities from the church colleges on the basis of their approach to the Christian religion, so also one cannot sharply distinguish the two on the amount of public financing that they received or on the basis of how they were controlled. State governments provided very little in the way of financial resources. Furthermore, a number of states gave aid to church colleges.[81] Since the Christian religion and higher education had been directly associated in America throughout its history, and since Protestantism commanded very wide respect in the generation between the Second Great Awakening and the Civil War, it was natural that the denominations would seek to exert the maximum possible influence in the new state universities. In many cases the denominations exercised greater administrative authority over the universities than did the state governments. For example, during at least part of the time before the Civil War, one or more denominations directly controlled the universities of Tennessee, North Carolina, Vermont, Kentucky, Miami,

Indiana, and Alabama. In a number of other cases, the denominations largely influenced the environment of the state universities.[82]

Probably no denomination exceeded the Presbyterian in the amount of control it exerted over a large number of state institutions. At Miami, for example, most of the faculty were Presbyterian ministers, many of the trustees were Presbyterian ministers or laymen, and until 1885 every president was a Presbyterian minister. As the Miami historian noted, "Though Miami University was created by the federal congress and established by the State of Ohio, it could not have been more Presbyterian if founded by John Knox."[83]

Although antebellum state universities operated as Protestant institutions, many denominational leaders opposed them because they believed them to be insufficiently religious or feared that they would become so. The church colleges doubted that state universities would emphasize Christian values sufficiently in teaching and in upholding moral standards to assure that students would not lose their religion. Professors at Emory and Davidson (NC) had the state universities in mind when they argued that education without religion "may illumine but it cannot heat; it may shine, but it cannot burn; nor can it infuse the warmth of moral life and religious hope into the world," and that ". . . the great sin of the mother of mankind was a thirst for intellectual knowledge without a corresponding desire for holiness." Similarly, Michigan Methodist leaders in 1857 expressed great concern that their young people might enroll in the state university: "We are compelled to fear . . . that it [the university] is so defective in those moral and religious restraints and influences which ought always to be thrown around students of literary institutions that it cannot be patronized by our citizens without imminent peril to . . . those youths who may be sent there." President Haven, who faced similar expressions of concern by certain church leaders during his presidency of the Ann Arbor school in the 1860s, expressed with insight the real nature of this concern when he suggested that "it is not a Godless education that they fear, but a Christian education not communicated through the forms and channels over which they preside."[84]

While the denominations often opposed the state universities, the universities in turn sometimes sought to limit the effectiveness of the church colleges or to eliminate them altogether. In Georgia, North Carolina, and South Carolina, the state universities for many years were able to influence their legislatures to prevent the founding of any denominational schools. Also, in Michigan the state university interests before 1855 convinced the legislature to give the university a monopoly of the degree-granting power and to place maximum valuation and income allotments upon the already established church colleges.[85]

The key to sound higher education in the antebellum period — as well as in later periods — was free competition between rival institutions and dialogue between prominent points of view. American higher education soon came to accept the former but only rarely has realized the latter. The public university, in particular, has an obligation to serve as a sounding board for all prominent points of view. On such controversial issues as religion, unfortunately, the free exchange of views has not regularly occurred. During the antebellum period, when orthodox Christian belief was prominent, most state institutions would not have tolerated an honest hearing for unorthodox views — those of agnostics or even of Unitarians, for example. Today the problem is reversed, for as Andrew Ten Brook, a University of Michigan professor, realized as early as the 1870s, the likelihood that the university would fall under the control of some parochial religious group was much smaller than the likelihood that evangelical Christianity would be forced out of the university. Ten Brook's fair view on the role of religion in the state university was that "in the state universities the question of religion may always be embarrassing. . . . If nothing is taught upon which men do not think alike, then teaching may be suspended for no subject can be traced far in any direction without ramifying into disputed territory."[86]

While scholars agree that the Christian religion dominated higher education before the Civil War, they disagree on whether the colleges of this period served the country well. During the 1950s and 1960s, the most influential educational historians expressed mostly critical comments about the antebellum colleges. A summary of their judgments would run something like this: The first half of the nineteenth century represents the low point in the history of American higher education, for this era witnessed the unfortunate proliferation of countless numbers of poor, weak colleges by competing Protestant denominations. These religious groups established institutions that were intellectually inferior and morbidly moralistic in their emphasis on evangelical piety and paternalistic discipline. Consequently, the students often rioted, the colleges became very unpopular with their larger constituencies, the enrollments declined, and many schools went out of existence. The salvation of higher education came only with the reforms of the late nineteenth century, when many institutions gradually began to discard the anachronistic religious requirements and classical curriculum and to replace them with a broader range of relevant courses, more highly trained professors, and an intellectually open environment. The result was a popular and democratic system of higher education that for the first time began to serve the real needs of the American public.[87]

Historians writing in the 1970s, by contrast, sharply challenged the validity of the above view. They argued that the older historians viewed the antebellum Christian liberal arts college from the perspective of the later secular university with which they identified, and that they too easily based their conclusions on a limited number and variety of sources. The most telling point of the younger scholars is that an increasing number of recent monographic studies provide data which show that many of the previously accepted views were inaccurate.

The results of this historiographical revolution present the old-time college in a favorable light. They show that the pre–Civil War college was less dominated by narrow, sectarian purposes than by broad, Christian ones; that the college served local needs as much as denominational ones; that in most respects it was very popular with its constituent groups; and that the supposed proliferation of needless colleges is explained more by the high number of "paper" institutions that never developed into legitimate colleges (80 percent of identifiable colleges failed either to open at all or to survive beyond a very brief period) than by an excessive number of fully operating institutions (most colleges that survived long enough to develop a full four-year program and actually to award degrees became permanent institutions).[88]

3

New Colleges and New Programs

The pre–Civil War period witnessed (1) very limited collegiate opportunities for blacks and white women, (2) only beginning efforts at significant curricular reform and expansion, (3) very few specially trained professors, and (4) only a slight hint of the extent to which athletics later would emerge as a major extracurricular activity. After the war, however, there began to appear an increasing number of colleges not only for blacks and women but also for groups outside the Protestant mainstream, many of whom had recently come from Europe. Of course the denominations that had been most active in college-founding before the war — the Congregationalists, the Presbyterians, the Methodists, and the Baptists — continued to found colleges in the newly developing regions in the West. Gradually most colleges, following the lead of Harvard, began to allow students to choose from an increasingly broad range of courses that were taught by professors whose training had become increasingly specialized. Intercollegiate athletics, especially football, not only began to surpass the literary society as the dominant extracurricular activity but also — for better or worse — captured the fancy of the general public to a degree never previously realized by a college program.

Higher Education for Blacks

Very few black students pursued college work before the Civil War. Of those who did advance beyond the elementary curriculum, most studied in apprenticeship, teacher training, or non-degree programs. It is doubtful whether even fifteen blacks enrolled in American colleges before 1840. The first recorded black college students were two Gold Coast seamen, Bristol Yamma and John Quamine, who, with the encouragement of Newport, Rhode Island, clergymen Samuel Hopkins and Ezra Stiles, enrolled at Princeton in the mid-1770s with the idea of preparing for missionary service in their African homeland.[1] With some notable exceptions (e.g., Oberlin, Western Reserve, and Berea), few colleges routinely admitted qualified blacks. Representative of the reluctance of the northern colleges was an incident at Union in which officials agreed to admit a black student, but only on the curious condition that he swear that he had no Negro blood in his veins. One major philanthropist, Gerrit Smith, after 1835 granted aid to colleges that freely admitted eligible blacks. He gave Oneida Institute more than $3,000 and three thousand acres of land in Vermont, and he contributed to Oberlin large amounts of money and twenty thousand acres of land in Virginia.[2] Of the black students that gained admittance to college, fewer than thirty graduated in the period before the Civil War. The first two blacks to earn baccalaureate degrees — both in 1826 — were John Russworm at Bowdoin and Edward Jones at Amherst.[3]

Most of the early black students gained admittance to college with the sponsorship of either the colonizationists or the abolitionists. The goal of the colonizationists was to train black leaders who then would migrate to Liberia and other parts of Africa to practice their skills. The colonizationists, however, directed most of their efforts toward educating American blacks after they had moved to Liberia. They established no college in this country. The abolitionists, by contrast, founded several antebellum educational institutions in the North and one in Kentucky. The most notable of these were Lincoln (PA), Wilberforce (OH), and Berea. The Presbyterians founded Lincoln, and the Methodist Episcopal Church began Wilberforce, but Berea opened apart from denominational affiliation under the leadership of two southern abolitionists.[4]

Wilberforce and Berea were exceptional schools. Most of the original students at Wilberforce were mulatto children of southern planters; legally they could not obtain an education in the South. After the Civil War, the African Methodist Episcopal Church assumed control of the institution, thus making it the first black controlled campus in the country. Berea was the first college in slave-holding territory to invite blacks to enroll; even more dramatic was its identification as an anti-slavery institution in a slave state.[5]

Berea began through the efforts of John Fee, a native of Kentucky and the son of a slaveholder. Fee became thoroughly converted to the anti-slavery cause while enrolled at Lane Seminary in Cincinnati. Subsequently he served as an agent of the Congregationalist-sponsored American Missionary Association. Later, with a fellow abolitionist, Cassius M. Clay, he purchased a large tract of land in the Kentucky mountains where he began his school in the hope that it would be "to Kentucky what Oberlin is to Ohio, an anti-slavery, anti-caste, anti-tobacco, anti-sectarian school — a school under Christian influence; a school that will furnish the

best possible facilities for those of small means who have energy of character that would lead them to work their way through this world."[6]

The college operated as an integrated institution until 1904, when the
Supreme Court upheld the controversial Kentucky school segregation
law — although not without a famous dissent from Justice John Marshall
Harlan of Kentucky. Harlan argued:

> I am of the opinion that in its essential parts the statute is an arbitrary inva-
> sion of the rights of liberty and property guaranteed by the Fourteenth
> Amendment against hostile state action and is, therefore, void. . . . The capac-
> ity to impart instruction to others is given by the Almighty for beneficent
> purposes and its use may not be forbidden or interfered with by government.

The outraged white students at Berea sent a letter to their former school-
mates expressing their dismay: "Our sense of justice shows us that others
have the same rights as ourselves, and the teachings of Christ teach us to
'remember them in bonds as bound with them.'" Berea remained segregated until the Kentucky legislature in 1950 revoked the earlier law.[7]

When during the Civil War flocks of freedmen began following the
Union armies, northern generals appealed to the public to help meet the
needs — including the educational needs — of the former slaves. Consequently, for four years northern missionaries literally followed the trail of
the Union army, establishing Sunday schools and elementary schools for
the largely illiterate freedmen. At the end of the war, the federal government's Freedmen's Bureau, led by the humanitarian general Oliver
Howard, cooperated closely with the missionary groups. The bureau gradually assumed responsibility for providing elementary education for the
blacks by opening four thousand schools; this freed the missionary groups
to concentrate on establishing secondary and collegiate institutions.[8]

The church groups worked diligently. They opened more black Protestant colleges during the next twenty-five years than have been founded in
all other periods. A dozen began by 1868, and forty of the fifty-four private Negro colleges in existence in the 1970s first admitted students during the quarter century following the Civil War. The most effective of
these church groups was the American Missionary Association of the
Congregational Church. The association combined dedication with skill in
raising money; immediately after the war it raised $250,000 to found some
of the best black colleges including Atlanta, Fisk (TN), Hampton (VA),
Howard (Washington, DC), Talladega (AL), and Tougaloo (MS). The
Methodist Episcopal Church North founded New Orleans (which later
merged with the Congregationalist's Straight to form Dillard), Clark (GA),
and Claflin (SC). Schools begun by the northern Baptists included Shaw

(NC), Virginia Union (VA), and Morehouse (GA). Later in the century, black denominations began to found their own colleges; in general, they were less affluent than those sponsored by white denominations and thus were considered less prestigious. Because of the large number of denominations and agencies involved in founding colleges, the geographical distribution of these institutions was not always ideal. Certain cities (e.g., Nashville, New Orleans, and Atlanta) acquired more colleges than they needed, while other areas suffered neglect.[9]

Meanwhile, increasing numbers of black students enrolled in northern colleges. During the generation following the war, approximately two hundred blacks graduated from northern institutions. Of this total, seventy-five graduated from Oberlin alone, while the remainder was distributed among approximately fifty other schools.[10]

Although black colleges today include state institutions and private schools that are secular, before 1900 to be a black college meant in almost every case to be a private Protestant institution. During the immediate post–Civil War period, black colleges placed major emphasis upon training ministers and religious leaders. Because the blacks had largely separated from the white churches to form their own, they needed more and better-trained ministers immediately. Even the early technical schools that were less likely to train ministers presented a strong religious orientation. The historian of Hampton, for example, in 1918 described his school as "essentially a spiritual enterprise conceived as a form of missionary service."[11]

The early years of Shaw typify the black colleges in their emphasis on ministerial training. Shaw was founded by Henry Tupper, a graduate of Amherst and Newton Seminary. Following service in the Civil War, Tupper obtained the support of the American Home Baptist Society in New York to train talented freedmen in biblical knowledge so that they might become leaders in the new black Baptist denominations. Accordingly in December 1861, he formed a class in a room in an old hotel where his first pupils were six deacons and ministers who studied first to read and then to interpret the Scriptures. Similarly, at Morehouse during one of its early years, 150 of 245 enrollees were preparing for the ministry.[12]

Leaders in the early black educational efforts hoped that their students would go forth to spread the Christian faith in Africa as well as among the Afro-Americans. Many believed that God had allowed the blacks to be brought to America to hear the Christian gospel and then to take it back to their ancestral homeland. The Christian colleges were to be a key instrument in providing the missionary training; thus, well into the twentieth century, schools such as Fisk and Howard listed "African redemption" among their major purposes. The Methodist colleges, black and white, also were very active in promoting African missions. Bishop William Taylor in the 1880s and 1890s inspired hundreds of black and white Methodist students to volunteer for service in Africa. Central Tennessee (Walden) organized in 1887 a "training school for Africa" with a building, staff, and curriculum that included studies in African agriculture and health.[13]

Gradually, the curricula of these schools broadened, and they began to prepare trained Christians for a variety of other vocations. By 1900, the percentage of black college graduates who entered the ministry—11.3 percent—was not significantly different from the percentage of ministerial graduates in other colleges. By comparison, of the 1,900 students who had graduated from thirty black colleges in the South by the end of the century, 37.2 percent had become teachers in black schools, 4 percent had entered the medical profession, and 3.3 percent had entered the legal profession.[14]

While many white colleges — especially those in the West — enrolled a majority of their students on the preparatory level, the degree to which the southern black "colleges" operated as elementary and secondary schools before 1900 was unmatched. As late as 1920, approximately 80 percent of the pupils in these institutions studied as grade-school and high-school scholars. It should be noted, however, that the schools offered unusually excellent precollegiate training. The colleges sponsored by the northern denominations in particular attracted as teachers highly dedicated graduates of New England colleges.[15] By contrast, the schools run by the black denominations and the local governmental units were greatly inferior.[16]

Most of the early black colleges, then, enrolled very few students who were prepared to study on the college level. For example, the enrollment at Wiley in 1887–88 included only one liberal arts student out of two hundred scholars; the others pursued a variety of preparatory, industrial, and other non-college-level programs. While the Wiley situation was extreme, it was not altogether unrepresentative. A thorough study of black education by Thomas Jones for the Federal Bureau of Education in 1916 identified as legitimate colleges only Howard and Fisk. Thus when scores of black institutions used the term "college" or "university" in their titles, they, like many of the white institutions, were proclaiming the ultimate goal of the founders rather than describing current reality. One of the founders of Fisk explained this practice of naming schools ambitiously by describing the thinking of the Fisk founders:

> Here was Fisk University . . . with the majority of its classes in the primary grades. Very well, Moses was Moses as truly in the bulrushes as when . . . he refused to be called the son of Pharaoh's daughter. . . . The name is in the interests and purpose, in the faith of what is to be, and in the hope of final achievement. Let us wait two hundred years and then ask whether or not this child was rightly named university.[17]

If in the modern period the black colleges more appropriately wear the college label, they still struggle with the problem of enrolling quality students.[18] The impact of the Civil Rights Movement led numerous primarily white schools to recruit vigorously distinguished black students, many of whom otherwise would have enrolled in black colleges. At the same time, the legacy of segregated public schools continued to affect negatively the educational preparation of the average black college enrollees. For example, the students at Morehouse — one of the better black colleges — in 1965 had an SAT median score of 800; consequently, many of them needed remedial work, and half of the student body spent five years to complete the undergraduate course.[19]

Historically, black colleges have attracted much less financial aid than have white schools. In their beginning years, many of them operated with almost no resources. For example, Morehouse originally met in a church basement, and Philander Smith (AR) first held classes in "an open dilapidated church." Until the mid-twentieth century, the black colleges relied heavily upon northern whites for philanthropic support. After the Civil War, blacks were unable and white southerners were unwilling to finance quality educational programs for blacks. Through the end of the nineteenth century, the missionary societies of northern denominations provided the major source of outside support.[20]

By the turn of the century, however, several foundations were making major contributions to black colleges, with the most significant aid coming from the John F. Slater Fund and the General Education Board Fund. Slater, a Connecticut businessman, in 1882 created a million-dollar fund, the income from which was to be used to assist students in black colleges, thereby "conferring on them the blessings of a Christian education." During its first half century, the fund's administrators distributed approximately $2 million to students in nearly fifty black schools. The Slater Fund was the first philanthropic organization devoted exclusively to black education. No foundation, however, contributed more money to black education than did the General Education Board which John D. Rockefeller established in 1903. By the 1930s the fund had allocated more than $32 million to the black colleges. After World War II the General Education Board increasingly concentrated its giving for black education to a limited number of schools, most notably Howard, Fisk, and the Fisk-related Meharry Medical College.[21]

Perhaps the most unique fund-raising method in black schools was designed by George White of Fisk. He combined his interest in university finance and vocal music to organize and lead the Fisk Jubilee Singers, a talented ensemble that, beginning in 1871, toured the North and Europe singing spirituals and making speeches in promotion of the college. The first tour raised $20,000 (including more than $4,000 from one concert in the Tremont Temple, Boston), thus allowing the school to pay its debt and purchase its present property site; the tour also produced much public acclaim, an increased demand for concerts, and an enlarged appreciation for the skills of blacks generally.[22]

Financial contributions from the North as well as the presence of northern teachers in the black colleges sometimes aroused suspicion among southern whites. For example, James Vardaman, an early-twentieth-century Mississippi governor and senator, expressed concern that "what the North is sending South is not money but dynamite. This education is ruining our negroes. They're demanding equality."[23]

In the mid-twentieth century, the United Negro College Fund emerged as the most important innovation in fund-raising for black colleges. Black educational leaders organized this agency because of declining support from the old foundations and because of a growing desire to be less dependent financially upon northern whites. Accordingly, both church-related and independent private colleges[24] engaged in annual cooperative fund-raising efforts that by 1960 netted for the institutions a yearly income equal to that which they would have realized from an endowment of $40 million.[25]

Colleges for Women

As was true with the black institutions, women's colleges founded before 1900 almost invariably operated as aggressively Christian institutions. For example, Mr. and Mrs. Henry Durant combined their wealth and evangelistic fervor to found Wellesley (MA) to train missionaries and other Christian workers in the style of Oberlin. They wrote as the original statute of the institution, "The college was founded for the glory of God and the service of the Lord Jesus Christ, in and by the education and culture of women." They required that every trustee, administrator, and instructor be a member of an evangelical church and that the instructors be able to teach the Bible classes in which each student would participate throughout her college course.

Mount Holyoke (MA) held to a similar purpose. It developed from one of the most advanced seminaries (i.e., secondary schools) to one of the most effective colleges, and its famous founder, Mary Lyon, described it as "a school for Christ. . . . It is designed to cultivate the missionary spirit among its pupils; — the feeling that they should live for God, and do something — do something as teachers, or in such other ways as providence may direct." In general, such religious foundations characterized the other women's colleges, both in the East and elsewhere in the country. Also, more than American colleges in general, the women's institutions determined to apply Christian ethics to societal problems.[26]

The establishment of colleges for young ladies represented the culmination of a long process of convincing society that women should have educational opportunities equal to those of men. Before the nineteenth century most people did not consider it necessary — or even desirable — for women to receive even the most elementary formal schooling. Only a few young girls joined their brothers in "dame" schools, where they obtained beginning instruction in reading and writing. By the eve of the American Revolution, however, New England girls were attending advanced elementary, or "master's," schools.[27]

While very few separate schools for girls existed before 1820, the number of such private institutions increased sharply after that date. The best of them included Emma Willard's Troy Female Seminary (NY), Catherine Beecher's Hartford Female Seminary (CT), and Lyon's Mount Holyoke Seminary. Troy and Mount Holyoke each trained approximately 1,200 students during the middle half of the nineteenth century. Gradually, these and some of the approximately one hundred other private secondary schools for women increased the scope and quality of their curricular offerings to the point where their academic programs became part secondary and part collegiate in nature. They convinced those who were willing to examine the data that women as well as men could pursue college-level work.[28]

Other female seminaries operated on a much lower level. In some the curricula were superficial — even frivolous; in some the courses of study were not continuous; and in some the proprietors were more interested in making a profit than in developing the intellectual and spiritual abilities of their pupils. For these reasons and others the academies received wide criticism. Note the following satirical critique of a school run by a Madame Cancan in the late 1850s:

> Madame Cancan still lives and still ogles and teaches,
> And still her light sermons on fashions she preaches;
> Still keeps of smooth phrases the choicest assortments;
> Still lectures on dress easy carriage deportment;
> And spends all her skill in thus moulding her pets
> Into very-genteelly-got-up marionettes.
>
> Yes! Puppet's the word, for there's nothing inside
> But a clockwork of vanity, fashion, and pride!
> Puppets warranted sound, that without any falter
> When wound up will go just as far as the altar;
> But when once the cap's donned with the matronly border,
> Go! The quiet machine goes at once out of order.

The average school, of course, was not *this* bad, just as it was not as good as Beecher's Hartford Seminary or Mount Holyoke. It generally fell below the academic level of the boy's institutions, although it probably exceeded them in teaching cultural appreciation, in its emphasis on practical training, and in developing skills for parental leadership and interpersonal relations.[29]

Both the educational leaders who wished to found colleges for women and the young women who wished to enroll in such institutions — or even in coeducational colleges — met with considerable opposition. Many opponents of higher education for women believed that women were mentally inferior to men and thus could not compete with them in the rigorous collegiate disciplines. Others thought that a woman's physical as well as intellectual constitution would break under such a strain. Many would have agreed with the sentiment of Rev. John Todd who argued, "As for training young ladies through a long intellectual course, as we do young men, it can never be done. They will die in the process." He lamented that, where this was tried:

> The poor thing has her brain crowded with history, grammar, arithmetic, geography, natural history, chemistry, physiology, botany, astronomy, rhetoric, natural and moral philosophy, metaphysics, French, often German, Latin, perhaps Greek, reading, spelling, committing poetry, writing compositions, drawing, painting, etc., etc., ad infinitum. Then, out of school hours, from three to six hours of severe toil at the piano. She must be at the strain during school hours, study in the evening till her eyes ache, her brain whirls, her spine yields and gives way, and she comes through the process of education, enervated, feeble, without courage or vigor, elasticity, or strength. Alas! must we crowd education upon our daughters, and, for the sake of having them "intellectual," make them puny, nervous, and their whole earthly existence a struggle between life and death?

Even some who believed women capable of competing with men in colleges thought the practice unwise on the practical grounds that it would lead to a reduction in the number and quality of marriages. As one opponent observed, "Man loves a learned scholar but not a learned wife."[30]

Gradually these arguments received less credence as more people observed women successfully completing college work. Furthermore, even in the nineteenth century it appeared unjust to prevent able women from pursuing their intellectual interests. Perhaps the most convincing argument for the higher education of women was that they gradually began to dominate the elementary teaching profession and thus needed the opportunity to become as well educated as possible.

The most effective of the early advocates of women's colleges was Catherine Beecher. In her *True Remedy for the Wrongs of Women*, she argued vigorously for female institutions that would match the existing men's colleges in curriculum, quality of instruction, and physical resources. She also emphasized the importance of an applied curriculum, particularly in the areas of domestic science and teacher education.[31]

Several institutions claimed to be the earliest female college. Wesleyan (GA) cited the earliest date (1836), but some critics doubt that it was operating as a bona fide college as early as were Mary Sharp (TN) and Elmira (NY), which opened in 1851 and 1855 respectively. Actually, during the middle part of the century there were many women's institutions that, like many of their male counterparts, were in the process of developing from primarily secondary to collegiate institutions. They actually operated on both levels for many years. It is difficult, therefore, if not impossible, to try to determine when such institutions actually became "colleges."[32]

Very few institutions for black women developed because there was little need for them. Some black women gained admittance to the white coeducational institutions such as Oberlin, where the first Afro-American woman graduated in 1862. The primary reason for the relative absence of black women's colleges, however, was that most of the black colleges freely admitted women as well as men. Nevertheless, in 1881 Spelman (GA) opened as the first institution for black women.[33]

If by the late nineteenth century there were many institutions in which young women could pursue college-level work, there were only a handful of women's institutions operating with levels of funding, quality of faculties, and admissions requirements that could compare with those found in the most prestigious men's institutions. The earliest of these elite colleges was Vassar (NY), which opened in 1865. During the Civil War, Matthew Vassar, a wealthy Quaker, noted that there was not in the world, as far as he knew, a single fully endowed college for women. He determined, therefore, "to be the instrument in the hands of Providence of founding and perpetrating an institution which shall accomplish for young women what our colleges are accomplishing for young men." Accordingly, Vassar opened on a grand scale with an endowment of $400,000 (three times as much as any women's college had held previously), a large new building, a faculty of eight men and twenty-two women, and a student body of 353. The fact that Vassar's wealth had come from his brewery investments embarrassed the early college leaders, but not the students who sang his praises:

> Then there's Matthew Vassar,
> Our love shall never fail,
> For well we know that all we owe
> to Matthew Vassar's ale.[34]

Other elite eastern women's colleges that opened in the nineteenth century included Wellesley in 1870, Smith (MA) in 1871, Radcliffe (MA) in 1879, Bryn Mawr (PA) in 1885, Barnard (NY) in 1889, and Mount Holyoke in 1893. Collectively these institutions were known as the seven sister colleges, and in prestige they served as the female counterpart to the Ivy League. Academically, the women's colleges exceeded the men's in some areas. For example, Vassar, Wellesley, and Smith all developed excellent departments of fine arts and English literature, and Wellesley became the first college to offer a major in art history.[35]

Most of the alumni of the women's institutions became teachers, missionaries, or homemakers — or some combination of these three vocations. The percentage of graduates entering the teaching profession included nearly 80 percent at Wellesley by 1893, and nearly 70 percent at Mount Holyoke during its first half century. By the late nineteenth century, women held most of the common-school teaching positions in this country; since most teachers were not college graduates, those who did hold college degrees provided as a group the best elementary instruction.[36]

Very few women received formal theological training. The first woman to graduate from a theological school was Antoinette Brown Blackwell, who finished the three-year course at Oberlin in 1851. Women, however, found no difficulty in becoming foreign missionaries. In fact, during the modern period of foreign missions (the nineteenth and twentieth centuries), the clear majority of Protestant missionaries have been women. Missions was probably the first profession in which women achieved status equal to men. When a woman went to a foreign field, she found much more freedom to exercise her leadership and creative skills than if she had remained in America. Even when married to a paternalistic husband, the missionary wife could organize an elementary school for girls; indeed, in many cases she was asked to do this.[37]

Graduates of the early women's colleges found the mission field especially appealing because there they could exercise in a practical way with few limits their zeal in promoting both the Protestant faith and the cause of women's rights. Typical of the experiences of the graduates who pursued missionary careers was that of Isabel Trowbridge Merrill, who graduated from Vassar in 1900. While speaking to the College Girls of America organization later in her life, she advised the young women considering career opportunities:

> The life of a missionary is the happiest, most joyous, most satisfying one I can know. A college girl's whole training is toward activity, and what else can give her so great pleasure and satisfaction as to be in an environment

that calls out all her powers and gives her a chance to live such a vital life and a life that tells. Oh girls, it pays so many times over.[38]

The early critics of higher education for women were correct when they predicted that women who went to college would be less likely to marry than their sisters who remained at home. A study of approximately two thousand college graduates in 1895 found that of those over twenty-five, 33 percent were married, and of those over forty, 55 percent were married; by contrast, 80 percent of all women over twenty were married. It should be noted, however, that these statistics showed a much higher marriage pattern among women who had attended coeducational institutions than among those who had graduated from women's colleges.[39]

In part, the nineteenth-century movement to found women's colleges in the East and South arose as a conservative response to the growing practice of coeducation in the western colleges and, later, the western state universities. After Oberlin admitted four women to its collegiate program in 1837, it became the best-known coeducational institution in the country, with women comprising between 10 and 25 percent of its enrollment in the early years. Many other western Protestant colleges quickly followed Oberlin's example, so that by 1873, of the ninety-seven institutions admitting women, sixty-seven were located in the West.[40]

By contrast, coeducational institutions at this time numbered only five in New England, eight in the Middle Atlantic states, and seventeen in the South. Before the Civil War, no coeducational college of any type existed in Georgia, the Carolinas, or Virginia. When the institution that ultimately developed into Texas Christian moved in 1873 from Fort Worth to Thorpe Spring, it decided to admit women. This was a sufficiently novel practice in the Southwest that the institution advertised its uniqueness in the school name, "Add Ran Male and Female College."[41]

In the late nineteenth century some institutions, especially in the East, began to think that their earlier insistence upon separation of the sexes for education may have been extreme but they still retained a reluctance to accept fully the idea of coeducation. These institutions adopted a mediating position whereby they located women's colleges adjacent to men's colleges. Thus there arose such "coordinate" institutions as Radcliffe (1879) near Harvard, Barnard (1883) near Columbia, and Pembroke (1891) near Brown. The coordinate college remained a rarity, however, and neither it nor the women's college would in the long run become the primary means of providing collegiate education for the nation's women. It was the coeducational institution that mounted in popularity, with the number of liberal arts colleges admitting women growing from 30 percent in 1870 to more than 50 percent in 1880 and 65 percent by 1890.[42]

Colleges Founded by the Newly Rich
and the New Immigrants

After the Civil War, as America was becoming the leading industrial power in the world, an increasing number of entrepreneurs acquired vast wealth. Some of them chose to give large sums either to transform a small college into a major institution or to launch a new university. Some of the new wealth went to the major women's colleges but most of it went to male or coeducational institutions.

Cornelius Vanderbilt, because of railroad and water transportation investments, possessed much money; his wife and her pastor possessed much interest in Central University of Nashville, which had been founded by the Methodist Episcopal Church in 1872. Consequently, the Vanderbilts contributed $1 million to the college in the 1870s. In appreciation, the school renamed itself after him. Other family members contributed an additional $10 million by 1895.[43]

The Washington Duke family of North Carolina so successfully developed their tobacco business that by 1889 they produced half of the cigarettes sold in America. Duke loved the Methodist church in which he had been converted as a youth, and he wished to express his appreciation by contributing a large sum to the denomination's educational work. He also wished to see a college located in his own town; therefore, when Trinity, the small, struggling Methodist college in Randolph County, North Carolina, needed financial strengthening, Duke and his son Benjamin offered to contribute $85,000 if it would relocate in Durham. The college agreed to move to Durham, and the gifts that Benjamin Duke continued to bestow upon the school reached $2 million by 1925. The family benevolence did not stop there, for a second son, James, created an endowment fund of $100 million, thus establishing what then came to be known as Duke University as a major educational institution.[44]

Like the Duke family, Asa Candler was a devout Methodist millionaire. He had earned his wealth from the manufacture and distribution of Coca-Cola. His gifts and those of his son, Howard, after him transformed small Emory College in Atlanta into the distinguished Emory University.[45]

Southern Baptist institutions benefiting from unusually large gifts included Stetson, Baylor, and Wake Forest. Stetson assumed its present name to honor John Stetson, of the Stetson hat manufacturing family. Stetson's generous gifts to the Baptist academy in his winter home of Deland, Florida, allowed the school to reorganize itself as a collegiate institution. John Hardin gave $1.25 million to Baylor in 1936, and while that institution was already well established by then, the gift represented the largest single contribution in its history. The Wake Forest endowment, which had reached only $100,000 by 1884, sharply increased with the gifts of Jabez Bostwick. Bostwick's contributions began in 1885 and culminated in a $1.5 million stock contribution from his will in 1923.[46]

Few nineteenth-century Americans were as wealthy as John D. Rockefeller, and it was perhaps inevitable that the dedicated Baptist churchman would found a great university. He had long held an interest in higher education, and for years he had offered significant aid to a variety of institutions. His former Cleveland pastor, Augustus Strong, had become president of Rochester Theological Seminary and argued that Rockefeller should found a great Baptist institution in New York. Other Baptist ministers, such as Thomas Godspeed and Fredrick Gates, pleaded for establishing the university in Chicago. The pro-Chicago leaders won, primarily because they were able to raise $400,000 to supplement Rockefeller's $600,000 gift. Rockefeller wished to establish a Baptist institution, and to appoint William Rainey Harper, a Baptist biblical scholar at Yale, to the presidency. He could not have both, however, as Harper was not in favor of making the institution orthodox Baptist. Apparently Rockefeller wanted Harper more than he wanted the college closely tied to the Baptist Church, for the University of Chicago was established as an institution that was neither Baptist nor unequivocally Christian, but whose orientation was broadly religious with a slight preference for the Christian faith. By 1910, Rockefeller had given $35 million to his creation, including $1.5 million for a university chapel that he desired to be the central and dominating physical feature of the campus, just as "the spirit of religion should penetrate and control the university."

While the new Chicago institution chose not to evangelize its students, it did agree to allow evangelical groups to work with the students on terms set by the university. Thus, when YMCA leader John Mott asked Harper for the privilege of organizing a chapter at Chicago similar to those which existed in most other collegiate institutions, Harper declined but invited Mott to participate along with other groups in the university-created Christian Union. The union was a broadly religious organization which started from a Christian framework but was careful to avoid denying the spiritual value of other faiths.[47]

Some other new, well-endowed institutions clearly defined themselves as religious in nature but not Christian. Stanford (CA) sought to be as religious as Chicago, while avoiding the latter's modest preference for the Christian faith. While Stanford's founders established voluntary religious services, they expressly forbade the university to offer "sectarian" instruction. They wished to tie the institution to no other religious creed than belief in "the immortality of the soul, the existence of an all-wise benevolent creator, and the idea that obedience to his laws is the highest duty of man."[48]

If Chicago wished to give slight preference to the Christian faith and Stanford only to promote religion in general, Johns Hopkins, founded in Baltimore in 1876 by a Quaker merchant of the same name, sought to avoid all official religious influences. It wanted to avoid the suspicion that it was opposed to religion, however. Accordingly, the leaders of the new institution established a voluntary fifteen-minute chapel service and provided a building site and secretarial salary assistance for the YMCA chapter.[49]

One of the most interesting philanthropists of Christian higher education was Daniel Pearsons, a Chicago financier. When Pearsons retired in 1890 at the age of seventy, he chose to devote the remainder of his life to giving from his accumulated wealth to small Christian colleges in the West and South. His conviction was that such institutions provided the best training for future leaders. He studied carefully each potential recipient institution to assure himself of its viability. If his assessment was favorable, he offered the college a sizable grant on the condition that it in turn raise significant monies from its constituency and that it broaden the base of that constituency. For example, Pearsons offered Beloit $100,000 on the condition that it raise an additional $400,000 within a prescribed period of time. In this manner he gave approximately $5 million to forty southern and western colleges.[50]

Foundation philanthropy has not been broadly helpful to Protestant higher education. In general, the foundations have given aid to a limited number of already well-endowed colleges. Between 1923 and 1929, for example, of the one thousand institutions in the United States, thirty-six received 80 percent of the $100 million given by the five largest foundations. Most of the recipient institutions were ones that were becoming secular. Sometimes this secularization was explicitly rewarded, as in the case of the early-twentieth-century Carnegie Pension Fund. This fund proposed to aid colleges in establishing retirement programs for their instructors, but only when the institutions held no church affiliation. A few foundations, however, such as the Lilly Endowment, which was established in 1937, showed special interest in supporting church-related colleges.[51]

While the industrialization of America during the second half of the nineteenth century produced multimillionaires who could afford to create major centers of learning, the continuing immigration to the New World in the same period brought ethnic and religious groups who chose to found their own colleges. Before the Civil War, most newcomers had emigrated from the British Isles and Germany; however, the post-war pattern became more complex. In addition to the sharply increasing number of Roman Catholics and Jews from southern and eastern Europe and the continuing influx of people who could identify with the older major Protestant denominations and colleges, there began to pour into the Mid-

west and the north central states Protestant separatist groups such as the
Scandinavian Lutherans, the Dutch Reformed, the German and Russian
Mennonites, and the German Brethren. Because these groups were more
determined than most to retain their unique cultural practices and religious beliefs, they preferred to found their own colleges rather than to
allow their young people to attend state institutions or colleges sponsored
by other denominations.

Most of the early Mennonite and Brethren leaders in this country distrusted advanced learning under any circumstances. According to a historian of Brethren higher education, most Brethren in the mid-nineteenth
century viewed high schools and colleges as "worldly places where the
young will at best puff up with proud knowledge and at worst desert the
church." When the young people of the German groups became increasingly interested in higher education, church leaders reluctantly and gradually concluded that maybe higher education per se was not evil. Certainly it would be better to fund church colleges to train their young
people than to lose them.

Sometimes the churches came to this conclusion belatedly. The eastern
Mennonites, for example, were especially slow to change on this issue.
The very large and influential Lancaster County, Pennsylvania, Mennonite Conference originally opposed the existence of Goshen (IN) which
began in 1902; and during the fifteen years preceding the opening of Eastern Mennonite (VA) in 1917, in the words of one Mennonite bishop,
"Much of the best talent was lost to the church because hundreds and
even thousands were getting their education in schools where the principles of the Bible were neither encouraged nor recognized."[52]

Consequently, the Brethren founded Juniata (PA) in 1876, Ashland
(OH) in 1878, Bridgewater (VA) in 1880, McPherson (KS) in 1887, Man-
chester (IN) in 1889, LaVerne (CA) in 1891, Elizabethtown (PA) in 1899,
Messiah (PA) in 1909, and Upland (CA) in 1920. The Mennonites were
even slower, opening Bethel (KS) in 1893, Bluffton (OH) in 1900, and
Tabor (KS) in 1908, in addition to the aforementioned Goshen and Eastern
Mennonite.

The early Scandinavian and Dutch immigrants recognized the need for
educated ministers and teachers, but, like the German Anabaptist groups,
they were fearful of higher education in institutions not of their faith. Acceptable European universities were too distant and the existing American institutions too untrustworthy. So the Scandinavians and the Dutch
began their own colleges to train their own leaders in their own regions; in
so doing they were following the example of their spiritual forebears such
as the German Lutherans who founded several eastern colleges before the
Civil War and the colonial Dutch who began Rutgers.[53] Sometimes the im-

migrants established schools as much to train godly teachers as to prepare preachers. The Lutherans remembered the advice of their sixteenth-century founder who had proclaimed, "We can take magistrates and princes as we find them, but not schools, for schools rule the world."[54]

The Swedes and the Norwegians were the most active Scandinavian groups in founding colleges. The Swedish Lutherans began Augustana (IL) in 1860, Gustavus Adolphus (MN) in 1862, Bethany (KS) in 1881, Luther (NE) in 1883, and Upsala (NJ) in 1893. North Park (IL) opened in 1891 as the Swedish Covenant school, and Bethel (MN) began in 1871 as a Swedish Baptist institution. The Norwegian Lutherans founded Augustana (SD) in 1860, Luther (IA) in 1861, Augsburg (MN) in 1869, Saint Olaf (MN) in 1874, Concordia (MN) in 1891, Waldorf (IA) in 1903, and, with the German Lutherans, Pacific Lutheran (WA) in 1894. The Danish Lutherans began Dana (NE) in 1884 and Grand View (IA) in 1896, and the Finnish Lutherans founded Suomi (MI) in 1896.

The schools begun by the Dutch included Hope (MI) in 1851 and Northwestern (IA) in 1882 by the Reformed Church and Calvin (MI) in 1876 by the Christian Reformed Church.

Slowly but surely the immigrant colleges assimilated American culture. Among the Scandinavians, the Swedish Lutherans led the way. From their beginning years, Augustana of Illinois and Bethany offered instruction in English as well as Swedish. Augustana by the 1890s admitted many "Americans" as commuter students, even though their habits were not controllable by the faculty; also, in 1898 the faculty recommended that morning chapel be conducted in English. The earlier vision of Augustana as an entirely Swedish Lutheran religious institution was changing. Sometimes the colleges made special efforts to retain the old-world culture for the Swedish students. For example, at Bethany as late as the 1920s Swedish American enrollees were expected to study the Swedish language.[55]

Among the Dutch, the weekly *DeHope*, with many Hope faculty members on its editorial board, served both to preserve the old-world culture and gradually to aid its readers in adapting to their new environment. Its purpose was to help Hollanders become Americans "by assimilation and not absorption."[56]

German and Russian Anabaptists faced a special problem in the acculturation process. Whereas the Scandinavians and the Dutch brought with them a tradition of participating in the culture of the home country, the Anabaptists brought an attitude of separation from and nonconformity toward the prevailing culture of any country in which they resided. For them, the acculturation process was not only a matter of adapting to the American setting but also of adapting to secular culture in general. For many decades after the beginning of the Anabaptist colleges, a sizable portion of the church members greatly distrusted them, partly because the colleges themselves were a part of the suspect ungodly culture and partly because within the denominations the colleges represented the greatest force leading to cultural change. Even such an issue as mode of dress could cause great controversy, as it did at Goshen early in the century when the Mennonite and Amish-Mennonite students began to dress more conventionally than they had in their home communities. Their home churches often criticized them as "dressy" and thus "worldly." Sometimes the students would leave the church, with the membership blaming the college for the desertion.[57]

The New Curriculum and Its Effects

During the second half of the nineteenth century, America's Industrial Revolution transformed American society. The United States changed from a primarily rural, agricultural country to a primarily urban, technological one. As we have already seen, the wealth resulting from these economic changes helped create a number of well-endowed colleges and universities.

The same societal changes that produced the country's new wealth also demanded that colleges reform their curricula away from traditional classical studies and toward more practical courses that would prepare students for the new roles that many of them must assume. In the new technological society, Harvard paved the way for the Protestant colleges when, beginning in 1869 under President Charles Eliot, it began to discard its required curriculum and to allow its students to choose from a broad variety of curricular options those which best met their vocational and personal goals.

Harvard was not the first to adopt such an elective system. At Union under President Eliphalet Nott, students since early in the nineteenth century had been able to choose widely from classical and other types of courses, and, regardless of their choices, they all received the same degree. The significance of the change at Harvard, however, is that when it introduced the elective system, the practice spread to nearly every other college. By 1886, Harvard retained almost no course requirements, and a student needed only to pass eighteen courses — one-quarter of them with a C or better — out of a total curriculum of 153 full and sixty-one half-courses taught by sixty-one professors.[58]

The Protestant colleges followed the Harvard example with varying degrees of completeness and speed. By 1890, one college out of three still maintained a totally prescribed curriculum, and the average institution offered a curriculum that was 84 percent required. A 1901 survey of approximately ninety-seven colleges showed that forty-six of them operated with at least 50 percent election. By 1940, the curriculum in the average college was only 40 percent prescribed.

Frequently colleges adopted the elective system sooner in theory than they could implement it in practice. It was one thing to agree with the philosophy of election and quite another to locate funds to hire additional professors to teach all of the new courses. Even affluent Harvard had adopted the elective system a full generation before it became a practical reality under President Eliot.[59]

One significant consequence of the elective system was that the Protestant schools and others began to introduce biblical literature courses into their formal curricula. In one sense this was not an innovation. The colleges had always offered Bible study as a part of the extracurriculum. Also, the classical studies included — even if indirectly — some instruction in biblical subjects, primarily through the courses in mental and moral philosophy. The difference between religious study in the old curricula and the new courses was something like the difference between a topical sermon that draws upon the Bible to illustrate and give authority to major points and an expository sermon that starts with the biblical text and develops its applications from it. In a few places, such as McPherson, Bible courses appeared as early as the 1880s. More typically, however, colleges added them in the 1890s and 1900s. Such was the case, for example, at Wellesley, Carleton, Franklin, Colorado College, Alabama, Columbia, and Barnard. Some colleges, particularly in the West, introduced Bible courses as late as the second or third decade of the twentieth century.[60]

While the more cautious Protestant colleges were gradually accepting larger degrees of election, institutions such as Harvard, which had been less inhibited in adopting election, began to recognize that students often graduated with courses of study severely lacking in unity and design. Many agreed with Eliot's successor at Harvard, Abbott Lawrence Lowell, that "the best type of liberal education in our complex world aims at producing men who know a little of everything and something well." Consequently, at Harvard and elsewhere in the early twentieth century, colleges began to require their students to choose a course or courses in each of several broad areas (thus the beginning of general education requirements) and also to select a block of courses in one discipline or area (thus the beginning of the requirement to graduate with a "major").[61]

While the elective system contributed to the decline in the integration of learning in the late-nineteenth-century college, the influence of German scholarship upon the increasing number of American professors who obtained their advanced training in that country did also. German universities taught that a trained intellectual should be less a generalist concerned with broad, universal meanings than a specialist concentrating on gaining scientifically accurate mastery of a narrow area of investigation. These German ideals of research and specialization became increasingly accepted in America as larger numbers of scholars returned from their German training. The number of Americans who had studied in Germany increased from three hundred on the eve of the Civil War to ten thousand by World War I. The desire of these professors to pursue more specialized areas of inquiry fitted nicely into the elective system and its encouragement for the instructors to offer more—and, by implication, increasingly specialized—courses.

As professors gained greater expertise in more restricted areas of learning, they relied increasingly upon the lecture rather than the recitation mode of teaching. The growing number of students enrolled in college in the late nineteenth century made lecturing the practical as well as the philosophically preferable method of instruction. Increasingly, the aim of the classroom became discovering new truths rather than discussing traditional ones. To facilitate this new aim, a number of colleges and universities began to introduce laboratories, greatly enlarged libraries, research and seminar courses, and graduate programs. By 1870, Yale and Harvard operated well-developed graduate programs with doctoral students; by 1890, twenty-five universities offered graduate fellowships; and by 1910 the graduate schools enrolled six thousand students. In general, the schools adopting these innovations most completely were large, well financed, and, as we shall see in the next chapter, in the process of changing from primarily religious to primarily secular institutions.[62]

While most of the Protestant schools did not introduce graduate programs or actively promote research, most did begin to give an increased emphasis to the library. As new professors came to their teaching positions with increasingly specialized and research-oriented graduate training, and as they began to teach specialized courses, they desired larger libraries for their own use and also for students, whom they now encouraged to engage in independent and specialized scholarship.

The growth in prominence of the Oberlin library exemplified the general trend. In 1874, the Oberlin collection numbered only 9,400 volumes, a retired minister on a small stipend supervised it, and students and faculty could enter the area housing it for only short periods each day. This began to change in the 1880s, however, and by the end of that decade the library contained 36,000 volumes, which the students were using with much greater frequency.[63]

With the growth of the elective system and the specialized research function, the concept of a uniform college education began to break down. Causing further confusion was the fact that the old admissions procedures were no longer practical. Increasingly, pre-college students obtained their training in public high schools instead of preparatory divisions of the colleges. As the colleges developed individualized curricula, high school officials complained of the difficulty, if not impossibility, of preparing students for widely differing college programs. Also, with the sharply increasing number of students applying for admission, college officials no longer could personally interview all applicants.

The confusion resulting from these changes led the colleges and high schools to cooperate in establishing academic standards and admission requirements. To do this, they formed regional associations. Thus were born the New England Association of Colleges and Secondary Schools in 1885, the Middle States Association of Colleges and Secondary Schools in 1889, the North Central Association of Colleges and Secondary Schools in 1895, the Southern Association of Colleges and Secondary Schools in the 1890s, the Northwest Association of Secondary and Higher Schools in 1917, and the Western College Association in 1924. These associations defined standardized criteria necessary for an institution of acceptable quality. As schools applied for membership in the associations, they were required to meet these standards. The associations gave the high schools guidelines on how to prepare students for college, and they gave the colleges information about the quality of the high schools in which their applicants had studied.[64]

Athletics and Fraternities

During the late nineteenth century, extracurricular activities on the nation's campuses increased in importance even as they became less directly related to the curricular programs. In the older days when literary societies dominated the extracurricular, debates and orations on important issues effectively complemented the work of the classroom. By 1900, however, college leaders found it difficult to demonstrate that the newer activities were equally appropriate. Many did not even attempt such a justification; Woodrow Wilson, then president of Princeton, found the growth of the new programs very disturbing and complained that "these side shows are so numerous, so diverting, so important if you will—that they have swallowed up the circus. . . ."

Not all college officials objected to the new activities, however. One early and articulate proponent of the idea that colleges should organize well-developed extracurricular programs, particularly in athletics, was Phillip Lindsley, president of the University of Nashville from 1825 to 1850. Lindsley argued that students could not spend all of their time studying. Human bodies needed the invigorating effect of physical exercise. Colleges often faced discipline problems, he thought, because, left to themselves, students devised destructive rather than constructive diversionary activities. It was the responsibility of the colleges, therefore, to provide wholesome activities of several types for all of the students all of the time. "Keep your youth busy," he urged, "and you will keep them out of harm's way."[65]

Gradually, the literary society became merely one of many types of activities in which a student could participate. The decline of the societies occurred most rapidly in those institutions which gave an early and enthusiastic reception to intercollegiate athletics and fraternities. They declined more slowly in the small colleges, particularly those in the West. At Shaw, for example, well into the twentieth century both intramural debating and contests with other members of the Pentagonal Debating League (Morehouse, Knoxville, Talladega, and Johnson C. Smith) attracted greater student interest than did intercollegiate athletics. Some institutions, like Taylor, not only continued their earlier interests in the literary societies but applied the society emphasis on oratory to reform causes such as those promoting peace and prohibition. Particularly noteworthy were the nationwide student contests of the Intercollegiate Prohibition Association. The general trend, however, was away from debating and oratory, and the most significant activity to replace them was organized athletics. After the Civil War rowing revived, and track and field, lacrosse, archery, polo, and even boxing and wrestling appeared on a limited number of campuses; but it was baseball and especially football that captured the enthusiasm of college students and the general public across the nation.[66]

Baseball became the first organized sport to be played widely on an intercollegiate basis. Although competition in the diamond game began at least as early as the twenty-six-inning Amherst–Williams contest of July 1, 1859, baseball suddenly became very popular during the Civil War; both northern and southern troops enjoyed it immensely. After the war ended in 1865, returning veterans took the new game home—and to college—with them. Consequently, baseball's popularity grew rapidly on campuses and in towns throughout the country—in the West nearly as early as in the East.[67]

The early form of baseball favored the offense. Pitching was slow with no emphasis upon speed or curves, the ball was lively, and defensive players sought to catch the ball without the aid of gloves. Consequently, early scores more closely resembled the results of later basketball contests than of modern baseball games. For example, Wabash defeated DePauw in 1866 by a score of 45 to 32, and a year later the Princeton sophomores triumphed over Yale's second-year men in New Haven by a 58 to 52 count.[68]

Not all colleges accepted the sport immediately. Some opposed it for financial reasons (equipment for the sport was quite inexpensive, although travel costs were a factor). Others thought it might be detrimental to morality and the promotion of Christianity (the non-college teams did tend to attract ruffians as players). Still other colleges thought it dangerous and counterproductive of academic excellence. For example, an 1868 edition of the Albion paper criticized baseball as a "finger destroying" sport that distracted students from higher literary interests.[69]

While baseball was the first big sport to invade the college campus, it did not remain the leading one for long. By the 1870s, college football not only surpassed baseball in prominence, it attracted the interest of the general public to a degree never before realized by any college activity. Beginning with the November, 1869, Rutgers–Princeton game (which resembled soccer more than modern football), the sport spread quickly throughout the East. By the early 1890s, games between Ivy League schools attracted crowds of more than thirty thousand, and Ivy League players upon graduation were often recruited as coaches for other colleges. In the 1890s, more than one hundred former Yale, Princeton, and Harvard players were coaching at other schools. Thus, what had begun as primarily an Ivy League sport became a national phenomenon by the early years of the twentieth century. In 1914, gridiron teams played on 450 campuses.[70]

The enthusiasm that the early game attracted was matched by its violence. In the era before the development of strict regulations and protective equipment, Ivy League teams of the 1870s "kicked not only the ball, but each other." Also tolerated was the practice of "jumping on an opponent's stomach with both feet. . . ." Without effective protective equipment, players died from the violence almost like soldiers in a war, with fatalities from college games reaching a peak of forty-four in 1903.[71]

Responsible educational leaders cried out in protest. President Eliot of Harvard thought that football was to academics what bullfighting was to agriculture. Professor George Groff, a Bucknell faculty member and physician, in 1894 referred to the "barbarous" game of football as a "travesty of athleticism." President Nicholas Murray Butler of Columbia agreed: "This is madness and slaughter." Dean Shailer Mathews of Chicago described football as a "boy-killing, education-prostituting, gladiatorial sport. It teaches virility and courage, but so does war." A college game, he continued, "should not require the services of a physician, the maintenance of a hospital, and the celebration of funerals." Even John L. Sullivan, the famous heavyweight boxer, noted after watching an Ivy League contest that "there's murder in that game."[72]

Most college officials and medical doctors agreed that the game should be radically altered, if not abolished. At this point Theodore Roosevelt, Walter Camp, and others led a movement to save the sport by ridding it of its most brutal aspects. President Roosevelt had been a sickly asthmatic as a youth and lamented the fact that he had not been able to participate in football at Harvard. Throughout the rest of his life, he repeatedly sought to develop and demonstrate his physical fitness. Camp, later known as "the father of American football," enrolled at Yale in 1876 and made the varsity team in every sport. He was instrumental in beginning the dynasty of Yale teams that thoroughly dominated the sport for the rest of the century.[73] Roosevelt's warning at a 1905 White House conference on football that the kicking, punching, biting, and scratching must end or he would abolish the sport by executive order did result in some improvement; but more was accomplished by the persistent efforts of Camp over several years to lead in the establishment of strict regulations (e.g., eligibility rules and neutral officials with power to penalize unnecessarily dangerous play). Gradually football changed from a violent form of soccer to a relatively humane game that added running with the ball, passing the ball forward, and retaining possession of the ball by advancing it at least ten yards in four plays.[74]

Although baseball and football appeared earlier, it is basketball that has become the most popular sport at the Christian colleges. Basketball was invented in 1891 by James Naismith, a young theological graduate of McGill (Canada) while he was enrolled in the YMCA training school (now Springfield College) in Springfield, Massachusetts. Professor Luther Gulick, chairman of the physical education department, explained to Naismith how not only his Springfield students but participants in YMCA gymnasium activities throughout the country experienced boredom with the lack of an indoor winter sport that could compete in excitement with football, baseball, and track. When Gulick gave Naismith the responsibility for leading a physical education class, he labored intensely to develop a new game that would challenge the students more than the traditional gymnasium activities, yet be less rough than the outdoor sports. Considerable experimentation led to the development of basketball—the only sport of strictly United States origin.

Basketball was an instant success and spread nationwide through the YMCA gymnasiums and the college coaches who had studied at or lived in Springfield. C. O. Beamis, a native of Springfield, was probably the first coach to introduce the game on the college level when he taught the sport to his students at Geneva in 1892. Two former Springfield educators, H. F. Kallenberg and Amos Alonzo Stagg, coached (and Kallenberg refereed!) the first men's intercollegiate game, which was won by Chicago over Iowa, 15–12, in 1896. Women competed in collegiate basketball nearly as early as the men, even if they usually played a less strenuous form of the game.[75]

If the early stages of intercollegiate athletics were full of controversy, such also was the case with the other major new extracurricular activity of this period, the fraternity. Technically, the Greek fraternity movement began with the Phi Beta Kappa chapter at William and Mary in 1776. For a time it featured not only literary interests but also such characteristics of modern fraternities as oaths, rituals, secrecy, comradeship, a hand-grip, and a desire to expand to other campuses (Yale and Harvard added chapters in 1779, Dartmouth in 1787, and Union in 1817). Soon, however, with the encouragement of faculty members, Phi Beta Kappa evolved into the scholarly honor society that it is today.[76]

The students' desire for secret fraternal organizations controlled by themselves continued, and the old fraternity idea revived at Union in the 1820s with the establishment of the first three fraternities that have continued to the present: Kappa Alpha (1825), Sigma Phi (1827), and Delta Phi (1827). From the New York college, the movement spread rapidly throughout the East, into the South beginning with Emory in 1841, and across the Appalachian Mountains where, in the middle 1830s, the Alpha Delta Phi chapter at Miami (OH) became the first western fraternity. Because the fraternity movement began at Union and because such a large number of fraternity chapters (four hundred by the mid-twentieth century) trace their origins to Miami, both of these institutions claim the title, "mother of fraternities."[77]

Almost invariably the faculty of a college fought vigorously against the students' attempts to introduce fraternity chapters; frequently, however, the faculty conceded to the students after a bitter battle. For example, at Union in 1832 President Nott strongly denounced the budding fraternities and warned that "the first young man who joins a secret society shall not remain in college one hour." Union lifted this ban a year later. In the late 1860s, President McCosh of Princeton viewed the fraternities on his campus as counterproductive to student democracy, discipline, and morality. He determined that if he "failed to conquer this evil," he would resign. The fraternities continued, and so did McCosh for the next two decades.[78]

It was not only college authorities who opposed the development of college fraternities. In a number of institutions the non-fraternity men — probably motivated by opposition to the social elitism implied by fraternity membership — formed "anti-secret" societies. Typical of the sentiment of these anti-secret student groups is the following statement from the constitution of the Hamilton (NY) Anti-Secret Organization: "Believing that secret societies are calculated to destroy the harmony of college, to create distinctions not founded on merit, and to produce strife and animosity, we feel called upon to exert ourselves to counteract the evil tendency of such associations. . . ." Hamilton's group joined similar organizations at Williams, Union, and Amherst to form the "Anti-Secret Confederation." At

Wittenberg (OH), nearly as soon as two fraternities appeared, thirty-seven opposing students prepared a thoroughly researched petition calling for college officials to abolish the new student groups.[79]

Sometimes the differences between students and the administration continued long after the fraternities appeared to be well established. By 1870, Ohio Wesleyan had housed Greek societies for seventeen years, yet the trustees suspended all "secret-college fraternities not purely literary." The trustees at Wofford took similar action in 1906 after a full generation of fraternity activity on its campus, and the struggle continued for a decade. After nine Wofford students went to Columbia in 1913 to accept initiation into one of the previously discredited fraternities, they accepted dismissal by the trustees and transferred to Duke. When approximately fifty more Wofford students organized fraternities two years later, however, the trustees, tired of the battle and probably fearful of losing so many students, relented and again officially allowed the fraternities.[80]

Students displayed cleverness as well as persistence in their battles with faculties. For example, the Quakers as a society had opposed secret organizations, but at Whittier (CA) in the 1930s Richard Nixon and other students gradually transformed the traditional literary societies into functional, if not nominal, fraternities.[81] The most effective tactic employed by fraternity leaders in their struggles with faculty members was their widespread practice of affiliating local chapter units with the national collegiate fraternity movement. The intercollegiate nature of the fraternal societies was what gave the local chapters their great negotiating strength. Officials of individual colleges often feared to oppose the student groups alone lest they lose their students by transfer to less hostile colleges.

How does one explain the great attraction of fraternities to students and the equally strong reaction against them by school officials? The students enjoyed the sense of power that the fraternities gave them. It was fun to know something that the faculty and administrators did not; it was also satisfying to see the faculty and other students threatened by what in many ways could be defended as good organizations. The fraternities, after all, often gave their members a sense of security, loyalty, and fellowship; they provided experiences in self-government; they sometimes prodded members to greater studiousness; and through their rituals they often promoted moral integrity and the pursuit of religion. The religion promoted by fraternities, however, was usually of a vague, nonspecific variety, as suggested in the following verse by Ernest Crosby:

> No one could tell me where my soul might be,
> I searched for God but He eluded me,
> I sought my brother out and found all three.[82]

Fraternity leaders often exaggerated the virtues of their organizations. For example, many chapters would have viewed as one of their major purposes the claim of the original Phi Beta Kappa chapter that it provided a haven for the free discussion of all issues: "Now then you may for a while disengage yourself from scholastic laws and communicate without reserve whatever reflection you have made upon various objects; remembering that everything transacted within this room is transacted *sub rosa,* and detested is he that discloses it."[83] College students, of course, had always found ways to discuss their innermost feelings in settings apart from the faculty. A major attraction of the fraternity was that it provided an organization to taunt the faculty officially with this reality.

Faculties opposed the fraternities for several reasons. They realized that the Greek societies would reduce their ability to control the lives of the students. Many of them believed that to acknowledge the fraternities officially would be to abandon their God-ordained responsibility to guide the religious and moral development of the students. College officials also shared the concern of the anti-fraternity students that the new organizations would lead to an anti-democratic elitism. Furthermore, they worried that the introduction of fraternities would upset the off-campus constituencies. Particularly was this the case when a college was affiliated with a denomination that officially opposed such secret societies as the Masons.[84] In general, throughout the past century, the more conservative the theological orientation of a college and its constituency, the less it has received pressure to introduce fraternities and the easier it has been for it to resist whatever pressure has arisen.

While growing democratization, expanding affluence, and curricular and extracurricular development brought major changes to American higher education in the late nineteenth century, the colleges and universities at the same time began to feel the early blasts of the intellectual winds that would come to full force in the new century, largely bringing down the spiritual underpinnings of the old-time college. This ideological revolution is the subject of the next chapter.

4

The Movement toward Secularization

In his 1967 dedicatory address at the opening of Oral Roberts University, evangelist Billy Graham, sensing the university's potential greatness, warned: "If ORU ever moves away from faith in the Bible and faith in God and putting God first, then let us this day pronounce a curse on it. This institution was built by the prayer and the dedication and the money of women and men who love God, who believe the Gospel, and who believe the Bible is the word of God."[1] Graham's concern came from his knowledge that the best-endowed colleges in America have tended to move from a Christian to a secular orientation. By the late twentieth century, even at most church-related colleges, secular modes of thought had come to dominate over the Christian worldview.[2] Students of the subject use terms like "nonaffirming colleges," "Protestant-change colleges," and "post-Protestant colleges" to describe those previously Christian institutions that have become largely nonreligious in nature.

Gradually, beginning in the late nineteenth century, American higher education in general changed its spiritual direction to the point that by the 1980s it exerted a primarily negative effect upon the spiritual development of its students. Whereas during the nineteenth century the great majority of colleges and universities included religious aims among their institutional goals, they identified such purposes only half as frequently by the second decade of the twentieth century. By the 1960s, widespread agreement existed among scholars that the degree of commitment to religious values by the average college student actually declined during four years of study. A major study by Kenneth Feldman and Theodore Newcomb in 1969 showed that entering freshmen almost invariably listed religious values as their highest values, but religious faith became significantly less important to them by the time they were seniors. A 1962 study of National Merit Scholars produced similar results. In response to the

113

question, "Do you personally feel the need to believe in some sort of religious faith?" 90 percent of the honor students responded in the affirmative as entering freshmen, whereas only 60 percent did so by the end of their junior year. A 1968 study comparing college students with employed non-college students of the same age found two and one-half times as many collegians as noncollegians valued religion less than they did in high school. Not only did most colleges and universities grow in the degree of their secularization; after 1945 an increasing percentage of young people chose to enroll in such institutions rather than the continuing Christian colleges.

The process of secularization did not proceed at a uniform rate in all institutions, yet one still can chart the general course of the secularization process. The major state universities and a limited number of elite private institutions led the secularization movement in the late nineteenth century. They were followed by the second line state universities and more of the elite private institutions. After the First World War, most colleges of the major denominations began to follow the trend. By contrast, most of the institutions that remain clearly Christian today are aligned with conservative Protestant denominations (e.g., Assemblies of God, most Baptists, Christian Reformed, Church of God, Churches of Christ, Evangelical Friends, Free Methodist, Lutheran, Mennonite, Nazarene, and Wesleyan) or, in some cases, transdenominational evangelical constituencies.

Some scholars have observed that the secularization process in higher education is an outgrowth of the secularization of America in general during the same period. To a certain extent this is true; however, one must note that the colleges secularized more than did society as a whole. Before the Civil War, the colleges, as agents of a church dominated by orthodoxy, were much more Christian in their convictions than was society. By contrast, higher education today is considerably more secular than is the populace in general.[3]

Sources of Secularization

The changes that took place in American thought beginning in the late nineteenth century were so sweeping that they might properly be called a revolution. Before this intellectual revolution, nearly all of the leading thinkers as well as laypersons subscribed to a supernatural worldview. Few argued against the idea that the Divine Creator intervenes directly in human affairs in miraculous as well as natural ways, and that he revealed himself supremely through the incarnation of his Son, Jesus Christ, by whose atoning death he seeks to restore sinful humanity to himself. Like the changes in the economy wrought by the Industrial Revolution, the dramatic changes in this prevailing mode of thought occurred gradually and moved forward on several fronts simultaneously. As the Industrial Revolution witnessed interrelated changes in industrial production, agricultural production, and transportation, the intellectual revolution saw simultaneous challenges to the traditional worldview coming from such fields as biblical interpretation, theology, philosophy, sociology, psychology, economics, and particularly the biological and physical sciences.[4]

Higher criticism as a method of biblical interpretation became especially popular in Germany, where so many American scholars were studying during the late nineteenth century. It gained prominence through the promotion of such thinkers as Friedrich Schleiermacher (1768–1834), Albrecht Ritschl (1822–89), and Adolf von Harnack (1851–1930). Higher criticism contended that a scholar could best understand the Bible and all other books recording the literature and history of ancient peoples by studying them in the historical context of their societies. The orthodox did not automatically reject this approach to biblical interpretation, for they believed that when one pursued it in an attempt to gain a more precise knowledge of God's purpose, it could be very worthwhile. What they did vigorously protest, however, was the tendency of many of the higher critics to combine their approach with an underlying assumption that the Bible was primarily a human book. This assumption became increasingly common in American colleges and universities as more and more of the American graduate students in Germany returned to assume positions in higher education in this country.

One such returning scholar, Benjamin Baker, became pastor of the university church at Yale; he observed in 1920 that "there is no greater service men like ourselves can do for our age than to sweep away the fogs and obscurities which gather around the figures of Jesus and Paul." Professor William Clarke of Colgate also represented this new trend when he wrote:

> Hitherto I had been using the Bible in the light of its statements, but now I find myself using it in the light of its principles. . . . I am not bound to work all its statements into my system; nay, I am bound not to work them all in; for some of them are not congenial to the spirit of Jesus and some express truth in forms that cannot be of permanent validity.

An increasing number of intellectuals, then, began to look to the Bible more as a source of religious history and general wisdom and inspiration than as the unique source of divinely revealed truth.[5]

At the same time, philosophers and thinkers in other areas also began to develop new conclusions about how best to search for truth. A system of thought known as logical positivism began to gain acceptance. Applied first in the natural sciences, logical positivism accepted as valid only those things which could be verified by the scientific method. The orthodox criticized this epistemological approach and labeled it "scientism," or the worship of the new god of the scientific method.

Another increasingly influential approach to truth, developed in Germany, was relativism. First, scholars had become less concerned about searching for universal meanings and more concerned with discovering new, limited bits of factual knowledge. Then, they developed the concept that one no longer could find universal truths. Belief in absolute eternal verities such as those expressed in the Bible increasingly gave way to a philosophy of relativism that suggested that what is true for one may not necessarily be true for another, and vice-versa.

Those who accepted much of the new thought but did not wish to give up all of their traditional Christian beliefs embraced a form of theology called liberal Protestantism. Such a view allowed its adherents to continue to embrace the moral and ethical teachings of the Judeo-Christian tradition while rejecting the supernatural elements of that faith, including the divinity of Jesus. Those who downgraded the supernatural aspects of Christianity often placed a heavy emphasis upon its sociological dimensions. The result was a revival of the social gospel that had characterized much evangelical effort before the Civil War. In 1903, Timothy Dwight, president of Yale (grandson of the earlier Yale president of the same name), compared the emphasis of preachers at his university during the first half of the nineteenth century with those that appeared at the end of the century: "The thought of the personal soul of the individual man . . . is less prominent than it was in the earlier days." By the turn of the century, he continued, the important question asked at Yale about one's religion was "What are its outgoings in efforts for other men?" Similarly, George Harris, president of Amherst, noted that at his college there now was "preaching on the real human Christ and on the service of man to man. Sermons are ethical and spiritual rather than theological . . . and irrational doctrine is discarded, but faith, hope, love, and character are exalted."[6]

Perhaps no college surpassed Oberlin in its social-gospel emphasis. When Theodore Roosevelt stopped there during his 1912 presidential campaign, he noted, "This is the community of the applied square deal . . . what I preach, you put in practice." Nationally known social-gospel leaders identified with the Ohio school. Washington Gladden of nearby Columbus made regular lecture appearances there, and Walter Rauschenbusch and Josiah Strong enrolled their children in the college. Also, an impressive number of social science professors and leaders in state universities and colleges actively participated in the social-gospel movement. Many institutions of higher education that are predominantly secular now gave considerable emphasis to liberal Protestant theology and social-gospel activity at some period between their orthodox Christian past and the present.[7]

Of the several factors influencing the transformation in the intellectual orientation of higher education from religious to secular, none caused greater controversy nor effected more sweeping change than did the gradual acceptance of Darwinian biology. Darwinism presented a novel perspective that invited reevaluation of traditional values in all the disciplines. As one measure of its impact, science began to surpass classical studies as the most prestigious intellectual subject.[8]

Following the publication of the *Origin of Species* in 1859 and its companion piece, *The Descent of Man,* in 1871, few American colleges rushed immediately to embrace the new thought. A reporter from the New York *Observer* in 1880 asked the presidents of Yale, Rochester, Princeton, Lafayette, Amherst, Union, Williams, Brown, and Hamilton whether they permitted their professors to teach that "man at least as far as his physical structure is concerned" was evolved from the animal kingdom, and each of the presidents responded negatively. Gradually, however, college presidents began to look the other way while the science professors accepted and taught the evolutionary theory. At Amherst, for example, when President Seelye reluctantly allowed Benjamin Emerson to teach physical science in a naturalistic manner, the instructor expressed appreciation that "the old fellow left us alone." Even in those institutions whose presidents quickly encouraged evolutionary teaching (e.g., Harvard, Johns Hopkins, Cornell, Stanford, Chicago), battles still usually occurred within the faculties over the new theory. The late-nineteenth-century Harvard science faculty, for example, contained both the best-known American proponent (Asa Gray) and the best-known critic (Louis Agassiz) of evolution.[9] Generally, the proponents of evolution won these battles and took the theory into the classroom.

Almost invariably, the first generation of scientists to embrace Darwinism attempted to reconcile it with the Christian faith. Asa Gray insisted that Darwinism was not harmful to religion as long as one accepted the view that the Creator designed the process. Professor Albert Wright of Oberlin argued that nothing in the theory *necessarily conflicted* with the Christian faith, and Joseph LeConte of the University of California proudly declared the ideal Christian man to be at the apex of the evolutionary process. President McCosh of Princeton, one of the most significant early converts, accepted evolution as "the method by which God works."[10]

Others thought differently. While Louis Agassiz allowed for evolutionary development within the biblical kinds, he insisted that the differing species resulted from separate acts of creation by God. James Dwight

Dana of Yale, one of the most respected geologists of the late nineteenth century, steadfastly rejected Darwinian thought. At the end of his career in 1890, he announced in his last public statement: "Science has made no real progress toward proving that the divine act was not required for the creation of Man. No remains of ancient man have been found to indicate a progenitor of lower grade than the lowest of the existing tribes." President Frederick Barnard of Columbia, himself a scientist, insisted in 1873 that if organic evolution were true, then one could no more confidently proclaim the existence of God or the immortality of the soul. "If the final outcome," Barnard argued, "of all the boasted discoveries of science is to disclose to men that they are more evanescent than the shadow of the swallow's wings upon the lake . . . give me then, I pray, no more science. . . ."[11]

The first generation of evolutionists believed they were helping save Christianity by accepting Darwinism. President McCosh of Princeton announced that he was "happy to report that there is little disposition in this college toward skepticism or scoffing. I do my best to guard against these, but, I do this not by keeping the young men ignorant of prevailing errors. . . . This is the most effective of all means to produce infidelity." Even President Andrew D. White of Cornell, whose book, *A History of the Warfare of Science with Theology in Christendom* (1896), greatly helped defeat orthodoxy in academic circles, held strongly as a liberal Protestant to what he saw as the essence of Christianity. He viewed those who opposed the new theory as joining the long, pathetic tradition of anti-intellectual zealots throughout history who have fought the discovery of new truth by wrongly tying the Christian faith to outmoded scientific theories. Later White must have been greatly dismayed to note that his campaign to save Christianity by liberalizing it only helped establish an atmosphere congenial to the secularism and relativism that he hated.[12]

John Fiske and Henry Drummond joined White as the most effective spokesmen in persuading American Protestant leaders to combine evolution with their traditional Christian beliefs. Fiske, a lecturer at Harvard and probably the leading American popularizer of and proselytizer for Darwinism, expressed his view in *The Destiny of Man Viewed in the Light of His Origin* (1884). Drummond's *Natural Law and the Spiritual World* (1883) exerted perhaps even more influence than did the work of Fiske in converting American Protestant theologians to Darwinism. To an unusual degree, Drummond combined evangelical zeal with his argument that evolution was God's way of doing things. Yale undergraduate William Lyon Phelps in 1887 brought Drummond to his campus where the author spoke nightly for two weeks. "I have never seen so deep an impression made on students by any speaker on any subject as that made by Henry Drummond," Phelps recalled.[13]

Not all of the early professors and students who accepted Darwinism sought to make it compatible with the biblical record. One Michigan State freshman wrote home that his professor "is a strong evolutionist" who "succeeds in converting many of his students to this theory and although he reconciles it to the Bible, they, when once set thinking, do not always." Some university leaders attempted no such reconciliation either for themselves or for their students. President Eliot of Harvard, a chemist, held to a rather ambiguous concept of God as a glorious "transcendent intelligence." David Starr Jordan, Stanford president and a biologist, was critical of the atheistic evolutionist, but, like Eliot, Jordan did not subscribe to a personal Christian deity. Rather, he believed in an abstract "power that made for righteousness."

In general, the evolutionary theory was accepted earlier and more completely in the state universities than in the denominational colleges and seminaries, in the church colleges under loose control than in the church colleges under tight control, and in the North and West than in the South. It also gained acceptance more easily at an institution if its first advocates there were known for their Christian piety and dedication (such as William L. Poteat, a biologist and later president at Wake Forest).[14]

Methodist and Baptist colleges in the South voiced some of the strongest criticisms of the theory during the nineteenth century. For example, when in the 1880s the West Virginia Methodists not only lost control of the state university at Morgantown but also discovered that professors there were teaching evolution, they expressed great dismay. The annual conference committee on education declared, "No college which permits its professors to insinuate skepticism into immature and impressionable minds, who antagonize scripture with science falsely so-called, can expect any favor from Christian parents." Given this distrust of the state university, it is not surprising that the Methodists three years later began West Virginia Wesleyan college at Buckhannon. One of the most widely publicized cases of professorial dismissal for teaching the new evolutionary ideas occurred at Vanderbilt, when Alexander Winchell lost his position even though his acceptance of the idea of evolution stopped short of including man. Before the turn of the century, most southern professors who felt strongly about promoting the theory had moved North.[15]

Although evolution suffered many defeats, it gradually gained acceptance in most institutions, including many of those that for years had bitterly resisted it. This happened in large part because year after year increasing numbers of science instructors in more and more colleges had received their training in graduate schools where the predominant professors and textbooks expressed sympathy for the evolutionary hypothesis.

While the decline in the acceptance of Christian orthodoxy by the leaders of thought has been the primary source of secularization in higher education, there have been other, more indirect causative factors. Beginning about 1850, American society became increasingly pluralistic. The immigration of Irish Catholics and German Catholics and Jews at mid-century, followed by the larger influx of eastern European Catholics, Orthodox Christians, and Jews between 1890 and 1915, reduced the Protestant religious consensus. No longer would Protestant denominations so easily dominate public institutions, including the state colleges and universities. This growing religious pluralism combined with the new systems of naturalistic thought to lead to the modern concept of the separation of church and state. In the state universities, this separation meant that the Christian faith ceased to be the integrating center of the educational process.

Marks of Secularization

As the new ideological influences began to gain acceptance on many campuses, the philosophical orientation of those institutions began to change. No longer did they operate from Christian premises and promote Christian purposes. The rate and degree of change has varied from college to college, but the process of change has been remarkably uniform; therefore, the characteristics marking that change have been similar.

The ultimate measure of the extent to which a given college in a given period — past or present — has moved toward secularism is how completely the college personnel still believe that the central act of history (and thus the key to ultimate meaning and truth in the universe) is the supreme revelation of God to humanity through Christ. When doubt begins to grow on this primary issue, many of the later stages in the secularization process follow quite naturally. For example, as key decision-makers begin to believe that the Christian religion is merely one of the many good systems of thought and that Jesus was only a good man, there remains little reason to hire only Christian scholars rather than good and knowledgeable scholars of all religions; to maintain a Bible requirement for all students instead of a course in religion or values in general; or to commit precious college resources to maintaining a carefully planned program for campus-wide Christian worship. Very few, if any, institutions have moved quickly from being predominantly Christian to being predominantly secular. Almost invariably they have gone through an intermediate step in which they seek to promote religious values in general without giving specific preference to the Christian religion.

Colleges in this transition, regardless of when the change has occurred, usually have displayed the following marks:

1. The public statements about the Christian nature of the institution begin to include equivocal rather than explicit phrases;

these statements often describe Christian goals in sociological but not theological terms.

2. The faculty hiring policy begins to place a reduced emphasis upon the importance of the scholar being a committed Christian, and subsequently fewer professors seek to relate their academic disciplines to the Christian faith.

3. The importance of the Bible and the Christian religion in the general education curriculum declines.

4. The previously strong official institutional support given to religious activities in general and the chapel service in particular declines.

5. The institution begins to reduce and then perhaps drop its church affiliation or, if it be an independent institution, it tends to reduce its interest in identifying with interdenominational and parachurch organizations.

6. Budget decisions begin to reflect a reduced emphasis upon the essential nature of Christian programs.

7. An increasing number of students and faculty members join the college community in spite of rather than because of the remaining Christian influences, and the deeply committed Christian students begin to feel lonely.

One can tell much about the religious orientation of a college by carefully examining its catalog. A college with decidedly Christian purposes will usually say so unmistakably. For example, note the following statement at the beginning of the 1980–81 Concordia (Moorhead, Minnesota) catalog: "The integrating element for the curriculum and life in the liberal arts college of the church is the revelation of God in Jesus Christ. . . . This concept of our shared life in Christ . . . involves the entire program of the college for all of life is to be viewed as under the lordship of Jesus Christ." On the other hand, denominational colleges that have begun moving in the direction of secularization often describe themselves as church-related rather than Christian because of a fear that the latter term suggests a narrow or sectarian intellectual orientation. Some colleges proclaim a continuing connection with the Christian religion by identifying with its broad social principles as opposed to its specific theological ones. For example, one college currently notes that it retains a "basic Christian outlook in the values it espouses," and another states that "the focus of . . . its church-relatedness is the enhancement of human dignity in the world." Still other colleges frankly describe their relationship to the Christian faith as a historical but not current one.

Some Protestant college catalogs contain misleading claims about the religious nature of their institutions. In some cases, colleges simply neglect to update their philosophical positions. In other cases, the neglect is intentional and is meant to avoid communicating to the constituencies the precise nature of the institutions. This sometimes occurs when denominational colleges seek to placate church constituencies that subscribe to a greater degree of orthodoxy than do the colleges. The old academic proverb, "Nothing lies like a college catalog," contains some truth, but it is probably less true now than in former years, since colleges have become increasingly sensitive recently about possible legal action or governmental intervention resulting from misleading catalog statements.[16]

In addition to examining college catalogs, another way to trace changes in the religious nature of an institution is to compare the earlier and later written histories of the college. When a college has changed from Christian to secular, almost invariably its later historians, as compared to its earlier writers, show much less enthusiasm for—and sometimes less understanding of—the intensity and pervasiveness of the Christian faith in the beginning years.

As late as the 1880s, most church-related colleges still required religious qualifications for faculty members; this requirement also existed in most state institutions for faculty who taught in controversial fields. By the turn of the century, many colleges began to discard this employment policy. For example, early in the twentieth century Oberlin hired a Unitarian candidate over a Methodist one to fill a German instructorship because the Unitarian was apparently better qualified academically. Such a decision probably made sense for a liberal Protestant institution such as Oberlin had become because liberal Protestantism and Unitarianism then expressed similar theological views. In reaction to this tendency, other institutions began to reaffirm earlier practices of hiring only Christians. For example, the trustees at West Virginia Wesleyan in 1900 resolved that "hereafter, no teachers . . . shall be employed . . . who are not active Christians," and the school has abided by this resolution through the time of the writing of its latest history in 1965.

By the mid-1960s, the Oberlin position had become more typical than the West Virginia Wesleyan one, for by mid-century even most church-related colleges no longer formally required evidence of Christian faith on the part of their new appointees. Today, intense debate continues on this issue in colleges whose constituency includes both strong conservative and strong liberal forces. For example, the college and denominational leaders of the Lutheran Church in America—the most liberal branch of American Lutheranism—have been struggling recently with the results of their hiring practices. During the 1960s, when it was difficult to hire qualified instructors, their colleges began to employ some non-Christian faculty members. Today 15 percent of the non-Lutheran faculty members identify themselves as indifferent or opposed to religion.[17]

Usually, a secularizing institution chooses no longer to maintain a meaningful general education requirement in biblical studies. Some institutions that were secularizing at the time of the growth of the elective system simply failed to introduce courses in biblical studies to replace the older courses in mental and moral philosophy, natural theology, and evidences of Christianity. Others that did add such courses either did not require them or later broadened the requirement by choosing between a Bible course and a wide range of other religious and metaphysical subjects (e.g., "Living Religions of Asia," "Patterns of Religious Experience," or "Religion as Story"). Such a curricular arrangement often suggested that the college, while continuing to believe that the study of religion was important, no longer believed that the Judeo-tradition was uniquely important in understanding the meaning of the universe. Some colleges and universities — particularly the state-owned ones — even adopted the curious position that the Christian religion was no longer an appropriate area for intellectual inquiry.

A decrease in the strong institutional support given to religious activities has been one of the more visible symptoms of a decline in the Christian orientation of colleges. It often has followed gradually after the appointment of increasing numbers of noncommitted Christians to the faculties. This mark appears in something as simple as a decrease in the tendency to open faculty meetings with prayer or as basic as the reduction and then elimination of campus community worship services. Repeatedly, the secularization battle has been fought most visibly on the issue of required chapel. Usually the practice of required chapel continued well into the period of secularization, so that required chapel — or even chapel at all — seemed somewhat out of place. Frequently when a secularizing school continued chapel, it did so to provide a sense of institutional unity. Nevertheless, chapel services in secularizing institutions usually became increasingly unpopular with the students because the students saw the requirement as inconsistent with the changing position of the institutions and because this reduced commitment made the colleges reluctant to allocate sufficient resources to guarantee quality programming.[18]

Sometimes, growth in the size of the student body beyond the seating capacity of the chapel provided the occasion for giving up required chapel. If a college's growing secularization was not itself a sufficient force to cause the institution to abandon required chapel, the contemplation of the expense necessary to provide an enlarged facility did. The value of required chapel no longer continued to rank sufficiently high on the list of institutional goals to warrant a major financial investment to continue it. Even the building of a new chapel has not always been an indication that a college was not moving in the secular direction, for sometimes a college has accepted an unsolicited gift of a chapel from a well-meaning philanthropist so as to be able to retain his good will for future gifts. Under such circumstances, the existence of a new chapel building did not assure that it would serve its intended purpose.[19]

When a college has abandoned its chapel program, it usually has done so slowly. First, the frequency and maybe even the length of the chapel services are gradually reduced. Then required chapel is changed to voluntary chapel, often with impressive sounding rationales such as, "We don't want to force religion artificially on anyone anymore" — as though a chapel requirement is more akin to the medieval state-church system than to the other graduation requirements of the college. Usually when a college ends its practice of required chapel, what it is saying is, "We don't think that Christian worship is very important anymore, certainly not as important as other requirements such as English composition or physical education activities." This isn't always the case, however. Calvin in 1971 "decontrolled" chapel attendance because of an abundance rather than a lack of Christian instruction in other parts of the college program. As the college's historian noted: "Intelligent and spiritual members both of the student body and faculty have never been convinced that chapel is a necessary element in a Christian college whose classrooms professedly embody a religious spirit."[20]

Compulsory chapel disappeared first at the newer state universities — led by Wisconsin in 1869 — and then at most of the other major state universities by the turn of the century. Harvard moved to a voluntary system in 1886, and many of the other older private schools followed its example by the 1920s. A large majority of the state colleges also abandoned required chapel before 1930. Most of the smaller church colleges continued their regular religious services into the mid-twentieth century. By the eve of World War II, compulsory chapel still existed at 91 percent of church-related colleges, 56 percent of independent colleges, and 11 percent of state institutions. By comparison, at the same time chapel services of either the voluntary or the required type continued to operate in 100 percent of church-related colleges, 84 percent of independent institutions, and 27 percent of state institutions.[21]

A close correlation has existed between the attitude of the faculty and students of a college toward the sponsoring denomination and the extent to which that denomination continued to proclaim an orthodox Christian theology. Secularizing denominations have tended not only to produce secularizing colleges but also colleges that wish to be free of denominational control. For example, church-college relations tend to be much more positive in Lutheran, Episcopalian, Southern Baptist, and the small evangelical and fundamentalist groups than they do in the other major Protestant denominations. The colleges of the latter churches usually are more liberal theologically than are their denominations. Frequently, as the ideological gap between college and church widens, the two reduce and then end their relationship. When the official divorce occurs, it is merely the culminating act of a secularizing process that had been taking place for many years. An important related factor in the separation of church and college is the extent to which the denomination operates with a congregational polity. This factor helps to explain why so many of the earliest church colleges to go independent originally had been associated with the Congregational church.[22]

A development related to the disassociation of church and college but one that is not necessarily a mark of secularization in itself has been the reduced role of ministers in the governance of the colleges. Until the late nineteenth century, most colleges regularly selected ministers for presidents. This pattern ended at Harvard in 1869, Denison in 1889, Illinois in 1892, Yale in 1899, Princeton — in the person of Woodrow Wilson — in 1902, Marietta in 1913, Bowdoin in 1918, Wabash in 1926, and Oberlin in 1927. Similarly, clerical influence on boards of trustees has sharply declined over the years. In the early days of Pomona (CA), which opened in 1887, clergymen — especially Congregationalist ones — dominated the governing board. Gradually, however, they were replaced by ranchers, lawyers, and businessmen, so that only two preachers continued on the board by 1930. Between 1884 and 1926, the percentage of clergymen on governing boards declined by 50 percent at Amherst, by 60 percent at Yale, and by 67 percent at Princeton. Additionally, a well-known study of fifteen private colleges showed similar results: the clergy representation on the boards of these institutions declined from 39 percent in 1860 to 23 percent in 1900 to only 7 percent by 1930.[23]

The Process of Secularization: The Universities

Higher education began moving away from a Christian orientation even before the Civil War, when Harvard embraced Unitarianism. Although the roots of Harvard's movement toward the Unitarian faith began as early as the presidency of Edward Holyoke in the eighteenth century (1737–1769), a more decisive turning point came in the early 1800s when, within a two-year period, the university appointed Unitarian Henry Ware as the Hollis professor of divinity and elected Rev. Samuel Webber, a virtual Unitarian, as president. A few years later, Harvard reinforced its earlier decisions by appointing an unquestioned Unitarian, John Kirkland, to succeed Webber. By 1831 the fourteen Harvard faculty members included six Unitarians, only one Calvinist, three other Protestants, three Roman Catholics, and one Sandemanian. President Josiah Quincy, who succeeded Kirkland in 1829, vigorously defended the school against its trinitarian critics. He charged the Calvinists particularly with seeking not only to rid Harvard of Unitarianism but also to put Calvinism back in control of the institution. Later, President Eliot made the curious claim that the best way to keep Harvard nonsectarian was to appoint only Unitarians to professorships and key positions. Harvard Divinity School, which began in 1816, became even more completely Unitarian than did the college. Before 1870, the seminary hired only Unitarians, and most of the students were preparing for the Unitarian ministry.[24]

Frequently it is easier to start a new institution than to change the orientation of one already established. Just as Yale began a century earlier largely in reaction to the loss of Congregational influence at Harvard, so in the early nineteenth century Amherst and Andover Seminary arose in reaction to the growing Unitarianism at the nation's oldest college. Noah Webster wrote that the professed purpose of Amherst was to "change the progress of errors which are propagated from Cambridge." Andover began in 1808, even before the official beginning of Harvard Seminary, as a place to train orthodox ministers. President Timothy Dwight of Yale long had wished to establish a similar seminary at his institution. Yale realized his goal, however, only after his death. In the 1820s, Dwight's prize pupil, Nathaniel W. Taylor, became the first incumbent of the Dwight professorship of theology and thus the first instructor in the Yale Divinity School.[25]

The family of Oliver Wendell Holmes Sr. exemplifies the transition from trinitarianism to Unitarianism in the New England intellectual tradition. Holmes's father, Abiel, served as the longtime orthodox minister of the First Congregational Church of Cambridge. Throughout his tenure there (1772–1829), he steadfastly refused to allow Unitarian doctrine to be promoted, even though that position contributed to his demise as minister. Oliver was born in 1809 and grew to manhood while the struggle raged. He attended Harvard during the early period of Unitarian success there, graduating in 1829. He became a committed Unitarian, but, unlike others of that faith, he went beyond the mere neglect of orthodoxy to fight it openly and vigorously. One of his most famous literary accomplishments, "The Deacon's Masterpiece, or the Wonderful One-Hoss-Shay," describes in parable form the downfall of Calvinism. Holmes despised the old theology which he thought only had the effect of

> Scaring the parson into fits,
> frightening people out of their wits.[26]

Antebellum Unitarianism appeared at other colleges but succeeded nowhere else. President Asa Merser of Brown gradually embraced the

Unitarian faith and consequently was forced to resign after twenty-four years as president and thirty-nine years of institutional affiliation. While a student at Bowdoin in 1824, Henry Wadsworth Longfellow noted that only a handful of students joined him as members of the college Unitarian Society: "We are as small as a grain of mustard seed."[27]

In general, the major state universities and the best-endowed private institutions were the earliest to break with the Christian conception of higher education. Harold Bolce, a researcher in the early twentieth century, visited and studied American colleges for more than two years. In 1909, after attending classes, interviewing faculties and administrators, and studying written records, Bolce reported with dismay that relativistic philosophies were replacing Christian ones in the classroom:

> There is a scholarly repudiation of all solemn authority. The decalogue is no more sacred than a syllabus. . . . From the college standpoint there are no God-established covenants. What happens at the primaries is more to the point than what took place in Palestine.
>
> They teach young men and women plainly that an immoral act is merely one contrary to the prevailing conceptions of society; and that the daring who defy the code do not offend any Deity, but simply arouse the venom of the majority — the majority that has not yet grasped the new idea.[28]

Despite the general momentum toward secularism, many state institutions remained considerably religious well into the twentieth century. The first set of rules for Arkansas State, which began in 1909, resembles those in vogue at church colleges before the Civil War. Frank Strong, president of Kansas, in his 1902 inaugural address argued that the state university should provide Christian, even though non-sectarian, training. The country, he stated, needed educated Christian men, and the university because of its "very atmosphere, by the purity of life of its Faculty, by the moral and religious wholesomeness of its entire . . . influence," should promote the "deepest spiritual life and growth."[29]

Even into the mid-twentieth century some state institutions maintained religious claims. For example, promotional literature issued by the University of South Dakota on the eve of the Second World War referred to its faculty as Christian men and women and advertised with approval the fact that sorority and fraternity pledges were required to attend church each Sunday. As late as the 1950s, Mississippi State collected student fees to support the YMCA chapter. In general, the black state colleges maintained required attendance at religious services later than did the predominantly white state institutions. This happened in part because several state legislatures encouraged it as "a good and safe thing" for blacks, but also because

Afro-Americans were religiously homogeneous, overwhelmingly they were Baptists and Methodists. In 1945 one researcher found compulsory religious exercises in eleven of the nineteen black state colleges surveyed. Some of them also required attendance at prayer meetings.[30]

Those who wished to retain Christian influences in the universities fought a steadily losing cause. Some within the universities and especially the church college leaders lamented this loss and expressed their protest publicly. President Noah Porter of Yale reacted against the new theories gaining acceptance at his institution. He perceived that "hasty and super-ficial generalization characterizes . . . the brilliant reminiscing of the elo-quent scientific lecturer, in the flippant theories that characterize our his-toric and literary criticism, and the confident dogmatism of our one-sided theorists in psychology, ethics, and sociology." Yale's most controversial professor was William Graham Sumner, who used as a textbook the writ-ings of Herbert Spencer, the man considered by many to be the most dan-gerous anti-Christian of the age.[31] Sometimes the church college com-plaints came from narrow sectarians who resented the fact that their denominations no longer controlled the state universities. In other cases, the critics simply lamented the fact that the Christian religion in general received less emphasis in the universities.

The criticisms of the church college leaders frequently were very pointed. The Geneva catalog of 1878 stated that "the determined attempts to secularize . . . higher institutions of learning should be met by the most uncompromising action by all truly Christian colleges." Presidents W. D. Goodman of Baldwin (now Baldwin-Wallace) and Blanchard of Wheaton complained that leaders of the new thought, while claiming a growing ob-jectivity in the search for truth, frequently displayed the worst form of in-tellectual narrowness. Goodman argued that positivists who deny a first cause and rationalists who refuse to acknowledge the legitimacy of truth obtained through spiritual experience limit themselves in an unscientific way: "This exclusion of any kind of knowledge is unscientific though done in the name of science. To refuse to investigate the supernatural is a form of scientific bigotry." Blanchard was no less severe:

> The discussion of what is vaguely called "the modern method" of educa-tion . . . means no Bible and no religion of Christ. The study of psychology is the study of dead men's brains to learn how those brains, while living, se-creted thought. Yet these brave champions of liberalism and materialism are really the most intolerant, narrow, and bigoted men . . . they cry up "sci-ence," "method," "new education," and whatever fine words are used to cover and conceal the intended complete divorce of education from God and His Word. . . . Christianity speaks now in whispers in common school associations and state universities.[32]

If the church colleges were critical of the secularizing tendencies of the larger universities, university spokesmen sometimes responded in kind with criticisms of church schools. Few opposed the church colleges more vigorously than did President White of Cornell. He accused them of being petty in their criticism, mediocre in their teaching, and narrow-minded. Perhaps he reacted so strongly because the church college leaders viewed his institution as one of the most secular universities in the land. White claimed that Cornell was a Christian university, but a nonsectarian one. In fact, the New York school was neither Christian nor godless. The misunderstanding existed because some denominational leaders equated nonsectarianism with atheism, while White confused nonsectarian Christianity with a Christianity that was moving in the direction of Unitarianism. Cornell students viewed the battle between White and the church colleges less seriously than did the president, and they lightheartedly formed such "tongue-in-cheek" organizations as the Young Men's Infidel Association and the Cornell Young Men's Heathen Association. The press publicized this student activity, and many readers became outraged.

Other university leaders joined the attack. President Eliot of Harvard proclaimed in 1891 that it was "impossible to found a university on the basis of a sect," and that great universities taught religious tolerance, in contrast to the many small, narrow church colleges that presumably did not. Even more extreme was the view of Professor John W. Burgess of Columbia, who argued that church colleges should die and that there would be no need for them if the secondary schools in every large town added two or three years to their preparatory programs. Students completing such local courses could then go directly to a university. Church colleges, Burgess added, are merely ridiculous imitations of universities. President Jordan of Stanford—the institution that YMCA leader John R. Mott in 1901 cited as the "most irreligious" university in America—viewed the church school as "a small university, antiquated, belated, arrested, starved. . . ." President Harper of Chicago not only agreed that the church colleges were intellectually inferior; he claimed that they failed in the very area in which they professed to be strong, namely the promotion of sound religion. More typically, he argued, they merely encouraged hypocrisy.[33]

The running battle between the universities and the church colleges was much more than a philosophical debate. The period after the Civil War when the universities were becoming secularized was also the period when it was not yet clear whether the university or the church college would ultimately emerge as the dominant form of American higher education. At the turn of the century, the church colleges still enrolled approximately half of all college students; thus the battle between the two types of institutions was fought in large part over the question of which would win the largest share of public support and student enrollment.

The universities secularized for a variety of reasons. One reason was their quest for a larger worldview than the denominational emphasis of a particular church. Such a concern reflected the growing American sensitivity to the separation of church and state. Another reason universities excluded religious concerns was because such concerns often involved great controversy and were difficult to organize so as to please everybody. Some could not conceive of nonsectarian religion and assumed that the only alternative to sectarian faith was to dismiss religion altogether. Others wished to deemphasize the Christian faith and to replace it with other value and belief systems.

During the early part of the twentieth century, the universities exhibited more opposition than neutrality toward religion. Some institutions viewed religious studies and student religious societies as inappropriate. For example, the University of Oregon voted against creating a chair of religion in the Department of Philosophy because the governing board feared that such a position stood in violation of the state's need for religious neutrality. Furthermore, the west coast university would not let the YMCA and YWCA chapters construct a building on campus and did not favor formal religious exercises of any type on university property.[34]

During the second generation of the twentieth century, university officials began to recognize that their earlier tendency to suspend religious instruction and activity was an undue reaction to the sectarian control of some universities during the nineteenth century. Consequently, after about 1930, these officials significantly increased their interest in religion. Typical of those who apologized for the earlier extreme position was Robert J. Sproul, president of the University of California, who in 1932 stated:

> Is religion itself a legitimate field of learning in the university? Is it a specific experience of the race, a necessity for each growing citizen, and a way of cultural growth for the future, or is it only a vestigial activity, and an antiquated pre-scientific anachronism? For my part I believe that religion (not the sects) is basic to morals, central in our American culture, unique as a dynamic within the individual, able to save us from ourselves and lead us out into nobility. I believe that without religion we are forced to substitute weak conventions for permanent values and abiding standards; that without religion, civilization, with no adequate reinforcement for the great strains that come upon it must yield inevitably to disintegration and decay.

Accordingly, religious programs began to appear on the university campus. Some institutions appointed chaplains and religious counselors, and many added courses or even departments of religion. By 1940, 80 percent of the state institutions and nearly all of the independent colleges offered at least one course in religion, and 30 percent of the state institutions and 85 percent of the independent colleges listed departments of religion.[35]

While the universities by the middle period of the twentieth century acknowledged the value of religion more than they had during the first part of the century, they did not necessarily give more support to the Christian religion in particular than had been the case before 1930. They did not view the Christian faith — or even religion in general — as the integrating whole of the educational process as had their intellectual forebears in the old-time college. Although the exclusion of the study of religion in the universities was less pronounced by mid-century than it had been earlier, nevertheless secular values and, in places, even hostility toward religious faith largely characterized the intellectual orientation of the institutions.

One widely publicized study of the religious orientation — or lack of it — of a prominent institution is *God and Man at Yale*, published in 1951 by the brilliant but highly controversial observer William F. Buckley, who attended Yale in the late 1940s. His book discusses more than just religion, but religion figures prominently in it. Buckley observes that, in the intellectual battle between Christianity and agnosticism and atheism, Yale, by mid-century, did not maintain an atmosphere of detached impartiality but rather an antireligious bias. The strongest such bias, he argued, existed in the social science departments; however, even the Religion Department did little to counter the prevalent trend. This profile, even if somewhat exaggerated by Buckley, nevertheless probably represented not only Yale but the situation in the universities in general at mid-century.[36]

In measuring the extent of the success of secularization in higher education, one should note not only the number of institutions that have accepted a secular worldview but also the number of students who are enrolled in these colleges and universities. Those institutions which have secularized most completely have, in the aggregate, enrolled a sharply increasing percentage of the college student market.[37]

The Process of Secularization: The Church Colleges

Nearly all of the church colleges remained essentially orthodox before 1900. In the New England colleges, for example, students talked regularly about religious issues and attended class prayer meetings and daily chapel services. One of the high points of the year in New England and elsewhere was the annual day of prayer for colleges, celebrated since the colonial period on the last Thursday of January. Despite the fact that some student humorists referred to the special day as "the day of whist" for colleges in reference to those who took advantage of the day off from classes to loaf and play cards, most of the students participated in the services of special religious emphasis that day; and across the nation countless churches devoted their mid-week prayer services on that evening to earnest, heavenly petitions on behalf of the college students and their institutions.[38]

If the church colleges did not become more secular in the late nineteenth century, they did become more denominational. Before the Civil War, the colleges had served community needs and drawn upon community resources. In the years following the war, however, they began to attract their students as well as their financial support from denominational constituencies statewide and beyond. As more and more local communities developed public high schools, there became less need to rely upon the community colleges to provide preparatory education for young people. Also, the significant increase in per capita wealth brought by the growth of the economy meant that more families could afford to send their young people to residential colleges away from their home communities. As the young people went away from home to college, they often chose institutions of their own denominations. At the same time, colleges added more denominational representatives to their boards, and they solicited more funds from the wealthy members of their denominations. The peak of denominational influence came in the 1890s and did not sharply subside until about 1930, when the church colleges began to move in a secular direction. The secularization of the church colleges, then, occurred primarily during the second generation of the twentieth century and continues to the present.[39]

Scholars of American higher education have concluded that by the 1960s the traditional church colleges had become more influenced by secular than by Christian thought. Myron Wicke believes that the major period of change began about the end of World War II. Earl McGrath suggests that some colleges consciously broke their religious links while others merely allowed the secular influences to "wear them away." George Buttrick observes that the typical church-related college of the 1960s tended to "dismiss the Bible as a vague and sentimental affair called 'religion,' as an unwarranted intrusion, as 'indoctrination,' or at best as a matter for private conscience." Manning Pattillo and Donald Mackenzie concluded that "the difficulty is that many academic people do not think of religion as concerned primarily with the truth about ultimate reality. Rather it is regarded as a moral code, as a set of ideals, or as a quaint and antiquated body of ideas which educated people are supposed to have outgrown." Robert Pace predicted that, except for the evangelical and fundamentalist colleges, the church-related institutions in this country would no longer be recognizable as Protestant by the turn of the twentieth century. Christopher Jencks and David Riesman thought that one could almost make such a statement already, for "in most church-related colleges official religious influence is quite dead."[40]

It will surprise some to note that despite the secularizing trend, the great majority of church-related institutions — 87 percent according to the Pattillo and Mackenzie survey — continued into the 1960s to require the completion of course work in religion and theology.[41] This fact is not necessarily inconsistent with the secularizing trend, for even state universities in recent decades have discovered that they can offer such courses as a part of a secular curriculum with the instructors usually teaching only from a historical or sociological viewpoint.

While the general trend since the early twentieth century has been for the colleges associated with major denominations to move gradually in a secular direction, some institutions have reversed that pattern. For example, King (TN), a Southern Presbyterian institution, was on the brink of financial collapse in early 1979. It agreed to a proposal presented by a committee of conservative Presbyterians to rescue the college financially on the condition that they be allowed to "make the school unapologetically and enthusiastically an evangelical institution of higher Christian education." Accordingly, the evangelicals hired Wheaton dean Donald Mitchell as president.[42]

One can understand the secularization process better by tracing its development in specific institutions. The cases of Oberlin, Franklin, and Ripon illustrate the general trend. Secularization occurred at Oberlin somewhat earlier than at most church colleges. The steps in the process of change at the Ohio college included (1) a gradual acceptance by professors and students of the theory of evolution and a gradual decline in their confidence that the biblical record was divinely inspired; (2) a gradual acceptance of the liberal Protestant interpretation of the Christian faith; (3) a gradual willingness to hire non-Christians as instructors; (4) the abandonment of the senior Bible requirement; and (5) a gradually increasing desire to upgrade the general academic quality and reputation of the institution without a concurrent and equivalent desire to sustain the previous religious zeal.

Before the Civil War, Oberlin could claim probably the most evangelically intense student body in the country, but by the eve of World War I, it enrolled a student body that was much more motivated by intellectual than religious goals. For example, a 1911 survey of a majority of the Oberlin students on the goals they sought to realize in college showed that they ranked "development of mental powers" as the most important and "development of religious life" as below average. By the latter item the students undoubtedly meant the experience of conversion and the growth of personal piety. They certainly did not mean by it Christian social activism,

for this pursuit busily occupied both the students and faculty, led especially by Professor, and later President, Henry Churchill King. More than
any other individual, King directed the turn-of-the-century transition of
Oberlin into an institution dominated by the liberal Protestant, social-
gospel emphasis. Gradually the pursuit of learning and the acquisition of
knowledge replaced social-gospel idealism as the dominant purpose of
Oberlin. This goal of acquiring knowledge gradually ceased to be associated with liberal Protestantism and increasingly became combined with
secular thought.[43]

In 1900, Franklin College operated as a typical northern Baptist college.
Its primary institutional purposes included a desire to train "worthy and
willing Christian workers." Most of its students — 80 percent — professed
the Christian faith, and the college sponsored strong YMCA and YWCA
organizations and regular prayer meetings.[44]

In the early 1920s this orthodox pattern at Franklin remained intact; the
Biblical Literature Department had expanded its offerings to ten courses.
The college desired that the students not only receive a "technical knowledge of the Bible and kindred subjects," but also that they be "offered the
opportunity of acquiring a deeper religious conviction and of fostering a
religious enthusiasm and zeal." Every student completed a minimum of
six hours of study in biblical literature and attended daily chapel services.
The catalog described the student religious activities as strong.[45]

By 1950, the six-hour Bible requirement had changed to a three-hour
course and the daily chapel requirement to one chapel and two convoca-
tion services, both voluntary, per week. The catalog contained no explicit
statement of religious purpose.[46]

By the 1970s, the college held voluntary chapel irregularly, and required no Bible or religion course, although all students did enroll in one
on the formation of values. The religion courses presented Christianity as
a slightly preferable option to other faiths, but the Christianity being presented was a different variety from the one students had studied earlier in
the century. The Philosophy and Religion Department announced that the
purpose of such courses was to help students understand the contribution
of the Judeo-Christian tradition to the formation of the modern world of
thought and culture. Today one need not be a Christian to be hired at
Franklin, not even in the Philosophy and Religion Department, and a
large minority of the faculty is indifferent to religion. Franklin consultants
told the institution in the early 1970s that its purpose was unclear and that
it should seek to determine it. Subsequently the trustees developed a statement defining Franklin as "a personal college" which seeks the "development on the part of each student of a value system which will enable him
to deal effectively with the complexities of modern life."[47]

Ripon College in 1883 described itself as a Congregational and Presbyterian college with "the earnest purpose to conduct the institution on distinctively Christian principles and to have it pervaded with a strongly moral influence." In 1904, the college repeated this statement and announced that each student was expected to attend religious services once daily and would have opportunities to participate in "plenty of other religious services." In 1926, the college described its aim as that of having "the simplicity of the Christian life permeate the institution"; it listed an even broader array of Bible courses than that contained in the 1904 catalog and proclaimed that such courses "are pursued in the spirit of reverent scholarship."[48]

As had been the case at Franklin, by mid-century the religious climate had changed. The formerly sizable Bible Department appeared as only a single course in the new Department of Philosophy and Theology. Also, the four-per-week chapel services of 1926 had been reduced so that "ordinarily two religious chapels and two convocations [were] held each month."[49]

By the late 1970s, Ripon described its primary mission as being "to foster the growth and integration of intellect and character." A recent institutional statement of goals contained no reference to the Christian faith. In the 1978–79 catalog section on affiliation, however, the college acknowledged its historic ties to the Congregational church and that the college related currently more to the Judeo-Christian tradition in general than to a particular denomination. The tone of the catalog suggested that the college offered opportunities for study in, reflection on, and worship in the Christian religion for anyone who desired them, but that pursuit of truth in this area was not necessarily more important than the pursuit of truth in any other area.[50]

Secularization occurred more slowly in the elite women's institutions than in their male counterparts. Except for Vassar, which abolished compulsory chapel in 1926, the leading eastern women's colleges continued such required religious services into the mid-twentieth century. Perhaps the religious influence continued this long at the women's colleges because of their relatively late founding by individuals who held intensely spiritual goals for their institutions. In the modern period at Vassar, "about the only vestige of religious formalities is the more or less nondenominational Protestant-Sunday services at which attendance is voluntary and the congregation may or may not outnumber the choir." The other women's colleges have followed Vassar's example to a considerable degree.

Students at black colleges maintained regular church attendance habits much later than did students in predominantly white colleges. As late as 1945, more than 90 percent of the students in black colleges attended church at least twice a month, even though only one third of the blacks viewed their fellow students as being religious. Apparently, church attendance served a greater social purpose for blacks than for whites, and this may explain the regularity of their attendance. When measured in terms of deep commitment to Christian beliefs, however, little difference apparently exists between the black and the white colleges, for as one student of religion in black colleges noted in 1973: "the remaining doctrinal ties [between the churches and the colleges] have little influence on the ideological stance of students and faculty. Practically no one thinks of these colleges as instruments to perpetuate religious doctrines."[51]

In many ways, the church-related colleges of the late twentieth century resembled the denominations with which they were affiliated. The denominations with the largest membership and influence tended to have the largest number of colleges (see table 2).[52] The Episcopal church fit this pattern less well than any other major denomination, for despite its progressive attitude toward education, its affluence, and the contribution of its members to society, it operated only a limited number of four-year, accredited institutions. In general, the denominations with the most democratic polity maintain the loosest relationships with their colleges. For that reason, college counting was especially difficult in a denomination such as the United Church of Christ, the denominational home of the many colleges that identified previously with the Congregational church. While Pattillo and Mackenzie counted twenty-four United Church of Christ colleges, the denomination itself listed thirty without including most of the older, very well known, historically Congregational eastern institutions. Of the schools then claimed by the United Church of Christ, none dated its origin earlier than 1829 (Illinois College), and none was much larger than two thousand students (Franklin & Marshall enrolled 2,040 in 1976).

Perhaps no denomination represented a broader variety of theological expression than did the Quakers, and this wide spectrum of opinion was reflected in the Friends colleges, with Swarthmore (PA) and Haverford on the left as Protestant-change colleges; Friends (KS), George Fox (OR), and Malone (OH) on the right as evangelical institutions,[53] and Whittier, Guilford (NC), Wilmington (OH), and Earlham (IN) in the center. No denomination maintained a larger block of primarily orthodox colleges than the Southern Baptist Convention. The Southern Baptist colleges hired almost no non-Christians as professors and very few non-Baptists as religion instructors or administrators. One of the most liberal Southern Baptist institutions was Wake Forest. In the late 1970s it maintained a weekly voluntary worship service in its 150-seat chapel rather than its 1,300-seat auditorium. The North Carolina institution required one course in religion for all students; however, the course need not be on the Christian religion. An institutional statement of purpose declared the college's intent to shape the school's

Table 2. Denominations Affiliated with the Protestant Colleges (1966)

Methodist Church	102
Southern Baptist Convention	52
United Presbyterian Church in U.S.A.	51
United Church of Christ	24
American Baptist Convention	22
Presbyterian Church in U.S.A.	20
Lutheran Church in America	19
Disciples of Christ	18
American Lutheran Church	13
Lutheran Church–Missouri Synod	12
Seventh-Day Adventists	12
Episcopal Church	11
Society of Friends	11
Other (50 religious bodies)	111
	478

policies and practices by Christian ideals and stated that all students should be concerned for spiritual, moral, and physical development.[54]

Almost invariably, church colleges in the late twentieth century reflected a more liberal orientation than did the church groups affiliated with them. In the major denominations, the colleges tended to be less orthodox and more secular than the church creedal statements, the church membership, and the church leadership. Frequently churches complained of the trends in their colleges. For example, a comprehensive study of the Methodist Episcopal colleges in 1932 lamented that many of the institutions failed to give serious thought to their stated purposes and even operated in violation of them. Also, in the 1950s, a formal proposal by the General Conference Commission on Higher Education of the Methodist Church implied a continuing concern with the secular drift in the denominational institutions of higher education when it proclaimed, "Every institution of learning identified with the Church should rededicate itself openly to its historic mission as a Christian school." The resolutions even called for the colleges to hold public services of rededication for this purpose.[55]

The movement toward secularization has caused more pain in some institutions than in others. Probably least affected have been those institutions that because of a western location or another reason began late and also affiliated with a relatively liberal and democratic denomination. By contrast, the process of change has created great difficulty in some of the older colleges of the American Baptist Convention. For example, in Maine, where the state Baptist convention has long been more conservative than the denomination and where Colby and Bates had increasingly accepted liberal Protestant thought, the Baptists responded with great vigor. As noted by the Colby historian, "In Baptist churches from Kittery to Caribou, the modernism and secularism of the colleges were being denounced. One Baptist pastor in a rural community told a mother he would rather see her son dead than enrolled in either Colby or Bates." Accordingly the state convention in the 1930s officially broke with the colleges.[56]

Varieties of Protestant Higher Education by 1980

Before discussing the different types of Protestant colleges following the major period of secularization, perhaps it would be useful to note the overall size and general character of these institutions. One of the best and most thorough of the modern studies of Protestant and Catholic liberal arts colleges, that of Pattillo and Mackenzie in 1966, identified 1,189 private colleges and found 817 of them to be church related. Approximately 475 of these operated in association with a Protestant denomination and perhaps twenty-five more with an independent Protestant constituency. If one added to them all of the Bible institutes and Bible colleges in operation then, the number would increase to 750; however, if one included only the accredited Bible colleges — in other words those generally recognized undergraduate theological institutions which have general education components — then the result was approximately 550 Protestant colleges. The 1965 enrollment for the individual church-related liberal arts colleges varied from only nineteen to more than 22,000, with an average of 1,297.[57]

When compared to the enrollment in higher education in general, the percentage of the nation's college students enrolling in church-related institutions in particular and private institutions in general had continually declined. As recently as the 1950s, private institutions enrolled approximately 50 percent of the students in four-year programs. That figure declined from 48 percent in 1954 to 43 percent in 1962 and 30 percent in 1978.

When one includes the junior colleges — whose enrollments grew very rapidly after mid-century — then the private sector by 1965 compared even less favorably, constituting only approximately one third of American higher education, with enrollment in the church-related higher educational institutions comprising only 17.3 percent of the total enrollment. By

1978 the private institutions could claim only 22 percent of the total higher education enrollment.[58]

In recent years, church-related colleges appear to have achieved more, relatively speaking, with their resources than has higher education in general and the public institutions in particular. Although church-related colleges enrolled only 17.3 percent of the students in 1965, they conferred 25.6 percent of the degrees, employed 22 percent of the full-time faculty members and 32 percent of the general administrative staff, and owned 42 percent of the total library volumes. They received only 15 percent of the current income for education and general expenses, but they held 22 percent of the annual endowment and 35 percent of the scholarship dollars, and they awarded 37 percent of the scholarships. Furthermore, studies in the modern period have shown that church-related colleges produce a disproportionately high percentage of American college professors, researchers, scientists, and doctors.[59]

In general the late-twentieth-century church-related liberal arts colleges, when compared to the large public institutions, (1) provided more school spirit and unity; (2) experienced more personal friendliness between students and faculty; (3) more successfully challenged the students to offer their time and abilities in service to other people and to society in general; (4) offered a more personalized education with the students being treated as individuals and the professors placed greater emphasis upon teaching than research (despite this emphasis, the professors were as active in research and publication as were professors in the small state colleges); and (5) offered their students greater opportunities for participation in a broad variety of co-curricular activities.[60]

In classifying the major types of Protestant colleges, one could, as a careful scholar of Christian higher education recently did, identify institutions by the closeness of the denominational relationship.[61] The most useful approach, however, when dealing with the secularization process, is to identify institutions on the basis of the degree to which they have moved from being orthodox to secular. Within this frame of reference, most institutions could be identified as (1) essentially secular even if nominally Christian, (2) generally religious, (3) liberal Protestant, or (4) conservative Protestant. This spectrum of colleges, as it existed in 1980, is the basis of the discussion of the remainder of this chapter.

The primarily secular college at its best is an objective and tolerant "multi-university" where any and all views on all issues, metaphysical or otherwise, may be presented and respected. At its worst, the secular college indoctrinates the religion of humanism and agnosticism.

While the secular university usually does not provide a planned dialogue to assist its students in developing an overall worldview, the generally religious college at its best intentionally confronts the students with "the ultimate dialogue," namely that between the differing doctrines on the relationship between God and man. At its worst, the generally religious college makes an end of the dialogue and gives the impression that, while it believes religion to be important, specific religious truth is relative.

The liberal and the conservative colleges at their best would agree with the importance of intentionally structuring intellectual dialogue on the differing doctrines of God and man. However, they would do more than the religious college to influence the outcome of that dialogue, because they believe that Christian answers to questions raised by the dialogue are more valid than others as a basis for developing a worldview and making a life commitment.

The liberal and conservative colleges differ from one another in how they explain the Christian voice in the dialogue. Liberals emphasize the ethical and moral teachings of Jesus, believing that they best interpret how God wishes humanity to live and thus provide the context in which all knowledge should be sought. Conservatives agree that Jesus' moral teachings are basic but add to this the foundational belief that the key event of history is the incarnation of God in the person of Jesus Christ, perfect God and perfect man, through whose atoning death each person, estranged from God, may be reconciled to the Creator. Liberals are less certain about the divinity of Jesus and the authority of the Bible—particularly its supernatural elements—than are conservatives. The liberal Protestant colleges at their worst are ideological way stations between orthodoxy and secularism, and while they may insist that in higher education secularism does not necessarily follow a liberalized Christianity, the conservatives with dismay and the secularists with glee remind them that this is what usually has happened. Conservative Protestant colleges at their worst seek to bypass any dialogue over the differing doctrines of the relationship between God and humanity and simply to tell their students what is truth.

The secular institutions include nearly all of the state universities, most of the elite private colleges, and an embarrassingly large number of church-affiliated institutions. Among the private schools, the tendency is for an institution to become increasingly secular as it becomes increasingly independent of denominational financial support, governance, and recruitment of students, and as it achieves higher academic standing. As the major denominations have watched their colleges become less Christian and an increasing percentage of their young people enroll in state universities, they have begun to identify less with their own colleges and more with the more orthodox denominational student centers near the state campuses.

In a very limited number of predominantly secular institutions (e.g., Miami University of Ohio), religious views are given a fair chance to compete with the prevailing secularism.[62] More typically, however, the intellectual balance of power weighs heavily against Christianity. In the state institutions it is often thought that the modern concept of the separation of church and state precludes a serious institutional commitment to explore the religious dimensions of life. Others at state institutions and elsewhere simply think such explorations are irrelevant for the modern mind. More frequently than secular educationalists would like to admit, a religious emphasis fails to appear in modern higher education primarily because its advocates are outmuscled in the struggle for influence. Whatever the explanation, impressionable young students clearly receive the message that knowledgeable and intelligent people no longer consider serious intellectual inquiry into religion to be a necessary task for the contemporary scholar.

Only a limited number of colleges actively wish to promote serious religious inquiry without favoring the Christian religion. In institutions as well as in individuals, deep religious commitment usually is made to a specific faith rather than to religion in general. When zeal for promoting the Christian faith wanes, institutions become reluctant to commit their limited financial resources to support well-developed programs for serious student inquiry into a broad variety of faiths. The seriously religious although not specifically Christian colleges include Pomona and Wellesley. Pomona, which began as a Congregationalist college, still wishes to be known as a religious institution and attests to that desire by providing (with the other schools of the Claremont Colleges cluster) Jewish, Catholic, and Protestant chaplains who serve the students on a full-time basis and direct the Center for Religious Activities. In addition, Pomona supports a very active religion department with six professors and a wide-ranging curriculum that emphasizes sociological, philosophical, and comparative religious studies.[63]

Wellesley believes that a student's search for personal and spiritual values is sufficiently important that it provides a college chaplain and staff of counselors who have developed a religious program, including corporate worship that embraces many faiths. The counseling staff itself represents several religious traditions. While participation in all religious programs and services is voluntary, the college does encourage such involvement. Similarly, the college offers the academic study of religion on an optional basis. A student may meet a general education requirement with a course in religion but need not do so. The Department of Religion and Biblical Studies offers a broad range of courses on a variety of religious faiths, with the biblical studies emphasizing the historical and literary critical method.[64]

Sometimes the generally religious college will describe itself as "truly Christian," by which it means that it is supportive of a broad variety of Christian and non-Christian faiths. Rarely, however, do such institutions promote their general religious concerns as vigorously throughout the totality of their program as do the Christian — particularly the conservative Christian — institutions.

A college whose religious orientation probably lies somewhere between that of "generally religious" and liberal Protestant is Texas Christian. It attempts to provide a campus environment "in which religion, especially the Christian religion, functions as the integrating center of learning. Students of all creeds and faiths are welcome, university religious activities are varied in style, celebrating many traditions and honoring them all." The university requires one course in religion and holds "university vespers" each Sunday evening in the chapel. The institution, in other words, desires religion to be the center of the university, for the Christian religion in particular to receive some preference, and for all other religions to be held in respect.[65]

In 1958, even while many church colleges were rapidly secularizing, the Commission of Higher Education of the National Council of Churches issued a classic statement entitled "What Is a Christian College?" which discussed the characteristics that should be found in a liberal Protestant college. The report called attention dramatically to the distance that was developing between mainline denominations and their colleges. It defined a Christian college as one that attempts to develop the whole personality of every student in accordance with the life and teachings of Jesus Christ. It suggested that a college could call itself Christian if the majority of its continuing personnel — and all of those that direct and implement policy — were consciously and actively Christian. The National Council statement also suggested that in a Christian college "the Christian faith is the preeminent discipline, and that the requirement for the study of it should be at least equal to the requirements in any other area . . . , and should as far as possible be sustained throughout the student's four year career." Finally, the report also stated clearly that a church college should present chapel services as part of its total curricular program, with the entire student body in regular attendance.

The statement of faith contained in the report did not differ much from a statement of, say, the National Association of Evangelicals — at least not in what it explicitly said. It was not clear, however, on the issues of the divinity of Christ, the authority of the Bible, and supernaturalism. It was clearer than most conservative Protestant statements on the ethical obligations of Christians and the brotherhood of man.[66] American higher education would be very different if all, or even most, of the colleges associated with denominations belonging to the National Council of Churches would follow its higher education commission's blueprint for a Christian college.

While conservative colleges criticize the less orthodox ones for not emphasizing sufficiently the traditional Christian worldview in their educational programs, the more liberal institutions charge the conservative colleges with not combining sufficient rigorous intellectual inquiry with their practice of the faith. As one such critic of the conservative schools noted, "Many a 'secular' professor honors an unacknowledged faith better by his honest confrontation of fact than another who advertises his 'little churchinesses' and offers only Mickey Mouse courses." The continuing Christian colleges do not deny that such teaching takes place in their institutions; neither do they usually approve of it. They would argue, however, that instruction of this type is less characteristic of their institutions than their liberal Protestant and secular critics imply. In fact, representatives of the conservative colleges argue that their institutions probably expose students to a broad variety of opinions on controversial religious and philosophical topics more effectively and objectively than do most other colleges and universities. The advantage that they claim is that usually they openly acknowledge their assumptions, whereas many professors in the secular and secularizing institutions mistakenly assume that because they do not have pro-Christian presuppositions, therefore they have none at all. In addition, Christian professors usually know non-Christian views in their disciplines better than non-Christian professors understand Christian interpretations in their areas of study; therefore, Christian professors can present a broader variety of perspectives. This is true in large part because most Christian professors have studied in secular graduate institutions and therefore know secular systems of thought quite well. Non-Christian instructors in secular institutions, by contrast, often have experienced little or no exposure on a sophisticated level to Christian worldviews.[67]

No longer then, by the last generation of the twentieth century, did the avowedly Christian colleges sit at the apex of the country's educational structure. That mid-nineteenth-century reality was now gone. Some of the old colleges continued to operate as unapologetically Christian institutions, and to their ranks were added many others during the last century; but the Christian colleges of 1980, although growing in program quality and public respect, did not hold the same position of prestige in society that they once did.

5

The Response to Secularization

Because American higher education has secularized more than have the churches or society in general, it is not surprising that Christian students, denominations, and parachurch organizations have sought to counter the trend. The methods they have used to promote the Christian faith have varied from period to period. During the quarter century following the Civil War, the denominations responded by concentrating their efforts less upon the state universities — where they were losing their influence, anyway — and more upon the church colleges, with the result that the latter became increasingly denominational in nature. Meanwhile, on the campuses of both public and private colleges, the largely student-led YMCA and YWCA chapters (collectively known as the "Y movement" or the "Ys") became unusually popular organizations.

Between 1890 and 1925, as increasing numbers of students from the major denominations began to enroll in state universities, the denominations decided again to devote major attention to the public centers of learning. While now acknowledging the largely secular nature of the state institutions, the major denominations sought to reduce this influence first by creating "satellite schools" (Bible chairs or Bible schools with dormitory facilities) at the universities and later by establishing the more common denominational foundation centers. Meanwhile, intercollegiate student religious societies, which now included the missionary-oriented Student Volunteer Movement as well as the Ys, reached the peak of their influence. Also in this period the smaller religious groups, in part as a response to the general secularization pattern, began to organize autonomous Bible institutes and Bible colleges, thus creating a largely new form of higher education.

After 1925, the old student societies as well as a large majority of church colleges became increasingly secular; consequently, there sprang up to

145

take their places new student organizations, led by the InterVarsity Christian Fellowship and Campus Crusade, and also new fundamentalist liberal arts colleges.

The YMCA and Other Student Christian Organizations

It probably was coincidental that during the middle of the nineteenth century the universities entered the beginning stages of secularization at the same time that Christian students began to develop the most influential and widespread student religious organization in American history. It was not mere coincidence, however, that the YMCA and the YWCA organizations reached the peak of their influence when the universities became more secular at the turn of the century. College Christian associations grew so rapidly partly because they filled the religious void left on the campuses as the universities withdrew from their former official promotion of the Christian religion. For example, the historian of the University of North Dakota observed that there the Ys became the most efficient agency of moral and religious training only after the state university backed away from its earlier direct support of religion. Also, the Northwestern historians frankly state that for many years the YMCA and YWCA chapters "kept alive the school's religious character." By the turn of the century, then, as stated by Professor Roswell Hitchcock of Union Seminary, the Christian associations were "the great religious fact in the life of the colleges."[1]

The Y movement swept the collegiate world and received widespread public approval. The movement prospered on both the state university and Christian college campuses. Denominational leaders, university and college presidents, and faculty members all highly acclaimed it.[2] Through the famous summer conferences and other means the movement had a great unifying effect among college students nationally. Before the turn of the century, nothing—not even the fraternity and sorority movements or intercollegiate athletics—did more to promote intercollegiate unity and fellowship.

College histories and contemporary catalogs in institution after institution—both public and private—describe the Ys as the largest, most active, and most influential of all student organizations.[3] By 1884, the 181 colleges with Y organizations counted as members nearly 30 percent of their total enrollment. During the peak period at the turn of the century, the membership percentage grew even higher. For example, membership in the Christian organizations included nearly 50 percent of the students at Furman in 1910, 50 percent of the students at Mississippi State in 1909, and two-thirds of the student body at the University of Alabama in 1887. Even as late as 1946, when the influence of the Ys was largely gone at most campuses, two-thirds of the students at Pennsylvania State (which historically had maintained one of the most effective chapters) still attended the programs of the local organization.[4]

The Ys' impact in black colleges matched that in the white schools. The Howard chapter began in 1869, two years after the institution opened; and the Christian association quickly became the most influential organization in the lives of the students there and in the many other new black colleges. Furthermore, just as the most able adults assumed roles of leadership in the black denominations, so also the best students accepted positions of leadership in the campus Y organizations.[5]

Originally, the YMCA maintained no direct connection with college students. George Williams and eleven fellow clerks founded it in 1844 in London to meet the practical needs of city youth in a period of rapid urban growth. It began to spread to the college campuses in America in 1858, when students at the Universities of Virginia and Michigan founded chapter units. During the next twenty years, students in approximately forty colleges organized local associations of the interdenominational, student-led organization. A very influential promoter and organizer of local chapters was Robert Weidensall who visited many colleges during the early 1870s, organized YMCA chapters in twenty-four of them, and became known as the "father of the American student YMCA movement." As early as the 1870 Indianapolis YMCA convention, the local campus units had heard a call to organize into a national organization. The series of events leading to national organization, however, began in 1875, when Luther Wishard transferred from Hanover (IN) to Princeton. There, he in particular and Princeton in general generated the activity and enthusiasm that led to the formal organization of the nationwide YMCA college movement in 1877.[6]

During the next decade, an increasing number of women in the coeducational institutions found it awkward—even humiliating—that their only opportunity for organized Christian fellowship existed in an organization whose title suggested that it was for men only. As women assumed increasingly active roles in the local units—for example, at Lawrence (WI) in 1882-83, both the president and the corresponding secretary were women—they gradually organized local chapters of the Young Women's Christian Association. By 1885, nearly two thousand female students had enrolled in approximately seventy YWCA units. The next year the women followed the example of the men a decade earlier and officially organized their local chapters into the national YWCA.[7]

The Y movement in America grew from forty chapters in 1877 to 181 chapters and 10,000 members in 1884, 345 chapters and 22,000 members in 1891, 628 chapters and 32,000 students in 1900, and 731 chapters and

94,000 students in 1920. The peak period coincided with the national leadership of John Mott.[8]

As a leader, Mott was unusually gifted in many ways. Converted as a Cornell undergraduate in 1886 during the visit of Englishman J. K. Studd to America, Mott assumed the leadership of the Cornell YMCA, and, believing that God placed him there "to do a work akin to that of the Wesleys at old Oxford," he built it into the largest and most effective local chapter. After graduation in 1888, the national YMCA recruited him as a field secretary, and he immediately threw his vast reservoir of energy and organizational skill into the movement. As he developed independent financial resources, he was able to commit himself completely to his evangelistic work. He traveled incessantly, bringing intense spiritual enthusiasm to campus after campus, especially through personal interviews with students, for which he allotted large periods of time. Mott probably influenced more young men than did any other person in this turn-of-the-century period. He was the most widely known figure in the academic life of the country — and probably the world. In addition to his extensive Y work, he intensely promoted evangelism, social justice, international peace and goodwill, and ecumenicity through a variety of denominational, missionary, and church federation activities. Unceasing activity during his long life took him to eighty-three countries, where governmental leaders repeatedly honored him. His awards included the Nobel Peace Prize. Kenneth Scott Latourette, the dean of American church historians, described him as the greatest Christian missionary since St. Paul.[9]

The Y movement in the colleges differed from previous student Christian movements in its effort to become a widespread intercollegiate fellowship and in its emphasis upon the practical application of the Christian faith. Before the Civil War, collegiate religious organizations had emphasized primarily personal piety and theological debate on the local campus. The Christian associations, by contrast, expanded their influence through a national organization, dynamic intercollegiate summer conferences, and a core of traveling secretaries who moved from campus to campus.[10]

In this period before the colleges developed student affairs programs, the Y chapters provided a wide range of services. Chapter members met new students as they arrived on the incoming trains, and they helped them adjust to college life. They published student handbooks, provided book-exchange services, operated employment bureaus and loan programs especially for poor students, assisted ill students, and, in some cases, conducted free tutorial services.[11]

The Y members also sought to serve off campus through "neighborhood work" in which student groups held religious services in poorhouses, jails, rescue missions, and Sunday schools in an effort to lead their hearers to

Christian commitments. Frequently they achieved success. For example, in 1898, eighty students from the YMCA chapters in Minnesota reported nearly four hundred conversions. Similarly, the University of Michigan chapter in the early period was known as "a persistent soul-winner of an organization."[12]

The evangelistic work also succeeded on campus. During its first seven years (1877–84), the national Y office reported that approximately seven thousand students experienced Christian conversion on the 181 campuses where Y chapters existed. Most of these decisions, the report stated, occurred directly as a result of YMCA work.[13]

In addition to student services and off-campus evangelistic programs, the local chapters regularly conducted prayer and Bible study meetings. The Bible studies proved sufficiently popular that by 1908 approximately one-fourth of all students enrolled in colleges with chapters were engaged in Bible studies using texts published by the association.[14]

The best financed local chapters erected their own buildings, sometimes with gymnasiums, and hired adult secretaries (or directors), some of whom served on a full-time basis. By 1896, forty colleges and universities employed full-time secretaries, and four years later twenty-seven college chapters operated their own campus buildings.[15]

One of the most important aspects of the Y program was the promotion that it gave to missionary activity through its foreign missionary arm, the Student Volunteer Movement (SVM); for thirty years after its official founding in 1888, John Mott headed it as well as the total Y operation. The SVM developed from the famous conference for YMCA student leaders held at Mt. Herman, Massachusetts, in the summer of 1886. Luther Wishard, secretary of the Princeton chapter, with the assistance of C. K. Ober, a recent graduate of Williams, organized the conference with unusual skill and enthusiasm. He persuaded Dwight Moody to address the delegates, hoping that the presence of the evangelist would positively affect the registration. It affected Mott, then a Cornell undergraduate, who stated that he "wanted to go [to the conference] so badly that he considered selling his new *Encyclopedia Britannica* if necessary to obtain the money to study under Moody."

In addition to featuring Moody, Wishard wanted to challenge the delegates seriously to consider foreign missionary service. Knowing that a senior student by the name of Robert Wilder had created great interest in missions at Princeton, he enlisted him to attend the conference and seek to generate similar enthusiasm among the 235 students who came as representatives from ninety-six colleges. The efforts of Wishard to promote the cause of missions at the conference succeeded dramatically, as one hundred of the delegates dedicated their lives to foreign missionary service.

Ober suggested that a team of the delegates should travel nationwide to campuses during the next school year to share the story of the Mt. Herman meeting and to seek to generate an even broader base of student interest in missionary activity. The team selected included Wilder and a fellow Princetonian, John N. Forman, a son of missionary parents. Their college meetings were as successful as the Mt. Herman conference itself, for during the 1886–87 school year and the subsequent summer, 2,100 additional college students dedicated themselves to foreign missionary service. This dramatic result led to the formal organizing of the Student Volunteer Movement and the adoption of its famous slogan: "The evangelization of the world in this generation." During the next half century, at least 13,000 SVM members became foreign missionaries. They constituted one of the best-trained groups of foreign evangelists in the history of the Christian church, and, at least until the decline of the movement, they displayed a concern for both the temporary and the eternal needs of the people to whom they ministered.[16]

The SVM did not operate as a missionary-sending agency; rather, it sought to generate interest in missions, to challenge students to offer themselves for missionary service, to lend support and encouragement to students once they made such a commitment, and then to work closely with the denominational and independent missionary boards. SVM units on individual campuses regularly offered study classes in missions, and they kept informed of the work of the movement across the country through the periodic visits of traveling secretaries, the monthly publication, the *Student Volunteer,* and other literature. The most dramatic activity, however, in the SVM program was a quadrennial national conference that regularly attracted thousands of students.[17]

The SVM, like its parent organization, reached its peak between the 1890s and the First World War, and then began to decline during the 1920s. After the war, both the SVM and the Christian associations began to concentrate less on evangelism and more upon social concerns such as international peace and goodwill between nations, race relations, international student relief and other forms of economic development, and ecumenicity in church organizations. As the Ys and the SVM decreased their evangelistic thrust, they found that the remaining "social Christianity" by itself could not generate the enthusiasm of the earlier years.[18]

The decline appeared at least as early as the 1920 student missionary conference at Des Moines. Even though the conference was very well attended, the students displayed more cynicism than enthusiasm. They reflected both the nation's general reaction to the World War and the growing distrust of traditional religion. Worldwide evangelist Sherwood Eddy sensed this attitude and spoke sharply to the delegates:

My friends, I am speaking to you, if you are out on the sidelines. This is my word to you today. Get off the sidelines of criticism and get in the game. . . . Some of you said to me yesterday, "Why do you bring this piffle, these old shibboleths, these old worn-out phrases, why are you talking to us about the living God and the divine Christ?" All right, we will call him a personal God if you like. . . . Perhaps the trouble is that you haven't yet found or don't know very well that living God, that living Father, or that great living Christ.

In July, 1931, William Miller, an extensive traveler for the Student Volunteer Movement, noted his great shock at the lack of missionary interest in the church colleges as well as the state universities.[19]

Accordingly, the number of enrolled missionary volunteers declined from nearly 2,800 in 1920 to 34 in 1937 and 25 in 1938; the number of volunteers who sailed abroad decreased from 637 in 1921 to 38 in 1934; the attendance at the quadrennial convention dropped from the 5,400 students from 950 colleges in 1920 to 1,700 students from 400 colleges in 1932; and the budget fell from $94,000 in 1924 to $14,000 in 1937.[20]

The Y movement also declined. Between the two world wars, the YMCA and the YWCA college chapters decreased in absolute numbers even though college enrollments mounted sharply. In 1920, approximately 1,000 colleges and universities enrolled 600,000 students; by 1940, 1,700 institutions enrolled 1,500,000 students. Meanwhile, the number of Y chapters fell from 731 college chapters in 1920 to only 430 in 1940, and the student membership dropped from 94,000 in 1921 to 51,000 in 1940.[21]

Several factors contributed to the decline of the Y and SVM movements. One was the growth of the university pastorate movement with its denominational fellowship houses. Also, many of the student services provided by the Ys during their most prominent years had become part of the college-administered student services programs. Moreover, the Ys faced growing competition from the rapidly expanding number of extracurricular activities of all types. The primary cause for the decline of the Christian associations, however, was that they were losing their sense of spiritual authority and evangelical mission.

As the Y movement declined, the university pastorate movement assumed an increasingly important role in ministering to the spiritual needs of students on the state and independent campuses. Beginning at about the turn of the century, many of the major denominations started to realize that not only were an increasing percentage of students from their churches enrolling in state universities, but also that these institutions were becoming increasingly secular. For example, the editor of the *Lutheran Witness* warned that "the typical university teaching . . . [was] unsettling to religious convictions [and that] a professor could undo in half an hour what it had taken years to build up." Furthermore, church leaders believed that because of the mounting enrollments, local churches of their denominations near the campuses could no longer satisfactorily meet the needs of the students, even with the help of the Christian associations. Therefore, the denominations began to establish their own student centers, staffed with their own clergymen, on locations immediately adjacent to the university campuses. The Presbyterians, led by Joseph Wilson Cochran, secretary of the Board of Education of the Presbyterian Church U.S.A., introduced the university pastorate movement at the University of Michigan in 1905 and established similar centers at the University of Kansas later in 1905, the University of Illinois in 1906, the University of Wisconsin in 1908, the University of Colorado in 1908, the University of Arkansas in 1909, and the University of Nebraska in 1909. Other denominations quickly followed the Presbyterian example, and by the 1930s denominational student centers operated on the campuses of at least 100 state and independent universities. The purposes of the movement have been to assist students to grow spiritually as much as the professors were helping them grow intellectually; to urge students to continue their loyalty to the denominations in which they had grown up; and to assist in developing future lay and clerical leaders for the denominations. A few denominations, led by the Disciples, have offered academic instruction in biblical literature at their student centers.[22]

In addition to denominational student centers, another movement that has arisen to succeed the YMCA in ministering to students on the secular campuses is the InterVarsity Christian Fellowship. It follows the tradition of the old Christian associations more than did the university pastorate movement, for it is interdenominational, international, and largely run by student members of the local, autonomous campus chapters with the assistance and counsel of traveling secretaries. With the assumption by the universities of comprehensive student services programs, however, there has been no need for the InterVarsity chapters to duplicate the earlier efforts of the Christian associations in this area. The objectives of InterVarsity have included the promotion of Christian maturity in its members by means of Bible study, prayer, and preparation for witnessing; evangelization on the campuses and stimulation of interest in foreign missionary activity; and the promotion of both Christian maturity and evangelism through an organizational periodical and a variety of carefully written books and pamphlets published at the organization's press in Downers Grove, Illinois.

If InterVarsity is a spiritual descendent of the early Christian associations, in a direct organizational sense it traces its origin to the Cambridge Intercollegiate Christian Union (CICCU), which developed from the English revivals in the late nineteenth century. Between the world wars, the Cambridge Union considered joining the ecumenically oriented national Student Christian Movement (SCM) in England. The climactic decision of the Cambridge students not to join the Student Christian Movement came in 1927 when representatives of CICCU asked the SCM: "Does the SCM consider the atoning blood of Jesus as the central point of their message?" The answer was, "No, not as central, although it is given a place in teaching." Subsequently, the CICCU chose not to join but rather to expand its evangelical witness to other campuses, thus marking the beginning of the InterVarsity Christian Fellowship. The movement spread to Canada in 1928 and to the United States in 1938. The University of Michigan, which earlier had organized the first YMCA chapter and hosted the first denominational student center, now formed the first InterVarsity chapter in the United States. Two years later, in 1940, the InterVarsity Christian Fellowship of the United States of America organized, with Stacey Woods serving as general secretary.[23]

Just as the Student Volunteer Movement arose as the missionary arm of the YMCA, so the Student Foreign Missions Fellowship (SFMF) became the branch of the InterVarsity Christian Fellowship that specializes in challenging students with the need for Christian evangelism in other countries. In a manner very similar to the SVM, the Student Foreign Missions Fellowship enlisted volunteers for foreign service; provided the recruits with fellowship, direction, and encouragement; and planned widely publicized, triennial missionary conferences. The SFMF maintained a separate existence until 1945, when it merged with InterVarsity. The first international missionary convention following the merger was held in 1946 at the University of Toronto, where 575 students from 151 schools in eight countries attended. After 1948, the conferences met at the University of Illinois. While students flocked to the InterVarsity missionary conventions in greater numbers (they regularly filled the 17,300-seat University of Illinois Assembly Hall) than those who earlier attended the SVM conventions, nevertheless a much smaller percentage of the students on the secular campuses participated in the activities of InterVarsity and other evangelical organizations such as Campus Crusade for Christ and the Navigators than were enrolled in the YMCA and YWCA chapters at the turn of the century.[24]

In 1951, William Bright organized at UCLA an organization that spread from that campus to become with InterVarsity one of the two most effective evangelical student organizations on the secular campuses. Today Campus Crusade for Christ operates many ministries, but the most important one continues to be its aggressive program of campus evangelism. During the 1976–77 school year, the organization's 1,500 full-time campus staff members explained the gospel message to approximately 150,000 students, 8,600 of whom professed faith in Christ. In addition, the staff members trained college students in witnessing techniques, and the chapter members led an additional 10,000 students to make Christian commitments. The staff members and students employed as their principal witnessing method an explanation of Bright's "Four Spiritual Laws." This technique was very simple — some say too mechanical — and the program achieved its greatest success on the large state university and private campuses that maintained strong athletic, fraternity, and sorority programs. By contrast, Campus Crusade experienced less success in intellectually oriented, elite schools like Harvard, Yale, and Stanford, where Inter-Varsity with its low-key and more cerebral approach is more likely to be effective.

The career of a Campus Crusade staff member was intense, somewhat Spartan, and often short. A new recruit enrolled for eleven weeks of detailed training at the organization's attractive headquarters near San Bernardino, California. The typical new staff member was young — usually middle-to-late twenties — had worked previously as a student member of a Campus Crusade chapter, and raised his or her own financial support (during the late 1970s the usual support was $460 per month plus 17 percent for fringe benefits). The training of the worker as well as the specific techniques that he or she employed in the field was highly programmed. This fact plus the limited income made it difficult for the organization to attract many seminary graduates. More typically, a staff member was a college graduate with a major in almost any discipline.

In 1966, Campus Crusade began a sports ministry program called Athletes in Action. Its purpose was to capitalize on the broad exposure and public acclaim given to athletes in order to present the Christian gospel. It organized high-quality teams in wrestling, gymnastics, track and field, weight-lifting, and soccer, but its greatest success was realized in basketball. During the 1976–77 basketball season, more than one hundred thousand people attended Athletes in Action games and listened to the Christian testimonies at halftime.[25]

The idea of athletic evangelism is at least as old as 1952, when Taylor sent a "Venture for Victory" basketball team to Taiwan at the invitation of Oriental Crusades missionaries and with the active encouragement of Madame Chiang Kai-shek. The Venture for Victory program expanded to include Christian athletes from a variety of colleges and later operated under the name of Sports Ambassadors as a division of the Overseas Crusades Mission. Taylor gained even greater recognition as a school that used athletics as a means of promoting evangelism in 1964 when football coach Robert Davenport — who had worked with Bright in the earliest days of Campus Crusade—developed the Wandering Wheels bicycle program which has been widely imitated elsewhere.[26]

During the 1970s, Bright expanded his campus-based program to include evangelistic efforts in a variety of other areas. He was able to do so because of his mounting success as a fund-raiser (e.g., the organization received $42 million in 1977). A close student of the movement suggested that by the late 1970s Bright was raising and spending more money for evangelism than was anyone else in the country.[27]

The Bible College Movement

The Bible college[28] movement arose in the late nineteenth and early twentieth centuries as a response to the widespread revivalism of Dwight Moody and others, as a reflection of the American movement toward popular education, and as a reaction to the growth of liberal thought in American Protestantism in general and its colleges in particular. Moody was the single most significant leader of what might be called "The Third Great Awakening" (approximately 1875–1915) which, like the earlier major awakenings, stimulated a renewed interest in Christian education and missions. The first two Bible schools, Nyack in New York City and Moody in Chicago, sought to provide quick, practical training for the sharply increasing number of young people who wished to become "full-time Christian workers," even if only as laypeople. They received encouragement from Moody and Nyack founder A. B. Simpson, both of whom believed deeply that if the Christian message was to reach all classes in all countries, the efforts of the regularly trained clergy must be supplemented by those of the less well trained but often more zealous Christian lay workers.

In this turn-of-the-century period before the development of universal secondary education, many of the young zealots were unprepared for admittance to a college or seminary. They were reluctant to commit eight or ten years to such study when their leaders advised them that such extensive preparation was not necessary for all workers. Such young people were advised to enroll in a Bible training school for a year or two, during which they would study theology and practical evangelistic methods. Then let them labor among the neglected lower classes in the American urban ghettos, use their training to improve the level of Sunday-school instruction in church schools across America, and travel abroad to evangelize the most ignorant classes in less-developed countries. The earliest Bible institutes, then, came into existence to serve as an auxiliary means of securing Christian workers.[29]

Although neither Nyack nor Moody was founded primarily to counter the growth of liberal theology, many of the Bible schools that followed them were motivated by this purpose. Indeed, one of the leading historians of fundamentalism has suggested that the early Bible institutes served the interdenominational fundamentalist movement like the headquarters of a denomination. As the major denominations and their colleges became less orthodox, the individual churches that separated from them, as well as the small denominations which had never operated educational institutions of any type, looked to Moody and the other early Bible schools as models for their own schools. By 1960, most of the Bible colleges with denominational affiliations represented groups that had withdrawn directly or indirectly from a mainline denomination in reaction to growing liberal tendencies. In that year the independent Disciples branch (formally known as the North American Christian Convention) of the Christian Church/Disciples of Christ tradition, several Baptist groups, and the combined Holiness and Pentecostal denominations each could claim between thirty and thirty-five Bible colleges. About 1900, and again in the 1920s, the conservative branches of the Disciples of Christ disassociated from the original group, and, although they did not organize into a formal denomination, the member churches did cooperate for a variety of purposes including higher education.

The Baptist groups with Bible colleges include the General Association of Regular Baptists, the Conservative Baptist Convention, the Baptist Bible Fellowship, and the Freewill Baptist Convention, all of which are branches that developed from the old Northern (now American) Baptist Convention. At mid-century even the Northern Baptist Convention relied upon the Bible colleges for nearly one-fourth of its ministers. The Bible college movement did not become nearly as popular among Southern Baptists, primarily because the Southern Baptist Convention remained largely orthodox. The Southern Baptists, however, did begin a few Bible colleges in remote areas to train practicing ministers who in most cases had not graduated from college, and more recently they opened Criswell Bible College in Dallas.

The Holiness and Pentecostal groups represent a continuation of the nineteenth-century variety of Methodism. Eight of the nineteen United States Pentecostal colleges in 1960 operated as institutions of the Assemblies of God, the largest Pentecostal denomination. The Assemblies of God originally entered the field of higher education with one- to three-year Bible institutes. By 1975, the denomination numbered thirty Bible colleges and four liberal arts institutions among its thirty-four institutions of higher education in the world.[30]

While there never has been a Bible college with a liberal Protestant theological orientation, the schools have varied widely in the degree to which they have fought the liberal institutions. During the early years, perhaps the most aggressive of the fundamentalist Bible schools was Northwestern, begun in 1902 in Minneapolis by William Bell Riley, pastor of one of the largest churches in the then Northern Baptist Convention, the First Baptist Church of Minneapolis. Riley, who added to the Bible school a seminary program in 1935 and a liberal arts college nine years later, announced that one of the major reasons for founding his schools was the fact that the "eastern seminaries were largely modernistic." It was "probably past dispute," he argued in 1917, "that there are not three English speaking schools in the entire Northland, belonging to any of the greater denominations . . . that are without an infection of that infidelity known as 'Modernism.' "[31]

Although the Bible college movement is primarily a North American innovation (it has been transplanted abroad by missionaries), the leaders of the earliest Bible schools found inspiration in the efforts of nineteenth-century English religious leaders. Perhaps the first Bible institute was the London Pastor's College, supported by Charles Spurgeon and the Baptist church made famous by his preaching, the Metropolitan Tabernacle in the Southwark section of London. Spurgeon began the institute to train poor ministers who could not afford a classical education. Moreover, Spurgeon doubted the desirability of the elite universities as places to train ministers because in such institutions "the fervor of the generality of the students . . . lagged far behind their literary training."

As a teen-ager in Ontario, A. B. Simpson admired the preaching of a visiting London minister, H. G. Guinness. Later, when Guinness began the East London Institute for Home and Foreign Missions in 1872, the young man who later was to found the first American Bible institute carefully observed its work. Its philosophy challenged the traditional idea that only highly cultured and university-trained workers should become foreign missionaries. Guinness admitted the need for the thoroughly trained workers required of most societies, particularly for performing such tasks as Bible translation, teaching, and administration.

> But were they the only men needed? . . . Did the 90% of the population of China who cannot read or the savages of Central Africa or the New Hebrides demand teachers of a higher stamp than did the working classes in these missionary sending countries? Should we not esteem it a great waste of resources to insist that home and city missionaries should be classical scholars? And are not workers of all classes required among the heathen as much as at home?

During its first sixteen years, the institute accepted eight hundred of the three thousand young men who applied for admission, and five hundred of these eventually completed their training and became lay Christian workers in England or on the mission field.

Both Simpson and Moody highly regarded another unorthodox promoter of foreign missions, J. Hudson Taylor. Taylor was an English Methodist who went to China in 1853 and shortly thereafter began operating a "faith mission" with more than nine hundred missionaries. Taylor not only recruited and sent abroad workers without college and seminary training, he also sent them without guaranteeing their salaries. By the end of the century, Taylor's China Inland Mission numbered more missionaries than did any of the other thirty-eight societies operating in the Asian country.[32]

When Simpson opened the first American Bible institute in New York City in 1882, he announced that it would be a school similar to the one Guinness operated in London. Simpson gathered forty students that first year to study the Bible and evangelism methodology on the rented back stage of the Twenty-third Street Theater. In many ways Simpson was an unlikely person to lead such a humble institution, for he was an 1865 high honors graduate of Knox College, Toronto, and had successfully served Presbyterian churches in Louisville and New York City. Yet the pastorate of respectable Presbyterian churches did not satisfy him, and he supplemented his New York parish work with preaching in the poor immigrant sections of Manhattan. Increasingly, he became concerned about the inadequacies of Christian programs for lower classes in this country and abroad. Consequently, he desired to open a training school to "prepare people who might not otherwise go to college to minister to people abroad who might not otherwise hear the gospel." He resigned his New York pastorate in 1881 to begin his work of training the "foot soldiers of God's army."

Meanwhile Moody was developing similar thoughts. In a famous January 1886 address, he called for "gap men" who could fill the void between the frequently neglected lower classes and the formally trained clergymen. Moody, himself a layman, realized that such individuals, when sufficiently motivated and industrious, could be very effective. His own evangelistic career as a Sunday-school recruiter, a YMCA worker, and an urban mass evangelist had always concentrated on the large population centers. Thus he knew intimately the physical and spiritual poverty of the immigrants and other industrial workers in the urban slums of America.[33]

Essentially, Simpson and Moody sought to develop schools to provide minimal training for the type of Christian workers who in earlier eras had pursued their spiritual endeavors with no training at all. These "gap men" streaming forth from Nyack, Moody, and the other early Bible schools were the turn-of-the-century counterparts of the earlier Wesleyan Sunday-school teachers in England, and the Methodist circuit-riders and Baptist farmer-preachers on the American frontier.

If Simpson and Moody shared a similar vision, nevertheless they applied that vision somewhat differently. While both desired to train the common people of America to take the gospel to the common people of this and other countries, Simpson emphasized foreign missionary activity and Moody gave priority to training home workers. Also, Moody was much more successful than Simpson—and all the other early Bible school leaders as well—in raising funds to support his institution. Before his evangelistic career, the youthful Moody had demonstrated uncommon success as a Chicago businessman, and thereafter he displayed great skill in raising funds from his business friends to promote his religious activities. Moody established his school on a solid financial basis at its beginning with the assistance of such affluent Chicago businessmen as T. W. Harvey, a millionaire lumber dealer; John Farwell, a dry goods merchant; and Cyrus McCormick, the agricultural machinery manufacturing magnate. Fortunately, upon Moody's death the management of the institute's business affairs passed to the able Henry Crowell, a leading executive of the Quaker Oats Company and other business enterprises. Crowell developed a very large network of regular donors whose contributions then and to the present have endowed the institution to such an extent that it has never charged tuition, but only room, board, and fees. Crowell's success was matched by the efforts of Reuben Torrey, who provided academic and spiritual leadership for the school. Moody hired the Yale graduate as superintendent beginning in 1889, and Torrey continued in that position for the next two decades.[34]

Moody's personal fame as an evangelist, the solid financial and academic base established by Crowell and Torrey, and the institute's central location in one of the most rapidly growing cities in the world combined to bring Moody Bible Institute quickly to a position of leadership in the Bible school movement. If Yale, Princeton, and Oberlin each gained reputations in the nineteenth century as mothers of many liberal arts colleges, Moody became known as the mother of numerous Bible institutes and colleges. Shortly after Moody's death, religious leaders from many parts of the country came to Chicago to study the Moody program with the goal of returning to their homes to found "little Moodys" in their regions.[35]

Two examples of the many Bible schools that began because of the Moody influence are Boston (later Gordon College) in 1889 and the Bible Institute of Los Angeles (later Biola) in 1908. The Boston school began when Moody held his Boston revival of 1887 in a tabernacle built immediately adjacent to A. J. Gordon's Clarendon Street Baptist Church, with the church serving as an auxiliary facility. Although Gordon had graduated from the most prestigious institutions of his denomination (Brown and Newton Seminary), he chose to follow Moody's example and founded what became the third permanent Bible school. On the West Coast, the still infant Bible Institute of Los Angeles in 1912 recruited Reuben Torrey for a leadership position. Torrey proceeded to use his skills to help his new institution develop the reputation that it long maintained as the leading Bible college on the West Coast.

In addition to Moody, Nyack, and the Boston school, other Bible colleges that began in the nineteenth century include Western Baptist (MO), a black institution, in 1890; School of the Evangelists (later Johnson in Tennessee), the first Christian Church Bible school, in 1893; Friends (later Cleveland Bible College and then Malone College), sponsored by the evangelically oriented Ohio Quakers, in 1894; Northwest Christian (OR), founded by the Christian Church (Disciples) in 1895; Berkshire Christian (MA) in 1897; Free Church (later Trinity Seminary) in Chicago in 1897; Azusa (CA), originally a Friend's institution, in 1899; God's Bible College (OH) in 1900; and Bethel (later Providence Barrington Bible College and then Barrington College, Rhode Island) in 1900.[36]

Although the Bible colleges gradually developed entrance requirements comparable to those of the liberal arts colleges (by 1950 the majority required high school graduation for admission as regular students), during their early decades they placed much more emphasis upon Christian character than educational attainment. For example, Boston maintained no age or formal schooling requirement; rather, "if the record [of the applicant] as a Christian was good and he or she showed a real desire to do Christian work, he was accepted."[37]

The early Bible schools offered very limited curricula. A typical school usually listed some courses in the liberal arts and a large amount of work in biblical studies, theology, and practical Christian training. The early curriculum at Nyack was broader than that at most schools. Its liberal arts offerings included English, logic, speech, language and literature, mental and moral philosophy, natural science, ancient and modern history, and geography; these supplemented its curriculum in theology (e.g., Bible, Christian evidences, New Testament Greek, systematic theology, church history, pastoral theology, and history of Christian work) and "practical" subjects (e.g., homiletics, foreign missions work, Sunday-school work, home missions work, vocal music, and personal evangelism). Dwight Moody's advice on the desirable curriculum suggests what probably was offered to the students in most of the early schools, including his own: "Never mind the Greek and Hebrew, give them plain English and good scripture. It is the sword of the Lord and cuts deep." Moody students listened to Bible lectures in the morning and engaged in practical work in Chicago during the afternoons and evenings.[38]

Every Bible college from the beginning of the movement to the present has made the English Bible the heart of its curriculum. The schools have increased their requirements in the liberal arts, as will be noted later, but they have usually done so by increasing the length of their programs rather than by reducing the Bible requirements. Almost invariably, each Bible college student has majored in biblical studies with perhaps a second major. Today those colleges that meet the requirements of the Bible college accreditation standards must enroll each of their three- and four-year students in a minimum of thirty hours of biblical studies. Some schools greatly exceeded this minimum standard; for example, Big Sky (MT) required fifty semester hours of biblical studies in all of its three- and four-year programs.[39]

Whether or not they have listed it as a formal part of their curricula, the schools invariably have given major attention to developing in their students a pietistic lifestyle. President Joseph Ramseyer of Fort Wayne (IN) undoubtedly represented the Bible college leaders in general when he argued that intellectual knowledge should never be valued above spiritual illumination because one can never acquire the most important knowledge apart from instruction by the Spirit of God. The Bible college educational process was designed to produce holy students as well as students who were knowledgeable about holy things.[40]

It is difficult to exaggerate the extent to which the early Bible schools emphasized foreign missionary activity. Many of them included this emphasis in their original titles (e.g., Moody at its inception was called "The Bible Institute for Home and Foreign Missions of the Chicago Evangelism Society"). The Student Mission Band at Fort Wayne began during the school's first year (1904) to study the mission fields of the world and to pray for missionary efforts. It included the entire student body in its membership, thus making it easily the most important extracurricular activity. Forty percent of the 2,500 students who attended Nyack between 1882 and 1902 eventually entered foreign missionary service in forty countries. The intense missionary emphasis of the early Bible schools joined other forces, including the efforts of the Student Volunteer Movement in the liberal arts colleges and universities, to allow the United States by the early twentieth century to surpass England as the supplier of the majority of both personnel and funds for Protestant foreign missions.[41]

So great was the missionary emphasis at the Bible colleges that they were producing by the mid-twentieth century a probable majority and by 1980 a large majority of the Protestant missionary recruits in this country. Indeed, this large number of missionary trainees has been one of the unique features of the Bible college movement. While many schools contributed significantly to the production of missionaries (e.g., Columbia of South Carolina sent 750 and Lutheran of Minnesota sent four hundred of its graduates to the mission field during the four decades before 1960), the champion missionary producer has been Moody — which continues to be the largest Protestant missionary training school in the world. By 1952, 3,300 Moody graduates had served as missionaries in ninety-four countries. In that year, 2,300 of them were active, as were 2,700 Moody missionaries in 1960. The Moody historian claims that by mid-century 5 percent of the total Protestant missionary staff in the world and approximately 13 percent of all evangelical missionaries from North America had studied at the school.[42]

While not all Bible college alumni could become missionaries, studies show that a high percentage — perhaps even a majority — have entered full-time Christian service, and probably an even higher percentage originally planned such a career. For example, of the thirty-two graduates of the 1952 class at the Bible institute in Cleveland, sixteen planned to be pastors, eleven missionaries, three pastors' wives, and one a song evangelist. One comprehensive study of the class of 1946 in forty-three representative Bible colleges showed that 29 percent became ministers and an additional 27 percent missionaries. More recently, a 1980 American Association of Bible Colleges survey found 52 percent of the graduates entering a full-time Christian ministry.[43]

"Practical training" — now known as Christian service — has been a part of the curricula of most schools since their beginning years. Most Bible school leaders would have agreed with F. W. Farr of the Nyack Bible Institute when he said in 1887: "It is best to know and to do, but it is better to do without knowing than to know without doing. . . . In order that we may know and do we must be taught and trained. . . . Teaching imparts knowledge and fills the mind. Training imparts skill and shapes habits." Similarly, the 1946 catalog of Grace (NE) expressed how vital practical service has been to the realization of its goals: "The only way to train for Christian service is to do it." Accordingly, Bible colleges have usually been located in cities where they can exert a wider influence and find more opportunities for Christian witness than would be possible in rural areas. In Boston in 1914 the Bible institute claimed that its students constituted "the largest body of city missionaries in New England." In Chicago the Moody students were no less busy. Their early record of service, while proportionately higher than that at most schools, probably reflects the general Bible school pattern; between 1889 and 1916 the Moody students taught approximately 1.5 million Bible classes, conducted eight thousand other public meetings, made more than two million calls to homes and visits to hospitals, counseled individually four million people, distributed thirty million pieces of literature, and led more than 500,000 people to an initial or renewed Christian commitment. Even by the mid-twentieth century, nearly one-half of the schools required Christian service activities of all students, and approximately three-fourths of all Bible school students enrolled in such programs.[44]

Bible colleges are not the only institutions that have placed major emphasis upon Christian service. Liberty Baptist (VA) in the 1980s required each student to complete one Christian service assignment each semester. Many of these assignments took place in the very large and nearby Thomas Road Baptist Church, the institution from which the college developed. Although most Christian liberal arts colleges have offered Christian service opportunities as voluntary rather than required activities, they often have attracted wide interest. For example, during a recent year at Wheaton a majority of the students participated in one or more of the college's many evangelism and social service activities. Similarly, at Bob Jones (SC) during a period in the late 1950s, ministerial candidates held 33,000 public services, counseled personally 137,000 people, recorded nearly 17,000 conversions to Christ, and distributed 3.5 million tracts.[45]

During the century-long history of the Bible college movement, the educational programs of the institutions have grown in both quality and breadth. Scholars traditionally have viewed Bible colleges as academically inferior to Christian liberal arts institutions. Many of the liberal arts colleges, however, also began with very modest academic programs, and at the time they were being compared to the Bible colleges most had had a longer period of time to develop. Also contributing to the Bible colleges' reputation for inferiority is the fact that an unusually broad range of institutions have called themselves Bible schools. Over the years, the Bible school spectrum has included everything from churches offering a few night classes as an extension of their Christian education programs to highly sophisticated collegiate institutions with programs of greater quality than those of many liberal arts institutions.

Growth in the quality of instruction has followed growth in the quality of the instructors. In the early years, most instructors possessed Christian service experience, Christian maturity, and a pious lifestyle, but not often academic achievement. By mid-century, however, the great majority of instructors held academic degrees. One comprehensive study of 536 full-time faculty members in 47 Bible colleges in 1946 found 80 percent with undergraduate degrees, 25 percent with masters degrees, and 11 percent with earned doctorates. By 1979, faculty members in the accredited schools had completed an average of nearly eight years of post-secondary study.

During the first generation of the Bible school movement, most institutions recruited primarily non-high-school graduates who studied in what were frequently "Bible training" schools for brief periods, usually not exceeding two years. During the 1920s and 1930s some schools began to expand their programs from two to three years, thus allowing for greater specialization in pastoral studies, missions, Christian education, and music; however, even as late as 1950, half of the schools still offered only one course of study. The curricular expansion was accompanied by a modification in institutional nomenclature as many schools began to change their names from Bible training schools to Bible institutes. Also, during this period, an increasing number of students became interested in combining their Bible institute work with study in a liberal arts college. The Bible schools responded by assigning credit hour value to their courses and by offering an increasing number of liberal arts courses. They made these changes both to ease the process of transfer for students going on to complete a liberal arts degree and also to satisfy students more completely with their own curricular offerings.[46]

The most significant mid-century development in the academic organization of the Bible college movement was the tendency for institutions to evolve from Bible institutes to Bible colleges and even, in a few cases, from Bible colleges to Christian liberal arts colleges. The changes have come in large part in response to student requests such as that expressed in the following complaint: "Why should a student have to spend years of his time studying in a Bible institute, only to receive a diploma, whereas the same years if spent in a secular school would lead to the granting of a degree . . . ?" Accordingly, between the 1930s and the 1960s, many Bible schools—led by Cleveland, Columbia, and Boston—enlarged their general education curricula sufficiently to justify calling themselves Bible colleges. By 1960, approximately half of the schools in North America identified themselves as Bible colleges rather than Bible institutes.[47]

As an educational institution, a Bible college occupies an intermediary position between a Bible institute and a Christian liberal arts college. Like a Bible institute, its students all earn majors in religion and all experience in their academic programs significant practical Christian service. Like a Christian liberal arts college, however, the Bible college enrolls all of its students in a series of general education courses. The Christian liberal arts college student can choose from a wider variety of general education courses and major disciplines; however, the academic experience of a Bible college student compares closely to that of a student who majors in religion in a Christian liberal arts college. A Bible college curriculum is generally four years long and results in an A.B. degree, whereas a Bible institute program is shorter—frequently three years—and results in a diploma.[48] By the late twentieth century, among the institutions accredited by the American Association of Bible Colleges, the trend was to replace the traditional three-year diploma programs with two- and four-year degree programs. Almost all of the accredited schools offered a four-year baccalaureate degree, more than half offered two-year degrees, and less than one-third continued to offer the old diploma programs.

A very limited number of institutions, including Biola and Northwestern, combined the characteristics of a Bible college with those of a well-developed Christian liberal arts college. At Biola, all students completed thirty hours of Bible as a graduation requirement and participated in Christian service assignments each term. The college offered a wide variety of liberal arts majors, and students majoring in disciplines other than Bible usually took five years to graduate. Added to the 2,300 undergraduate students were 650 enrollees in Talbot Seminary and 150 students in the affiliated Rosemead School of Psychology. For Biola, the combination of Bible college and liberal arts college was the philosophical ideal, not a transition stage from Bible college to liberal arts college.[49]

The effort to organize the Bible college movement for the purpose of improving and unifying standards began as early as 1918, when James Gray, president of Moody, called a meeting of Bible institute representatives for this purpose. Nothing came of his effort but thirteen years later another Moody official, Clarence Benson, led in the establishment of the Evangelical Teacher Training Association (ETTA), which might be considered the forerunner of the American Association of Bible Colleges. Benson and other ETTA leaders believed that the Sunday-school movement, while well-intentioned, had failed to realize its goals because of the inadequate preparation of its teachers. As John Vincent, the nineteenth-century leader of the movement, had observed, "The Sunday school is strong at the heart and weak at the head." The American Sunday School Union began in this country in 1825 as an import from England where forty years earlier Robert Raikes, a Gloucester printer, founded the Sunday-school movement. Raikes sought to help the many children in his hometown who were forced to work four to six days a week by opening a school to educate them in secular and biblical subjects during a five-hour session each Sunday. In America, the Sunday-school movement exerted its greatest initial influence on the frontier, where it was taken by home missionaries and where untrained laypeople did most of the teaching.

The purpose of the ETTA, then, was to use the existing structure of the Bible schools to improve the quality of the nation's Sunday-school instruction, and by the end of its first decade, more than one hundred schools had affiliated with the association. The association identified a "standard training course" which ideally the well-trained Sunday-school teacher would complete. This curriculum called for the completion of the equivalent of one academic year of study in biblical and related subjects. Of course, not all Sunday-school teachers could devote a year to full-time study; accordingly, the association encouraged them to complete a "preliminary training course" involving approximately six credit hours of study in a school or under a graduate of the standard training course. The association set standards for institutions as well as individuals. It designated as "gold seal schools" those Bible schools that (1) required high school graduation for admission, (2) required college graduation for faculty status, (3) provided residence dormitories for day students, and (4) owned a library of at least one thousand books.[50]

The effort to create an organization that would establish standards for the total program of the Bible colleges finally succeeded in the late 1940s under the leadership of presidents Howard Ferrin of Providence Barrington and Safara Witmer of Fort Wayne, and Dean Samuel Sutherland of Biola. These men led in the organization of the Accrediting Association of Bible Institutes and Bible Colleges (AABIBC). The organizational meetings took place in Minneapolis during the annual meeting of the National Association of Evangelicals in 1946 and at Winona Lake, Indiana, in 1947. The new organization profited greatly from the help given by John Dale Russell, assistant commissioner of the United States Office of Education, who displayed unusual interest in helping the Bible schools.

Since the quality of the work offered in the many institutions calling themselves Bible schools varied greatly, the leaders of the new association believed that they must establish rigorous standards for those schools seeking initial membership. In 1948 the AABIBC accredited its first twelve schools, and the same year the United States Office of Education acknowledged the organization as the only accrediting body in the field of undergraduate theological education. Thus the Office of Education began to recognize the schools approved by the AABIBC just as it recognized the seminaries approved by the American Association of Theological Schools.

Students from AABIBC member schools began to find it much easier to transfer credits to another institution. Shortly after the establishment of the AABIBC, Carroll Newson, associate commissioner of Higher Education for New York State, declared: "The New York State Department of Education recognizes the AABIBC as maintaining acceptable standards for four year higher institutions and recommends for transfer purposes full credit for courses which are appropriate to the degree requirements of the institutions to which credit is being transferred. . . ." Among the earliest institutions to accept work completed at Bible institutes and colleges were New York University, Texas Wesleyan, Wheaton, and Taylor.

Not all of the Bible schools accepted the accreditation movement as desirable, however. For example, L. H. Maxwell, whose Prairie Bible Institute in Alberta, Canada, was widely respected among Bible college officials in the United States, frankly stated:

We are not personally concerned about becoming uniform with others, or in becoming accredited. God has given us a special method of Bible study second to none, and we are content to do what God wants us to do without having to adjust to that which others feel led to do. . . . We are convinced that many of the present trends will ultimately take these very Bible institutes into modernism. . . .[51]

In the late 1950s the Accrediting Association of Bible Institutes and Bible Colleges shortened its name to the Accrediting Association of Bible Colleges (AABC) and hired President Witmer of Fort Wayne as its first full-time executive secretary. In his new position, Witmer traveled widely to visit many of the Bible colleges in North America. He criticized freely major weaknesses he saw in the colleges but also served as their leading spokesman to the "outside world," which he believed too little appreciated the significance of what Bible colleges were achieving. While Witmer acknowledged that the schools were understaffed, under supported, inadequate in their ability to integrate general education disciplines with biblical values, and lacking in academic respectability and creativity, he also argued with logic and passion that higher education in general should accept the Bible college philosophy of education as a viable option. He lamented that "while Bible college education ranks first in values . . . it is frequently regarded as inferior and only partially evolved as an acceptable type of college education." Additionally, he argued that since the Bible college offers both a Bible education and a college education, it provides an integrated worldview in contrast to much of modern education. Most modern education, he added, takes a compartmentalized approach that gives no overarching meaning to the sum of its curricular parts. In the late 1950s and early 1960s, Witmer was generally recognized as the leading authority on the Bible colleges; some even referred to him as "Mr. Bible College."[52]

Meanwhile the AABC continued to grow. The number of North American institutions accepted as fully accredited members increased to thirty-six in 1960, forty-seven in 1969, and seventy-seven in 1980. In each case, accredited and candidate members represented approximately 20 percent of the Bible institutes and colleges. By the late twentieth century, the AABC manual listed the following standards for its member schools: (1) a desirable student-faculty ratio of 15:1, with the maximum allowable being 25:1; (2) a minimal academic training for faculty members of the first graduate or professional degree beyond the baccalaureate; and (3) a high school graduation requirement for admission.[53]

By the end of the century, nearly all of the schools accredited by the AABC were Bible colleges rather than Bible institutes. A notable exception was

Moody Bible Institute which maintained with conviction its traditional identification. Yet, Moody continued to be recognized as the leader of the Bible
college movement because of the breadth of its Bible and applied curriculum, the size of its faculty and staff (more than five hundred full-time employees in 1969), the number of its alumni and the size of its student body,
the size of its annual budget, and its extensive off-campus services to a wide
variety of individuals (e.g., the radio-broadcast ministry on WMBI in
Chicago and elsewhere, the correspondence division which frequently enrolled as many as 120,000 students, the Moody Institute of Science Films, and
the widely read *Moody Monthly* magazine and Moody Press publications).[54]

During the two decades after the early 1960s, five of the six regional accrediting associations accepted as members a total of eleven Bible colleges
including Bethany (Assemblies of God), Biola, Pacific Christian (Independent Disciples), and Simpson (Christian and Missionary Alliance) in California; Western Baptist (General Association of Regular Baptists) in Oregon; Northwest College of the Assemblies of God in Washington; St. Paul
(Christian and Missionary Alliance); Northwestern in Minnesota; Philadelphia; Gulf Coast (Church of God) in Texas; and Johnson.[55]

One of the major reasons that Bible colleges have experienced such a
struggle to improve their academic programs is that throughout much of
their history they have operated with very limited financial resources. Typically, the schools have recruited their students from the lower to middle
socioeconomic classes, and the students have been preparing for careers
that offer more spiritual challenge than financial reward. Consequently,
the schools charged minimum fees. As late as the 1940s, approximately half
of the Bible colleges charged no tuition fee at all, although sometimes they
asked the students to contribute labor as well as room and board expenses.
In 1978–79, one of the largest Bible colleges, Baptist of Missouri, charged a
tuition of only eight dollars per credit hour. The colleges balanced their
books by relying on the voluntary services of ministers of nearby churches
and by asking their full-time employees to subsidize the educational expenses of the students by accepting substandard salaries. Sometimes the
colleges could offer able instruction despite these limitations, but usually
the academic environment they produced was less than excellent. This situation has gradually improved since the organization of the AABC.[56]

Like American higher education in general, the Bible college movement
witnessed significant growth during the twentieth century. While many of
the leading Bible colleges began before 1920, the great majority of the contemporary institutions came into existence after 1940. The recent Bible college enrollment pattern compares favorably with the enrollment figures of
graduate theological schools. For example, by mid-century only one theological seminary—Southwestern Baptist Theological Seminary (TX)—

could match Moody's overall enrollment of approximately 1,650. The largest accredited Bible colleges in 1980 were Biola, 2,345; Baptist of Missouri, 1,721; Moody, 1,341 (plus 1,975 in the evening subcollegiate program); Southeastern College of the Assemblies of God (FL), 1,255; Central, an Assemblies of God school (MO), 1,094; Northwest College of the Assemblies of God, 825; Baptist of Pennsylvania, 823; Southwestern Assemblies of God College (TX), 713; North Central (MN), an Assemblies of God school, 701; St. Paul, 658; Bethany, 645; Multnomah (OR), 633; Toccoa Falls, a Christian and Missionary Alliance school (GA), 619; Columbia, 587; Valley Forge Christian, an Assemblies of God school (PA), 535; Cincinnati, 522; Free Will Baptist (TN), 513; Nazarene (CO), 510; Philadelphia, 509; and Washington (MD), 500. The average enrollment in the accredited schools was approximately 425 (accredited seminaries, by comparison, average 293 students). Most schools, however, are much smaller. While some Bible college leaders claim that the existence of many small institutions allows the movement to serve more geographical regions and to place a larger number of students in meaningful Christian service assignments, the AABC manual suggested that efficiency of operation was not possible with an enrollment of less than several hundred.[57]

In the 1980s enrollment maintenance began to be a major concern of Bible college leaders. The growth pattern of the early 1970s had not continued, and many seminars and discussion groups at Bible college professional meetings focused on this problem. While the general spiritual awakening of the previous two decades had affected Bible college enrollment positively, its effects were offset by factors that concerned higher education in general, namely the declining supply of college-age students and the downward turn in the economy. Partly as an effort to aid the student recruitment effort, the AABC in the late 1970s conducted a comprehensive study of the demographic characteristics of incoming Bible college students. It showed that many students did not enroll immediately upon high school graduation (only 52 percent of the new students were younger than 19); most came from homes with modest incomes (44 percent reported 1975 family income of less than $10,000 and 67 percent less than $15,000) and non-urban locations (40 percent came from communities of less than 10,000 population, and 64 percent less than 50,000); and almost none (1.5 percent) planned to enroll in seminary following their Bible college study.[58]

Fundamentalism and Higher Education

Any discussion of fundamentalism must begin with the issue of definition, for the word suggests very different things to different people. To many who identify with the movement, fundamentalism refers to those spiritually minded Christians who most faithfully practice God's biblical commands. For some Christians who react negatively to the term, it refers to those to the right of them on the theological spectrum, particularly those who are somewhat difficult to get along with or somewhat insensitive and unthinking in their zeal. For example, one Wheaton student defined a "fundy" as "a person who will ask you in the shower at 7:30 A.M. what the Lord has done for you this morning."[59] Many nonevangelicals use the term to characterize all Protestant individuals, churches, and organizations that still maintain an orthodox approach to Christianity. Finally, to a wide variety of observers the term describes those conservative Protestants who are aggressive in fighting liberal Protestantism and who proudly accept the fundamentalist label; this latter definition is the one that I will assume.

During the early decades of the twentieth century, as most of the major denominations became increasingly influenced by liberal Protestant thought and as their colleges gradually became secularized, Wheaton gained a reputation as the leading fundamentalist college. Wheaton earned this reputation because of its dogged determination to resist secular influence and because its nondenominational nature made it attractive to students from orthodox homes in a broad variety of denominations. On the eve of World War I, the still new Christian and Missionary Alliance, which at that time operated only Bible schools, identified Wheaton as "the officially recognized college of the Alliance" for its young people who desired a baccalaureate degree. One Wheaton historian observed that, by the 1920s, the list of Wheaton supporters "read like a Who's Who of Northern Fundamentalism." Lyman and Milton Stewart contributed heavily to the college; they were the wealthy oil men who financed the publication of *The Fundamentals,* the apologetic series that gave the movement its name. Also, serving as trustees or members of the board of reference during the 1920s were Fleming Revell, the leading fundamentalist publisher and a brother-in-law of Dwight Moody; William Blackstone, author of the widely distributed book on the Second Coming, *Jesus Is Coming;* and William Bell Riley, the vocal Baptist fundamentalist. When the death of Charles Blanchard in 1925 brought to an end the second of the long-lasting Blanchard presidencies, the trustees clearly demonstrated their orientation by naming as president an unequivocal fundamentalist, J. Oliver Buswell Jr., a young but aggressive leader of the orthodox wing of the Northern Presbyterians.[60]

While some schools looked to Wheaton as their model, others viewed the Illinois college as a leading example of what they did not want to become. For example, when Elam J. Anderson interviewed for the presidency of Northern Baptist–sponsored Redlands (CA) in 1938, he learned that a part of the trustee board had determined that the next president must be a fundamentalist, and that Redlands must become "the Wheaton of the Southwest."[61] He responded that "if that is the purpose of the trustees, then I must withdraw my candidacy. While I am sympathetic with much of Wheaton's program, I have a deep conviction that the method of compulsion both in doctrine and conduct is not only non-Baptist, but also contrary to sound principles of education."[62]

If Wheaton was the best-known fundamentalist college in the 1920s, Williams Jennings Bryan was the best-known fundamentalist spokesman. During Bryan's participation in the widely publicized Scopes evolution trial at Dayton, Tennessee, in the summer of 1925, he expressed the wish that a men's college would be established in the scenic hill country surrounding Dayton. Shortly after the trial he died, and his followers thought that the development of a major fundamentalist university near Dayton would serve as an appropriate memorial. The Depression, however, severely restricted the fund-raising abilities of the project promoters, and the resultant college which opened in 1930 has developed into a modest-sized liberal arts college rather than a large university.[63]

It is appropriate that Bryan wanted to establish a clearly orthodox college, for his almost continuous travels throughout the country afforded him the opportunity to learn about and closely identify with the continuing Christian colleges. For example, when he spoke at Taylor in the early 1920s, he began his address with high praise for the school:

> Parents all over this nation are asking me where they can send their sons and daughters to school knowing that their faith in God and in morality will not be destroyed. I find that this is a college where they teach you the Bible instead of apologizing for it, and I shall for this reason recommend Taylor University to inquiring Christian parents.[64]

Although the fundamentalist movement has been especially associated with conservative factions in the Baptist, Presbyterian, and Disciples of Christ denominations, it also existed within the denomination claiming the largest number of Protestant colleges, the Methodist Church. Near the turn of the century and just before the peak of the fundamentalist-modernist battles of the 1920s, the theological division within Methodism was between the holiness advocates, who wished to perpetuate the early-nineteenth-century style of Methodism, and those who favored a more restrained form of worship. The latter thought this restraint appropriate since the denomination's constituency had become largely middle rather than lower class in socioeconomic standing. Between 1890 and 1920 the holiness movement was at its peak. Many contemporary holiness and holiness-pentecostal denominations had their origins in this period. The movement thrived on summer camp meetings led by popular preachers like Henry Clay Morrison, who later served as the first president of Asbury (KY). Asbury operated, as did Taylor, as one of the few colleges representing the sizable holiness branch of Methodism. Although holiness Methodist families existed throughout the country, holiness Methodist colleges did not; therefore, Asbury attracted many students from great distances. During Morrison's presidency, for example, students came from forty-seven states and eighteen foreign countries. By 1920, Asbury's leaders thought it necessary to preach against modernism as well as for holiness, with the result that they sounded increasingly like the more Calvinist fundamentalists. Morrison, a crusading religious orator in the style of Bryan, attacked the Protestant liberals for proclaiming what their theology was not rather than what they did believe: "The modernists are as yet up in the air. They have some hesitation as to where they shall light and with whom they shall settle down for permanent abode and active service. As yet they have no inspired Bible, no divine atoning Christ able to save from sin, no system of theology, no fixed creed, no hymnology, no enthusiastic evangelism to win sinners from the ruin of their wickedness to a Savior. The fact is that there is a question in their minds as to whether there is any real sin or a need of a Savior."[65]

Because the fundamentalists fought what at the time appeared to be a losing battle over such critical issues as the divinity of Christ and the trustworthiness of the biblical record, the struggle was very tense. Christian grace, rationality, and due attention to issues other than theology sometimes suffered. With the passage of time and the appearance of new conservative Protestant leaders, these undesirable aspects of the battle — particularly when they continued for several decades — looked increasingly embarrassing. Consequently, many of the new leaders, without discarding their orthodox theology, chose to disassociate themselves from the emotionally laden word "fundamentalist" and instead called themselves "evangelical." This new theological label became the preferred one of the majority of orthodox Protestants after World War II. (By the 1980s probably no more than 10 to 15 percent of the estimated 40 million evangelicals would have called themselves fundamentalists.)

The major factor distinguishing recent fundamentalists from the more moderate evangelicals was the degree to which the former chose to separate from liberal Protestants and, in some cases, from other orthodox Protestants. The evangelicals did not insist that orthodox Protestants withdraw from the large, theologically mixed denominations. Rather, they thought it appropriate to seek to win the denominations back to their earlier orthodoxy. The fundamentalists, by contrast, thought it a violation of the separation commandment in 2 Corinthians 6:14 for an orthodox Christian to be associated with a denomination or any other group that was not completely administered and populated by fellow orthodox believers.[66] George Dollar, a fundamentalist historian writing in the 1960s, identified the following colleges as examples of evangelical institutions: Barrington, Columbia Bible, Houghton (NY), Kings (NY), LeTourneau (TX), Nyack, Oral Roberts, Taylor, and Wheaton. Clearly fundamentalist schools, according to Dollar, included Baptist Bible of Pennsylvania, Baptist Bible of Colorado, Baptist Bible of Missouri, Bob Jones, Maranatha Bible (WI), Midwestern Baptist Bible (MI), and Pillsbury Baptist Bible (MN). Colleges between these two types who, presumably, would favor separating from most of the major denominations but would not wish to make a major issue of the fact, would, in Dollar's opinion, include the following: Asbury, Biola, Cedarville (OH), Covenant (TN), Detroit Bible, John Brown (AR), Moody, Philadelphia College of the Bible, Tennessee Temple, and Washington (DC) Bible.[67]

Among those institutions that accepted the fundamentalist label, the generally acknowledged leaders included Tennessee Temple, Baptist Bible of Missouri, Liberty, and Bob Jones. Tennessee Temple was founded in 1946 by Lee Roberson as an extension of his Highland Park Baptist Church in Chattanooga. The Tennessee Temple "schools" included a Bible college and a seminary as well as a liberal arts college, with total enrollment exceeding 2,300 by 1971. The sponsoring Highland Park Baptist Church, in addition to its variety of programs in Chattanooga, organized the fundamentalist Baptists in the southeastern United States into an organization called the Southwide Baptist Fellowship.[68]

One fundamentalist institution that was more significant than well known is Baptist Bible of Missouri. Its 2,500 students in the late 1970s gave it an enrollment rarely matched in Bible college history. The school is the approved institution of the Baptist Bible Fellowship (BBF), a loose confederation of over 3,500 churches that militantly promote the importance and autonomy of the local church. Despite their insistence upon congregationalism, BBF members recognized the value of some cooperation, and they created the Missouri school for the sole purpose of training workers for their many churches.

The college was organized in 1950 by more than one hundred ministers who previously had been associated with the World Baptist Fellowship empire of J. Frank Norris, the longtime minister of the First Baptist Church of Fort Worth. By mid-century, personality clashes and organizational disputes resulted in the aging Norris losing most of his following among Baptist fundamentalists. Those who dropped away reorganized themselves into the Baptist Bible Fellowship. Principal leaders of the new group included G. B. Vick, minister of Detroit's large Temple Baptist

Church, and W. E. Dowell, minister of the High Street Baptist Church of Springfield, Missouri. When the leaders of the reorganized group agreed on the desirability of establishing a Bible college, they chose to locate it in Dowell's home town and to select Vick to commute from his pastorate in Detroit to serve as the school president.

Few colleges have been organized with as close a relationship to the basic purpose of the supporting denomination as was Baptist Bible. The school described itself as "a training center to prepare young men and women to fit into the fellowship's congregation building thrust." The local churches were multifaceted and heavily growth-oriented; therefore, there have been sufficient positions in the BBF system for all graduates. Furthermore, the fellowship wanted all of its new ministers to have graduated from the school because, according to Vick, "Preachers, even fundamentalists, who have not been trained by us, don't think like we do."[69]

One of those who did think like the BBF ministers and who graduated from the three-year course at Baptist Bible was Jerry Falwell, who by the 1970s had become one of the best-known preachers in America. Consistent with the church-growth emphasis of the BBF, the young Falwell began Thomas Road Baptist Church in Lynchburg, Virginia, and led its growth from thirty-five church members in 1956 to 17,000 members in 1980. Also consistent with the BBF emphasis that he learned while in college, Falwell developed a comprehensive church program including a day-school academy, a Bible institute, a correspondence school, a seminary, and a college. Falwell was able to build his college and other programs in part by soliciting funds from his radio and television ministry, which by 1980 included nearly seven hundred television and radio stations. Approximately eighteen million weekly listeners sent contributions totaling $1 million a week, with much of the income going to pay the cost of the broadcasts. This widespread media exposure brought Falwell not only funds but also students — in numbers totaling three thousand by 1978. Falwell has never hesitated to set high goals, and his enrollment targets included ten thousand by 1988 and fifty thousand by 2000. He also boasted that his school would eventually schedule Notre Dame in football.[70]

Liberty may some day be the largest fundamentalist college, but through much of the twentieth century the holder of that title was Bob Jones University (BJU). The school was founded by the evangelist of the same name in 1926. During the first quarter of this century, Bob Jones Sr. preached 12,000 sermons to more than fifteen million people. According to his biographer, 300,000 of these "came forward" to make spiritual commitments and 100,000 subsequently joined a Christian church. BJU, then, like Oral Roberts University in a later era, was built upon a broad publicity base of religious crusades conducted over many years in many geographic regions. Jones states that during his evangelistic travels he became increasingly disturbed with the many reports of how students from Christian families left home to study in college—including church colleges in the process of becoming secular—and then returned without their faith and/or their purity. He described listening to the account of an aged couple who had served as home missionaries in the Northwest, where they helped found a college of their denomination and then gave sacrificially of their meager funds to support it. Naturally they sent their son to study there, but to their surprise the institution in the meantime had hired non-Christians as faculty members. These skeptical instructors led their son astray, and he became a "drunken atheistic bum." Their appeal to the evangelist was this: "Brother Bob, my wife and I are old. You are a young man. Go up and down this country, and tell this story, and warn the people that the educational drift of this nation is atheistic." Jones's reaction to this and similar pleas was not merely to go up and down the country uttering jeremiads but to found a Christian college with sufficient "safeguards" surrounding it to assure that it would not, like the church college mentioned above, ever move in a secular direction. Accordingly, when Jones opened his institution in Saint Andrews Bay, Florida, in 1926, he not only provided it with an orthodox creed but added the following proviso at the end of the statement of belief: "This charter shall never be amended, modified, altered, or changed." In 1933 he purchased the property of Centenary College in Cleveland, Tennessee, and moved the school there, where it remained until its relocation in 1947 to its present Greenville, South Carolina, campus.[71]

In several ways BJU represented both the best and the worst in fundamentalist higher education. Its very attractive $50 million campus served five thousand students (1974) who came from nearly every state and approximately twenty-five foreign countries. The physical plant included a 3,600-seat dining commons and a seven-thousand-seat amphitorium where the entire student body met seven mornings a week for chapel and worship services. During the middle decades of this century, the school's record in training large numbers of young men to minister to large numbers of people and to lead large numbers of people to make initial Christian commitments may be unmatched. Also, in some ways its academic program and facilities were superior. Outside critics observed that the BJU movie and television studios and its art gallery were among the best on any college campus in the country. Only UCLA, USC, and Boston University operated cinema-production programs comparable to that at BJU. The technically excellent films produced in its studios include *Wine of Morning, Red Runs the River,* and *Flame in the Wind.* In 1973 an essayist in the *National Review* expressed utter astonishment at the quality of the university art museum which he described as containing "an array of pictures (medieval, renaissance, baroque, and eighteenth century) that is nothing short of incredible. How is it possible in a short space of twenty years to assemble such a collection at a time when old masters, especially with names like Botticelli, Rubens, Rembrandt, Titian, Tintoretto, have become so scarce and so expensive so as to be almost unavailable?" The collection of sacred art, just like the university's emphasis upon excellence in the fine arts in general, is due largely to the efforts of Bob Jones Jr., who presided over the school between 1947 and 1971.[72]

On the other hand, Bob Jones University encouraged some of the criticism made against it both by other Christians and those outside the Christian faith. For example, the catalog descriptions of the institution in places were unnecessarily aggressive, defensive, and boastful. The first page of the catalog, carrying the heading, "Important," stated that the university holds the privilege of suspending any student at any time who "in the opinion of the University does not fit into the spirit of the institution regardless of whether or not he conforms to the specific rules and regulations of the University." Also, the BJU motto read, "Bob Jones University is determined that no school shall excel it in the thoroughness of its scholastic work; and, God helping it, it endeavors to excel all other schools in the thoroughness of its Christian training." In some respects the college matched its motto; in others it clearly did not, yet because of its sweeping claim it invited others to examine it closely. Many, for example, doubted whether the quality of the faculty was commensurate with the claims of the institution for academic supremacy. In 1978, only 14 percent (36 of 257 regular faculty appointees) held earned doctoral degrees (this did not include the sixty graduate assistants who taught half-loads). Admittedly this is only one index of academic quality, but it is one which is easily measurable. Another quantifiable standard is the number of library volumes, which was 155,000. In both of these areas, Bob Jones ranked low for colleges of its size.[73]

Some of the things for which Bob Jones received criticism were not necessarily bad, only different. For example, some objected to the university practice of paying faculty members only small cash salaries (based upon family need), but then supplementing this income with on-campus room and board accommodations and hospital privileges. Such a remuneration plan may not be orthodox, but it is no more inappropriate than are, say, similar plans for ordained instructors in Roman Catholic institutions.[74]

Historically, a number of traits have characterized fundamentalist higher education and still are apparent in it. Perhaps the most important of these is an emphasis on evangelism. Fundamentalist schools have stressed not only the training of ministers but, more specifically, the training of "soul-saving" ministers. One of the primary purposes for founding

Bob Jones was to serve as "a fundamentalist base for future evangelism"; twenty-five years later this base was well in place with 1,200 of the three thousand Bob Jones students being trained as ministerial evangelists. *Time* magazine duly noted: "Bob Jones University has demonstrated that it is possible to take the enthusiasm of a religious revival, transfer it to a campus, and sustain it without missing a beat." While today a smaller percentage of BJU students enters the ministry, the number of such ministerial students is still significant.

During his lifetime, the founder of the school gave special attention to the younger men, to whom he referred affectionately as his "preacher boys." He gave them weekly instruction in the practical aspects of the ministry, including evangelism. In the weekly sessions, he counseled them to "have pure minds and hearts, be honest with people, deal fairly and kindly with them, dress neatly and appropriately, preach from the Bible, know the Scriptures, respect womanhood. . . ." He also warned them severely against the temptations of money and women. According to Jones's biographer,

> He blasts away at young ministers who would go out just to preach for money or who make decisions to serve God on the basis of income. He thunders at them, like a prophet of yesteryear, to be gentlemen in every respect in relation to girls and ladies, and verbally threatens any young preacher who would go out to hold a meeting or to conduct a service and then become sinful with some single "fancy female" who flatters his ego and entices him to ruin all the good he has accomplished.[75]

Each time the class met, the hundreds of preacher boys sang their theme song:

> Souls for Jesus is our battle cry
> Souls for Jesus, we'll fight until we die;
> We never will give in
> While souls are lost in sin,
> Souls for Jesus is our battle cry.[76]

A similar evangelistic emphasis has characterized the other fundamentalist colleges. During the first twenty-six years of Tennessee Temple, one-third of its graduates — nearly one thousand students — entered the ministry. President Dowell of Baptist Bible of Missouri represented the conviction of the people at his institution when he stated that "the only hope of America is the establishment of thousands of independent soul-winning churches." One cannot even gain admittance to the Missouri college without expressing the desire to become a Christian worker. At Liberty, soul saving was an integral part of the theoretical and applied curriculum. All first-year students took classes in Christian evangelism, in which they learn the basic techniques and methods of personal soul winning. Many of the students participated in the evangelistic thrust of the Thomas Road Baptist Church, which conducted intensive revival campaigns each fall and spring.[77]

In the late twentieth century the fastest-growing program of the large fundamentalist churches — as well as many other conservative Protestant churches — was the Christian day-school movement. Consequently, the fastest-growing program in fundamentalist colleges was that of preparing teachers for the growing number of Christian elementary and secondary schools. For example, Tennessee Temple began such a program in 1964. Within eight years, it had become the largest division in the college. Whereas in 1950 most of the elementary and secondary students enrolled in private schools attended Catholic, Lutheran, and Christian Reformed institutions, most of the private schools established since then have been operated by fundamentalist organizations. The director of the Association of Christian Schools International claimed that by the late 1970s more than one million students were enrolled in more than five thousand such schools, with additional ones opening at the rate of two per day. Baptist Bible of Missouri considered it so natural for a church to operate a day school that it required every pastoral candidate for the bachelors degree to take a course in the history and philosophy of the Christian day-school movement. The great growth of Christian schools developed only in part because of governmental decisions calling for the integration of public schools. More significant has been the reaction against the 1962 and 1963 Supreme Court decisions banning group devotional exercises from the public schools, the decreasing quality of public education, the reduced role of ethical instruction, the increasing public school problems with personal and academic discipline, the proliferation of illegal drug usage, and the increasing national affluence that made it possible for middle-income families to afford private school tuition charges.[78]

Another characteristic of fundamentalist colleges was their tendency to use authoritarian leadership styles. Most such schools were founded in the middle half of the twentieth century by unusually aggressive and dynamic men who then continued to lead the schools they founded. Their followers often deferred to them more completely than they would to the leaders of a college that had existed for a century or longer. For example, E. C. Haskell, chairman of the deacon board of Highland Park Baptist Church in Chattanooga, the sponsoring church of Tennessee Temple, described why he generally accepted the view of Lee Roberson, the church's pastor and the founder and president of the school: "I know of no man that I consider to live closer to God than Dr. Roberson; and if this is what he thinks should be done then I will not ask questions." Sometimes, however, lesser officials and instructors in the fundamentalist colleges did ask questions, with the result that what might be an engaging debate on other campuses becomes a traumatic crisis in a highly authoritarian institution. At Bob Jones, for example, in 1953, the registrar, three deans, and a dozen teachers resigned, charging the founder-president with demanding that "the tiniest facet of his thought be considered red letter gospel." The response of Bob Jones Sr. was to preach a sermon on Judas.

An authoritarian leader often works with few people able or willing to assist him in developing his thinking, and when he adopts an extreme interpretation of the biblical commandment for separation from the world, he may end up withdrawing from and denouncing the very people and institutions who should be his natural allies in the promotion of Christian higher education. Bob Jones Jr. for years criticized evangelical institutions with even greater emotional fervor than that used in fighting the original enemies of his college, the modernists. He once observed that "Satan's three forces in his war against God are modernism, neo-orthodoxy, and the new evangelism. Of these three, the last group is the most dangerous." He also accused fellow fundamentalist Jerry Falwell of being a tool of Satan. In 1980 the newspaper of Falwell's conservative political lobby, *Moral Majority*, described a letter written by Bob Jones Jr. to the 1980 BJU graduates calling Falwell "the most dangerous man in America today as far as Biblical Christianity is concerned," and his Moral Majority program "one of Satan's devices to build the world church of Antichrist."[79]

Fundamentalist colleges also tended to be associated with Baptist "super churches." A close correlation exists between the fundamentalist church emphasis on growth and bigness in general (e.g., church membership, big buildings, bus fleets, Sunday-school enrollment, radio and television broadcasts on increasing numbers of stations to increasing numbers of viewers who send in increasing numbers of dollars) and their establishment of colleges designed to enroll increasing numbers of students. This growth emphasis is related to a desire for mass evangelism organizations that multiply results; it is also a religious form of boosterism. One example of this phenomenon is the relationship between Temple Baptist Church of Detroit and Baptist Bible of Missouri. Temple Baptist Church was the leading sponsor of Baptist Bible. The pastor of one was the president of the other. In 1955, *Life* magazine identified the Temple Baptist Sunday school as the largest in America. The 1973 *Christian Life* listing of the one hundred largest Sunday schools in America found that twenty-three of them were led by ministerial graduates of Baptist Bible. A later *Christian Life* poll showed that each of the three fastest-growing Sunday schools during the 1968–77 decade have operated fundamentalist colleges. These included the First Baptist Church of Hammond, Indiana, which grew from 3,300 to 14,000 members and sponsored Hyles Anderson; Highland Park Baptist Church of Chattanooga, which grew from 2,400 to 8,000 members and directed Tennessee Temple; and Thomas Road Baptist Church of Lynchburg, Virginia, which grew from 2,600 to 6,400 members and administered Liberty.[80]

Still another characteristic of fundamentalist colleges was their concern to protect the purity of the Christian faith more than — and sometimes at the expense of — intellectual freedom. Bob Jones III frankly admitted this to be the case at his institution. "We're unusual in our objectives to teach the student what he believes. Most schools would be appalled at this statement, but committed as we are, we don't throw out a bunch of theories to them about the religion of the world and philosophy and this sort of thing." The official biographer of Billy Graham suggests that a significant factor in Graham's decision to leave BJU after one semester in attendance was the lack of intellectual freedom that he experienced there: "Dr. Bob knew exactly what was true and false in faith, ethics, and academics. He also stated publicly that his institution had never been wrong. Independent thought was so discouraged that many alumni say in retrospect that there was almost thought control." Bob Jones Sr. used to tell the students in chapel that "if you don't like it here you can pack your dirty duds and hit the four-lane highway." Graham, among others, accepted that option.

Fundamentalist colleges frequently hesitated to allow their students to attend local churches not directly affiliated with the college; to protect them they frequently provided Sunday worship services as well as weekday chapel services on campus. Tennessee Temple required all of its students to attend the affiliated Highland Park Church because:

> Students are not always wise in their choice of churches while at school nor in their discernment of truth and error. On several occasions students have become involved in Baptist churches which were pentecostal and have been diverted into the error of tongues. With so many heresies about, it seemed advisable that rather than making a "black list" of churches not to attend, it would be a wiser course to require the students to go where there were no such pitfalls for novices in the Christian faith.[81]

The colleges also defined very specific belief and behavioral expectations for their faculty members. Tennessee Temple, at least as recently as the 1970s, required its faculty to join the Highland Park Baptist Church unless employed by another church, to fill out a weekly activity report verifying attendance at one week-night and two Sunday services, to believe in eternal security and premillennial eschatology, and not to play cards, go to the movies, participate in mixed bathing, wear shorts, or — for men — grow a beard or wear long hair. Other fundamentalist institutions held similar faculty requirements. Consequently, the schools were forced to hire faculty heavily from the ranks of their alumni — or from the graduates of a limited number of similar institutions — so as to obtain people who are willing to submit to the severe restrictions on their personal freedoms. For example, at Bob Jones in the mid-1960s, 130 of 150 regular faculty members had taken at least part of their academic training at BJU.

The colleges sometimes found it difficult to recruit people who are both competently trained and willing to comply with school standards. In 1969, President Vick of Baptist Bible of Missouri stated that he probably would not hire an instructor unless he possessed a baccalaureate degree from an accredited institution and was willing to work towards a master's degree; "Nevertheless," he observed, "we know the dangers, we're aware of history; and we are not going to sacrifice our convictions on anybody's academic altar." Bob Jones Sr. noted another concern about graduate school training: it tends to make people more analytical, more questioning, and less inclined to accept automatically enthusiastic responses and approaches. On one occasion he remarked — probably half seriously — "Every time we add one of these Ph.D.'s to the faculty we have to pray and work harder to keep the evangelistic fires burning."[82]

Since the 1960s, at least, fundamentalist colleges have tended to promote conservative political views and candidates. Bob Jones granted honorary doctoral degrees to Billy James Hargis and George Wallace, governor of Alabama. Senator Strom Thurmond of South Carolina and the school found each other sufficiently acceptable for Thurmond to serve as a member of the board of trustees. In the late 1970s, President Falwell of Liberty organized Moral Majority, a political lobbying organization that used its vast influence to support conservative political candidates as well as some causes that evangelical Christians generally supported. Moral Majority crusaded not only for conservative political candidates but against liberal ones. For example, senators Birch Bayh, Frank Church, George McGovern, and Gaylord Nelson found Moral Majority campaigning against their 1980 reelection bids. The lobbying effort was sufficiently successful to attract a cover story by *Newsweek* magazine.[83]

During the middle part of the twentieth century, probably no conservative Christian college attracted greater attention for its promotion of conservative politics than did Harding (AR), a Churches of Christ institution. Beginning in 1936, when returning China missionary George S. Benson assumed the presidency of Harding, that institution developed a national reputation as an outspoken proponent of the free-enterprise economic system. Benson was appalled at the growth of government involvement in and control of the economy during the early New Deal years. After he appeared before the House Ways and Means Committee in 1941 to call for the government to transfer funds from New Deal relief agencies to defense purposes, he began to attract increasing attention to himself and his institution. By 1954 his weekly newspaper column appeared in more than three thousand newspapers, and his weekly radio program, "Land of the Free," was heard on 365 stations. Donations began to pour into the college from people across the nation who supported the causes that Benson advocated.[84]

Although most evangelical colleges have been less aggressive than Harding in promoting specific political perspectives, members of their communities in recent years have shown a clear preference for conservative candidates.[85] For example, a poll of Wheaton students in the 1960s on the political preference of their parents showed that 61 percent favored conservative Republicans, 20 percent liberal Republicans, and only 7 percent Democrats.[86]

The quality of the fundamentalist institutions, like that of the Bible colleges, was limited by the meager financial bases from which most of them operated. Since fundamentalist organizations represented denominations and individuals that withdrew from the mainline denominations in the twentieth century, they had to start anew in developing their own colleges. Consequently, from the standpoint of tradition and financial resources, many of these schools functioned at a level of development comparable to that reached a century earlier by the colleges of the denominations from which they separated. In too many cases, limited resources have caused the institutions to hire inadequately trained professors to direct courses whose quality was defended because of the Christian character of the teachers.

The student Christian associations, the university pastorate movement, the Bible schools, and the fundamentalist colleges were the most direct and the most novel responses to the secularization of higher education. They were not the only ones, however, for the twentieth century has witnessed the founding of a number of traditional liberal arts colleges by new conservative, if not clearly fundamentalist, groups (e.g., the Churches of Christ, the Nazarenes, and the Church of God denominations). These new evangelical colleges together with the Bible colleges, the fundamentalist colleges, and the continuing Christian colleges are the subject of the next chapter on the mid- to late-twentieth-century period of Protestant higher education in America.

6

The Reconstruction of
Christian Higher Education after 1945

Never since the skeptical 1790s had Christian colleges experienced the degree of demoralization that they did during the second quarter of the twentieth century. The secularizing pattern first hit the Christian colleges with intensity in the 1920s and the situation worsened during the 1930s, for added to the growing secularization were the effects of the nation's worst economic depression. The continuing Christian colleges were often the less affluent ones, and it is a testimony to their dedication that so many employed highly sacrificial and sometimes creative measures in the largely successful struggle to survive. For example, at Abilene Christian, in 1931–32, faculty members voluntarily returned 50 percent of their salaries to allow the school to balance its budget, while Greenville used its chemistry laboratory as an industrial plant to employ impoverished students in the manufacture of a variety of household toiletries, medicines, and flavorings, which additional students then sold at 30 percent commission throughout the country.[1] By the 1940s the Christian colleges were beginning to recover. Although the movement toward secularization continued, the stimulus of war production ended the Great Depression, and the GI Bill brought a record number of enrollees to colleges of all types.

The recovery process continued steadily after World War II and the Christian colleges became stronger than they had been at any time since the secular revolution. The recovery did not come because secularizing institutions returned to their earlier orientation (very few did) or because many new, well-developed Christian colleges came into existence (except for a limited number of colleges like Oral Roberts and Pepperdine in California, most of the new colleges began with very modest resources). Rather, the recovery came because of factors that benefited higher education in general (a relatively prosperous economy, the increasing popularity of attending college, and the new and expanding forms of government aid to students and institutions); because of the decline in the number of additional colleges to begin the secularization process; and because cooperative efforts through such organizations as the Christian College Coalition and the American Association of Bible Colleges allowed the Christian colleges to achieve greater influence and an increased public awareness of their growing quality and clearly defined goals.

The Emerging Line-up
of the Continuing Christian College

Enough time had passed since the peak period of the secularization challenge for most of the historically church-related colleges to decide whether they were generally accepting of or generally resistant to secular influences. Since so many colleges chose to accept these influences, the Christian college line-up of 1980 was considerably different from that of 1920. The continuing Christian colleges included those affiliated with the smaller evangelical denominations, a number of independent evangelical colleges, most Southern Baptist and Lutheran institutions, some Presbyterian colleges, and a few colleges affiliated with other major denominations and traditions. There were perhaps two hundred such continuing Christian liberal arts colleges plus the Bible colleges.

The Southern Baptists maintained probably the largest denominational network of continuing Christian colleges. Approximately sixty institutions identified with that denomination. Baylor with its ten thousand students was not only the largest of the Southern Baptist colleges but also the largest Protestant college that seriously sought to integrate the Christian faith with its educational program.[2] Southern Baptist colleges with leading academic reputations included Wake Forest, Richmond, Baylor, Furman, Mercer, Stetson, Mississippi, Louisiana, and Samford.[3]

The number of colleges associated with the several Lutheran denominations nearly equaled the Southern Baptist total and included thirty-eight senior colleges, ten junior colleges, and five Bible colleges. The largest of these, with 1980 enrollments of more than two thousand, were Valparaiso, Pacific Lutheran, St. Olaf, California Lutheran, Concordia of Moorhead, Minnesota, Wagner, Wittenberg, Gustavus Adolphus, Augustana of Illinois, Augustana of South Dakota, Capital, and Luther. The most selective in admitting students included Augustana of Illinois, Gettysburg, Gustavus Adolphus, Muhlenberg, Pacific Lutheran, St. Olaf, and Valparaiso.[4]

In general, the denominations associated with continuing Christian colleges supported their institutions much better than did the denominations whose schools were more secular. For example, of the major denominations, none contributed as much to the operating budgets and building programs of its colleges as did the Southern Baptists and Lutherans. The Missouri Synod Lutheran Church provided from one-fourth to one-half of the operating expenses for its synodical colleges. Also noteworthy was the practice of the Christian Reformed Church, which required all of its individual members, by virtue of their membership, to support the denomination's higher education program.[5]

A comparison of the Christian college line-ups of 1920 and 1980 showed great contrast not only because many secularizing institutions had departed but also because new liberal arts colleges had appeared. While Protestant groups founded far fewer colleges after 1920 than they did between the Civil War and World War I, nearly all of the new institutions declared a clearly Christian orientation.[6]

Some new colleges were founded by the major denominations. For example, Valparaiso began in 1925 as the first comprehensive college of the Missouri Synod Lutherans; the Southern Baptists added Grand Canyon in 1949; the American Baptists opened Eastern in 1952 and Judson in 1963; and the Lutheran Church in America and the American Lutheran Church together founded California Lutheran in 1959. For the most part, however, the new liberal arts colleges, like most of the Bible colleges, were founded by new evangelical denominations or independent groups that separated from the mainline denominations in protest over the latter's growing liberal theological orientation.[7] For example, the General Association of Regular Baptists founded Grand Rapids Baptist in 1941 and acquired Cedarville in 1953; the Reformed Presbyterians (Evangelical Synod) began Covenant in 1955; and the Churches of Christ established seventeen currently operating institutions including David Lipscomb in 1891, Abilene Christian in 1906, Harding in 1924, and Pepperdine in 1937. Abilene and Pepperdine, as the leading schools of the 2.5-million-member Churches of Christ confederation, have become two of the largest Christian colleges in the country; in 1980 the Texas school enrolled 4,372 students and the California institution 7,298 students. Pepperdine was named for its original benefactor, George Pepperdine, who developed the chain of Western Auto Supply stores.

The Pentecostals became the latest major American religious group to enter the field of higher education. Like the older Holiness movement (leading denominations include the Wesleyan Church, the Free Methodist Church, the Anderson, Indiana-based Church of God, the Church of the Nazarene, and the Salvation Army), the Pentecostal movement (major denominations include the Assemblies of God, the Cleveland, Tennessee-based Church of God, the Pentecostal Holiness Church, the United Pentecostal Church, the Church of the Foursquare Gospel, and the Church of God in Christ) has historic connections with Methodist ideas. The Holi-

ness movement—especially the Wesleyan and Free Methodist churches—
began founding colleges in the late nineteenth century, with Roberts Wesleyan, Houghton, Spring Arbor, Seattle Pacific, Greenville, and Asbury
appearing at that time. By contrast, the Pentecostal liberal arts colleges developed only since World War I, with the best known of these being Lee,
begun in 1918 by the Cleveland, Tennessee Church of God; Emmanuel,
begun in 1919 by the Pentecostal Holiness Church; Evangel, begun in 1955
by the Assemblies of God; and Oral Roberts, begun independently by the
evangelist in 1965.

The reluctance of Pentecostalism to accept liberal arts education is illustrated by comparing the twentieth-century record of its largest predominantly white denomination, the Assemblies of God, with that of the
largest Holiness denomination, the Church of the Nazarene. During this
period, very few denominations opened more new liberal arts colleges in
this country than did the Nazarene church. It founded Bethany, Trevecca,
Point Loma, Olivet (IL), Northwest Nazarene, and Eastern Nazarene, before or during World War I; and Mt. Vernon and Mid-America in the
1960s. By contrast, the 1.3-million-member Assemblies of God relied primarily on Bible college education; at mid-century it was the largest Protestant denomination in the country without a liberal arts college. When the
church leaders finally opened Evangel in 1955, they created considerable
controversy throughout the denomination.[8]

The founding and development of Oral Roberts University (ORU) represented the culmination of the entry of Pentecostalism into higher education; however, its significance was even greater than this, for never since
the late nineteenth century had a Christian college been so well funded at
its inception and so quickly become a leading Christian college in this
country. Only six years after the school opened in 1965, ORU could claim
a student body of one thousand coming from forty-nine states and
twenty-three foreign countries, a library of 121,000 volumes, a physical
plant valued at more than $30 million, and full regional accreditation. The
school developed so rapidly because of the financial base and publicity
provided by the Oral Roberts Evangelistic Association. In the early 1970s
the association was supplying the school with over half of its operating
budget and nearly all of its capital funds. Enrollment grew to 1,800 in
1972, 3,500 in 1975, and 4,000 in 1978. Also, in the late 1970s the university
opened graduate programs in business, theology, medicine, dentistry, and
law.[9]

Roberts desired his school to be the university of the entire charismatic
movement rather than a narrowly denominational school of one or more
of the traditional Pentecostal churches. As some Pentecostals have believed that all converts to the charismatic movement must leave their tra-

ditional denominations and join one of the historical Pentecostal churches, it was symbolically significant when Roberts in 1968 transferred his membership from the Pentecostal Holiness denomination to the Methodist Church, with which he had identified as a youth. Roberts succeeded in his desire for a broadly interdenominational university; by 1972 less than 50 percent of the students came from Holiness or Pentecostal churches, and by 1976 over forty denominations were represented in the student body.

Most of the ORU faculty sympathized with the president's emphases on the ministry of the Holy Spirit and physical health. These emphases helped to make the university's general education program unique. For example, every student enrolled in a two-hour course on the Holy Spirit taught by Roberts, and every student participated in a physical education class each semester. Also, if a student was overweight, he or she, like those who performed inadequately in the classroom, had to demonstrate satisfactory progress toward removing his or her deficiency in order to continue in school.[10]

The educational feature of ORU that attracted the broadest attention was its modernistic application of technology to the learning process. The heart of the institution's academic program was the fourteen-acre learning resources center that combined library, laboratories, classrooms, and office space in an interrelated system housed under one roof. This learning system earned high praise from the Carnegie Commission and the Ford Foundation, the latter referring to it as "one of the most creative facilities on the American campus today." The institution itself claims that it is the first university to install a computerized information retrieval system whereby students, whether in class, the library, dormitory study lounges, or their own dormitory rooms, have direct-dial access to the audiovisual materials prepared for the courses in which they are enrolled. The college used the system most extensively for its large-enrollment, general-education courses.

Other campus facilities of note included the 11,000-seat basketball arena and the aerobics center, custom designed for the effective application of Kenneth H. Cooper's nationally famous aerobics program. President Roberts early believed that his athletic teams—particularly his basketball team—would zoom to the top nationally just as dramatically as other aspects of the college have progressed. During the school's initial year as an NCAA member in the major college division, the basketball team earned a ranking among the top twenty teams in the nation. Roberts stated that he views athletics as an attention-getting means to an end: "Sports are becoming the number one interest to people in America. For us to be relevant, we had to gain the attention of millions in a way that they understood and they would then tune us in on TV to hear us preach the gospel."[11]

Athletic participation at ORU was not just for the talented few. In fact, probably no school in the nation except the military academies combined a high quality, intercollegiate program with emphasis upon the physical fitness of each student. In describing the school's insistence upon regular vigorous activity by all, Roberts explained: "We don't want to turn out 'educated monsters' who . . . house their minds in weak bodies."[12]

The futuristic architecture of the campus buildings helped make the college a major tourist attraction. By the mid-1970s, ORU had become the most frequently visited site in Tulsa and one of the leading attractions in Oklahoma. Perhaps the most striking structure was the 200-foot, blue and white, space-needle-like prayer tower, which housed the prayer groups that received thousands of requests per month.[13]

Much of ORU's success has been due to the wide publicity it achieved through the founder's national television broadcasts that began in the 1950s. Since then, other television evangelists also have sought to capitalize upon their media publicity to found Christian colleges. The evangelist with the greatest potential for matching Roberts's success in college founding was Billy Graham, who after due consideration decided against opening his own institution. Early in his career (1947–51), Graham briefly had succeeded William Bell Riley as president of Northwestern in Minnesota. By 1980, the most successful of the other "television colleges" had been Liberty Baptist, the school founded by Jerry Falwell (see chapter 5). The most obvious failures were Rex Humbard's Mackinac, which operated for only one year on Mackinac Island in northern Michigan, and Jim Bakker's Heritage in South Carolina.[14]

In addition to the "television colleges," a few other unusual types of Christian colleges were appearing. Very few Christian institutions offered engineering curricula, primarily because of the costliness of the necessary laboratory equipment. While such schools as John Brown, Geneva, and Valparaiso operate programs of varying degrees of thoroughness, no Christian college has placed such a high percentage of its resources in technical education as has LeTourneau (TX). The school was founded by Robert G. LeTourneau, an inventor-industrialist widely known for designing heavy-duty earth moving equipment and off-shore drilling platforms and then donating most of his earnings to missionary and evangelistic organizations. LeTourneau operated his school as a technical institute from its beginning in 1946 to 1961, when it became a liberal arts college, adding baccalaureate programs in electrical engineering technology, industrial management, mechanical engineering technology, welding engineering technology, and flight technology; and two-year programs in automotive technology, aviation technology, and design technology.[15]

Only a limited number of Christian colleges concentrated on educating students from the lower socioeconomic classes. Some colleges that serve denominations with a large percentage of lower-class membership have in a de facto manner achieved this purpose; such, for example, has been the case at Anderson, Evangel, and the several Nazarene institutions, at least in their early years. Still fewer institutions have offered their programs at a lower cost than that charged in the public universities, and only a handful have existed primarily to educate youths so poor that they could not pay for their training.

College of the Ozarks (MO) joined the earlier tradition of Berea and Berry in specializing in educating impoverished mountain youth in exchange for their commitment to work for the college. The income from a sizable endowment base and gifts provided scholarships for all of the students, and each student agreed to work 15 to 20 hours per week in one of a broad variety of college employment opportunities (e.g., meat processing; furniture manufacturing; clerical, instructional, and personnel assistance; campus maintenance; on-campus and off campus construction; the specialty gift plant; the dairy; the farm; the kitchen and bakery; the food services; the restaurant; the airport; the theater; and the electrical, plumbing, print, sheet metal, machinery, and engineering shops). The students often carried a reduced academic load while working, but still were able to graduate in four years by studying throughout the summers.[16]

In the 1960s and 1970s John Snyder, Frank Nelsen, Ron Sider, and others called for the development of "satellite" Christian colleges located adjacent to large public universities. These Christian colleges or centers would provide dormitory and dining facilities, spiritual support services, and limited instruction by qualified evangelical instructors, especially in biblical studies, theology, philosophy, and apologetics. The students would register in a regular university program and would pay very little more for the alternate educational experience.

The satellite idea is still largely experimental. One of the best North American examples of such a school has been Conrad Grebel, established by the Mennonites in 1961 at the University of Waterloo, Ontario. The Grebel professors, most of whom are Mennonite by confession, hold joint faculty appointments with the two institutions. They offer a curriculum that complements rather than duplicates the university's offerings (e.g., biblical studies, peace and conflict studies, interdisciplinary values-oriented courses such as "Quest for Meaning in the Twentieth Century"). Many Waterloo students join the 115 students who reside in the Grebel dormitory in taking Grebel courses and/or participating in its chapel and counseling programs. The university pays the college for the instruction of its students.

The idea of a Christian satellite college related to a state university did not develop only in the late twentieth century. For example, through much of the century the Methodists operated Wesley College at the University of North Dakota, and the Southern Baptists established Southern Illinois College of the Bible at Southern Illinois University in 1938. In each case, the university granted credit for work offered by the satellite school. Another variation of the satellite model has existed at Northwest Christian at least since the 1930s. Northwest Christian combined its Bible college curriculum with the course offerings of the adjacent University of Oregon to allow their baccalaureate graduates to earn a double major in biblical studies and a liberal arts area.[17]

The Emerging Identity of the Continuing Christian College

As the institutional composition of the surviving Christian college community became increasingly evident, so also did the character of the continuing Christian college movement. These emerging character traits by the 1980s included (1) a growing quality; (2) an enlarged intellectual openness within the realm of orthodoxy; (3) an increasing effort to integrate faith, learning, and living; (4) a continuing effort to promote spiritual nurture and character development; and (5) an increasing degree of intercollegiate cooperation.

While the improvement in the quality of Christian higher education came gradually, public recognition of this improvement grew sharply, beginning in the 1970s, perhaps in part because of the increasing publicity given to evangelical Protestantism in general since 1975. The intellectual community as well as the general public began to show greater recognition of and appreciation for Christian higher education. Kenneth Briggs, religion editor of the *New York Times,* cited the favorable enrollment trend,[18] the financial stability, and the improved academic standing of evangelical schools. Robert Pace, in his Carnegie Commission study, was even more specific when he described the orthodox colleges as "the fastest growing group presently among Protestant colleges" and stated that in academic quality they now match the mainline Protestant colleges. Carl Henry believed that the campus resources of the evangelical colleges comprising the Christian College Coalition (see table 3, pp. 199–201) had become the best they have been since the secular revolution. Coalition president John Dellenback saw these schools as "far stronger" than they were in 1970 and as continuing their improvement in the 1980s.

One of the most important measures of success for a college is its ability to inspire students to achieve their maximum potential. David Riesman observed in 1981 that the evangelical colleges send a much higher percentage of their graduates to graduate or professional schools than would be expected based upon their SAT scores. Also, in the alumni data noted in the 1966 Pattillo and Mackenzie study, the only college to rank high in each of the three categories of producing younger scholars, physicians, and seminarians was Calvin, an evangelical institution with only a moderately competitive admissions policy.[19]

In their efforts to improve, many Christian colleges received able assistance from the Council for the Advancement of Small Colleges (renamed the Council of Independent Colleges). The council began in 1955 to assist small independent colleges in achieving regional accreditation.[20] Later it concentrated on providing small colleges with highly practical and modestly priced training skills and management services. The organization has been heavily funded by external support from individuals, the federal government, and foundations (especially the W. K. Kellogg Foundation). Many of the member colleges are evangelical Protestant and Catholic institutions.

Many observers continued to look to Wheaton as the intellectual leader of the evangelical colleges affiliated with either a small denomination or no denomination at all. Some thought it the intellectual leader of the continuing Christian colleges of all types. Students found it difficult to gain admittance to Wheaton, and, once accepted, found the academic environment very rigorous. For example, during the late 1960s, new enrollees entered with an average college board (SAT) score of approximately 1,200, and nearly 75 percent of them had graduated in the top 10 percent of their high school classes. One Wheaton student suggested that the competition for grades that he experienced as an undergraduate was more intense than that which he faced in his graduate work at the University of Wisconsin Law School. Knowledgeable and keen outside observers noted that at Wheaton, "The college creates discussion as intense, perhaps, as any to be found on American campuses, and as consistently directed to ultimate issues." *Time* magazine noted that during the 1920–1976 period, Wheaton alumni ranked eleventh among all four-year colleges in earning Ph.D. degrees and that the school's number of National Merit Scholars in 1979–80 placed it with the very best four-year institutions of similar size.[21]

In the 1970s, Wheaton attracted attention—even controversy—when it invited the Billy Graham Evangelistic Association to build the Billy Graham Center on its campus. The center houses documents recording Christian evangelism and missions in the past and it promotes such efforts in the future by hosting a broad variety of training sessions and conferences. The archival division of the center of course contains the papers of Billy Graham and his evangelistic association, but it also includes those of hundreds of other organizations and individuals. In fact, the center with its archives, library, and museum has become one of the world's largest resource centers for the study of the history of evangelism and world missions.

The decision to locate the Graham Center at Wheaton involved risk for the college. While the Billy Graham Evangelistic Association paid the $13.5 million to build the five-story, 200,000-square-foot structure, the college accepted the obligation to raise a $15 million endowment to maintain it. Some of the faculty feared that the center would become a financial liability for the college. The administrative staff and trustees, however, remained confident that as a symbol as well as a continuation and expansion of the Billy Graham ministry, the center would be a long-range boon to the outreach and public relations efforts of the institution.[22]

While by 1980 the Christian colleges were able to develop the financial base to support good — sometimes excellent — undergraduate programs, they had not yet acquired the larger resources necessary to achieve financial independence or to develop graduate programs of sufficient quality and quantity, except in theology. One could point to individual programs of note (e.g., the Baylor School of Medicine, the several able law schools affiliated with Christian colleges, the growing emphasis upon psychology and communications in the seminaries, and the potential of the new professional programs at Oral Roberts and Regent [VA]); nevertheless, the statement still held that save for theology, and especially in the liberal arts, Christian graduate education remained largely undeveloped.

Christian educators had long been aware of this deficiency, and at least since the days of William Jennings Bryan and Charles Blanchard of Wheaton in the 1920s, plans to found a Christian university had been considered seriously. In the late 1950s and early 1960s, Billy Graham, Carl Henry, and others discussed the feasibility of developing such an institution at Gordon because of the latter's large campus (eight hundred acres) and location near "the educational capital" of the country, Boston. One of the reasons for the creation of the Christian College Consortium in 1971 was to provide an organizational base for continuing study of the Christian university idea. In the post–World War II period, however, the vision of what Carl Henry has called a "Christian Johns Hopkins" remained in the dream stage.[23]

By 1980, the continuing Christian colleges had become increasingly willing and able to expose their students to a broad range of perspectives in all areas, including those which directly consider Christian values. For example, instruction in the religion departments, while retaining the earlier commitment and biblical literature emphasis, now followed a more strictly academic approach and included a broader curriculum. Also, while science professors believed in the divine creation of the earth and of man, they differed widely on the method and the timetable used by the

Creator. Some accepted theistic evolution (i.e., macroevolution). A larger number believed in progressive creation, thus allowing for microevolutionary activity within — but not across — the several biblical "kinds." Few evangelical scholars insisted that God created the world in six days of twenty-four hours each.

The Christian college professors also disagreed widely on the age of the earth and the earliest man. One group placed the origin of man somewhere between 6,000 and 15,000 years ago by interpreting genealogical passages in the Bible as being without generational gaps. Others, including many members of the evangelically oriented American Scientific Affiliation, believed it possible that the original man, Adam, was created as early as 100,000 years ago and certainly before the time of the earliest human or humanlike forms found by archaeologists. Regardless of how they interpreted the facts, science instructors usually advised their students that there is no single orthodox Christian approach to the broad subject of origins.[24]

Few themes have received greater emphasis in Christian colleges after 1970 than the integration of faith and learning. While there have always been Christian teachers in secular as well as religious institutions who have sought to realize this idea, the unique element of the modern period is the conscious, overt effort of many Christian colleges to stimulate their faculty members better to achieve it.

While Christian colleges are seeking to apply the faith and learning principle to their entire curricula, secular institutions, since they discarded their Christian orientation, have not been able to find another philosophical center. A half century ago, Dean Bernard Loomer of the University of Chicago Divinity School noted that "there is . . . no concerted and sustained effort to make a university out of the pluralistic and atomistic departments within the so-called university. . . . Few if any universities can set forth a meaningful statement of goals and purposes that would withstand careful scrutiny and be relevant to the needs of our culture." That Loomer's observation in 1951 is still applicable is seen from the widespread recognition that the general education programs in American higher education today are generally lacking in unity and values and barren of meaning.[25]

One of the earliest institutional leaders of the integration emphasis was Calvin, the Christian Reformed college that has been influenced greatly by Abraham Kuyper (1837–1920), the influential Netherlands political (he served as prime minister from 1901 to 1905) and religious leader and reformer as well as educational theorist. Kuyper founded the Free University of Amsterdam not just to produce and teach orthodox theology but also to place all learning on a scriptural base. He defended vigorously the sacredness of what often were called secular areas of investigation, believing that the Christian church had as great an obligation to influence these dimensions of life as the theological area. Otherwise, he argued, the church "bears only a partial witness in its society. To have an institute or a seminary in which only ministers are trained and the rest of professional life is untouched, would be like furnishing an army with only one kind of weapon and expecting it to take successfully to the field."[26]

One could cite numerous examples of the gradually increasing impact of the integration principle. The Christian College Coalition identified the faith and learning idea as its most important emphasis. Also, during this period Christian scholars in Christian colleges as well as secular institutions organized by academic disciplines to help themselves integrate their faith and their particular fields. These organizations, most of whom now count a membership of hundreds or thousands, include the American Scientific Affiliation, the Association of Christian Mathematicians, the Christian Association for Psychological Studies, the Conference on Faith and History, the Conference on Christianity and Literature, Christians in the Visual Arts, the Evangelical Philosophical Society, the Evangelical Theological Society, the Society of Christian Philosophers, the Association of Christian Librarians, the Fellowship of Christian Economists, the Christian Sociological Society, the National Association of Christians in Social Work, and the Christian Nurse Educators.

Other noteworthy integration examples included Goshen's study-service trimester requirement and the conferences of Christian professors and other environmentalists at the Au Sable Trails Institute of Environmental Studies in Michigan. Goshen students combined the Christian service ideal with the opportunity to live in and to study a foreign culture, usually in an underdeveloped part of the world. At the Au Sable conferences, Christian environmentalists discussed how to apply the biblical mandate for stewardship of world resources to the contemporary ecological crisis. The most significant results of the integration emphasis, however, probably were taking place in countless classrooms as individual professors adapted their teaching methods to reflect their increased determination to "think Christianly" about their disciplines.[27]

While the degree of attention given to the integration of faith and learning in the classroom was an innovation of this period, the Christian colleges also continued many of the older forms of religious emphasis, including chapel services, Christian social service programs, gospel teams, and revivals. Following the example of the largely urban Bible colleges, more rural liberal arts schools began to form gospel teams in the early-to-middle decades of the twentieth century when automotive transportation became more widely available. A typical gospel team consisted of a small group of

students with musical and/or speaking ability. The team would participate in or lead services of churches in the geographic area of the college.
Frequently the institution employed some of the best musicians — usually
male vocalists — to invest their summer vacation traveling, singing, and
promoting the Christian gospel and the college. For example, the Crusader
Male Quartet of Eastern Nazarene traveled nearly ten thousand miles in
fourteen states to appear in more than 150 churches besides radio performances and hospital visits during the summer of 1937.[28]

While revivalism had become a less regular, less intense, and less characteristic form of religious expression in the Christian college of this period than it had been in the nineteenth century or the early twentieth century, it still existed — sometimes dramatically so — especially in colleges
associated with churches that emphasized emotional religious experiences. Through the whole of the twentieth century, few colleges matched
the emotional fervor that broke loose periodically at Asbury. One early-
twentieth-century Asbury student later recalled his first impressions:
"There was more noise along with their religion than I had been used
to. . . . They let a good deal of physical demonstration enter in. Back in
those days it was not unusual for a student to jump over a seat in his
ecstacy."[29]

One of the most widely publicized periods of college revivalism occurred in 1950, when the national news media flocked to Asbury and
Wheaton to interpret the proceedings to the world. At Wheaton they
found a nonstop confessional meeting lasting nearly two days and nights
during which the majority of the students apologized and/or testified
publicly. As observed by a *Time* reporter:

> Singly and in little groups, sweatered and blue-jeaned undergraduate stu-
> dents streamed onto the stage, filling up the choir chairs to await their turns.
> Hour after hour, they kept coming. All night long, all the next day, all
> through the following night and half the following day, students poured out
> confessions of past sins and rededicated themselves to God.

The nature of the confessions varied from cheating and pride to criticism
of teachers (a male student stated: "I want to apologize for making the faculty the butt of my corny jokes") and sins committed toward fellow students. One young woman sought forgiveness in this fashion: "I know it's
mostly fellows that say they have impure thoughts, but girls have them
too. And I want to apologize if I've ever tempted any of the fellows I've
had contact with. I know I've tried, and I'm sorry."[30]

More recently, in February 1970, a widely publicized revival began at
Asbury when a witnessing service continued uninterrupted for 185 hours,

closing down classes for a week and then continuing nightly for two weeks after the resumption of regular classroom activity. One student explained the effects of the episode on him: "The revival changed my life. I was a stagnant Christian before. Now I like to read the Bible, and my prayer life is revitalized, and I can really love people. And I'm not ashamed to talk about it." Subsequently, the majority of Asbury's one thousand students traveled on weekends to colleges in other states and Canada to tell what had happened at the Kentucky institution with the hope of inspiring similar movements elsewhere. The effort was effective, as revivals occurred at many other Christian colleges including Wheaton, Trevecca Nazarene, Taylor, Spring Arbor, Houghton, Azusa Pacific, Oral Roberts, Greenville, and Fort Wayne Bible College.[31]

That Asbury has been known as a major center of revivalism is partly explained by the nature of its student body. Historically, it has attracted a disproportionately large share of students preparing for a full-time Christian ministry. During the 1960–61 school year, for example, no college in the nation except Concordia (IN), at the time an institution exclusively for pre-seminary students, had a higher percentage of its graduates attending seminary. When the same 1960–61 poll ranked colleges in terms of the number rather than the percent of graduates enrolled in seminary, Southern Baptist and Lutheran schools headed that list with Baylor having the highest number (496).[32]

It is generally accepted that Christian college students display more friendliness, community spirit, and general decorum than do students on other campuses. What is less clear is whether the Christian college students display such traits because they come to college with them or because of the impact of the college environment; most likely, home and campus influences reinforce each other. Generally positive behavior has characterized Christian college students for a long time, probably since the period when most non-Christian students began enrolling in other types of institutions. One survey conducted in 1930 asked students at Houghton, Asbury, Taylor, Wheaton, Eastern, and John Fletcher (IA) the factors in college that most satisfied them. Except for "Christian influence," students ranked "friendliness" far ahead of everything else. More recently, on the basis of freshman responses on the National College and University Environment Scales, Wheaton ranked in the ninetieth percentile on propriety or orderliness in behavior, and in the ninety-sixth percentile on "community." The Wheaton environment reflects the atmosphere that exists at evangelical schools generally.[33]

As noted in chapter 2, students in the pre–Civil War Christian colleges frequently did not behave well. It has been common to blame the behavioral problems of the early-nineteenth-century period on the rigid rules.

During the 1964–74 period of major student unrest and misconduct, how-ever, the schools with the tightest discipline tended to remain quiet, while those with minimal demands experienced the most trouble. Probably in both periods the tendency toward student misbehavior in a college de-pended more upon the type of students enrolled than upon the nature of the institutions' regulatory systems.

In analyzing why Christian colleges remained calm during the general upheavals of the 1960s and early 1970s, one must begin with—but not end with—the observation that students on the Christian campuses possessed more of God's grace and Dad's discipline than did those on other cam-puses. For example, note the response of one Oral Roberts student to the question of why the students on that campus did not protest: "We're too busy seeking answers in the classroom to the world's problems and trying to help the needy people in the community in our spare time to even think about organizing demonstrations. That's a waste of time compared to what can be accomplished on the one-to-one level. I'd rather spend my time helping persons to feel big and important than in trying to make es-tablishments seem small and irrelevant."[34]

Also important in explaining the Christian college decorum is the fact that Christian college students came from the socio-economic classes that are least prone to use violence. The majority of them grew up in families that were Protestant and nonlabor; that resided outside of major cities; and that held conservative political views on domestic issues. The major public issue that stirred the secular university students to dissent and vio-lence was the Vietnam War; one reason that religious college students did not participate in the violent protest against the war was that most of them did not oppose it. With some notable exceptions (primarily at the Men-nonite, Quaker, and Brethren colleges), Christian college students' views on the war did not differ significantly from the Vietnam policies of the Johnson and Nixon administrations.

Probably the most important reason for the relatively nonviolent at-mosphere of the Christian colleges was the fact that they made it much easier than did the large secular universities for a student to receive per-sonal attention and to develop a satisfactory worldview and life commit-ment. In general, Christian college faculty members showed greater inter-est in teaching and guiding their students, in part because their schools placed minimal or no pressure upon them to conduct and publish re-search. Because they had more time to give to their students, the students acquired fewer of the emotional reactions that develop from a sense of neglect.[35]

While the Christian colleges have been proud of the character of their students and the social environment of their campuses, they sometimes have been disturbed by the excessive expectations of some parents who look for "safe" and even "miracle working" colleges for their young people. Houghton expressed the sentiments of many colleges when it warned parents of undisciplined young people that, while the college will provide a supportive environment, "the school does not offer itself as a reformatory for young people who are too wayward for home restraints."[36]

Still another characteristic of the continuing Christian colleges was the broadly based, inter-institutional cooperation in the promotion and protection of their religious interests. Colleges of the same denomination had always worked together in many ways, but after the secular revolution many institutions came to realize that their closest allies had become the continuing Christian colleges irrespective of denominational affiliation. This movement toward interdenominational cooperation came more easily for colleges affiliated with small denominations than for those related to the large, somewhat exclusive church groups (e.g., Churches of Christ and Independent Disciples, Lutherans, and Southern Baptists). Still, the movement toward cooperation among all continuing Christian colleges gradually attracted an increasing number from these latter groups, as indicated by their growing interest in joining the Christian College Coalition.

Among the organizations developed in this period by and/or for the continuing Christian colleges were the Christian College Coordinating Council for Admissions Officers; the Christian College Referral Service; the *Christian Scholars Review,* an interdisciplinary scholarly journal; the Christian College Consortium; and the Christian College Coalition.

The Christian College Consortium began in 1971 with the active encouragement of Carl Henry, editor of *Christianity Today;* Earl McGrath, director of the Temple University Higher Education Center; and the Lilly Endowment. The original member schools (Bethel of Minnesota, Eastern Mennonite, Gordon, Greenville, Malone, Messiah, Seattle Pacific, Taylor, Westmont, and Wheaton) sought to cooperate in a number of areas, including the more effective promotion of faith and learning integration, the more widespread promotion and explanation of the mission and record of the continuing Christian colleges, the development of cooperative national and international academic programs, and the continuing study of the feasibility of the Christian university idea.[37]

Probably the single most important contribution of the consortium was its founding in 1976 of the Christian College Coalition as a satellite organization with the specific task of protecting the religious and educational freedom of the Christian colleges. The coalition sought to provide a unified voice in the nation's capital for those evangelical Protestant colleges that previously had lacked such representation. The coalition initially identified its objectives as (1) the monitoring of public opinion, legislation, judicial activity, and governmental regulations on matters that could affect the freedom of Christian colleges to function educationally and religiously; (2) the development of unified positions on the critical issues for presentation to governmental agencies, other organizations, and those influential to the formation of public policy; and (3) the development of an offensive position on potential erosions of religious and educational freedom in the Christian college movement. In short, the organization worked partly as a lobbying group—although it would not choose that term to describe itself—and partly as a unifying and educational forum for Christian colleges.[38]

Table 3. Christian College Coalition Membership List (1984)

Anderson (IN) Church of God	Bryan (TN) Independent
Asbury (KY) Independent	Calvin (MI) Christian Reformed
Azusa Pacific (CA) Independent	Campbell (NC) Southern Baptist
Barrington (RI) Independent	Campbellsville (KY) Southern Baptist
Bartlesville Wesleyan (OK) Wesleyan	Central Wesleyan (SC) Wesleyan
Belhaven (MS) Presbyterian	Covenant (TN) Presbyterian Church in America
Bethany Nazarene (OK) Nazarene	Dordt (IA) Christian Reformed
Bethel (IN) Missionary	Eastern (PA) American Baptist
Bethel (KS) Mennonite General Conference	Eastern Mennonite (VA) Mennonite
Bethel (MN) Baptist General Conference	Eastern Nazarene (MA) Nazarene
Biola (CA) Independent	Evangel (MO) Assemblies of God

Fresno Pacific (CA)
Mennonite Brethren

Geneva (PA)
Reformed Presbyterian

George Fox (OR)
Society of Friends

Gordon (MA)
Independent

Grace (IN)
Grace Brethren

Grand Canyon (AZ)
Southern Baptist

Greenville (IL)
Free Methodist

Grove City (PA)
Presbyterian

Houghton (NY)
Wesleyan

Huntington (IN)
United Brethren in Christ

John Brown (AR)
Independent

Judson (IL)
American Baptist

King (TN)
Presbyterian

The King's College (NY)
Independent

Lee (TN)
Church of God

Los Angeles Baptist (CA)
Baptist

Malone (OH)
Society of Friends

Marion (IN)
Wesleyan

Messiah (PA)
Brethren in Christ

Mid America Nazarene (KS)
Nazarene

Mississippi (MS)
Southern Baptist

Mt. Vernon Nazarene (OH)
Nazarene

North Park (IL)
Evangelical Covenant

Northwest Christian (OR)
Disciples of Christ/Independent
Disciples

Northwest Nazarene (ID)
Nazarene

Northwestern (IA)
Reformed Church in America

Northwestern (MN)
Independent

Nyack (NY)
Christian & Missionary Alliance

Olivet Nazarene (IL)
Nazarene

Oral Roberts (OK)
Independent

Palm Beach Atlantic (FL)
Baptist

Point Loma Nazarene (CA)
Nazarene

Roberts Wesleyan (NY)
Wesleyan

Seattle Pacific (WA)
Free Methodist

Simpson (CA)
Christian & Missionary Alliance

Sioux Falls (SD)
American Baptist

Southern California (CA)
Assemblies of God

Spring Arbor (MI)
Free Methodist

Sterling (KS)
Presbyterian

Tabor (KS)
Mennonite Brethren

Taylor (IN)
Independent

Trevecca Nazarene (TN)
Nazarene

Trinity (IL)
Evangelical Free

Trinity Christian (IL)
Christian Reformed/Independent

Warner Pacific (OR)
Church of God

Warner Southern (FL)
Church of God

Westmont (CA)
Independent

Wheaton (IL)
Independent

Whitworth (WA)
Presbyterian

The significance of the Christian College Coalition grew beyond that of its original purpose of protecting religious freedom. As its membership continued to increase (by January, 1984, the number of member schools had grown from the original consortium group of ten to seventy-one colleges), so also did its reputation as the primary interdenominational confederation of continuing Christian liberal arts colleges. Its mere existence and dynamic nature provided the Christian college movement with enhanced unity, influence, and public recognition and appreciation. Increasing numbers of colleges that wished to be recognized as continuing to be clearly Christian institutions joined the coalition. Some colleges sought membership because of the encouragement that affiliation gave them in their efforts to resist the secularization process; others joined because of the hope that the explicit identification as an orthodox Protestant college would assist their admissions efforts in the shrinking student market of the 1980s. While the coalition was the child of the consortium, it was already on the way toward surpassing the parent organization in operation and significance.

In Partnership with the Government

Since the Great Depression, few factors have affected higher education of all types as dramatically as has the major increase in state and especially federal funding. The share of higher education income from public sources grew from only 21 percent in 1929–30 to 79 percent by 1973–74. This growth in public appropriations came not only because of the unprecedented increase in the number and size of public institutions but also because of the growing public aid to private education. Indeed, these resources help explain the improvement in quality of the contemporary Christian colleges that was described earlier in this chapter.[39]

Traditionally, public funds for higher education have come largely from the state governments for the state-owned institutions. Before the 1930s, the federal government maintained only minimal involvement in higher education. The limited early federal legislation benefiting education included the Northwest Ordinance of 1787, the first federal allocation of land for higher education; the Morrill Act of 1862, the first nationwide distribution of land for education; and the Hatch Act of 1887, the first federal program giving aid directly to institutions. Especially during the early national period, the central government considered founding a national university but established neither it nor any central educational agency — except for the military and naval academies — until creating the Office of Education in 1867.[40]

Since the 1930s, the federal government has sharply increased its revenue allocation to higher education. Whereas at the outset of the Depression the federal government supplied only 9 percent of the public appropriations for post-secondary education, by the mid-1970s it was furnishing 45 percent of the total. The first of the modern federal programs was the National Youth Administration (NYA), created during the 1930s when New Deal legislation provided assistance to many impoverished groups in American society. Between 1935 and 1943 the NYA distributed approximately $100 million to the majority of private and public colleges to provide work opportunities for needy students. The GI Bill of 1944 expanded upon both the precedent set by the NYA and also the practice during earlier American wars of rewarding faithful veterans with land or cash bonuses. The GI Bill provided each qualified veteran with funds to pay for post-secondary training in an institution of his or her choice, generally for a period equal to the veteran's wartime service plus one year. More than two million of the fifteen million World War II veterans enrolled in college under the GI Bill, with the result that by 1946 they comprised approximately one-half of all college students and by June, 1949, the Veterans Administration had issued nearly $4 billion in veterans' education payments. The federal government realized that tuition payments did not provide for all of the costs of educating students, and, accordingly, it gave war surplus land, buildings, and equipment to nearly seven hundred colleges. The GI Bill program continued well beyond the World War II period, as did the wartime practice of funding specialized military training and scientific research. Also, the innovative National Defense Education Act of 1958 passed through Congress as much for military reasons as for educational ones.[41]

By the 1960s, however, it was clear that an enlarged philosophy of federal aid was emerging in Washington. The Kennedy and Johnson administrations convinced Congress that it would serve the public interest for the federal government to help finance higher education costs for an increasing number of Americans, irrespective of what they had done or would do directly for the government. Accordingly, the Higher Education Facilities Act of 1963 and the Higher Education Act of 1965 introduced the idea of extensive federal assistance to public and private colleges for physical plant construction and aid to needy students. With the encouragement of these programs, many Christian colleges during the 1960s built instructional facilities and dormitories and expanded their financial aid services.

While in the modern period the federal government has dramatically extended its involvement in higher education, the state governments have added to their traditional appropriations to the state colleges and universities new forms of assistance that have benefited private as well as public institutions. By the mid-1970s only seven states provided no support of any type to the private colleges within their borders, and these states enrolled very few students in private colleges. Almost one-half of the states gave direct support to the independent schools, and approximately two-thirds provided aid to the students attending such institutions. The most common type of state aid to Christian and other independent colleges has come indirectly in the form of scholarships, loans, and grants to students. Also significant in some states has been the practice of allocating aid to institutions in proportion to the number of students enrolled or graduated. For example, in 1976–77, independent schools in New York received $300 for each two-year degree and $940 for each four-year degree awarded. Similar institutions in Georgia received $500 per student, and the private schools in Maryland collected 15 percent of the state institution subsidy rate.[42]

Response to the participation of church-related colleges in the federal and state aid programs varied widely. Among the most alarmed was C. Stanley Lowell, associate director of Americans United for Separation of Church and State, who argued in 1971 that if a religious college accepted public aid it must admit students and hire faculty without considering their religious orientation, and it could no longer require chapel services or religious studies. The American Civil Liberties Union policy statement of 1965 approved sharply limited forms of aid including scholarships, loans, and GI Bill assistance to students in other than theological schools and for research on nonreligious topics. Of the major denominations, the Southern Baptist Convention exercised the most caution in approving government aid for its colleges. The general pattern of the Southern Baptist schools was to allow aid to students but not to accept it, except in the form of loans, for the institutions. Some Southern Baptist colleges accepted much more public aid than did others, with the exact policy in each case depending upon the philosophy of the state convention and the degree of autonomy that the convention allowed the trustees of a given college. Furman and Stetson caused a national stir in the 1960s when their trustees chose to act contrary to the instruction of their state conventions and accept federal grants for science building construction. Furman, however, agreed to return its $611,898 grant when the South Carolina convention promised to provide similar funds.[43]

One of the bolder responses to the concept of public aid for private institutions was to propose tuition equalization grants to students enrolled in private colleges. In recognition of the declining percentage of college-bound youth enrolling in private institutions because of sharply increasing costs (the ratio between private and public college tuition grew from 3.5:1 in 1956–57 to 5:1 in 1974–75), the Carnegie Council in 1975 called for the federal government to provide grants on a matching basis with the states to pay private college enrollees approximately one-half the average subsidy provided per student in a state university (the state university subsidies in 1973–74 averaged approximately $2,000). Similarly, in 1975 the National Conference of Independent Colleges and Universities called for tuition equalization grants ranging from 25 percent to 75 percent of the state subsidy. By contrast, private colleges did not show enthusiasm for the legislation proposed by Senators Daniel Moynihan (NY), Bob Packwood (OR), and others whereby parents would receive up to a $500 annual federal income tax credit for tuition paid to enroll a child in an elementary, secondary, or post-secondary institution. The plan as proposed would greatly aid families with children in private, pre-college schools but would provide little, if any, advantage over present forms of assistance to families of private college students.[44]

Some traditionally Christian colleges sought the newly available tax funds so eagerly that they were willing to abrogate their denominational relationships, sharply reduce or eliminate their religious identities, and drop the mandatory nature of their chapel services and religious courses in an effort to guarantee the continuance of such assistance. Probably the most publicized case of this type was that of Methodist-related Western Maryland which in 1975 gave up, perhaps unnecessarily, much of its religious identity in order to qualify for state aid. The college agreed not to describe itself as church-related, to remain totally neutral in the spiritual development of its students, and to remove all religious symbols from the campus.[45]

Despite the broad spectrum of opinion on the use of public aid, nearly universal agreement existed among the Christian colleges on the following points: aid to individual students is acceptable whether they elect to attend public or private institutions (e.g., even such a staunchly independent school as Baptist Bible of Missouri distributed Basic Educational Opportunity Grants and GI Bill benefits);[46] aid to individuals clearly is preferable to direct aid to institutions; and as the state and federal governments reevaluate old and develop new programs of aid to private higher education, they must be careful to avoid violating the "free exercise" clause of the First Amendment by discriminating against the church-related institutions.

Often in American history the appearance of a new and controversial type of legislation leads to litigation to test its constitutionality. During the 1970s, the federal and state courts tried a significant number of cases on the issue of public aid to private colleges. Although the Supreme Court had been hearing similar cases involving private elementary and secondary schools since *Everson v. Board of Education* in 1947, challenges to aid for higher education did not appear until after the adoption of the 1963 and 1965 federal higher education acts and the expansion of the state aid programs. The 1971 case of *Tilton v. Richardson* was the first time the Supreme Court ruled on a suit challenging the constitutionality of federal aid to private higher education. The Court decided that federal aid programs (in this case, the Higher Education Facilities Act of 1963) could benefit such church-related colleges as were not "pervasively religious" in nature. Under *Tilton,* church colleges qualifying for aid included those that did not discriminate on religious grounds in faculty hiring and student admissions, did not maintain compulsory religious activities, did not "proselytize" religious doctrine in their courses, and met the generally acceptable standards for academic freedom. Prior to *Tilton,* the widespread assumption was that public funds could go to religious colleges if the aid served a secular (e.g., science building or dormitory construction) purpose. Now *Tilton* introduced the new philosophy, which the subsequent Supreme Court cases of *Hunt v. McNair* (1975) and *Roemer v. Board of Public Works* (1976) generally supported, that the nature of an institution's religious emphasis was also a factor in determining eligibility. A large number of the continuing Christian colleges likely did not meet all of the criteria established by *Tilton.* It is not clear, however, that the *Tilton* standard for receiving aid was universally applicable. Even if such were the case, there was little reason to believe that Christian colleges that might be barred from receiving direct governmental aid could not continue to accept students who received assistance under one or another of the federal student aid programs.[47]

The question of the constitutionality of state aid programs was even more complex because of the differing nature and philosophy of the fifty state constitutions, aid programs, and courts. Probably the most important cases came from Maryland, Kansas, and Missouri. In the 1976 *Roemer* case from Maryland, the litigants, represented by the Americans United for the Separation of Church and State, challenged the right of one Methodist and four Roman Catholic colleges to participate in the state program which, as mentioned earlier, distributed to the eighteen private colleges annual grants per pupil equal to 15 percent of the state appropriation per student in the four-year state colleges. In essence the Supreme Court approved the earlier ruling of the federal district court that the colleges in question qualified for the aid program because they met the eligibility criteria of the *Tilton* case.

The issue in the Kansas and Missouri cases was the validity of the state scholarship programs that aided students in religious as well as secular institutions. In *Americans United v. Bubb* (1974), the federal district court applied to the Kansas indirect aid program an even more severe set of eligibility criteria than those listed in *Tilton* for a direct assistance program. It ruled that five colleges did not qualify but could do so by taking remedial action. Accordingly, the five colleges dropped the disqualifying features of their programs, with three of them ending the mandatory nature of their chapel services.

By contrast, the related Mid-American Nazarene case met with a different result. In 1979 the Kansas Attorney General reversed the 1972 ruling of a predecessor that the students in the Nazarene school did not qualify for the state grants because the college chose to continue to require attendance at its chapel services. Also, in 1976 the Missouri Supreme Court sustained the state's tuition grant program that aided students in the seventeen church-affiliated colleges as well as the other private and public institutions. This case was significant partly because it was the first major ruling following the *Roemer* case and partly because the Missouri state constitutional provision calling for the separation of church and state was unusually explicit.[48]

Two major cases that indirectly affected the issue of aid to church-related schools were those of Grove City (PA) and Oral Roberts. Grove City beginning in 1977 refused to sign the federal form showing compliance with Title IX of the Education Amendments of 1972 which bans discrimination against women. Grove City based its action on the principle of institutional autonomy rather than on a desire to defend a questionable institutional practice. The Pennsylvania college had never received any direct aid, and for many years after 1979 it was to be in court with the government over whether the latter could deny aid to Grove City students because of the school's refusal to sign the compliance form. In past years the Grove City students received no federal financial assistance.

Meanwhile, Oral Roberts was battling, not with the government but with a professional accrediting agency. In 1981 an American Bar Association (ABA) accreditation committee recommended that accreditation not be granted the new but well-developed Oral Roberts Law School, primarily because it required a Christian commitment of students and faculty. Oral Roberts filed suit, and a federal court preliminary ruling determined that the ABA action violated the university's right to freedom of religion. The ABA reluctantly amended its standards on religion for religious institutions to require only that such schools advertise clearly their admission and employment policies to students, faculty, and others involved. While few Christian colleges operated law schools, all were very interested in the question of whether the government could withhold aid from students who attend a college that requires religious commitments from the faculty it hires and the students it admits.[49]

By the 1980s, a summary of the not always consistent results of the first decade of litigation over public aid to higher education included the following points: (1) Christian colleges are not automatically excluded from federal and state aid programs; (2) the courts are more sympathetic to aid for religious colleges than for religious secondary and elementary schools and are more willing to approve assistance to individuals than to institutions; (3) aid to religious institutions cannot be for specifically religious programs; (4) direct aid would probably be denied to pervasively sectarian colleges, although it is often difficult to determine equitably which colleges fit this category; (5) there had not yet emerged from these cases a clear set of universally applicable and specific principles because of an inherent conflict between the application of the establishment clause and that of the free exercise clause of the First Amendment (legislation that is too inclusive violates the former, while acts that are too restrictive violate the latter).[50] As the Christian college moves into the twenty-first century its relationship with government and the latter's resources will continue and in some ways become more regular; that, however, is one of the stories for the next chapter.

7

On to the Twenty-first Century

Never before the present period has the mainstream world of letters and journalism demonstrated such a contrast between its expressions of dismay toward the secular university and its general appreciation for the Christian college. At least since the appearance of Allan Bloom's *The Closing of the American Mind: How Higher Education Has Failed Democracy and Impoverished the Soul of Today's Students* (1987)[1] and Page Smith's *Killing the Spirit: Higher Education in America* (1990),[2] and with increasing intensity to the present,[3] the general modern critique of secular higher education has bemoaned the tendency to replace the character and values education dimension of learning with an intellectual conformity and an anti-religion bias. Even the traditionally elite institutions themselves are becoming aware of their growing barrenness, as noted recently by Columbia University professor Andrew Delbanco: "There is a nervous sense that something basic is missing—a nervousness that may account for the rise of compensatory institutions within the institutions such as the Center for Human Values at Princeton . . . or the Institute of Ethics at Duke. But what can it mean that thinking about ethics has become mostly an extracurricular activity?"[4]

By contrast, the media headlines in essays on faith-based higher education carry such headlines as "Christian Colleges Are Booming" (*Time*), "The Opening of the Evangelical Mind" (*The Atlantic Monthly*), and "Evangelical Colleges Gaining Ground in Secular World" (*Los Angeles Times*). Primarily the attention is upon the orthodox colleges and is inspired in part by the widely publicized enrollment growth statistics distributed by Robert Andringa, President of the Council for Christian Colleges & Universities (CCCU). This data shows an enrollment increase of 67.3 percent for the CCCU institutions and 2.1 percent for all colleges and universities for the 1992–2002 decade. The focus on enrollment increase has led to a closer study of the growing academic attainments of the intentionally Christian institutions. Also very significant is the growth of religious intentionality by the mainline church-related colleges and universities who are influenced by the broadly based 2004 UCLA Astin Study documenting the interest in the spiritual domain by the large majority of college students.[5]

During the late twentieth century a number of factors converged to contribute to the sharp increase in the quality of the Christian college and the heightened interest in finding an acceptable way to reintroduce a larger role for religion in the academy in general. These developments included (1) the rise of the evangelical churches simultaneous with the decline of the mainline denominations; (2) the emergence of the CCCU to give increasing structure, influence, and recognition to the Christian college movement; (3) the fascinating and highly publicized saga of Baylor University in its effort to become the primary model of a Christian research university; (4) the influential writings of higher education prophets such as Mark Noll (to the Christian colleges), George Marsden (to the secular universities), and Ernest Boyer (to all of higher education); (5) a growing opportunity within secular higher education for the consideration of the spiritual domain because of a declining faith in the worldview of modernism; (6) the sharply growing public interest in spirituality, especially among young people, since the 1980s; (7) the availability of unprecedented foundation monies — especially from the Lilly Endowment and the Pew Charitable Trusts — to stimulate study, discussion, networking, and program development on the role of religion in higher education; and (8) a growing partnership with Catholic colleges and universities in the common effort to preserve and at least partly recover an appropriate emphasis upon the dimension of faith in the study of the human condition.

In addition to enjoying the growing prosperity of its traditional campus-based programs, the turn-of-the-century Christian college has encouraged its regular students to study and engage in service projects abroad, and it has provided instruction in new forms (especially electronic courses) to new groups (primarily working adults) in new locations (almost anywhere). Also it has established linkages with and provided encouragement to the growing number of similar institutions worldwide. Meanwhile the Christian college has continued to carefully observe the federal and state governments with an eye both appreciative (especially for the significant student financial aid) and wary (because of the uncertain pattern of legislative and judicial actions).

The Recovery Continues

The United States Department of Education identifies approximately nine hundred religiously affiliated colleges and universities.[6] The traditional way of further distinguishing such institutions is to classify them by denominational connection, and while such categorizing continues to be helpful, it is less meaningful now than is a system of identification that focuses upon the degree to which the Christian worldview is the central organizing principle of a college's intellectual program. Perhaps the best-developed such typology is that offered by Robert Benne in his fine study, *Quality with Soul*; the summary chart of his schema appears as appendix B at the end of the book.[7] Benne's typology identifies two categories of Christian colleges, namely the "orthodox" and "critical-mass" institutions. A third type of church-related college, the intentionally pluralist, provides the Christian worldview an assumed but not a privileged voice, while the fourth type, ironically, does not even do that. It is the orthodox college, with its most distinguishing feature being that of employing only confessing Christians as scholars, that has been the most dynamic model in recent decades, and it is the Council of Christian Colleges & Universities that serves as the umbrella organization for the orthodox/evangelical Protestant institutions.[8]

Developing from its parent organization, the fourteen-member Christian College Consortium (which still exists) and changing from its previous name (the Christian College Coalition) in 1999, the CCCU developed at a rate that largely coincided with the growing prominence of the evangelical movement in general. Prospering especially during the presidential tenures of John Dellenback (1977–88) and Robert Andringa (1994–2006), the member institutions grew in number from 38 in 1977 to 77 in 1988 to 105 representing 27 denominations (plus 69 affiliate members) in 2004.[9]

Presently CCCU membership (see appendix C) is limited to North American, primarily undergraduate, liberal arts colleges, although a variety of other institutions — for example, Bible colleges, graduate seminaries, and universities, and especially overseas institutions (see section titled "New Constituencies and Extended Borders" in this chapter) — have become affiliate members. By the 1990s, the CCCU had gained recognition in the world of private higher education in general and in the Washington, DC, government-education network in particular, comparable to that of the Association of Catholic Colleges and Universities. Among the denominations with colleges joining the CCCU for the first time (or in much larger numbers) since 1984 are the Southern Baptists, the Christian Church and Churches of Christ (Independent), the Churches of Christ, the General Association of Regular Baptists, the Seventh-Day Adventists, and the Pentecostals. Additionally, many independent colleges and some former Bible colleges have joined the organization. The 2005 CCCU comprehensive institutional membership of 174 when identified by denominational affiliation includes sixty-one independent, twenty-two Southern Baptist, twelve

Nazarene, nine Presbyterian (six PCUSA), six Christian Church or Churches of Christ, five Assemblies of God, five Christian and Missionary Alliance, five Free Methodist, five Mennonite, four Wesleyan Church, three American Baptist, and three Christian Reformed. One Catholic university (Franciscan of Steubenville) and one Russian Orthodox institution (St. Petersburg School of Religion and Philosophy) are also members, but there are no institutions from the United Methodist, United Church of Christ, Episcopal, or Lutheran (some Missouri Synod Lutheran colleges have made inquiry) traditions. Of the evangelical denominations, the Nazarenes, the Seventh-Day Adventists, and the Christian Reformed have maintained close relationships with their denominations. Nevertheless, in general the evangelical denominations, like their mainstream counterparts, have loosened their formal organization connections with their colleges.[10]

The sharp growth in the number of independent CCCU colleges is noteworthy. It reflects both the general decline of denominational loyalty and the rise of the independent church movement in the late twentieth century. The Hartford Institute for Religion Research estimates that there are 35,000 independent or nondenominational congregations with a membership of ten million, thus making the movement larger than any Protestant denomination except for the Southern Baptists. Almost all (82 percent) of these independent congregations describe themselves as evangelical, fundamentalist, charismatic, or Pentecostal. Thus, the two largest Protestant groups of churches are also the two groups most represented in the CCCU institutions.[11]

In addition to the CCCU, the second major organization of orthodox colleges is the Association for Biblical Higher Education (ABHE), which until 2004 was known as the Accrediting Association of Bible Colleges. The change in name reflects a change in organization to better serve a changing constituency. While some Bible colleges continue to evolve into liberal arts colleges — for example, Crown (MN), Simpson (CA), Southeastern (FL), and Vanguard (CA) — others have added graduate programs. Meanwhile, hundreds of new institutions have come into existence since 1980, bringing the total of Bible schools and colleges to more than 1,200. The expanded ABHE organization has added to its traditional role of providing institution-wide, undergraduate theological accreditation, as it now also reviews graduate education for its members, offers church vocation and program evaluation for comprehensive institutions that hold general accreditation with another recognized accreditation organization, and provides general development services for its affiliate institutions. By 2005 the ABHE claimed 88 members and 45 affiliate members (see appendix D).[12]

The orthodox and critical-mass colleges worked cooperatively during the past decade in a number of Christian scholarship endeavors. These include the *Christian Scholars Review* (*CSR*), which is currently sponsored by 47 colleges (up from 26 in 1984), including Baylor, Grove City, Hope, Pepperdine, Saint Olaf, and Samford as well as 41 CCCU institutions.[13] Also Lutheran, Catholic, and evangelical scholars work together as editors, contributors, or readers for *Cresset*, published at Valparaiso as one of the older collegiate-based periodicals of religious thought in the United States, and *First Things*, published by the Institute on Religion and Public Life. The Lilly Fellows Program (LFP), also based at Valparaiso and designed to facilitate dialogue on the relationship between Christianity and the academic vocation, has involved, since 1991, a network of approximately 70 institutions led by Lutheran, Catholic, and evangelical colleges and universities, plus a few others (five Presbyterian, five United Methodist, two traditionally African American, one Disciples of Christ, and one Episcopalian). Influenced by the LFP, the most significant new common endeavor of the twenty-first century is the Lilly Endowment–funded Programs for the Theological Exploration of Vocation (PTEV) initiative, involving approximately 20 each of Catholic and evangelical colleges and 10 each of Lutheran, Presbyterian, and Methodist colleges out of a total of 88 institutions. For a complete list of the LFP and PTEV institutions, including those that have operated as pluralist colleges, see appendices E and F. In addition to the 88 PTEV grant recipients, more than three times as many other colleges applied for the grants. Never in the history of Christian higher education in America had so many colleges (375) applied for so much aid from a single program for the purpose of assisting in a campuswide effort to enhance the faith domain (in this case the relationship between faith and vocational purpose).[14]

It is possible that the Lilly PTEV program may do as much in the early twenty-first century to stimulate thoughtful spirituality in church-related higher education—and beyond—as the Carnegie Pension Fund did to discourage the same in the early twentieth century (see page 99). The results to date are encouraging even if preliminary. Nearly all of the earliest colleges to receive grants are now planning to make their programs permanent.

In general among the mainline PTEV institutions, those which have secularized the least and the most recently (e.g., such Midwestern Lutheran colleges as Luther, Concordia-Moorhead, and Augsburg) are the ones that have most easily developed broad-based programs. Yet no less significant are the efforts to reintroduce religious discourse into the academic arena in institutions where it had largely disappeared. "Some schools have taken steps that may appear small to an outsider, but signal a major opening internally to engage, in fresh ways, questions about their religious heritage," notes Christopher Coble, Lilly PTEV director.

College leaders comment how the program has given them a natural vehicle by which to "break the culture of silence" regarding the spiritual domain. For example, at Hendrix, the recent alumni are astonished by the freedom and naturalness with which the current students and faculty talk and think about religion in a reflective way. By contrast, some of the PTEV institutions that have never been silent about religion simply use their grants to strengthen existing programs, such as Howard's cooperative endeavor between the chaplain's office and the faculty to enhance the discipline-specific programs in ethics and spirituality.

Some of the PTEV colleges (e.g., Butler, Wake Forest, and Sewanee or University of the South) that have become independent of their founding denomination and have increasingly admitted students and hired faculty of other faith and non-faith traditions are using their grant in significant part to access how in this new environment of independence and pluralism they can best facilitate religious inquiry. As the president of Butler, Bobby Fong, asked in the immediate context of the national tragedy of September 11, 2001, "How can you serve a community well without a religious dimension?" Essentially such colleges are seeking both to communicate the idea that faith is and always has been a vital part of being human, and then to develop systems that best encourage individual religious inquiry without institutionally advocating a specific outcome.

Other major emphases in the PTEV colleges include new courses, faculty-development programs, and student service-learning programs. For example, Willamette and Macalaster are offering innovative academic experiences for interested students, while Furman and Davidson are introducing seminars to enhance the theological and vocational understanding of new and existing faculty. While nearly all of the colleges give major emphasis to student ministry programs, these become more nearly the sole focus at some of the more secular institutions. In most institutions the students have embraced the PTEV programs more eagerly than have the faculty, the denominations associated with the colleges appreciate the emphasis upon mentoring more and better-qualified ministerial candidates, and the institutional leaders appreciate the large degree of freedom that the program gives each individual institution to develop programs that best fit its environment.[15]

The number of liberal arts institutions that applied for the PTEV grants (375) is one indicator of the number of intentionally Christian colleges in the United States that now have a serious interest in facilitating the faith development of their students. That number compares closely, albeit on the high side, with the estimate of the Robert Andringa chart (see appendix A), which identifies approximately 250 Protestant liberal arts colleges that are "more or less intentional about integrating their faith with their mission." The Andringa chart also suggests that there are 150 other traditionally Protestant institutions "who have pretty much neglected their faith tradition." Perhaps the PTEV program will help to reduce the number of institutions in the latter category.

If the Christian colleges are becoming more prosperous, more focused on their traditional Christian worldview, and more ecumenical in working with similar institutions, are they also becoming more scholarly? The consensus answer is yes, but the commentators on this subject differ considerably in how they present their affirmative responses. George Marsden notes that since the 1980s the Christian colleges have accelerated their pace of recovery with better-qualified faculty, more academically strong colleges, more study centers, and more scholarly activity. Also, Richard Gathro, the executive vice president of the CCCU, observes that now in the early twenty-first century, "The overall quality of faculty on our campuses is the best that it has ever been." One further mark of academic development is a growing capacity to engage in self-criticism when writing authorized institutional history (note, for example, the recent histories of Point Loma and John Brown). As the evangelical academic community has become more scholarly, the general academy has joined the evangelical scholars in increasingly focusing upon American evangelicalism as a subject for study. Larry Eskridge of the Institute for the Study of American evangelism reports that since the early 1990s, the number of scholarly books appearing yearly on evangelicalism has increased three-fold.[16]

Within the evangelical colleges the single most significant vehicle for promoting the expansion of scholarly writing has been the faith and learning integration concept (see pp. 193–94). This integration idea, stemming especially from such centers as Calvin (led by Nicholas Wolterstorff and others), Wheaton (led by Arthur Holmes), and, more recently, Baylor (led by Michael Beaty and Douglas Henry) and affecting especially the humanities, sciences, and social sciences (led by philosophy and history), became widely influential within the orthodox institutions (such as those in the CCCU). The central concepts of this system are that "all truth is God's truth" and that humans should seek to apply God's truth to every area of learning and every social system.

The influence of the faith and learning integration model can be measured by its impact on the development of new professional organizations and college courses. The discipline-specific faith and learning integration organizations numbered approximately fifty by the early twenty-first century; and with their membership drawn largely but not exclusively from the orthodox colleges and their emphasis upon integration scholarship (and fellowship and mutual encouragement), they were in large part an application of the integration system of thought. Also, in our 2004 study of the curriculum of the church-related institutions, research assistant

Christopher Burns and I found that 50 percent of the CCCU member colleges offer a required faith and learning integration course (usually at the freshman or senior level).[17]

A second major recent system for bringing together faith and learning was the Christian vocation model. Developed at Valparaiso University and most commonly associated with Mark Schwehn and his book *Exiles from Eden* (1993), this vocational emphasis was a central principle of the Lilly Fellows Program. It has been especially influential in the critical-mass institutions (and the would-be critical-mass institutions), increasingly so in the twenty-first century as such thinking is at the center of the major Lilly Endowment Theological Exploration of Vocation (PTEV) Program. The vocation model of Christian scholarship places less emphasis upon the development of well-reasoned compelling arguments than upon a deep personal quest to find the best basis for practicing scholarship (or any other calling). Doing follows being. With a mature sense of being, then, the Christian scholar works at the scholarly task humbly, communally, and with a sense of intellectual openness.[18]

In many respects Schwehn's vocation model overlaps with the ideas of other major recent theorists of Christian scholarship: Douglas and Rhonda Jacobsen, Parker Palmer, and Ernest Boyer. The Jacobsens, while appreciative of the contributions of the Reformed model of integration especially in stimulating the renaissance in evangelical scholarship after 1975, argue that there are other viable approaches to doing Christian scholarship. Reflecting the Arminian and Anabaptist traditions of their institution, Messiah, the Jacobsens favor an approach to learning which values humility and dialogue more than apologetics, debate, and "waging war for the faith through the means of heavily footnoted books and rapier-like essays." Palmer offers that the best Christian scholarship is "transformational learning" in which the scholar continually seeks to develop personally by that which he or she learns and teaches. Boyer, a graduate of two CCCU institutions, Messiah and Greenville, rose to become one of the most respected voices in American education during the late twentieth century while serving as president of the Carnegie Foundation for the Advancement of Teaching and as Jimmy Carter's Commissioner of Education. His widely discussed book, *Scholarship Reconsidered: Priorities of the Professoriate* (1990), emphasized how American higher education had placed undue emphasis upon one form of scholarship, namely research and publishing, and too little emphasis upon another form of scholarship, namely classroom instruction. Thus the Schwehn-Jacobsens-Palmer-Boyer model of scholarship values research and publication (the leaders of this model all are masters of the craft) but never to the neglect of one's best effort in the classroom and never to the exclusion of the development of lived-out truth in the totality of one's life.[19]

Amidst all of the discussion of the recent progress of Christian scholarship, one voice, Mark Noll, stands out as a reminder of the degree to which evangelical scholarship and the evangelical movement in general still falls short. While acknowledging the recent improvement since the appearance of his *Scandal of the Evangelical Mind* (1994), Noll wonders why a group that can so readily voice the scriptural command to love the Lord thy God with all thy heart and all thy mind fails to seek to practice the latter as much as the former. Essentially Noll is calling for a greater balance in the values and allocation of resources by evangelicals in their total sense and practice of mission. Not a scold by nature, Noll is in fact a very generous and kind-hearted man. Arguably the premier evangelical scholar of the current generation, few scholars of any type are as erudite, productive, and irenic in combination as is he.[20]

Noll and the other major contributors to the enhanced reputation of evangelical scholarship received significant funding for their labors from mainline Protestant foundations much more than from the evangelical foundations, the latter of which remained largely focused on evangelism, youth ministry, and missions. Beginning in the late 1970s, the Lilly Endowment and the Pew Charitable Trusts became major funders of not only the projects of individual evangelical scholars but also evangelical academic conferences (e.g., "The Bible in American History" and "Reforming the Center: Beyond the Two-Party System in American Protestantism") and study centers (the Institute for the Study of American Evangelicals); of course, especially the Lilly Endowment was funding similar efforts in the critical-mass colleges and universities (see section titled "Enlarging the Faith and Learning Dialogue" in this chapter).[21]

In general, the state of Christian scholarship appears much better than it did in the 1980s because (1) the Christian academicians are producing more significant works of scholarship; (2) the Christian academic communities are less isolated, more readily identifying with the contributions of one another, and thus perceiving themselves as a part of a larger—and more significant—whole; and (3) there is a broadening definition of scholarship that allows the Christian colleges to better realize how well they had been doing all along in certain aspects of spiritually informed intellectual activity, namely collegiality and caring, incarnational teaching.

If the turn-of-the-century Christian colleges have continued to progress in reputation, resources, campus environment, and scholarship, which of them are exemplary in this development? Within the CCCU, among the generally recognized leaders are Calvin, Wheaton, and Gordon in scholarship; Taylor, Westmont, Calvin, Whitworth, John Brown, Azusa, and Seattle Pacific in campus community; Belhaven and Nyack in diversity development; and Union, Lee, Palm Beach Atlantic, Biola, Point Loma, Dordt, Northwestern (MN), Houghton, Oklahoma Christian, Bethel (MN),

Messiah, Goshen, Abilene Christian, Lipscomb, and Asbury in overall quality.[22]

CCCU schools that have repeatedly (since 1990) ranked high in the *U.S. News and World Report* (*USNWR*) "Best Colleges" rankings include Wheaton, Westmont, Erskine, Gordon, Goshen, Houghton, Whitworth, Seattle Pacific, Calvin, Taylor, Oklahoma Baptist, Messiah, John Brown, Asbury, Dordt, Covenant, Oklahoma Christian, Master's, George Fox, North Park, Northwest Nazarene, LeTourneau, Eastern Mennonite, College of the Ozarks, Bethel (MN), and Western Baptist. Also listed regularly in the recent *USNWR* rankings are (1) *Christian Scholars Review* (*CSR*) institutions: Pepperdine and Baylor, among the national universities, and also Saint Olaf, Hope, Samford, and Grove City; (2) PTEV or LFP institutions: Duke, Wake Forest, and Howard among the national universities, and also Davidson, Grinnell, Macalester, Sewanee, Furman, Occidental, Rhodes, Denison, Willamette, Wooster, Spelman, Wofford, Austin, Earlham, Hendrix, Gustavus Adolphus, Transylvania, Augustana (IL), Luther, Wittenberg, Alma, Concordia Moorhead, Georgetown, Guilford, Hastings, Westminster (PA), Roanoke, Mercer, Valparaiso, Butler, Hamline, Pacific Lutheran, Berea, Maryville, Elmhurst, and Augsburg; and (3) Southern Baptist, Lutheran, and independent institutions not already mentioned: Stetson, Bellmont, Ouachita Baptist, Texas Lutheran, and Berry.[23]

Among the colleges enrolling high numbers of freshmen National Merit Scholars are CCCU or CSR institutions Wheaton, Baylor, Saint Olaf, Furman, Calvin; and PTEV institutions Duke, Macalester, and Grinnell. Those with high endowments include CCCU or CSR institutions Baylor, Pepperdine, College of the Ozarks, Regent, Wheaton, Samford, Saint Olaf, Abilene Christian, Loma Linda; and PTEV or LFP institutions Duke, Grinnell, Wake Forest, Berea, Macalester, Howard, Earlham, Davidson, Furman, Occidental, Spelman, Sewanee, Rhodes, Willamette, and Mercer; and independent Berry. Those identified on the Carnegie Foundation listing of major doctoral-granting institutions in the mid-1990s include CCCU or CSR institutions Andrews, Baylor, Biola, Loma Linda, Pepperdine; and PTEV universities Duke, Howard, and Wake Forest. Institutions producing significant numbers of undergraduates who proceed to complete doctoral programs include CCCU or CSR institutions Baylor, Saint Olaf, Wheaton, Calvin, Hope, Abilene Christian, Mississippi, Oklahoma Baptist, Samford, Goshen, Grove City, Houghton; and PTEV or LFP institutions Duke, Wake Forest, Valparaiso, Wooster, Grinnell, Occidental, Macalester, Furman, Davidson, Earlham, Luther, Wittenberg, Gustavus Adolphus, Denison, Rhodes, Augustana (IL), Spelman, Pacific Lutheran, Concordia at Moorhead, Hendrix, Butler, and Berea; and Harding and Juniata. Among the institutions with high graduation rates are CCCU or

CSR institutions Wheaton, Saint Olaf, Pepperdine, Taylor, Grove City, Hope, Houghton, Calvin, Messiah, Westmont, Baylor, Franciscan of Steubenville; and PTEV or LFP institutions Duke, Wake Forest, Davidson, Grinnell, Furman, Sewanee, Macalester, Luther, Occidental, Augustana, Wofford, Spelman, Trinity, Austin, Rhodes, Valparaiso, Presbyterian, Wittenberg, Elmhurst, Wartburg, and Earlham.[24]

New Constituencies and Extended Borders

Since the decline of the nineteenth-century pre-collegiate academies (see pp. 60, 70–71, 132), the Christian college had educated primarily young undergraduate students within the confines of the campus boundaries. This changed sharply in the late twentieth century as the Christian colleges moved increasingly into graduate training, adult degree-completion programs (often at off-campus sites), and distance learning and other forms of electronic instruction, and also encouraged their traditional students to study and serve abroad for periods ranging from a month (e.g., January term) to a year. Furthermore, the Christian colleges of this country developed networks with similar institutions around the world.

A significant part of the enrollment increase in Christian higher education is due to the new programs. Some institutions (e.g., Indiana Wesleyan, Azusa Pacific, Biola, Wayland Baptist, and Dallas Baptist) have grown from small colleges to medium-sized universities by their investment in such ventures. Others who made major commitments to curricular innovation include Liberty, Grand Canyon, Regent, LaTourneau, Belhaven, George Fox, Spring Arbor, Roberts Wesleyan, Bethel (MN), Cornerstone, and several of the Nazarene institutions.[25]

The quality of the graduate programs in Christian higher education is often undervalued because of the tendency to place in a separate category its most important and best-developed component, namely the theological seminary. By the early twenty-first century, the largest ten (Fuller, Southwestern Baptist, New Orleans Baptist, Southern Baptist, Gordon-Conwell, Dallas, Southeastern Baptist, Asbury, Trinity, and Golden Gate Baptist) and nearly all of the largest twenty-five seminaries in America were evangelical or orthodox in nature, thus further accelerating the trend in place by 1980 (see n. 18 of chapter 6). Most of the recent student enrollment growth has been with women and minorities, and in evangelical, including Southern Baptist, seminaries. Additionally, among graduate institutions of all types, evangelical seminaries Fuller and Trinity have become the leading producers of dissertations on missions.[26]

Among the intentionally Christian universities, those with the broadest range of major professional and graduate programs are Baylor and Pepperdine. Baylor and Pepperdine both have highly regarded law and business schools. The Baylor graduate school lists more than sixty master's-level programs, and the Baylor 2012 Plan (see the end of the section titled "The Mainline Reassesses" in this chapter) intends to steadily increase the number of doctoral programs (fifteen in 2002) as a major component in its plan to become a premier Christian university. Especially noteworthy is the goal of adding doctoral programs in the humanities and social sciences, the thinnest curricular area in Christian higher education. Nearly two-thirds of Pepperdine's eight thousand students are graduate students with most of them enrolled in the schools of business and management, education and psychology, public policy, and law. Besides Baylor and Pepperdine, other institutions with law schools include Wake Forest, Mercer, Howard, Samford, Stetson, Willamette, Campbell, Mississippi, Regent, Valparaiso, and Capital. Samford has a sizable pharmacology program and recently opened one of the most significant new evangelical seminaries. Loma Linda's unusually extensive curriculum within the health sciences reflects the Seventh-Day Adventist holistic approach to human development. Andrews offers fifty master's and ten doctoral (mostly in theology and education) programs.[27]

Reflective of the recent movement of the CCCU institutions into graduate education is that a majority of them now use the term "university" in their name. Of the 102 United States members, sixty-nine offer master's-level programs while approximately twenty offer doctoral programs. Education at all levels is the most common curriculum, with Azusa Pacific, Baylor, and Regent (VA) offering doctoral programs for those pursuing careers in higher education. Even the Bible colleges have embraced advanced programs, as their constituency is increasingly expectant of a graduate degree for their ministry professionals. The M.A. rather than the M.Div. is the most common Bible college graduate degree with one-third of the Bible colleges now offering postgraduate instruction.[28]

One of the most significant new Christian universities, Regent University, operates almost totally as a graduate institution. Pat Robertson, televangelist and son of a Virginia senator, sought to found a graduate professional program to train Christian leaders in areas that could have the greatest impact in changing society. He began with communications in 1978 and added education, counseling, psychology, entrepreneur business, law, government, and theology, meanwhile developing a Washington, DC–area campus and an unusually large endowment base for a young institution. Enrolling 3,200 students in 2003–04, Regent operates with an evangelical theology broader than the founder's charismatic views, although the university is largely reflective of Robertson's political conservatism.[29]

Since 1990 the fastest-growing segment of higher education has been the working adult population, and most of the institutions emerging to serve this market with user-friendly programs have been small, often urban, evangelical or Catholic colleges with low endowments.

The most popular new curriculum has been the degree-completion program. Approximately one-half of college freshmen fail to earn the baccalaureate degree before assuming careers and/or family responsibilities, and when they discover that colleges would offer them a plan to complete their degree in a relatively short period of time (e.g., eighteen to twenty continuous months for the last two undergraduate years) in convenient locations with sometimes reduced formal classtime demands, moderate tuition fees, and financial aid packages, all while continuing their regular employment, many are interested.[30]

The more traditional colleges and universities — religious and secular — raised questions about the credibility of the new programs. Were they "bargain basement" programs that compromised quality and sometimes institutional mission to earn "easy money" (many of the programs employed high numbers of inexpensive, part-time instructors and in general required low maintenance) to enhance or even save their traditional programs? The defenders noted that innovative programs designed to bring the benefits of education to new population groups have always required time to develop quality controls.[31]

Among the evangelical institutions, the generally recognized leader in the field of nontraditional higher education is Indiana Wesleyan, which began its program in 1985, hired an aggressive young president, James Barnes, to promote it, and benefited from being in a state with a low college graduation rate and no community-college system. In the past decade, the IWU College of Adult and Professional Studies has come to maturity under the leadership of Mark Smith, being especially exemplary in quality control, the facilitation of student success, and a faith and learning integration emphasis commensurate with that of the traditional program. By 2005 the university's nontraditional programs enrolled more than nine thousand students in its nine regional campuses and seventy total program centers while maintaining a high graduation rate (80 percent).[32]

Distance learning (primarily online instruction but also interactive television, CD-ROM, and satellite modes) emerged in academe with much fanfare in the late twentieth century. The development of the World Wide Web offered the promise of replacing not only correspondence courses but much of the highly expensive on-campus forms of learning. By the early twenty-first century, about 8 percent of American undergraduate students were enrolled in one or more distance-learning courses, and more than 50 percent of all colleges — including about 50 percent of the CCCU colleges — were offering at least some electronic instruction.[33]

The initial enthusiasm began to fade, however, as it became increasingly clear that the students preferred the "face-to-face" (f-2-f) mode of learning. Still, electronic instruction is assuming a real although much more modest role in the learning process. Traditional classroom teachers are using computer technology to enhance their teaching, and traditional students are enrolling in limited numbers of e-courses.[34]

The greatest value of electronic instruction in Christian institutions is to serve those who have no easy access — or no access at all — to traditional modes of learning; these include many adult learners, advanced home-schooling students, missionary children in remote locations, and — in the spirit of the Theological Education by Extension movement introduced by missiologist Ralph Winter and others a generation ago — the minimally educated pastors and Christian workers in the less-developed parts of the world. Among the Christian colleges, many institutions use online instruction to a limited degree, but only a few use it extensively. Among the latter are Liberty, Regent (40 percent of its students), Grand Canyon, Indiana Wesleyan, and Azusa Pacific.[35]

One of the boldest ventures in nontraditional programming was the 2004 decision by Grand Canyon University to transform itself not just into a heavily online institution but also into the first for-profit Christian college in the United States. One major goal is to combine the profits of online instruction and the efficiencies of for-profit higher education to fund a low-cost, Christian mega-campus in Phoenix. The significance of the Grand Canyon experiment may lie less in its own development than in the influence that it has upon Christian higher education in general as the latter struggles with the issue of how to make its educational experience more affordable.[36]

Two new colleges have closely identified with the sharply growing home-schooling network of pre-collegiate education. Patrick Henry (VA) opened in 2000 with the explicit purpose of recruiting students from the approximately 500,000 families that teach their children at home; then, once on campus, it seeks to train them as conservative political activists with the majority of the students majoring in political science. Pensacola Christian is less political in orientation but does specialize in preparing curricular materials — known as A Beka Book — for thousands of home-schooled children and Christian schools.[37]

Meanwhile, both the predominantly white and the predominantly black Christian colleges have continued to work to make their programs available to all ethnic groups. Because of the higher cost of a private education, devout Christians of all races have enrolled primarily in public universities. Only 14 percent of evangelical college youth attend CCCU institutions, and only 12 percent of black students attend the approximately one hundred historically black colleges and universities (HBCUs). Within the CCCU institutions, the minority enrollment was 10 percent (5 percent

African-American, 2 percent Hispanic, 2 percent Asian) in 1991, while in
the HBCUs the white enrollment was 10 percent in 1976 and 13 percent in
1994 (the total white, Hispanic, Asian, and Native American enrollment
was 16 percent in the latter year). The white enrollment in the HBCUs was
very uneven, however, being especially high in the public HBCUs of the
upper South (from 17 percent to 92 percent in the fourteen institutions
with the highest percentages in 1994) and especially low in the private
HBCUs in the Deep South (less than 1 percent in the fourteen institutions
with the lowest percentages in 1994).[38] The CCCU institutions with the
greatest success recently in recruiting minority students include Nyack,
Houston Baptist, Andrews, Belhaven, Indiana Wesleyan, Howard Payne,
North Park, William Tyndale, and Warner Southern; also noteworthy are
LaSierra, LaVerne, Columbia, Averett, Mercer, and Texas Lutheran. In ad-
dition to the many HBCUs founded by mainline Protestant denomina-
tions after the Civil War, more recently the Seventh-Day Adventists
founded Oakwood (AL) in 1896, the Missouri Synod Lutherans began
Concordia Selma in 1922, and the Churches of Christ opened Southwestern Christian College (TX) in 1948.[39] Among the HBCUs, Howard and
Tuskegee operate especially effective chaplaincy programs, and Bethune-
Cookman has sought to work in close cooperation with the mostly white
CCCU. Perhaps the greatest contribution that the black colleges can make
to Christian higher education — and also to American Christianity in general — is, in the words of Samuel Dubois Cook, to "be prophetic voices and
agents," to "speak truth to power," both internally and to society in general as we all seek to overcome the "terrible evils that block progress toward the loving community of all of God's children." Also noteworthy is
Bacone, which to this day serves as a mission project of the American Baptist churches and their many work teams. Chartered by the Indian tribes of
Oklahoma, 60 percent of the college enrollees are Native American.[40]

   In addition to extending academic offerings to new types of students in
this country, the modern Christian college has also created many new
overseas study and service opportunities for its traditional students and
developed alliances of mutual support and cultural understanding with
similar institutions worldwide. Among American institutions, the Christian colleges and universities have long been leaders in promoting international awareness. Since the beginning of the modern missionary movement during the Second Great Awakening, through the YMCA/YWCA
and Student Volunteer Movement organizations and with the rise of the
Bible college, the Christian colleges have emphasized worldwide evangelistic concern and preparation for after-college missionary careers. What
has been new to the last generation is the number of students who live
overseas as a part of their undergraduate experience.

   While the number of all American students studying abroad doubled during the 1990s to 1.3 percent per year (or 5 percent of students during the four-year college period), Christian college students studied and/or served abroad at a higher than normal rate. Institutions with large numbers of students studying abroad included Baylor, Pepperdine, Wake Forest, Calvin, Wheaton, Messiah, Pacific Lutheran, Gustavus Adolphus, Concordia Moorhead, and Luther, while those with high percentages of students serving abroad included Goshen with its unique study-service program (see p. 194) and PTEV or LFP institutions Austin, Earlham, Goshen, Saint Olaf, and Wofford. Sometimes individual colleges developed a special relationship with a specific international institution (e.g., Malone with Hong Kong Baptist and Geneva with Christ College, Taiwan) with resultant student- and faculty-exchange programs.[41]

The CCCU has been very active in promoting international understanding. It is perhaps symbolically significant that six of its members include or imply "international" in their titles. Also, seven of the organization's eleven semester-long study programs are located at an overseas site (China, Costa Rica, Egypt, England, Russia, Australia, Uganda). Leaders among the CCCU colleges in the internationalization effort have been Gordon, Messiah, Calvin, Taylor, Andrews, and Eastern. Gordon offered well-developed travel/study courses, especially to Europe, for its students and others as early as the 1950s; the aforementioned Goshen program with its general-education requirement for a semester of studying and serving in a third world country has long been a model; Messiah hosted the influential 1986 CCCU conference on "Internationalizing the Curriculum" and produced a book of the same name; Calvin enrolls students from approximately sixty countries and offers approximately thirty-five off-campus courses each J-term; Taylor, which pioneered in overseas athletic evangelism in the 1950s and computer instruction for Wycliffe and other missions organizations in the 1970s, founded the first MK ("missionary kid") support group (MuKappa) in the 1980s. There are now MuKappa chapters on more than one hundred college campuses, where the MKs do much to facilitate cross-cultural appreciation.[42]

Few colleges reflect an international environment as much as Andrews, and few denominations operate as many liberal arts colleges in as many countries as does Andrews's supporting denomination, the missionary-minded Seventh-Day Adventist Church. Inspired by the teaching of church cofounder Ellen White, who emphasized that "the work of education and the work of redemption are one," the Adventist worldwide educational network has grown to 99 tertiary institutions — mostly liberal arts colleges (86 outside of the continental United States), 1,100 secondary schools, and 4,400 primary schools to serve the denomination's 13 million members (more than 12 million outside of the United States). With Andrews being the Adventist institution with the broadest graduate curriculum, it attracts many international Adventists seeking advanced theological or education degrees; these international students comprise eight hundred of the Andrews enrollment of three thousand—one of the highest percentages among American colleges.[43]

Andrews and Eastern operate model graduate programs to train leaders of humanitarian-aid organizations in the developing world. Both institutions offer instruction on both their American campus and at overseas sites, with Andrews yearly enrolling nearly two hundred students (mostly employees of the large, worldwide Adventist Development and Relief Agency) at four overseas sites that rotate periodically. Eastern has worked closely with World Vision to develop its School of International Leadership and Development and describes its Economic Development Program as the hallmark of the university.[44]

The late twentieth century witnessed a sharp rise worldwide in private colleges, including Christian colleges. The desire for higher education has outdistanced the ability of many governments to pay for it. Some countries such as Canada still discourage private colleges (except for Bible colleges); however, in Asia, Latin America, Central and Eastern Europe the growth is especially dramatic as governments are making it easier for nonpublic colleges to obtain charters. Even Africa is developing a meaningful private college system.[45]

It is difficult, if not impossible, to gauge the degree of growth of the Christian college movement worldwide in recent decades. Joel Carpenter has identified forty-one evangelical liberal arts colleges begun outside of the West since 1980. Robert Andringa believes the number of overseas Christian colleges to be anywhere from five hundred to two thousand. In many cases they evolve from Bible colleges and theological seminaries as local church leaders—in contrast to the Western missionaries—are encouraging a broader curriculum to facilitate national social and economic development.[46]

Many of the new international Christian colleges have sought membership with the CCCU, and to date the North American organization has accepted thirty-eight such institutions as affiliates. The majority of these international affiliates, like the plurality of the North American members, are interdenominational, and a description of some of them appears in appendix H. The newly developing overseas Christian colleges seek affiliation so eagerly because, in many cases, not being a Bible college, denominationally based, or government-owned, they have no natural local or national organization with which to identify. Being a member of the CCCU enhances credibility with government and accreditation officials, and it facilitates the recruitment of American students, professors, and other resources.[47]

By contrast with the blossoming overseas Christian liberal-arts-college movement, the overseas Bible colleges are much better linked to each other and to their North American counterparts. This should cause no surprise as throughout much of the twentieth century the United States and Canadian Bible colleges were the primary producers of overseas missionaries, and these international evangelists tended to reproduce the type of educational institutions with which they were most familiar and that could best facilitate their goals of evangelism and church planting. Beginning in the 1960s and following the model of the North American Accrediting Association of Bible Colleges (now the Association for Biblical Higher Education), the Bible colleges of the world founded regional accrediting associations in Africa, Latin America, the South Pacific, Asia, the Caribbean, Europe, and Euro-Asia with the worldwide umbrella organization of the associations being the International Council for Evangelical Theological Education (ICETE), which operates under the auspices of the World Evangelical Alliance. By 2003 the number of Bible colleges accredited by ICETE member organizations numbered 710.

The ICETE institutions offer primarily undergraduate programs. By contrast, Overseas Council International (begun in 1974) facilitates developmental activities in the most advanced evangelical theological programs (primarily graduate seminaries) in each region of the world. Among the best-developed of the one hundred Overseas Council institutions are Central American Theological Seminary (Guatemala), the best-developed evangelical seminary in Latin America; South American Theological Seminary (Brazil); Bangui Evangelical School of Theology (Central Africa Republic), the best-recognized program in French-speaking Africa; Nairobi Evangelical Graduate School of Theology (Kenya); George Whitefield College (South Africa); Evangelical Theological Seminary in Cairo (Egypt), the largest evangelical seminary in the Arab-speaking world; Odessa Theological Seminary, the leading evangelical seminary in the Russian-speaking world; China Graduate School of Theology (Hong Kong), one of the best doctoral-level theological programs in the world; South Asia Institute of Advanced Christian Studies (India); and Union Biblical Seminary (India). Additionally, in 1989 the Association of Theological Schools in the United States and Canada led in the organization of the World Conference of Associations of Theological Institutions (WOCATI); however, WOCATI remains in an early stage of development.[48]

Enlarging the Faith and Learning Dialogue

Since the 1960s the orthodox colleges have given major focus to the idea of bringing together the faith and knowledge domains in writing, thinking, and certainly in teaching (see pp. 193–94). What is new to the period since 1990 is that growing segments of the academy are increasingly acknowledging the extent to which they have secularized (see chapter 4) and are reassessing how they can best offer a fair hearing to the spiritual dimension of human existence.

While in recent years the evangelical liberal arts colleges have continued to embrace the general goal of faith and learning integration, they debated just exactly what the concept meant and how it could best be applied to the specific academic subjects. The Bible colleges meanwhile discussed — and decided one institution at a time — how much and in what disciplinary areas they wanted to become like the Christian liberal arts colleges. The "critical-mass" Christian colleges struggled with the idea of how they could be both Christian and pluralistic. A growing number of the more-or-less secular church-related institutions, while not necessarily wanting to return to their earlier — often nineteenth-century — mode of being a Christian college, did begin to reassess whether they had unduly eliminated religious discourse and should find ways to reintroduce its most vital elements. Other secular private institutions recognized but resisted the growing public interest in spirituality.

Meanwhile, at the turn of the century, a few of the public institutions were starting to ask how a state university could deal both honestly and objectively with the religious aspect of the human condition. Mostly, however, the public universities — and many of the elite private institutions — were operating in a postmodern void that was still leery of considering religious issues.

The growing general discourse included a specific body of major literature.[49] The most widely influential studies were the critical laments of the secularization of the academy, beginning with George Marsden's landmark *The Soul of the American University: From Protestant Establishment to Established Nonbelief* (New York, 1994) and also including Douglas Sloan's *Faith and Knowledge: Mainline Protestantism and American Higher Education* (Louisville, 1994) and James Burtchaell's *The Dying of the Light: The Disengagement of Colleges and Universities from Their Christian Churches* (Grand Rapids, 1998). Marsden focused on the secularization process in the elite, precedent-setting universities, beginning in the late nineteenth century; Sloan traced the subsequent movement in the mainline Protestant church-related colleges with special attention on their failed effort in the 1950s and 1960s to reunite faith and learning in the academy; while Burtchaell examined the related process of disassociation from the sponsoring denomination in Catholic and Protestant institutions alike. Also working effectively as a critique was Larry Braskamp's *Fostering Student Development through Faculty Development* (n.p., 2003), a careful survey of the chief academic officers of 250 Catholic and Protestant mainline church-related colleges and universities in which the collective responses themselves documented the significant degree of secularization in the traditionally Christian institutions.

While the literature of critique served the purpose of "consciousness raising," a second type of literature began to appear—especially near and after the turn of the century—that sought to move beyond the negative ethic of social criticism to the more positive ethic of presenting models and proposing workable solutions. Certainly there were strong elements of this second approach even in the critiques as Marsden's *Soul of the American University* called for the major institutions to more consistently implement their profession of pluralism when it involved religious discourse, and Braskamp's report encouraged a much greater emphasis upon educating the instructors (most of whom had studied in secular doctoral programs) in how to meet the holistic learning expectations of their students. The latter, as the aforementioned Astin study had shown quantitatively, and Colleen Carroll, *The New Faithful: Why Young Adults Are Embracing Christian Orthodoxy* (Chicago, 2002) and Naomi Schaefer Riley, *God on the Quad: How Religious Colleges and the Missionary Generation Are Changing America* (New York, 2005) had demonstrated in narrative form, were seeking an education that did not neglect the spiritual domain.

Among the many fine new studies pointing the way to a religiously informed learning are two works that could be used in faculty development programs, Caroline Simon et al., *Mentoring for Mission: Nurturing New Faculty at Church-Related Colleges* (Grand Rapids, 2003), and Richard Hughes, *How Christian Faith Can Sustain the Life of the Mind* (Grand Rapids, 2001). The Simon book is a helpful guide for those directing faculty-development programs while the Hughes book is a useful tool for introducing new faculty to a Christian higher learning that is both open in mind and gracious in spirit.

Multiauthor books growing out of major faith and learning conferences or study groups include Paul Dovre, ed., *The Future of Religious Colleges* (Grand Rapids, 2002); Andrea Sterk, ed., *Religion, Scholarship, and Higher Education* (Notre Dame, IN, 2002); and Stephen Haynes, ed., *Professing in the Postmodern Academy* (Waco, 2002). These and other works, such as Robert Benne, *Quality with Soul* (Grand Rapids, 2001), Richard Hughes and William Adrian, eds., *Models for Christian Higher Education* (Grand Rapids, 1997), and John Wilcox and Irene King, eds., *Enhancing Religious Identity: Best Practices from Catholic Colleges* (Washington, DC, 2000), sought to provide models for consideration by those institutions seeking to become more intentionally Christian or more intentionally inclusive of the spiritual domain.

In so many of the recent conferences and projects, Protestant and Catholic educators have been working together. Among the more significant recent works on Catholic higher education are Philip Gleason, *Contending with Modernity* (1995), Alice Gallin, *Negotiating Identity* (Notre Dame, IN, 2000), and David J. O'Brien, *From the Heart of the American Church: Catholic Higher Education and American Culture* (New York, 1994). Gleason (to Vatican II) and Gallin (since Vatican II) together present the definitive history of twentieth-century Catholic higher education in America. Since the tumultuous 1960s, Catholic institutions have pursued the same movement toward secularization that their Protestant counterparts had followed during the prior two generations. The O'Brien book with its positive tone points the way toward religious reconstruction in Catholic higher education.

Given the enhanced interest in religion as illustrated by the above literature, it is not surprising that two of the major journals of higher education each devoted an entire issue to the phenomenon. *Academe*, the publication of the American Association of University Professors, entitled its November–December 1996 issue "The Academy: Freedom of Religion or Freedom from Religion?" while *Liberal Education*, published by the Association of American Colleges and Universities, named its fall 2001 issue "Religion on Campus." It is an apt reflection of the evolving nature of the dialogue that the first issue emphasized the lack of religious discourse and the second issue (five years later) stressed its growing presence.

The Lilly Endowment provided the financial resources for many of the books, conferences, projects, and study centers[50] that appeared after 1990. Vice President for Religion Robert Lynn, together with a late-1980s conversation group that included David Ray Griffin, Joe Hough, Mark Schwehn, and Douglas Sloan, introduced the Lilly Initiative of the 1989–99 decade; however, the fuller development of the program came with Lynn's successor, Craig Dykstra,[51] who strongly believed that there should be a larger role for religion in the marketplace of ideas in the university. During the first decade of the initiative, Lilly, led by religion program director Jeanne Knoerle, awarded seventy grants totaling $15.6 million to support approximately forty-five projects. More recently the initiative has featured the Programs for the Theological Explorations of Vocation (see section titled "The Recovery Continues" in this chapter).[52]

The Mainline Reassesses

Beginning earlier than the faith and learning movement in the mainline colleges has been the related renewal movement in the mainline denominations. Of course, the mainline churches never secularized as much as did their colleges, but unlike their colleges they suffered significant enrollment losses—more than 20 percent during a period (1960–2000) when overall United States church membership was growing at a rate of 33 percent. The resultant loss of influence by the historic denominations was described baldly by one inside analyst: "If at one time the churches whose life flowed from the Reformation . . . were considered mainline, they are now clearly sideline. If once they set the religious agenda, . . . they are now increasingly ignored. On the one hand an energetic secularism pays them scant attention; on the other hand, an equally energetic fundamentalist — charismatic — evangelical wave has taken the center religious stage."[53]

Both church and college were influenced by an increasingly secularized society, and both church and college influenced each other. The churches' reduced emphasis upon an authoritative (and demanding) gospel gave greater freedom to the church college to proclaim alternate worldviews, and the educated alumni of the secularizing colleges often chose not to return to the churches. Sociologist Robert Wuthnow noted, "Between 1958 and 1982, the most serious declines in regular church attendance came . . . among younger people with at least some education. . . . Education seemed to have become associated with a kind of 'gap' in religious commitment that had not been there prior to the 1960s." Scholars Dean Hoge, Benton Johnson, and Donald Luidens reached the same conclusion in the mid-1990s, namely that the mainline decline primarily stemmed from a failure to retain the young adults, especially the well-educated ones.[54]

If the mainline colleges previously were influenced by the secularizing tendencies in the churches and society in general, perhaps they will be influenced in the opposite direction by the previously discussed growing contemporary interest in spirituality — especially among young people — and by the renewal movement in the churches. As noted by Christian educator Dorothy Bass, "Revitalization in main-line church-related colleges needs to be accomplished — and maybe only can be accomplished — as one element in the general revitalization of society in general including specifically the churches related to a college."[55]

So how much are the mainline churches reviving and how much will the revival affect their related colleges? By the early twenty-first century there were approximately thirty renewal (or confessing) groups in the mainline denominations with the largest being the United Methodist Confessing Movement with more than 630,000 members, the fastest-growing being the Confessing Church Movement of the Presbyterian Church of the United States of America with 420,000 members and 1,400 churches, and the umbrella organization being the Association for Church Renewal (founded in 1986). Studies by sociologists Rodney Stark, Roger Finke, and Jennifer McKinley suggest that the momentum in the mainline churches is with the renewal groups. The renewal clergy are younger, they are learning how to be more effective in church politics, they are much more effective at the grassroots level, and through evangelism they are enlisting most of the new members. One of the most optimistic observers of the movement is Methodist theologian Thomas Oden, who has stated flatly, "A reversal has occurred in our time," noting that just when the evangelicals and the Eastern Orthodox Church had largely given up on the major Protestant denominations, the renewal movement powerfully emerged in all of the mainline churches.[56]

If the evangelicals are thriving, the mainline churches are nudging toward orthodoxy, and the whole country is witnessing a growing spirituality, can the mainline colleges, influenced as they are by market realities and offers of renewal program funding, resist gradually shifting to a greater concern with serious religious initiatives? Already most of the major denominational college associations have introduced programs to assist colleges in their reevaluation of institutional mission or identity. Change is occurring; of course only time will tell how extensive the renewal will become.[57]

In general, the mainline colleges that have secularized the least are the ones most active in revitalization. More specifically, this includes the midwestern and western Lutheran colleges and the Catholic institutions. The Lutheran colleges are known for their emphasis upon teaching scholarship, exemplary chorale music programs, and a "two spheres" approach to the faith and learning issue. Thus, while the Lutheran colleges are experiencing revitalization, it is with a somewhat different type of emphasis than the integration focus of many of the CCCU colleges. Perhaps the most prominent recent advocate of the two-spheres philosophy often associated with Lutheran thinking has been James Nuechterlein, who at one of the classic "trialogues" of the 1980s among representatives from the geographically proximate Valparaiso, Notre Dame, and Calvin, argued for the critical importance of both faith and learning but as largely separate rather than largely blended components. He stated, "I think of the relationship between faith and learning less in terms of integration or transformation and more in terms of paradox and tension. . . . Faith and learning, while . . . not ultimately irreconcilable and while, indeed, they must for their mutual health inform each other at certain points, do exist largely on different planes and are incapable of essential fusion or integration."[58]

The most secularized Lutheran colleges are the Evangelical Lutheran Church of America (ELCA) institutions in the East; the most culturally isolated ones are the Missouri Synod Lutheran (MSL) colleges; the schools leading the renewal movement include Valparaiso, Saint Olaf, Concordia Moorhead, Luther, and Gustavus Adolphus; colleges that have become more intentionally Christian in recent years include Augsburg, Concordia Moorhead, Luther, and Roanoke.

Strong tensions continue to exist between the ELCA (about five million members) and MSL (about 2.5 million members) denominations, and this strain manifests itself in the relationships between the colleges of the two traditions. The MSL colleges (with Concordia River Forest as the traditional flagship institution and Concordia Wisconsin as the largest school) are doubtful of the theological purity of the ELCA colleges, while the latter question the intellectual openness of the former. More than any other institution, Valparaiso is the university that provides a bridge between the two traditions.[59]

In Catholic higher education, secularization and renewal are compressed into a shorter time span (a single generation) than has been the case with the Protestant colleges (a century); therefore, one can observe evidence of continuing secular growth and serious revival simultaneously in the former. The Cardinal Newman Society commissioned a study by the Higher Education Research Institute (UCLA) that showed that students at thirty-eight Catholic colleges in the 1997–2001 period graduated with a reduced devotion to the Catholic church and its teachings. Still, of course, there is contrasting evidence of a growing spiritual hunger in the students. The colleges themselves have declared their independence from the church (note the 1967 Land O'Lakes meeting led by President Theodore Hesburgh of Notre Dame) while Pope John Paul II responded through his *Ex Corde Ecclesiae* (1990), essentially designed to maintain control over the theology faculties and to assure that the Catholic colleges would remain at least critical-mass institutions.

What are the long-range prospects for Catholic higher education? Father Burtchaell of Notre Dame has received much attention because of his sense of doom. Alice Gallin, for many years a leader of the 230-member Association of Catholic Colleges and Universities, is more sanguine, preferring to view the changes since the 1960s as generally beneficial: "What we witness may be a shedding of a religious culture rather than a loss of faith."

The Catholic institutions that have secularized the most have been the large (frequently Jesuit) research institutions. As with the Protestant universities, the desire to compete for recognition as a publishing institution has made it tempting to hire established or promising writers irrespective of religious orientation. The institutions that have led the renewal movement include Notre Dame, Boston, Dayton, Holy Cross, and Fairfield. New or newly focused small colleges that have positioned themselves as centers of orthodox Catholicism include Ave Maria (MI, FL), Christendom (VA), Franciscan of Steubenville (OH), Magdalen (NH), Thomas Aquinas (CA), and Dallas (TX).[60]

Presbyterian higher education has long been a producer of leaders for American society and long has identified closely with the development of the American culture. Therefore, as society in general and its colleges in particular have become more secular, it is not surprising that the Presbyterian colleges have done so also. By 1990 the colleges and the churches were losing interest in one another to the point that the presidents of the nearly seventy Presbyterian colleges and universities stated that "the Presbyterian church could be close to the point where its involvement in higher education could be lost forever." More recently there is a larger basis for hope. Encouraging factors include the growing influence of the denomination's renewal movement, and the still strongly creedal basis of Presbyterianism. One Presbyterian scholar recently estimated that of the sixty-six Presbyterian colleges, nearly 45 percent have a denominational connection that is historic only, another 45 percent retain a partial connection, while about 10 percent still maintain a close connection.

Eight Presbyterian colleges participate in the CCCU or CSR (Belhaven, Grove City, King, Montreat, College of the Ozarks, Sterling, Waynesburg, and Whitworth) while twelve are LFP or PTEV institutions (Alma, Austin, Davidson, Hanover, Hastings, Illinois, Macalester, Maryville, Presbyterian, Rhodes, Whitworth, Wooster).[61]

Noteworthy examples of recent revitalization in Presbyterian higher education exist at Davidson, Waynesburg, and Eckerd. With the help of its PTEV grant, Davidson is preparing three to four times more ministerial graduates than it did a decade ago, placing a major emphasis upon training its faculty in theological understanding, and in general moving back toward being a critical-mass institution. Few colleges of any denomination have changed as completely from largely secular to orthodox in as short a time while growing sharply in enrollment and affluence as has Waynesburg during the tenure of President Timothy Thyreen. Eckerd began only in 1958 as a cooperative effort of the then two major branches of Florida Presbyterianism, and thus has not had to recover from the period of secularization. In addition to operating model programs of international and intergenerational learning, it infuses its curriculum with a values and "quest for meaning" emphasis, and it operates a comprehensive Center for Spiritual Life led by Duncan Ferguson, longtime leader in Presbyterian higher education.[62]

No denomination has produced more elite universities than have the Methodists; and there is no denomination where there is a bigger gap in worldview between the laity and the denominational colleges than in Methodism. One Methodist leader estimates that 25 to 30 percent of United Methodists are evangelical with some degree of understanding while 70 percent are conservative or moderate on theological issues. Yet most of the colleges are more or less secular. F. Thomas Trotter, Methodist higher education leader in both denomination and university, defends the Methodist educational institutions as they had become by the 1980s. He describes the denomination as having given birth to the colleges, raised them, and then as an act of love freed them from church control to pursue unfettered the love and truth of God. Bishop Will Willimon is not as pleased with this separation and, while noting with appreciation the contemporary trend of church colleges to partially reconnect with the denominations, is fearful that "our Methodist colleges and universities have gotten so far away from the church that they may not be able to establish a truly meaningful connection. That grieves me."

Still there are hopeful signs. On the grassroots level, the influential renewal movements are becoming increasingly effective in church politics. The renewal-related Asbury Theological Seminary is now producing one-sixth of the new United Methodist ministers, and the Foundation for Theological Education has prepared more than one hundred young evangelical scholars for academic positions in Methodist institutions.

On the national level, the church and college officials agreed to a noteworthy statement of increased cooperation ("An Educational Covenant of Partnership") at the 2000 General Conference, and four years later at an Institute of Higher Education they discussed more specifically how the relationship between the two entities might better realize John Wesley's goal of blending "knowledge and vital piety."[63]

Perhaps the most realistic expectation is that increasing numbers of Methodist colleges and universities will follow an active version of the intentionally pluralist model of a church-related college in which the students receive, among other views, a clear understanding of the best case that can be made for Christian theism. An example of an institution that articulates this approach is the University of Indianapolis.[64] LFP or PTEV Methodist institutions in addition to Indianapolis include Bethune-Cookman, Claflin, Columbia, Duke, Hamline, Hendrix, Millsaps, Morningside, Ohio Wesleyan, Simpson (IA), Williamette, and Wofford.

In degree of secularization, the United Church of Christ colleges are perhaps comparable to the Methodist institutions. Among its colleges with the greatest interest in bridging the faith and learning gap are Catawba, Dillard (which is also Methodist-related), and Elmhurst, all PTEV institutions; and Defiance, Elon, Lakeland, Northland, and Piedmont. One leader is Elmhurst, which established its Niebuhr Center (H. Richard is a graduate and former president; Reinhold is also an alumnus, and his statue graces the center of campus) to encourage the college to return toward a Niebuhr-type of religious earnestness.

The general Disciples and Northern Baptist traditions contain many orthodox colleges, but most of these are connected with groups that broke from the Disciples of Christ and the American Baptist Churches in the

United States during the early-twentieth-century Fundamentalist-Modernist conflict. Of the seventeen colleges listed on the Disciples of Christ higher-education website, one each participates in the CCCU (Northwest Christian), the LFP (Culver-Stockton), and the PTEV (Transylvania); Butler, with an earlier Disciples connection, is also a PTEV institution. Three of the sixteen American Baptist colleges are CCCU members (Eastern, Judson, and Sioux Falls), while Alderson-Broadus and perhaps Keuka would also view themselves as orthodox institutions. William Jewell is more nearly a critical-mass college.

The colleges of one small denomination, the Church of the Brethren, are worthy of mention because of their unusual combination of moderate secularization theologically and freedom from secularization in social practice. More specifically, while the Church of the Brethren colleges would not qualify for membership in the CCCU, nevertheless in many respects they serve as models for the entire Christian college community in their emphasis upon the Christian virtues of humility, service, peace witness, social justice, and distrust of power politics.[65]

Of the major denominations, the Southern Baptist Convention is the one whose colleges have secularized the least. Nevertheless, the Southern Baptist colleges have been going through their own type of reassessment with the major focus being whether to continue the governing oversight of the individual state conventions. During the 1990s, ten or more colleges (including Baylor, Furman, Grand Canyon, Houston Baptist, Ouachita Baptist, Samford, Stetson, Carson-Newman, Mississippi, and Meredith) altered or discarded their traditional relationship with their specific state Baptist organization, and by the early twenty-first century twice that number (or a large plurality of the colleges) had joined the CCCU.[66]

The major factor in the movement toward independence from the Southern Baptist denomination was a desire to escape the effects of the intense battle between the conservative and moderate wings for control of the denomination. Beginning in 1979, the insurgent conservative party led by Paul Pressler and Paige Patterson gradually secured control of the denomination, including the right to select the trustees of the major seminaries. Consequently, the colleges and universities led by Baylor in 1990 and Furman and Stetson shortly thereafter, began to seek a greater degree of independence.[67]

One Southern Baptist scholar described the colleges as fighting a two-front war in the twentieth-century ideological conflicts, battling against anti-intellectual fundamentalism in the church on one hand and secular trends in the academy on the other. By the late twentieth century, secularism in Southern Baptist universities had achieved its greatest impact at Richmond and, to a lesser extent, Wake Forest, both of whom had become free of Southern Baptist control earlier in the century. In the early twenty-first century, however, Wake Forest, in the way it was using its PTEV grant and with its hiring of evangelical scholar Nathan Hatch as president, was showing signs of becoming the primary example of a major Southern Baptist university that had partly secularized but was now reevaluating whether it wished to reconnect more completely with its Christian heritage.[68]

If the Southern Baptist colleges were increasingly disconnecting from their state conventions, they were increasingly relating to—perhaps even becoming a part of—the growing evangelical college network. Their presence in the CCCU grew from four in 1984 to twenty in 2005; their faculty members increasingly interacted with their evangelical-college counterparts in the academic faith and learning conferences and student personnel association meetings; Baylor since 1990 has sought to adopt an explicit model of faith and learning integration, and the evangelical Institute for Advanced Christian Studies in 2002 contributed the majority of its resources to the Baylor University Institute for Faith and Learning to create the Carl F. H. Henry Endowment for Christian Scholarship; and the evangelical monthly, *Christianity Today*, regularly and thoroughly reviewed the turn-of-the-century saga of Baylor in its efforts to become the premier intentionally Christian research university in America.[69]

Led by President Robert Sloan (1995–2005) and provosts Donald Schmeltekopf and David Jeffrey, Baylor developed a plan (articulated in its "Vision 2012") to enhance and give more specific theological definition to Baylor's already strong Christian orientation and to develop further Baylor's graduate school and research emphasis with the result that the institution would become the unquestioned premier Christian research university of the Protestant tradition in America. The Baylor plan attracted much interest in the evangelical community, especially among those who long had hoped for a fully developed, broadly recognized, seriously Christian university of the Protestant variety, and a number of its bright scholars began to relocate to the Waco institution. But the plan also attracted much opposition within the quite evenly divided Baylor faculty, many of whom were not pleased with the increased research expectations, what some of them perceived as a reduced level of religious freedom, and the not always deliberate process of implementing change. While the Baylor experiment is bold and promising, whether it will ultimately be successful is unclear. The initial comments of the newly appointed Baylor president, Frank Lilley, express a strong commitment to the Baylor 2012 plan.[70]

Southern Baptist institutions holding membership in the CCCU or CSR include Baylor, Bluefield, California Baptist, Campbell, Campbellsville,

Carson-Newman, Charleston Southern, Dallas Baptist, East Texas Baptist, Hardin-Simmons, Houston Baptist, Howard Payne, Judson, Louisiana, Mississippi, North Greenville, Oklahoma Baptist, Palm Beach Atlantic, Samford, Southwest Baptist, Union, Wayland, and Williams Baptist. LFP or PTEV member institutions include Baylor, Georgetown, Mercer, Samford, and Wake Forest.[71]

The External Governors

Not since the colonial era — when the few colleges often combined public and private features — has the government been so involved in supporting and regulating private, including church-related, institutions of higher education as has been the case since the Lyndon Johnson administration (1963–69).[72] The court decisions of the 1970s discouraged the granting of public aid to "pervasively religious" colleges with the result that some of the institutions — especially Roman Catholic ones — that had not yet become secular, decided — perhaps unnecessarily — to move in that direction to assure the continued flow of the governmental assistance. Even the colleges that did not secularize tended to loosen their denominational relationship.

By the latter decades of the twentieth century, most of the church-related colleges and universities were becoming increasingly confident that their general religious nature would not prevent the federal government aid from continuing to come to their students; at the same time, such institutions were becoming increasingly dependent upon that aid.[73] After 1980, the institutions that faced the greatest likelihood of losing government financial benefits were (1) those who were closely connected to a church — especially a specific, high-profile local church — or a highly visible ministry (e.g., televangelism); (2) those who were highly religious institutions in states that provided significant financial assistance to private education (e.g., tuition-equalization grants) but which had constitutions with greater limits on the ability of the government to aid religious organizations than does the federal constitution; and (3) those who were in non-compliance with a highly valued government and/or public social goal.

On another level of governance, the turn-of-the-century Christian colleges faced increasing pressure from the American Association of University Professors (AAUP) and some of the accrediting agencies to conform to the philosophy of the public universities. This challenge, however, has been partially reduced by the growing public criticism of secular higher education, including its undue restrictions on the free exercise of religion in the state institutions.

An example of a university with a close connection to a specific church known for its widely televised ministry was Liberty. The Virginia institution, associated with the televangelist Jerry Falwell and his Lynchburg

Thomas Road Baptist Church, sought Virginia tuition-assistance grants
for its in-state students. When in 1989 the Virginia Supreme Court ruled
that at Liberty "religion is so pervasive that a substantial portion of its
functions are subsumed in religious function," the university agreed to
modifications in course and chapel requirements and in the institutional
descriptions in its publications. This then was a striking case of a state
government and a Christian college negotiating institutional alterations in
exchange for eligibility for state funds. A decade later, in a somewhat less
restrictive judicial environment, the Virginia Supreme Court allowed another institution (Regent) begun by another televangelist (Pat Robertson)
to issue tax-exempt bonds to finance campus building projects.[74]

In recent years the federal courts have been less willing to disqualify
"pervasively religious" colleges from eligibility for public aid even while
they have allowed states to rule theological students to be ineligible to receive payments from state tuition-grant programs. For example, in *Mitchell v. Helms* (2000), a pre-collegiate case with implications for higher education as well, the Supreme Court argued that the constitutionality of public
aid should be determined primarily by the secular nature of the aid program rather than by the degree of religious orientation of recipient institutions. The plurality opinion of Justices Kennedy, Rehnquist, Scalia, and
Thomas sharply criticized the earlier "pervasive sectarianism" doctrine as
not only "unnecessary, but also offensive. . . . This doctrine, born of bigotry,
should be buried now." Consistent with *Mitchell v. Helms*, a year later the
Fourth Circuit Court ruled not only that Columbia Union, a Maryland Adventist college, was not pervasively sectarian and thus eligible for the
Maryland funding program, but also that being "pervasively sectarian"
was not a valid basis for disqualifying a college for state assistance.[75]

Meanwhile, in *Locke v. Davey* (2004), the Supreme Court, consistent
with its earlier decision in *Witters v. Washington* (1986), ruled that while a
state aid program may include theological students, it did not have to do
so to be in compliance with the free-exercise provision of the First Amendment. Joshua Davey, a student at Northwest, an Assembly of God college
in Washington, had sued the state of Washington when it denied him a
scholarship because of his major in pastoral studies and business management and administration. In 2003, Washington was one of eleven states
(also Alabama, Louisiana, Michigan, Missouri, New Jersey, New York,
Oregon, South Carolina, South Dakota, and Wisconsin) that prohibited
state aid for theological students. Some critics of these state constitutional
provisions — and the Supreme Court's willingness to tolerate them — compared them to earlier discriminating codes against Catholics ("Blaine
Amendments") and blacks (Jim Crow laws).[76]

Two cases from the early 1980s demonstrate the limits of the First

Amendment free-exercise-of-religion guarantees when they clash with the restrictions of the civil rights and equal-employment opportunities acts that prohibit discrimination based upon sex or race. While the restrictions, as they pertain to religious belief, generally exempt religious educational institutions, especially those directly connected to a denomination, they do not necessarily do so when the beliefs involve limits upon the eligibility of women and minorities for certain activities. In *EEOC v. Mississippi College* (1980), the Fifth Circuit Court stated that the federal government might prohibit a college from maintaining a policy of hiring only men for the religion faculty. More explicitly, in *Bob Jones University v. the United States* (1983), the Supreme Court upheld the Internal Revenue Service regulation calling for withdrawal of tax-exempt status for schools and colleges with policies of racial discrimination. The Bob Jones standard forbade students from interracial dating and marriage, and the court determined that a "fundamental national public policy" could override sincerely held religious beliefs regardless of the effect that such a ruling could have on the financial welfare or even survivability of a college.[77]

In the early twenty-first century, a major concern of many Christian colleges is that a federal higher education act or court decision might declare them ineligible for continued federal student aid because of a hiring policy that reflects an institutional belief that homosexual practice is morally wrong. The threat of accreditation removal by discipline-specific accrediting agencies in social work and psychology may be even greater. Increasingly the orthodox and critical-mass institutions are building defense coalitions to protect their employment policy interests.[78]

Meanwhile, the Christian colleges are watching with great care the relevant gay-and-lesbian court decisions. After the Washington, DC, Human Rights Act of 1987 declared it an "unlawful discriminating practice" for an educational institution to deny a person access to its services and facilities because of that person's sexual orientation, two gay organizations at Georgetown University sued the institution for (1) refusing university recognition, and (2) refusing the use of facilities and services that comes with such organizational recognition. The District of Columbia Court of Appeals ruled that the institution must grant the groups the facilities and services but not necessarily the recognition.

Later, major decisions have more completely upheld the rights of private organizations. In *Hurley v. Irish-American Gay, Lesbian and Bisexual Group of Boston* (1995), the Supreme Court upheld the right of organizers of the Boston St. Patrick's Day Parade to exclude marchers who wished to identify themselves as gay, while five years later the court ruled in *Boy Scouts of America v. Dale* (2000) that the scout organization, which instructs its members that homosexual conduct is not "morally straight," can deny the scoutmaster position to gays. Also in 2000, a federal court upheld the right of Baptist Memorial College of Health Science (TN) to terminate a lesbian employee. During the following year, American Christian educators followed closely the Trinity Western case across the Canadian border in which the British Columbia College of Teachers, which accredits teacher education programs in the province, withheld professional recognition for the Trinity Western program because the university "Community Standards" document contained a prohibition on homosexual behavior. When the university brought suit, the Supreme Court of Canada ruled for the university, declaring that the Trinity Western standard by itself was not a valid basis for denying accreditation.[79]

The federal and state governments are not the only external governors of the Christian college. For example, the AAUP has long exerted an extralegal but powerful control in its ability to influence both public opinion and accrediting agencies in their evaluations of Christian higher education. The AAUP began in part as a Progressive Era reaction by secular reformers such as John Dewey against the late-nineteenth-century Protestant dominance in American higher education. No organization has done more to promote the cause of academic freedom, but the AAUP focus has always been that of individual freedom rather than institutional freedom and, as pertains to religion, freedom from religion more than freedom of religion. It has focused much more on the restrictions of academic freedom at religious colleges than on the limits of religious expression at secular institutions. Since its original 1915 statement, the major AAUP pronouncements on academic freedom (most notably those of 1940 and 1970) have displayed a barely tolerating disdain toward the religious colleges.[80]

The most recent AAUP statement (1996) is somewhat more moderate in tone, undoubtedly reflecting the more accepting religious climate in the nation. Interestingly, in 2005, the CCCU, the Catholic higher educational agencies, and the independent colleges organizations actually were able to work together with the AAUP against a common threat—the possibility of greater government intervention and regulation, motivated in part by the public concern over the growing tuition expenses. Altogether, twenty-eight national higher education organizations signed the statement on academic rights and responsibility, which seeks to maintain the present level of self-governance in higher education.[81]

Fortunately, the actions of the Supreme Court and the regional accrediting agencies have moderated the effects of the AAUP posture toward religious institutions. In a Cold War–era case, *Sweezy v. New Hampshire* (1957), and elsewhere, the Supreme Court defended the idea of institutional academic freedom. The frequently quoted line from the Sweezy case came from the concurring opinion of Justice Frankfurter (together with Justice Harlan) that identified "the four essential freedoms" of a university, namely "to determine for itself on academic grounds who may teach, what may be taught, how it shall be taught, and who may be admitted to study." Of course, the court added that these freedoms are not absolute, but must be consistent with the constitutional limitations protecting individual freedoms. Although the regional accrediting associations have reflected much of the AAUP thinking on academic freedom, they have always had a broader agenda and have usually employed their considerable power with an evenhandedness. Particularly in recent years, they have tended to evaluate institutions on the basis of how well they were fulfilling their self-defined educational mission.[82]

In contrast to the AAUP record, the Christian colleges, especially the more orthodox ones, historically have placed greater emphasis upon institutional academic freedom than upon individual academic freedom. Reflecting their growing maturity in general, the Christian colleges are demonstrating a growing capacity to both understand and articulate a compelling apologia for the rights of religious colleges and universities and also to be increasingly insistent of clear communication, due process, and Christian charity in the implementation of their own processes of academic freedom. Particularly helpful in this area have been the recent writings of Calvin-related scholars George Marsden, Nicholas Wolterstorff, and Anthony Diekema.[83]

While in recent years the federal courts have shown a greater tendency to accommodate the interests of the religious colleges, and many of the mainline colleges are increasingly interested in religious learning, the state universities and even more so the secular private institutions have largely moved in the opposite direction, challenging the right of campus Christian organizations to select their officers from only Christians, to view homosexual practice as a moral wrong, and in general to receive recognition equal to that of other student organizations with specific ideas and goals. Scholar Candace DeRussy talks of "the campus war against faith," and lawyer David French states that, "in many ways, religious liberty is the new center stage in the battle for freedom on the secular campus." Both DeRussy and French are active in the aggressive and effective political action group, Foundation for Individual Rights in Higher Education (FIRE). The religious discrimination of the secular institutions most directly affects the Christian colleges in its traumatic impact upon the graduate programs of their present and future faculty members. Secular mentors often are free to discourage and even forbid the expression of religious perspectives in scholarly work with the threat of rejection of professional credentialing.[84]

In addition to the fate of religion on the secular campuses, the decisions of the courts on the role of religion in pre-collegiate education also have a direct impact on Christian higher education because of the general judicial trends that they demonstrate. Whereas in the 1960s and 1970s the Supreme Court was concerned that the public schools not violate the establishment clause of the First Amendment, in recent years it has focused more upon protecting the free-exercise rights of citizens in the public and private schools. In response to the prayer and Bible-reading decisions of the 1960s,[85] many local schools had overreacted; in an effort to avoid promoting a specific faith, they had disadvantaged the study of religion and voluntary religious expression in general. Just as *Widmar v. Vincent* (1981) had said that the University of Missouri must allow religious clubs to use the university facilities in the same way that other clubs do, so also *Westside v. Mergens* (1990), *Lamb's Chapel v. Center Moriches Union* (1993), and *Good News Club v. Milford* (2001) determined that a public school must not distinguish between religious organizations and other types of student and community groups in determining who could use the school facilities for their after-hours meetings. In a similar spirit of accommodation, *Zelman v. Simmons-Harris* (2002) determined that a publicly funded voucher program could be organized in a way to allow students to choose to use their stipend to attend a religious school. Collectively these cases reflect a growing judicial commitment to the neutrality principle with respect to religious organizations — government programs must not disfavor religious education any more than they must not favor it.[86]

EPILOGUE

Varieties of Religious Seeking

. . . the object of opening the mind, as of opening the mouth, is to shut it again on something solid. (G. K. Chesterton)

. . . God is light . . . the true Light . . . gives light to every man . . . seek, and you will find . . . the path of the just is like the shining sun that shines ever brighter unto the perfect day. (1 John 1:5; John 1:9; Matthew 7:7; Proverbs 4:18; NKJV)

A college is a company of seekers of the truth. A Christian college is a voluntary community of those who share the central conviction that the key to understanding the human condition is the incarnational idea that God has come to us in Christ. While we seek individually, we do so in a group context. The Christian college experience then is an especially focused period of truth-seeking, usually during the formative years, when the company of the committed develop a life-long practice of continual seeking and of being transformed by the truth that they find. Such is the Christian college ideal.

The pluralistic college or university is also a community of truth-seekers. A public university by definition is open to all religious and non-religious perspectives even while privileging none. A private college may choose to be pluralistic. The central conviction of a pluralistic college is the idea that the free exchange of ideas is the best environment for individual seekers to find the truth or at least a truth that works for them. Such is the pluralistic college ideal.

In practice, of course, all colleges, as all individuals, fall short of their ideals. Such is one of the universal realities that we seek to understand and from which we seek liberation in the ongoing, unending earthly quest for the ultimate.

While no model of seeking is perfect, some are more natural than others. Of the four types of colleges identified in the classic Benne typology in appendix B (1. orthodox; 2. critical-mass; 3. intentionally pluralist; 4. accidentally pluralist—or functionally secular), the first and the third are the purest models. The second represents a modification of the first; at its best the second is motivated by intellectual openness and a spirit of unity with all humanity, while at its worst it is unduly influenced by secular ideas of academic success and pluralism. The fourth represents a failure of the evenhandedness of the third. The third is the ideal model for a public university; the fourth is an ideal model for no liberal arts institution.

A model one college (orthodox) begins with an institutional commitment to a Christian worldview and then invites into its community of learning those scholars who, already of their own volition, have chosen this worldview as the framework through which they can best find truth.[1] The danger for the orthodox Christian college is that it will become more narrow than the Christian faith itself[2] and, with no in-house challenger, will compare an idealized form of its own tradition with the actual or the worst manifestations of other systems of thought. Also, Robert McAfee Brown, as interpreted by Bradley Longfield and George Marsden, worries that "an all-Christian faculty produces an anemic faith, unfortified by the give and take of genuine dissent." The best orthodox colleges recognize these risks and consider them worth living with to maintain campus unity (philosophically being a *uni*versity in contrast to the *multi*versity of the pluralistic institutions) and reduce the likelihood of secularization; and then to assure that their students receive a fair understanding of the other major worldviews they employ objective, fair-minded, no less than Christian, instructors, and regularly provide campus forums that present a variety of perspectives on primary issues.[3]

A model two institution (critical-mass) operates with a less clear and less consistent apologia or rationale than does the orthodox one, but its adherents nevertheless are among the "intentionally Christian" institutions, and they do provide some able blueprints for this type of college or university.[4] The danger for the critical-mass institution is that whether from inattention or philosophical indifference it can easily lack diligence in implementing its faculty personnel procedures both before and after the initial hiring process. The faculty hirees who do not believe in the Christian faith must at least believe in the great good of the Christian university rather than simply being glad to receive an appointment and then, once in the institution, become non-supportive of its goals or even seek to change it in a secular direction. Even more than the orthodox colleges, the critical-mass institutions with their unique combination of Christian commitment and diverse faculty hiring procedures need to give special attention to faculty development programs that instruct their new faculty in the history and philosophy of the college or university so that they might best be able to participate in and contribute to its vital perpetuation.

A model three institution (intentionally pluralist) may or may not be a religious institution but it values instruction about religion. It presents the Christian system of thought clearly and fairly as one worldview, and it does the same with other major explanations of life and meaning. Among these worldviews the institution by design seeks to remain neutral in influence, thinking that such neutrality is the best way to facilitate critical, independent, and mature thinking by its students. A desire that the students specifically develop some form of spirituality may or may not be an institutional goal. A state institution seeking to offer a fully developed system of instruction and wishing to comply with both parts of the First Amendment provision on religious freedom (which now usually means being as sensitive to not denying the free exercise of religion as it is to not promoting religion) will find this model to fit well.[5]

A danger for the intentionally pluralist system is that one specific worldview (whether religious or anti-religious) will become both dominant and zealous to control, thus driving out the institutional goal of religious neutrality. American history has shown that zeal by a dominant party often leads to structural control unless there are specific systemic provisions to prevent it. Thus the intentionally pluralist institution will need to carefully define its pluralist intentions in a widely available written document.

A second danger for the intentionally pluralist college is that its commitment to pluralism may come to reflect a preference for relativism. Of course, just because God does not love any one person more than any other person does not necessarily mean that no idea is more nearly correct than any other idea.

It is difficult to understand why a model four institution (functionally secular/accidentally pluralist/religiously dismissive) would want to continue to appear on a denomination list of church-related colleges unless there was a separate category (as there is with the UCC colleges) for an historical-only relationship. By design or by default a model four institution does not value religion as an important component of the human condition, or for some reason believes that religion alone of the primary elements of the human condition should not be considered seriously in the academy.

The irony of the typical secularized church-related college is that in an effort to become a credible (i.e., not sectarian) institution, it has lost its capacity to become a complete one (i.e., a college concerned with the whole universe of human thought and experience). One such secularized institution that sensed its lack and devised a modest plan to reengage the spiritual dimension appropriately called its proposed program "A Move toward Wholeness."[6] Perhaps given the changing zeitgeist of the twenty-first century, many formerly Christian colleges will seek to find a way of combining their modern independence and critical thinking skills with an epistemology that includes all of the human ways of knowing.

Providing training in the thoughtful approach to religious seeking is the essential business of the intentionally Christian college. So important is this human endeavor that Christian higher education must continue to seek new ways of making its services accessible to a larger percentage of the Christian scholars that would prefer to study in its institutions.

In short, Christian higher education needs a broader variety of undergraduate programs in a broader variety of price ranges, and it also needs a larger number of sites where its future professors can obtain their advanced graduate training in an environment that is supportive of the faith and learning framework in which they will be encouraged to teach during their careers in the Christian colleges.

One encouraging step is the recent growth of distance learning and user-friendly adult degree completion programs (see chapter 7, the section titled "New Constituencies and Extended Borders"); but at least some of the Christian colleges also need to review the ways in which the traditional residential program could be restructured to operate with greater economy. While there will always be a demand for the more expensive model (also called variously the full-service model, the Cadillac model, or the country-club model), most of the Christian colleges will want to respond to the growing public expectation of cost control by making at least limited adjustments, and some will want to make more radical changes both to fill a marketing need and also because of a missionary sense of service to "the least of these my brethren." The accrediting associations, with their recent emphasis on outcome assessment as opposed to delivery mode, are becoming increasingly sympathetic to cheaper delivery systems.[7]

The efficiency measures from which a Christian college might choose in an effort to reduce its costs include the following:

1. become essentially a junior college with its limited, large course enrollment curriculum;
2. adopt the approach of many large universities that offer very large sections (as large as a Sunday morning congregation) of many of the introductory general education courses;
3. offer pre-produced video instruction by master teachers;
4. limit the number of courses in a major to approximately the minimum number needed to complete the major;
5. reduce the more expensive components of the extracurriculum;

6. redefine the professorial workload to free the instructors from many of the time-consuming, extra-teaching demands and thus be able to teach a larger number of courses per year;

7. combine the old Woodrow Wilson tutorial idea at Princeton (whereby upperclassmen helped in the instruction of the lowerclassmen), the modern idea of internships, and the age-long idea of learning by teaching, to assist in the personalization of large enrollment classes and the overall learning and sense of service and community by the upperclassmen. Or better yet, employ graduate assistants who would offer an even higher level of instructional assistance and could do so as a part of a graduate program that would be preparing them to be able to teach in a faith and learning environment.

In addition to distance learning and less expensive approaches to traditional learning, the Christian college community could increasingly provide Christian learning components for the many Christian youth studying at the less expensive state universities. These components could include Christian residence centers (essentially a large building with apartment units and student development services including religious programming and faith and learning discussion groups), satellite colleges (Christian residence centers plus limited academic instruction in religious studies and faith and learning courses; see page 189), and academic services in cooperation with the long-standing evangelical and mainline student ministry centers (a Christian college working with such groups as InterVarsity Christian Fellowship, Campus Crusade for Christ, The Navigators, and the denominational foundation centers to complement the ministry programs of the latter groups with the college's academic instruction in those areas of religion which the students do not receive in their state university education).

Meanwhile there remains the long-standing issue of how to provide better advanced training opportunities for the future instructors in the Christian colleges. One of the reasons for the wide publicity of the recent Baylor struggles to grow quickly into a major university is the hope that the Baptist institution could become the long-awaited grand Christian university of the evangelical tradition. Whatever may happen with Baylor, perhaps it is more realistic to expect that the ultimate solution is likely to come from developments in a variety of institutions, as can be seen, for example, in the growth of graduate education in many Christian colleges (see chapter 7, the section titled "New Constituencies and Extended Borders"). Other possible ways of meeting this graduate training need include the following:

1. As previously mentioned in the discussion on undergraduate instruction efficiencies, seek to meet the need for cheaper undergraduate costs and the need for better and more graduate training opportunities in faith-informed scholarship in the same institutions by placing increasing numbers of graduate students in undergraduate teaching roles under the direction of master teachers.

2. Increasingly consider the idea of an "ecumenically orthodox Christian university" (EOCU) which would combine the efforts of all major branches of the Christian tradition.[8] Such an institution could come into existence most easily and fill the greatest need on the graduate level.

3. Given the growing relationship between the evangelicals and the Roman Catholics during the past generation, the higher educational institutions of the two groups could develop more formal, mutually satisfactory relationships for graduate training in some of the already well-developed Catholic universities.

4. Encourage some of the prospering and growing evangelical seminaries to expand their vision beyond a largely church focus so as to increasingly serve the Christian colleges by adding doctoral level programs in areas that are both reasonably related to seminary interests and that would meet the greatest need in Christian liberal arts training. These relevant but needy curricular areas include such values-oriented disciplines as economics, history, literature, philosophy, political science, and sociology.

How wonderful it would be if a generation from now the public universities would have become more truly pluralistic, the Christian institutions would have found ways to make their product — or at least the heart of the Christian college experience — accessible to the majority of Christian youth enrolled in college, and the students everywhere in increasing numbers would have come to value the relentless, honest, and even joyful search for truth in general and the source of that truth in particular.

APPENDIX A

Profile of U.S. Postsecondary Education

By Bob Andringa, Council for Christian Colleges & Universities

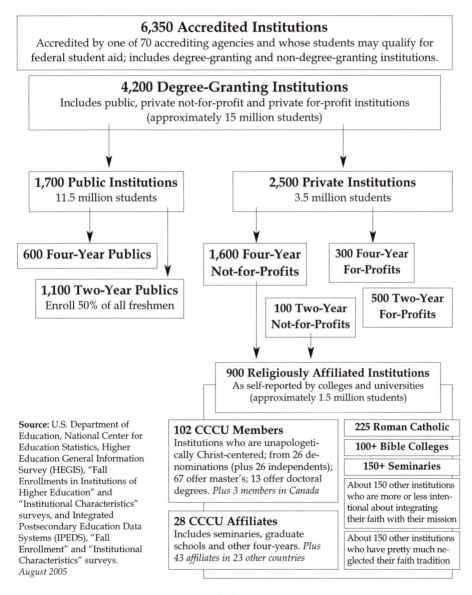

6,350 Accredited Institutions
Accredited by one of 70 accrediting agencies and whose students may qualify for federal student aid; includes degree-granting and non-degree-granting institutions.

4,200 Degree-Granting Institutions
Includes public, private not-for-profit and private for-profit institutions
(approximately 15 million students)

1,700 Public Institutions
11.5 million students

2,500 Private Institutions
3.5 million students

600 Four-Year Publics

1,600 Four-Year Not-for-Profits

300 Four-Year For-Profits

1,100 Two-Year Publics
Enroll 50% of all freshmen

100 Two-Year Not-for-Profits

500 Two-Year For-Profits

900 Religiously Affiliated Institutions
As self-reported by colleges and universities
(approximately 1.5 million students)

Source: U.S. Department of Education, National Center for Education Statistics, Higher Education General Information Survey (HEGIS), "Fall Enrollments in Institutions of Higher Education" and "Institutional Characteristics" surveys, and Integrated Postsecondary Education Data Systems (IPEDS), "Fall Enrollment" and "Institutional Characteristics" surveys.
August 2005

102 CCCU Members
Institutions who are unapologetically Christ-centered; from 26 denominations (plus 26 independents); 67 offer master's; 13 offer doctoral degrees. *Plus 3 members in Canada*

28 CCCU Affiliates
Includes seminaries, graduate schools and other four-years. *Plus 43 affiliates in 23 other countries*

225 Roman Catholic

100+ Bible Colleges

150+ Seminaries

About 150 other institutions who are more or less intentional about integrating their faith with their mission

About 150 other institutions who have pretty much neglected their faith tradition

Appendix B

The Benne Typology of Church-Related Colleges and Universities

	Orthodox	Critical-Mass	Intentionally Pluralist	Accidentally Pluralist
Major divide:	the Christian vision as the organizing paradigm		secular sources as the organizing paradigm	
Public relevance of Christian vision:	Pervasive from a shared point of view	Privileged voice in an ongoing conversation	Assured voice in an ongoing conversation	Random or absent in an ongoing conversation
Public rhetoric:	Unabashed invitation for fellow believers to an intentionally Christian enterprise	Straightforward presentation as a Christian school but inclusive of others	Presentation as a liberal arts school with a Christian heritage	Presentation as a secular school with little or no allusion to Christian heritage
Membership requirements:	Near 100%, with orthodoxy tests	Critical mass in all facets	Intentional representation	Haphazard sprinkling
Religion/theology department:	Large, with theology privileged	Large, with theology as flagship	Small, mixed department, some theology, but mostly religious studies	Small, exclusively religious studies
Religion/theology required courses:	All courses affected by shared religious perspective	Two or three, with dialogical effort in many other courses	One course in general education	Choice in distribution or an elective
Chapel:	Required in large church at a protected time daily	Voluntary at high quality services in large nave at protected time daily	Voluntary at unprotected times, with low attendance	For few, on special occasions
Ethos:	Overt piety of sponsoring tradition	Dominant atmosphere of sponsoring tradition — rituals and habits	Open minority from sponsoring tradition finding private niche	Reclusive and unorganized minority from sponsoring tradition
			(Dominantly secular atmosphere)	
Support by church:	Indispensable financial support and majority of students from sponsoring tradition	Important direct and crucial indirect financial support; at least 50% of students	Important focused, indirect support; small minority of students	Token indirect support; student numbers no longer recorded
Governance:	Owned and governed by church or its official representatives	Majority of board from tradition, some official representatives	Minority of board from tradition by unofficial agreement	Token membership from tradition
			(College or university is autonomously owned and governed)	

APPENDIX C

Council of Christian Colleges & Universities (CCCU)
U.S. Member Institutions (2005)

1. Abilene Christian University (TX)
2. Anderson University (IN)
3. Asbury College (KY)
4. Azusa Pacific University (CA)
5. Belhaven College (MS)
6. Bethel College (IN)
7. Bethel University (MN)
8. Biola University (CA)
9. Bluffton University (OH)
10. Bryan College (TN)
11. California Baptist University (CA)
12. Calvin College (MI)
13. Campbellsville University (KY)
14. Carson-Newman College (TN)
15. Cedarville University (OH)
16. College of the Ozarks (MO)
17. Colorado Christian University (CO)
18. Cornerstone University (MI)
19. Covenant College (GA)
20. Crichton College (TN)
21. Crown College (MN)
22. Dallas Baptist University (TX)
23. Dordt College (IA)
24. East Texas Baptist University (TX)
25. Eastern Mennonite University (VA)
26. Eastern Nazarene College (MA)
27. Eastern University (PA)
28. Erskine College (SC)
29. Evangel University (MO)
30. Fresno Pacific University (CA)
31. Geneva College (PA)
32. George Fox University (OR)
33. Gordon College (MA)
34. Goshen College (IN)
35. Grace College & Seminary (IN)
36. Greenville College (IL)
37. Hardin-Simmons University (TX)
38. Hope International University (CA)
39. Houghton College (NY)
40. Houston Baptist University (TX)
41. Howard Payne University (TX)
42. Huntington College (IN)
43. Indiana Wesleyan University (IN)
44. John Brown University (AR)
45. Judson College (AL)
46. Judson College (IL)
47. Kentucky Christian University (KY)
48. King College (TN)
49. Lee University (TN)
50. LeTourneau University (TX)
51. Lipscomb University (TN)
52. Louisiana College (LA)
53. Malone College (OH)
54. Master's College & Seminary, The (CA)
55. Messiah College (PA)
56. MidAmerica Nazarene University (KS)
57. Milligan College (TN)
58. Mississippi College (MS)
59. Missouri Baptist University (MO)
60. Montreat College (NC)
61. Mount Vernon Nazarene University (OH)
62. North Greenville College (SC)
63. North Park University (IL)
64. Northwest Christian College (OR)

65. Northwest Nazarene University (ID)
66. Northwest University (WA)
67. Northwestern College (IA)
68. Northwestern College (MN)
69. Nyack College (NY)
70. Oklahoma Baptist University (OK)
71. Oklahoma Christian University (OK)
72. Oklahoma Wesleyan University (OK)
73. Olivet Nazarene University (IL)
74. Oral Roberts University (OK)
75. Palm Beach Atlantic University (FL)
76. Point Loma Nazarene University (CA)
77. Roberts Wesleyan College (NY)
78. Seattle Pacific University (WA)
79. Simpson University (CA)
80. Southeastern College (FL)
81. Southern Nazarene University (OK)
82. Southern Wesleyan University (SC)
83. Southwest Baptist University (MO)
84. Spring Arbor University (MI)
85. Sterling College (KS)
86. Tabor College (KS)
87. Taylor University (IN)
88. Trevecca Nazarene University (TN)
89. Trinity Christian College (IL)
90. Trinity International University (IL)
91. Union University (TN)
92. University of Sioux Falls (SD)
93. Vanguard University of Southern California (CA)
94. Warner Pacific College (OR)
95. Warner Southern College (FL)
96. Wayland Baptist University (TX)
97. Waynesburg College (PA)
98. Western Baptist College (OR)
99. Westmont College (CA)
100. Wheaton College (IL)
101. Whitworth College (WA)
102. Williams Baptist College (AR)

Appendix D

The Association for Biblical Higher Education (ABHE)
U.S. Member Institutions (2005)

1. Alaska Bible College (AK)
2. Allegheny Wesleyan College (OH)
3. American Baptist College (TN)
4. Appalachian Bible College (WV)
5. Arlington Baptist College (TX)
6. Baptist Bible College (MO)
7. Baptist Bible College (PA)
8. Baptist University of the Americas (TX)
9. Barclay College (KS)
10. Bethesda Christian University (CA)
11. Beulah Heights Bible College (GA)
12. Boise Bible College (ID)
13. Calvary Bible College (MO)
14. Central Bible College (MO)
15. Central Christian College of the Bible (MO)
16. Cincinnati Christian University (OH)
17. Circleville Bible College (OH)
18. Clear Creek Baptist Bible College (KY)
19. Colegio Biblico Pentecostal (PR)
20. Colegio Pentecostal Mizpa (PR)
21. College of Biblical Studies–Houston (TX)
22. Columbia International University (SC)
23. Crossroads Bible College (IN)
24. Crossroads College (MN)
25. Crown College (MN)
26. Dallas Christian College (TX)
27. Davis College (NY)
28. Ecclesia College (AR)
29. Emmaus Bible College (IA)
30. Faith Baptist Bible College (IA)
31. Florida Christian College (FL)
32. Free Will Baptist Bible College (TN)
33. God's Bible School and College (OH)
34. Grace Bible College (MI)
35. Grace University (NE)
36. Great Lakes Christian College (MI)
37. Heritage Christian University (AL)
38. Hobe Sound Bible College (FL)
39. Johnson Bible College (TN)
40. John Wesley College (NC)
41. Kentucky Mountain Bible College (KY)
42. The King's College (CA)
43. Lancaster Bible College (PA)
44. Life Pacific College (CA)
45. Lincoln Christian College (IL)
46. Manhattan Christian College (KS)
47. Moody Bible Institute (IL)
48. Multnomah Bible College (OR)
49. Nazarene Bible College (CO)
50. Nebraska Christian College (NE)
51. Oak Hills Christian College (MN)
52. Ozark Christian College (MO)
53. Philadelphia Biblical University (PA)
54. Pillsbury Baptist Bible College (MN)
55. Puget Sound Christian College (WA)
56. Reformed Bible College (MI)
57. Rio Grande Bible Institute (TX)
58. Roanoke Bible College (NC)

59. Rosedale Bible College (OH)
60. Somerset Christian College (NJ)
61. Southeastern Baptist College (MS)
62. Southeastern Bible College (AL)
63. Southwestern College (AZ)
64. Toccoa Falls College (GA)
65. Tri-State Bible College (OH)
66. Trinity Bible College (ND)
67. Trinity College of Florida (FL)
68. Vennard College (IA)
69. Washington Bible College (MD)
70. Zion Bible Institute (RI)

Appendix E

Lilly Fellows Program Members (2004)

1. Abilene Christian University (TX)
2. Augsburg College (IA)
3. Baylor University (TX)
4. Belmont Abbey College (NC)
5. Benedictine University (IL)
6. Berea College (KY)
7. Bethel College–St. Paul (MN)
8. Bethune-Cookman College (FL)
9. Boston College (MA)
10. California Lutheran University (CA)
11. Calvin College (MI)
12. College of the Holy Cross (MA)
13. Columbia College (SC)
14. Concordia College (MN)
15. Concordia University at Austin (TX)
16. Concordia University–Portland (OR)
17. Concordia University–Seward (NE)
18. Culver-Stockton College (MO)
19. Davidson College (NC)
20. Dordt College (IA)
21. Eastern Mennonite University (VA)
22. Fordham University (NY)
23. Furman University (SC)
24. Geneva College (PA)
25. Georgetown College (KY)
26. Gordon College (MA)
27. Goshen College (IN)
28. Gustavus Adolphus College (MN)
29. Hope College (MI)
30. Houghton College (NY)
31. Illinois College (IL)
32. Indiana Wesleyan University (IN)
33. Loyola College in Maryland (MD)
34. Loyola Marymount University (CA)
35. Luther College (IA)
36. Mercer University (GA)
37. Messiah College (PA)
38. Midland Lutheran College (NE)
39. Morningside College (NE)
40. Mount Saint Mary's College (MD)
41. Pepperdine University (CA)
42. Presbyterian College (SC)
43. Rhodes College (TN)
44. River College (NH)
45. Roanoke College (VA)
46. Rosemont College (PA)
47. Saint Mary's College (IN)
48. Saint Mary's University of Minnesota (MN)
49. Saint Xavier University (IL)
50. Samford University (AL)
51. Seattle Pacific University (WA)
52. St. Olaf College (MN)
53. Texas Lutheran University (TX)
54. University of Dallas (TX)
55. University of Indianapolis (IN)
56. University of Notre Dame (IN)
57. University of Scranton (PA)
58. University of St. Thomas (MN)
59. University of the Incarnate Word (TX)
60. University of the South (TN)
61. Valparaiso University (IN)
62. Villanova University (PA)

63. Wartburg College (IA)
64. Westminster College (PA)
65. Westmont College (CA)
66. Wheaton College (IL)
67. Whitworth College (WA)
68. Wilberforce University (OH)

69. Wittenberg University (OH)
70. Wofford College (SC)
71. Xavier University (OH)
72. Xavier University of Louisiana (LA)

APPENDIX F

Programs for the Theological Exploration of Vocation Institutional Members (2004)

1. Alma College (MI)
2. Asbury College (KY)
3. Augsburg College (MN)
4. Augustana College (IL)
5. Austin College (TX)
6. Azusa Pacific University (CA)
7. Baylor University (TX)
8. Bluffton College (OH)
9. Boston College (MA)
10. Butler University (IN)
11. Calvin College (MI)
12. Cardinal Stritch University (WI)
13. Catawba College (NC)
14. Claflin College (SC)
15. College of Holy Cross (MA)
16. College of Saint Benedict (MN)
17. College of Wooster (OH)
18. Concordia College (MN)
19. Covenant College (GA)
20. Creighton University (NE)
21. Davidson College (NC)
22. Denison University (OH)
23. Dillard University (LA)
24. Dordt College (IA)
25. Duke University (NC)
26. Earlham College (IN)
27. Eastern Mennonite University (VA)
28. Elmhurst College (IL)
29. Evangel University (MO)
30. Fairfield University (CT)
31. Furman University (SC)
32. Geneva College (PA)
33. Georgetown College (KY)
34. Gordon College (MA)
35. Goshen College (IN)
36. Grinnell College (IA)
37. Guilford College (NC)
38. Gustavus Adolphus College (MN)
39. Hamline University (MN)
40. Hanover College (IN)
41. Hastings College (NE)
42. Hellenic College (MA)
43. Hendrix College (AR)
44. Hope College (MI)
45. Howard University (DC)
46. Indiana Wesleyan College (IN)
47. Lee University (TN)
48. Loyola University of Chicago (IL)
49. Luther College (IA)
50. Macalester College (MN)
51. Manchester College (IN)
52. Marian College (IN)
53. Marquette University (WS)
54. Maryville College (TN)
55. Mercer University (GA)
56. Messiah College (PA)
57. Milligan College (TN)
58. Millsaps College (MN)
59. Mt. St. Mary's College (MD)
60. Northwestern College (IA)
61. Occidental College (CA)
62. Ohio Wesleyan University (OH)
63. Our Lady of the Lake University (TX)
64. Pacific Lutheran University (WA)
65. Pepperdine University (CA)
66. Saint Louis University (MO)
67. Samford University (AL)
68. Santa Clara University (CA)
69. Seattle Pacific University (WA)
70. Seton Hall University (NJ)
71. Simpson College (IA)
72. Spelman College (GA)

73. St. Bonaventure University (NY)
74. St. John's University (MN)
75. St. Norbert College (WI)
76. St. Olaf College (MN)
77. Transylvania University (KY)
78. University of Dayton (OH)
79. University of Indianapolis (IN)
80. University of Notre Dame (IN)
81. University of St. Thomas (MN)
82. University of the South (TN)
83. Valparaiso University (IN)
84. Wake Forest University (NC)
85. Wartburg College (IA)
86. Whitworth College (WA)
87. Willamette University (OR)
88. Xavier University of Louisiana (LA)

Appendix G

Colleges and Universities Affiliated with the Major Denominations (2005)

Some church-related colleges wish to be known as Christian, some do not, while still others prefer a partial identity. A statement at the beginning of the "Directory of Schools, Colleges and Universities related to the Presbyterian Church U.S.A." reflects in general this mixed pattern among the colleges founded by the largest branches of the Protestant tradition: "Some [Presbyterian schools] are demonstrably Christian inside and outside the classroom; others tend to be more secular. Some claim their Presbyterian identity in a visible way; others are Presbyterian largely in an historical sense." Each of the following colleges appears on the website of its corresponding denomination or denominational association of colleges.

1. American Baptist–Related Colleges and Universities

Alderson-Broaddus College (WV)
Bacone College (OK)
Benedict College (SC)
Eastern University (PA)
Florida Memorial College (FL)
Franklin College (IN)
Judson College (IL)
Kalamazoo College (MI)
Keuka College (NY)
Linfield College (OR)
Ottawa University (KS)
Shaw University (NC)
University of Redlands (CA)
University of Sioux Falls (SD)
Virginia Union University (VA)
William Jewell College (MO)

2. Lutheran Educational Conference of North America

Augsburg College (MN) (ELCA)
Augustana College (IL) (ELCA)
Augustana College (SD) (ELCA)
Bethany College (KS) (ELCA)
California Lutheran University (CA) (ELCA)
Capital University (OH) (ELCA)
Carthage College (WI) (ELCA)
Concordia College (Bronxville, NY) (LCMS)
Concordia College (Moorhead, MN) (ELCA)
Concordia College (Selma, AL) (LCMS)
Concordia University (Ann Arbor, MI) (LCMS)
Concordia University (Austin, TX) (LCMS)
Concordia University (Irvine, CA) (LCMS)
Concordia University Wisconsin (Mequon, WI) (LCMS)
Concordia University (Portland, OR) (LCMS)
Concordia University (River Forest, IL) (LCMS)
Concordia University (St. Paul, MN) (LCMS)
Concordia University (Seward, NE) (LCMS)
Dana College (NE) (ELCA)
Finlandia University (MI) (ELCA)
Gettysburg College (PA) (ELCA)
Grand View College (IA) ELCA
Gustavus Adolphus College (MN) (ELCA)

Lenoir-Rhyne College (NC) (ELCA)
Luther College (IA) (ELCA)
Midland Lutheran College (NE)
    (ELCA)
Muhlenberg College (PA) (ELCA)
Newberry College (SC) (ELCA)
Pacific Lutheran University (WA)
    (ELCA)
Roanoke College (VA) (ELCA)
St. Olaf College (MN) (ELCA)
Susquehanna University (PA)
    (ELCA)

Texas Lutheran University (TX)
    (ELCA)
Thiel College (PA) (ELCA)
Trinity Lutheran College (WA)
Valparaiso University (IN)
Wagner College (NY) (ELCA)
Waldorf College (IA) (ELCA)
Wartburg College (IA) (ELCA)
Wittenberg University (OH)
    (ELCA)

3. Association of Presbyterian Colleges and Universities

Agnes Scott College (GA)
Albertson College of Idaho (ID)
Alma College (MI)
Arcadia University (PA)
Austin College (TX)
Barber-Scotia College (NC)
Belhaven College (MS)
Blackburn College (IL)
Bloomfield College (NJ)
Buena Vista University (IA)
Carroll College (WI)
Centre College (KY)
Chamberlain-Hunt Academy (MS)
Coe College (IA)
College of the Ozarks (MO)
College of Wooster, The (OH)
Cook College & Theological School
    (AZ)
Davidson College (NC)
Davis & Elkins College (WV)
Eckerd College (FL)
Grove City College (PA)
Hampden-Sydney College (VA)
Hanover College (IN)
Hastings College (NE)
Illinois College (IL)
Inter-American University of
    Puerto Rico (PR)
Jamestown College (ND)
Johnson C. Smith University (NC)
King College (TN)
Knoxville College (TN)

Lafayette College (PA)
Lake Forest College (IL)
Lees-McRae College (NC)
Lindenwood University (MO)
Lyon College (AR)
Macalester College (IL)
Mary Baldwin College (VA)
Mary Holmes College (MS)
Maryville College (TN)
Millikin University (IL)
Missouri Valley College (MO)
Monmouth College (IL)
Montreat College (NC)
Muskingum College (OH)
Peace College (NC)
Pikeville College (KY)
Presbyterian College (SC)
Queens College (NC)
Rhodes College (TN)
Rocky Mountain College (MT)
Schreiner University (TX)
Sheldon Jackson College (AK)
St. Andrews Presbyterian College
    (NC)
Sterling College (KS)
Stillman College (AL)
Trinity University (TX)
Tusculum College (TN)
University of Dubuque (IA)
University of Ozarks (AR)
University of Tulsa, The (OK)
Warren Wilson College (NC)

Waynesburg College (PA)
Westminster College (MO)
Westminster College (PA)

Westminster College (UT)
Whitworth College (WA)
Wilson College (PA)

4. Southern Baptist–Related Colleges and Universities

Anderson College (SC)
Baptist College of Florida, The (FL)
Baylor University (TX)
Belmont University (TN)
Blue Mountain College (MS)
Bluefield College (VA)
Brewton-Parker College (GA)
California Baptist University (CA)
Campbell University (NC)
Campbellsville University (KY)
Carson-Newman College (TN)
Cedarville University (OH)
Charleston Southern University
  (SC)
Chowan College (NC)
Clear Creek Baptist Bible College
  (KY)
Criswell College (TX)
Cumberland College (KY)
Dallas Baptist University (TX)
East Texas Baptist University (TX)
Gardner-Webb University (NC)
Georgetown College (KY)
Hannibal-LaGrange College (MO)
Hardin Simmons University (TX)
Houston Baptist University (TX)
Howard Payne University (TX)
Judson College (AL)

Louisiana College (LA)
Mars Hill College (NC)
Mercer University (GA)
Meredith College (NC)
Mid-Continent College ((KY)
Mississippi College (MS)
Missouri Baptist College (MO)
North Greenville College (SC)
Oklahoma Baptist University (OK)
Ouachita Baptist University (AR)
Palm Beach Atlantic College (FL)
Samford University (AL)
Southwest Baptist University (MO)
Truett-McConnell College (GA)
Union University (TN)
University of Mary Hardin-Baylor
  (TX)
University of Mobile (AL)
University of Richmond (VA)
Virginia Intermont College (VA)
Wake Forest University (NC)
Wayland Baptist University (TX)
William Carey College (MS)
William Jewell College (MS)
Williams Baptist College (AR)
Wingate University (NC)
Yellowstone Baptist College (MT)

5. Schools Related to the United Church of Christ

Catawba College (NC)
Deaconess College of Nursing (MO)
Defiance College (OH)
Dillard University (LA)
Doane College (NE)
Drury University (MO)
Elmhurst College (IL)
Elon University (NC)
Heidelberg College (OH)
Huston-Tillotson College (TX)

Illinois College (IL)
Lakeland College (WI)
Lemoyne-Owen College (TN)
Northland College (WI)
Olivet College (MI)
Pacific University (OR)
Piedmont College (GA)
Rocky Mountain College (MT)
Talladega College (AL)
Tougaloo College (MS)

Schools Historically Related to the United Church of Christ

Beloit College (WI)
Carleton College (MN)
Cedar Crest College (PA)
Fisk University (TN)
Franklin and Marshall College (PA)
Grinnell College (IA)

Hood College (MD)
Ripon College (WI)
Ursinus College (PA)
Westminster College of Salt Lake
   City (UT)

6. United Methodist–Related Colleges and Universities

Adrian College (MI)
Alaska Pacific University (AK)
Albion College (MI)
Albright College (PA)
Allegheny College (PA)
American University (DC)
Andrew College (GA)
Baker University (KS)
Baldwin-Wallace College (OH)
Bennett College for Women (NC)
Bethune-Cookman College (FL)
Birmingham-Southern College (AL)
Boston University (MA)
Brevard College (NC)
Centenary College (NJ)
Centenary College of Louisiana
   (LA)
Central Methodist College (MO)
Claflin University (SC)
Clark Atlanta University (GA)
Columbia College (SC)
Cornell College (IA)
Dakota Wesleyan University (SD)
DePauw University (IN)
Dickinson College (PA)
Dillard University (LA)
Drew University (NJ)
Duke University (NC)
Emory and Henry College (VA)
Ferrum College (VA)
Florida Southern College (FL)
Green Mountain College (VT)
Greensboro College (NC)
Hamline University (MN)
Hendrix College (AR)
High Point University (NC)

Hiwassee College (TN)
Huntingdon College (AL)
Huston-Tillotson College (TX)
Illinois Wesleyan University (IL)
Iowa Wesleyan College (IA)
Kansas Wesleyan University (KS)
Kendall College (IL)
Kentucky Wesleyan College (KY)
LaGrange College (GA)
Lambuth University (TN)
Lebanon Valley College (PA)
Lindsey Wilson College (KY)
Lon Morris College (TX)
Louisburg College (NC)
Lycoming College (PA)
MacMurray College (IL)
Martin Methodist College (TN)
McKendree College (IL)
McMurry University (TX)
Methodist College (NC)
Millsaps College (MS)
Morningside College (IA)
Mount Union College (OH)
Nebraska Methodist College (NE)
Nebraska Wesleyan University
   (NE)
North Carolina Wesleyan College
   (NC)
North Central College (IL)
Ohio Northern University (OH)
Ohio Wesleyan University (OH)
Oklahoma City University (OK)
Otterbein College (OH)
Oxford College of Emory Univer-
   sity (GA)
Paine College (GA)

Pfeiffer University (NC)
Philander Smith College (AR)
Randolph-Macon College (VA)
Reinhardt College (GA)
Rocky Mountain College (MT)
Rust College (MS)
Shenandoah University (VA)
Simpson College (IA)
Southern Methodist University (TX)
Southwestern University (TX)
Spartanburg Methodist College
   (SC)
Syracuse University (NY)
Tennessee Wesleyan College (TN)
Texas Wesleyan University (TX)

Union College (KY)
University of Denver (CO)
University of Evansville (IN)
University of Indianapolis (IN)
University of Puget Sound (WA)
University of the Pacific (CA)
Virginia Wesleyan College (VA)
Wesley College (DE)
Wesleyan College (GA)
West Virginia Wesleyan College
   (WV)
Wiley College (TX)
Willamette University (OR)
Wofford College (SC)
Young Harris College (GA)

Appendix H

Christian Liberal Arts Colleges outside of the United States:
An Annotated Sample List

This appendix, researched and written by David Tripple, is designed to illustrate the growing interest worldwide in Christian liberal arts education and the growing interest among United States institutions in encouraging such development. Many of the colleges and universities appearing here are orthodox in nature and recent in origin; others are historically significant. Most of the information in this section comes from the websites of the institutions.

North America/Canada

Redeemer University College (Ancaster, Ontario)
Opened in 1982, Redeemer University College was the first Canadian institution to join the Council of Christian Colleges and Universities (CCCU) in 1986. The university was originally of the Reformed tradition, but it is now an interdenominational institution. Students may choose from more than thirty majors in four broad divisions. Redeemer University College has approximately eight hundred students and forty full-time faculty members. In 1994, the university established the Dooyeweerd Centre for Christian Philosophy in order to translate and make available in English the works of Dutch Christian philosopher Herman Dooyeweerd (1894–1977).

Regent College (Vancouver, British Columbia)
Located on the campus of the University of British Columbia in Vancouver, Regent College was founded in 1968 as an interdenominational graduate school of theology. However, the institution emphasized training for lay Christians, rather than those pursuing a pastoral ministry. The student body, consisting of some seven hundred individuals, includes a variety of cultures, denominations, and vocations. The college offers four programs of study, with the highest academic degree being a Master of Theology. While the primary emphasis of the school remains to train lay people, Regent College now offers programs for those entering full-time Christian service.

Latin and South America

Universidad Evangelica Boliviana (Santa Cruz, Bolivia)
Universidad Evangelica Boliviana (UEB) located in Santa Cruz, emphasizes its role in providing Christian education to persons of all faiths. Founded in 1982 by World Gospel Mission worker Meredythe Scheflen, UEB was the product of international cooperation between seven national organizations and five North American missions. It was the first private university in Bolivia, as well as the first evangelical institution in Spanish-speaking South America. The school, a CCCU

affiliate, offers several graduate and undergraduate degrees and serves nearly two thousand students.

Universidad Christiana Latinoamericana (Quito, Ecuador)

Universidad Christiana Latinoamericana, established in 2000, has been a member of the CCCU since 2001. Founded by Methodist nationals, the school has a philosophy of owning no buildings. The university's president, Dr. Patricio Proano, earned a doctorate from Princeton University. Although a young institution, the school already claims approximately two thousand students.

La Universidad de Mariano Galvez (Guatemala City, Guatemala)

Named for a former president of Guatemala, La Universidad de Mariano Galvez in Guatemala City has established itself as a major evangelical university in Latin America. Founded in 1966, the school has multiple campuses throughout the country. While providing a wide variety of academic programs to approximately fifteen thousand students, the institution continues to remain true to its Christian heritage.

Universidade Metodista de Piracicaba (Piracicaba, Brazil)

The first Methodist university in Latin America, Universidade Metodista de Piracicaba (UNIMEP) can trace its roots back to 1748. Originally founded as the Kingswood School by John Wesley, UNIMEP later became the Piracicabano School in 1881 under the direction of American missionary Martha Watts. Maintaining a strong commitment to Methodism, the school acquired university status in 1975. UNIMEP emphasizes national and international cooperation within the Methodist denomination. A large university, more than fourteen thousand students attend classes on four distinct campuses.

Africa

Fourah Bay College (Freetown, Sierra Leone)

Established in 1827, Fourah Bay College is the oldest institute of higher education in western Africa. Originally founded by the Church Missionary Society, the school's original intent was to train Africans as teachers and members of the clergy. However, since 1966, Fourah Bay College has been a part of the University of Sierra Leone and is now largely secular. Facilities exist for Protestant, Roman Catholic, and Muslim worship. The school has experienced growth in recent years and estimates enrollment to be approximately three thousand students.

Uganda Christian University (Mukono, Uganda)

Located close to Uganda's capital, Kampala, Uganda Christian University is the first African affiliate member of the CCCU. The school is relatively young, having been established and licensed in 1997. Uganda Christian University is built on the site of Bishop Tucker Theological College, one of the oldest educational institutions in the nation. The school has strong ties to the Anglican Church, and approximately one thousand students study on campus.

Daystar University (Nairobi, Kenya)
Founded in 1967 by Dr. Donald K. Smith and S. E. M. Pheko, Daystar University has become the largest non-denominational, Christian liberal arts college in Africa. Historically, the institution has had close ties with both Wheaton and Messiah Colleges in the United States, and the university continues to emphasize international cooperation. The school highlights its role of providing biblical training to Africans without the high cost of overseas relocation. Daystar University has close to two thousand students on two campuses.

South Korea

Yonsei University (Seoul)
Korea's oldest Protestant university, Yonsei University was begun as Kwanghyewon hospital by a Presbyterian missionary doctor named H. N. Allen in 1885. Over the years, the institution underwent several changes before merging with Yonhi College in 1957. Now largely secular, Yonsei University claims nearly fifty thousand students in eighteen graduate schools and nineteen colleges. The university is recognized as one of Korea's leading teaching and research institutions.

Keimyung University (Daegu)
Keimyung University, originally Keimyung Christian College, began in 1954. A Presbyterian missionary, Edward Adams, joined with two local church leaders, Choi Jaehwa and Kang Ingu, to create an institution of higher education rooted in Christianity. Over the last fifty years, Keimyung University has grown to twenty-seven thousand students. The school also boasts the largest international exchange network in Korea, cooperating with nearly 125 universities in twenty-six countries.

Ewha Women's University (Seoul)
Founded by a Methodist missionary, Ewha Women's University has grown to become the largest women's university in the world. Mary F. Scranton, a missionary from Ohio, began the school in a small house in Seoul in 1886. Her efforts to bring higher education to women despite cultural discrimination succeeded. Today, Ewha serves twenty-one thousand students and has an extensive academic program, including fourteen graduate schools. Although now a research-focused, secular institution, Ewha remains committed to promoting Christian morals and values in its teaching.

Soongsil University (Seoul)
Soongsil University has remained faithful to its Christian heritage for more than one hundred years. Dr. William M. Baird, a Northern Presbyterian missionary, founded the school in 1897. Throughout its history, the institution has actively engaged the Korean culture from a Christian perspective. During the Japanese colonization of Korea, the university took a leading role in several independence movements, which ultimately led to a temporary closure of the school in 1938. Since reopening in 1954, Soongsil has experienced steady growth. Presently, ap-

proximately twelve thousand students attend the university's eight colleges and eight graduate schools.

Southeast Asia

Tokyo Christian University (Japan)
Tokyo Christian University (TCU) traces its roots back to 1881 and the founding of Kaisei Women's Mission School. Other institutions from which TCU has developed include Tokyo Christian College and the Kyoritsu Christian Institute. In 1990, TCU was founded with a firm commitment to train Christian men and women as pastors, missionaries, and Christian workers. Today, the university identifies itself by four characteristics: evangelical, interdenominational, global missions, and practical education. TCU is an affiliate member of the CCCU.

Doshisha University (Kyoto, Japan)
Doshisha University was founded by a young samurai named Joseph Hardy Neesima. In 1864, at the age of twenty-one, Neesima illegally left Japan to study in the United States. After attending Phillips Academy and Amherst College, he returned to Japan in order to establish an institution of higher learning based on Western thought and Christian teachings. In 1875, he opened Doshisha English School in his home with eight students. Today, the university serves nearly twenty-four thousand individuals on three campuses. The school continues to teach Christian values and emphasizes cross-cultural learning in cooperation with numerous institutions around the globe.

Asia and the Middle East

Serampore College (Serampore, India)
Founded in 1818 by three English Baptist Missionary Society missionaries, William Carey, Joshua Marshman, and William Ward, Serampore College was established as an institution open to all persons, regardless of caste or creed. Carey and Marshman were members of Serampore's first governing council. From 1857 to 1883, the institution was affiliated with the University of Calcutta. For a brief time at the end of the nineteenth century, the college served as a theological institute for the Baptist churches in Bengal. The school is currently affiliated with the University of Calcutta after rejoining in 1911, and it offers courses in the sciences and humanities.

American University of Beirut (Lebanon)
Founded in 1866 as a private, independent institution of higher learning, American University of Beirut (AUB) initially had a goal of providing medical training to individuals of any race or religion. Dr. Daniel Bliss, an American missionary serving in Lebanon, served as the first president of the school. The institution originally opened as Syrian Protestant College with the first sixteen students meeting in a rented house. Today, 6,900 students, representing sixty-seven countries, at-

tend courses at AUB. Additionally, the AUB Medical Center is one of the most prominent and respected medical institutions in the Middle East.

Jerusalem University College (Israel)
Formerly known as the Institute of Holy Land Studies, Jerusalem University College (JUC) was founded in 1957. Originally an independent graduate institution, the school now works with approximately one hundred colleges, universities, and seminaries around the world to provide Christian students with an opportunity to study in the Holy Land. JUC, together with many of its affiliate schools, is a member of the CCCU. Since its inception, more than sixteen thousand individuals have studied in some capacity at JUC. Approximately 1,200 students participate in either long- or short-term programs at the school each year.

Europe

Lithuania Christian College (Klaipeda, Lithuania)
Established in 1991 at the request of the Lithuanian Ministry of Education, Lithuania Christian College (LCC) is a joint venture involving Lithuanian, Canadian, and American foundations. LCC is an international affiliate of the CCCU and provides students with a unique, interactive learning environment. Currently, about six hundred students from sixteen countries can choose from three courses of study. LCC's English Language Institute provides night courses to help the local Lithuanian citizens become proficient in English.

Russian-American Christian University (Moscow)
Russian-American Christian University (RACU) developed after Russian educators asked the Christian College Coalition (predecessor of the CCCU) to develop a Christian liberal arts institution in Russia. The school held its first courses, four evening classes, in 1995. In 2003, the Russian Ministry of Education licensed RACU, making it the first private, faith-based liberal arts university to be accredited in Russia. This CCCU affiliate institution currently serves approximately one hundred students and provides degrees in business, economics, social work, and English.

International University of Vienna (Austria)
International University of Vienna (IU) was chartered in the United States as a private, degree-granting institution in 1980. One year later, the school was officially registered in Austria. IU follows a liberal arts model of education and offers undergraduate and graduate degrees in business administration and diplomatic studies. Although not exclusively Christian in nature, the institution does emphasize the role of Christianity in the development of the Western world. During the past twenty years the school has been able to present this worldview to students representing more than one hundred countries.

NOTES

Preface to the Second Edition

1. For the recent history of American Catholic higher education, see Philip Gleason, *Contending with Modernity* (New York, 1995), on the twentieth-century period to the Second Vatican Council; and Alice Gallin, *Negotiating Identity: Catholic Higher Education since 1960* (Notre Dame, IN, 2000).

2. *Taylor University: The First 125 Years* (Grand Rapids, 1973); and *Taylor University: The First 150 Years* (Grand Rapids, 1996).

3. In the present book, this usual limitation is mitigated by the outpouring of recent reflective literature on the relationship between religion and higher education.

4. Benne's typography originally appeared in his 2001 book, *Quality with Soul*, 49.

Preface to the First Edition

1. Such studies exist, however, for the Catholic colleges in the United States and the Protestant colleges of Canada. See Edward J. Power, *Catholic Higher Education in America: A History* (New York, 1972), and Donald C. Masters, *Protestant Church Colleges in Canada* (Toronto, 1966). Also useful on Catholic colleges are the many monographs by Philip Gleason and Andrew Greeley. For Protestant seminaries, see the important recent works of Robert Handy, Robert Lynn, and Natalie Naylor.

2. Carl Henry, "Faith Affirming Colleges," *Christianity Today*, May 1971, 32.

3. Manning M. Pattillo and Donald M. Mackenzie, *Church Sponsored Higher Education in the United States* (Washington, DC, 1966), 153.

Chapter 1

1. Walter Crosby Eells, *Degrees in Higher Education* (New York, 1963), 85.

2. Franklin Hamlin Littell, *From State Church to Pluralism: A Protestant Interpretation of Religion in American History* (Garden City, NY, 1962), xx, 32; Winthrop S. Hudson, *Religion in America* (New York, 1973), 129–30.

3. Merle Curti, *The Growth of American Thought* (New York, 1951), 50–53; Winthrop S. Hudson, "The Morrison Myth Concerning the Founding of Harvard," *Church History* (June 1939): 154; M. Kelley Brooks, *Yale: A History* (New Haven, 1974), 42; Brander Matthews, ed., *A History of Columbia University* (New York, 1904), 444; Arthur V. Chitty, *The Episcopal Church in Education* (Cincinnati, n.d.), 10.

4. Hudson, "Founding of Harvard," 50–51; Samuel Eliot Morison, *Three Centuries of Harvard, 1636–1936* (Cambridge, 1936), 24, 44–50, 64–68, 87–88.

5. Brooks, *Yale: A History,* 3–4, 31–33; Richard Watch, *School of the Prophets: Yale College, 1701–1740* (New Haven, 1973), 100–117.

6. Beverly McAnear, "College Founding in the American Colonies, 1745–1775," *Mississippi Valley Historical Review* (June 1955): 24–25.

7. See William H. Cowley, "European Influences on American Higher Education," *Educational Record* (April 1939): 168.

8. Douglas Sloan, "Harmony, Chaos, and Concensus: The American College Curriculum," *Teachers College Record* (December 1971): 229; Edwin S. Gaustad, *The Great Awakening in New England* (Chicago, 1968), 30.

9. Thomas J. Wertenbaker, *Princeton, 1746–1896* (Princeton, NJ, 1946), 10–20; Archibald Alexander, *Log College* (Philadelphia, 1851), 11.

10. Wilder D. Quint, *The Story of Dartmouth* (Boston, 1916), 17, 55; Merle Curti and Roderick Nash, *Philanthropy in the Shaping of American Higher Education* (New Brunswick, NJ, 1965), 33–35.

11. Jurgen Herbst, "From Religion to Politics: Debates and Confrontation Over American College Governance in the Mid–Eighteenth Century," *Harvard Educational Review* (August 1976): 273–75; Willard W. Smith, "The Relation of College and State in Colonial America" (Ph.D. diss., Columbia University, 1949), 158–63.

12. Cowley, "European Influences," 166–69; Kenneth S. Latourette, *A History of Christianity,* 2 vols. (New York, 1975), 1:552.

13. Wertenbaker, *Princeton, 1746–1896,* 80–85.

14. Douglas Sloan, *The Scottish Enlightenment and the American College Ideal* (New York, 1971), vii–ix, 36–39; Cowley, "European Influences," 169–70.

15. Curti, *Growth of American Thought,* 236; Henry May, *The Enlightenment in America* (New York, 1976), 62–64, 346–50.

16. McAnear, "College Founding in the American Colonies," 31; Wertenbaker, *Princeton, 1746–1896,* 94; W. D. Carrell, "American College Professors, 1750–1800," *History of Education Quarterly* (fall 1968): 289–90.

17. McAnear, "College Founding in the American Colonies," 31; Wertenbaker, *Princeton, 1746–1896,* 30, 43; Carrell, "American College Professors, 1750–1800," 299–302; Ernest Earnest, *Academic Procession: An Informal History of the American College, 1936–1953* (New York, 1953), 27.

18. Carrell, "American College Professors, 1750–1800," 292–99.

19. C. H. Cramer, *Case Western Reserve* (Boston, 1976), 13–14; Theodore Hornberger, *Scientific Thought in American Colleges, 1630–1800* (Austin, TX, 1945), 36; Wertenbaker, *Princeton, 1746–1896,* 99, 137.

20. Richard Hofstadter and Walter Metzger, *The Development of Academic Freedom in the United States* (New York, 1955), 155; Hudson, "Founding of Harvard," 154; Morison, *Three Centuries of Harvard, 1636–1936,* 84.

21. Jurgen Herbst, *From Crisis to Crisis: American College Government, 1636–1819* (Cambridge, 1982), 48ff.; John S. Brubacher and Willis Rudy, *Higher Education in Transition: A History of American Colleges and Universities, 1636–1976* (New York, 1976), 26–31.

22. Curti, *Growth of American Thought,* 8–83; Wertenbaker, *Princeton, 1746–1896,* 102–3; Morison, *Three Centuries of Harvard, 1636–1936,* 241.

23. Hornberger, *Scientific Thought in American Colleges,* 22–34.

24. Ibid., 23–60, 80–87; Stanley M. Guralnick, *Science and the Antebellum American College* (Philadelphia, 1975), vii–viii.

25. Hornberger, *Scientific Thought in American Colleges*, 35, 37, 67; Morison, *Three Centuries of Harvard, 1636–1936*, 27–28.

26. R. Freemen Butts, *The College Charts Its Course* (New York, 1939), 63, 65.

27. McAnear, "College Founding in the American Colonies," 30, 36.

28. Ibid., 32–33; James McLachlan, "The American College in the Nineteenth Century: Toward a Reappraisal," *Teachers College Record* (December 1978): 294; Wertenbaker, *Princeton, 1746–1896*, 116–17.

29. McAnear, "College Founding in the American Colonies," 32–33.

30. Ibid., 33–34; Charles E. Cunningham, *Timothy Dwight, 1752–1817* (New York, 1942), 10, 20; Hornberger, *Scientific Thought in American Colleges*, 16, 19, 21; Richard P. McCormick, *Rutgers: A Bicentennial History* (New Brunswick, NJ, 1966), 20; David C. Humphrey, *From King's College to Columbia, 1746–1800* (New York, 1976), 163.

31. Humphrey, *From King's College to Columbia*, 186–89; Henry D. Sheldon, *Student Life and Customs* (New York, 1901), 85–88; Quint, *Story of Dartmouth*, 68–69; McCormick, *Rutgers: A Bicentennial History*, 20; McAnear, "College Founding in the American Colonies," 28–29; Wertenbaker, *Princeton, 1746–1896*, 28–29.

32. Yale as well as Harvard suffered from significant student disorders more than did the other northern colleges. See McAnear, "College Founding in the American Colonies," 38.

33. Kathryn M. Moore, "Freedom and Constraint in Eighteenth Century Harvard," *Journal of Higher Education* (November 1976): 649–51.

34. William H. Cowley, "History of Student Residential Housing," *School and Society*, 1 December 1934, 708–12.

35. Brooks, *Yale: A History*, 42; Morison, *Three Centuries of Harvard, 1636–1936*, 28; Earnest, *Academic Procession*, 36.

36. McAnear, "College Founding in the American Colonies," 38–39; Herbert B. Adams, *The College of William and Mary* (Washington, DC, 1887), 15–16; Humphrey, *From King's College to Columbia*, 91–96.

37. Curti and Nash, *Philanthropy in the Shaping of American Higher Education*, 20–23.

38. Ibid., 4–19, 31–33; Wertenbaker, *Princeton, 1746–1896*, 3; Quint, *Story of Dartmouth*, 72; Chitty, *Episcopal Church in Education*, 8.

39. Curti and Nash, *Philanthropy in the Shaping of American Higher Education*, 28–29; Wertenbaker, *Princeton, 1746–1896*, 31–36; Chitty, *Episcopal Church in Education*, 10–11.

40. McLachlan, "American College in the Nineteenth Century," 295; Donald G. Tewksbury, *The Founding of American Colleges and Universities before the Civil War* (New York, 1932), 70, 72.

Chapter 2

1. McLachlan, "American College in the Nineteenth Century," 295; George P. Schmidt, "Colleges in Ferment," *American Historical Review* (October 1953): 19.

2. Clarence P. Shedd, *Two Centuries of Student Christian Movements* (New York, 1934), 36, 48; Cunningham, *Timothy Dwight, 1752–1817*, 300–302.

3. Brubacher and Rudy, *Higher Education in Transition*, 42–43.

4. Tewksbury, *Founding of American Colleges and Universities*, 16, 69–73; David B. Potts, "College Enthusiasm as Public Response, 1800–1860," *Harvard Educational Review* (February 1977): 41.

5. Tewksbury, *Founding of American Colleges and Universities*, 104–5.

6. Ibid., 115–16.

7. Butts, *College Charts Its Course*, 118; Sloan, "American College Curriculum," 231; James H. Fairchild, *Oberlin: The Colony and the College, 1833–1883* (Oberlin, OH, 1883), 151–53; Colin B. Goodykoontz, *Home Missions on the American Frontier* (Caldwell, ID, 1939), 381; Earnest, *Academic Procession*, 23.

8. N. A. Naylor, "Antebellum College Movement: Re-appraisal of Tewksbury's Founding of American Colleges and Universities," *History of Education Quarterly* (fall 1973): 270; Herbst, *American College Government*, xi–xii; Charles D. Johnson, *Higher Education of the Southern Baptists: An Institutional History, 1826–1954* (Waco, 1955), 47; William C. Ringenberg, "The Protestant College on the Michigan Frontier" (Ph.D. diss., Michigan State, 1970), 63, 66, 72–73.

9. David B. Potts, "American Colleges in the Nineteenth Century: From Localism to Denominationalism," *History of Education Quarterly* (winter 1971): 367–68; Potts, "College Enthusiasm," 31–37; Timothy L. Smith, *Uncommon Schools: Christian Colleges and Social Idealism in Midwestern America, 1820–1950* (Indianapolis, 1978), 3, 21–29, 59.

10. *General Catalogue of Oberlin College, 1833–1908*, 117; *Oberlin College Catalogue, 1858–1859*, 38; *Oberlin College Catalogue, 1864–1865*, 6–34; Clyde S. Kilby, *Minority of One: The Biography of Jonathan Blanchard* (Grand Rapids, 1959), 151–52; Charlie Brown Hershey, *Colorado College, 1874–1949* (Colorado Springs, Colo., 1952), 41; Smith, *Uncommon Schools*, 30.

11. John D. Wright, *Transylvania: Tutor to the West* (Lexington, KY, 1975), ix, x, 86, 155, 174.

12. Potts, "College Enthusiasm," 37–38; David F. Allmendinger, "New England Students and the Revolution in Higher Education, 1800–1900," *History of Education Quarterly* (winter 1971): 381–86; David F. Allmendinger, *Paupers and Scholars: The Transformation of Student Life in Nineteenth-Century New England* (New York, 1975), 1–22.

13. George P. Schmidt, *The Liberal Arts College* (New Brunswick, NJ, 1957), 274; *Beloit College Catalog, 1860–61*, 12; *Franklin College Catalog, 1847*, 5–7.

14. Albea Godbold, *The Church College of the Old South* (Durham, NC, 1944), 107–9; Walter Havighurst, *The Miami Years, 1809–1959* (New York, 1958), 32–33.

15. Godbold, *Church College of the Old South*, 120–23; *Beloit College Catalog, 1860–61*, 19; Thomas LeDuc, *Piety and Intellect at Amherst College* (New York, 1946), 24.

16. Godbold, *Church College of the Old South*, 71.

17. Hofstadter and Metzger, *Development of Academic Freedom*, 152, 293.

18. George P. Schmidt, *The Old Time College President* (New York, 1930), 190–91; Shedd, *Two Centuries of Student Christian Movements*, 122.

19. Wertenbaker, *Princeton, 1746–1896*, 165; Godbold, *Church College of the Old South*, 128–30; George B. Manhart, *DePauw through the Years*, 2 vols. (Greencastle, IN, 1962), 1:138.

20. Kilby, *Minority of One*, 84.

21. Tewksbury, *Founding of American Colleges and Universities*, 83–84; Johnson, *Higher Education of Southern Baptists*, 10; Godbold, *Church College of the Old South*,

ch. 2; William M. Glasgow, *The Geneva Book* (Philadelphia, 1908), 72; G. Wallace Chessman, *Denison: The Story of an Ohio College* (Granville, OH, 1957), 117.

22. McLachlan, "American College in the Nineteenth Century," 297; Goody-koontz, 362, 365; Shedd, *Two Centuries of Student Christian Movements*, 122; Godbold, *Church College of the Old South*, 196; Ringenberg, "Protestant College on the Michigan Frontier," 159; Claude M. Fuess, *Amherst: The Story of a New England College* (Boston, 1935), 242–43. For comparative data on the late-eighteenth-century period, see Donald O. Schneider, "Education in Colonial American Colleges, 1750–1770, and the Occupation and Political Offices of Their Alumni" (Ph.D. diss., George Peabody University, 1965); and Walter C. Bronson, *The History of Brown University, 1764–1914* (Providence, RI, 1914), 154.

23. Humphrey, *From King's College to Columbia*, 160.

24. Earnest, *Academic Procession*, 40; Cunningham, *Timothy Dwight, 1752–1817*, 266.

25. Earnest, *Academic Procession*, 41; for a vivid description of the dramatic influence of one of these powerful "old-time presidents" (Wayland), see Bronson, *History of Brown University, 1764–1914*, 207ff.

26. Shedd, *Two Centuries of Student Christian Movements*, xviii, 24–31, 40–41, 90; Morison, *Three Centuries of Harvard, 1636–1936*, 61–62.

27. Shedd, *Two Centuries of Student Christian Movements*, 48–61, 69, 71–74, 80.

28. Potts, "College Enthusiasm," 38; Curti, *Growth of American Thought*, 225; Godbold, *Church College of the Old South*, 59, 152, 198–201; Rockwell D. Hunt, *History of the College of the Pacific, 1851–1951* (Stockton, CA, 1951), 33; McLachlan, "American College in the Nineteenth Century," 296; Kilby, *Minority of One*, 152; *Beloit College Catalog, 1860–61*, 20; Ringenberg, "Protestant College on the Michigan Frontier," 102.

29. See, for example, Johnson, *Higher Education of Southern Baptists*, 11–12, 68–69, 98; and Godbold, *Church College of the Old South*, 56.

30. Parker E. Lichtenstein, "Berea College," in *Struggle and Promise: A Future for Private Colleges*, ed. Conrad Hilberry and Morris Keeton (New York, 1969), 52–53.

31. Warren H. Smith, *Hobart and William Smith* (Geneva, NY, 1972), 177; *Annual Report of the Directors of the American Education Society, 28 May 1860* (Boston, 1860), 6; Naylor, "Antebellum College Movement," 270; James Findlay, "Congregationalists and American Education," *History of Education* (winter 1977): 449–50; Allmendinger, "New England Students," 381–86; *Wake Forest Catalog, 1978–1979*, 13.

32. Daniel T. Johnson, "Financing the Western Colleges, 1844–1862," *Journal of the Illinois State Historical Society* (spring 1972): 43–53.

33. Wertenbaker, *Princeton, 1746–1896*, 271.

34. *Ripon College Catalog, 1864–65*, 16.

35. Sloan, "American College Curriculum," 240–41; Curti, *Growth of American Thought*, 362; Earnest, *Academic Procession*, 22.

36. Schmidt, *Old Time College President*, 93, 104–5, 107; Sloan, "American College Curriculum," 246–47; D. H. Meyer, *The Instructed Conscience: The Shaping of the American National Ethic* (Philadelphia, 1972), x–xiv, 6–11.

37. Schmidt, *Old Time College President*, 108–18, 144; Ralph Henry Gabriel, *Religion and Learning at Yale* (New Haven, 1958), 109–13; Rufus Jones, *Haverford College* (New York, 1933), 69; Meyer, *Instructed Conscience*, 147–56.

38. Guralnick, *Science and the Antebellum American College,* viii–xii, 141–42, 158–59; Potts, "College Enthusiasm," 39; Godbold, *Church College of the Old South,* 81; Sloan, "American College Curriculum," 233.

39. Guralnick, *Science and the Antebellum American College,* 153, 155; Theodore Dwight Bozeman, *Protestants in an Age of Science: The Baconian Ideal and Antebellum American Religious Thought* (Chapel Hill, NC, 1977), vi–xii, 76–81; Gabriel, *Religion and Learning at Yale,* 113–16; Hofstadter and Metzger, *Development of Academic Freedom,* 292; Wertenbaker, *Princeton, 1746–1896,* 95; Sloan, "American College Curriculum," 227.

40. Cunningham,*Timothy Dwight, 1752–1817,* 35–39.

41. Earnest, *Academic Procession,* 95.

42. Guy E. Snavely, *The Church and the Four-Year College: An Appraisal of Their Relation* (New York, 1955), 80–81; Matthew N. Young, *A History of Colleges of the Churches of Christ* (Kansas City, MO, 1949), 31; Glasgow, *Geneva Book,* 20.

43. Wertenbaker, *Princeton, 1746–1896,* 198–99; John Barnard, *From Evangelicalism to Progressivism at Oberlin College, 1866–1917* (Columbus, OH, 1969), 25; Earnest, *Academic Procession,* 45; Johnson, *Higher Education of Southern Baptists,* 10.

44. Frederick Rudolph, *The American College and University: A History* (New York, 1965), 281–82.

45. McLachlan, "American College in the Nineteenth Century," 303–4; Schmidt, *Old Time College President,* 226–27.

46. Sloan, "American College Curriculum," 242–48; Earnest, *Academic Procession,* 75–77.

47. Butts, *College Charts Its Course,* 129–31.

48. Eells, *Degrees in Higher Education,* 72–73.

49. Ibid., 73–78.

50. Schmidt, *Liberal Arts College,* 70–71; Schmidt, "Colleges in Ferment," 19; Wertenbaker, *Princeton, 1746–1896,* 300; Charles O. Brown, "Faculty of Olivet College, 1867–1876," manuscript, Olivet College archives.

51. Earnest, *Academic Procession,* 76; Wertenbaker, *Princeton, 1746–1896,* 300; Orin J. Oliphant, *The Rise of Bucknell University* (New York, 1965), 116; Ringenberg, "Protestant College on the Michigan Frontier," 92–93.

52. D. Elton Trueblood, *The Idea of a College* (New York, 1959), 34–36; Kilby, *Minority of One,* 96.

53. Sheldon, *Student Life,* 89–93, 125–35; Thomas S. Harding, *College Literary Societies, 1815–1876* (New York, 1971), 22; Brubacher and Rudy, *Higher Education in Transition,* 46–48.

54. Sheldon, *Student Life,* 125–35; Godbold, *Church College of the Old South,* 88.

55. Godbold, *Church College of the Old South,* 85–88; Ringenberg, "Protestant College on the Michigan Frontier," 119; Earnest, *Academic Procession,* 86; Manhart, *DePauw through the Years,* 129–30.

56. Kilby, *Minority of One,* 28–29; Barnard, *From Evangelicalism to Progressivism at Oberlin College,* 21–22; Wertenbaker, *Princeton, 1746–1896,* 201–4.

57. Harding, *College Literary Societies, 1815–1876,* 49, 101, 132, 158, 197–98, 232, 235–36; Codman Hislop, *Eliphalet Nott* (Middletown, CT, 1971), 181.

58. Godbold, *Church College of the Old South,* 94, 168; Barnard, *From Evangelicalism to Progressivism at Oberlin College,* 21; Oliphant, 66; Wertenbaker, *Princeton, 1746–1896,* 237–38.

59. The largest college library collection was the one at Harvard which numbered 13,000 volumes in 1800 and 122,000 in 1865 (Hornberger, *Scientific Thought in American Colleges,* 78; Brubacher and Rudy, *Higher Education in Transition,* 94–95).

60. Harding, *College Literary Societies, 1815–1876,* 56, 67–68; Godbold, *Church College of the Old South,* 79.

61. Harding, *College Literary Societies, 1815–1876,* 56, 83.

62. Vivian Lyon Moore, *The First Hundred Years of Hillsdale College* (Ann Arbor, MI, 1944), 93; Harding, *College Literary Societies, 1815–1876,* 1.

63. Harding, *College Literary Societies, 1815–1876,* 262, 296–98, 318.

64. Sheldon, *Student Life,* 145–47, 192–95.

65. Earnest, *Academic Procession,* 125–27; John J. Shipherd, Letter to Hamilton Hill, 17 August 1844, Michigan Historical Collection, University of Michigan; Butts, *College Charts Its Course,* 140; also see Cramer, *Case Western Reserve,* 160.

66. Sheldon, *Student Life,* 151; Fuess, *Amherst,* 220–22.

67. Schmidt, *Old Time College President,* 204–6, 222–25; "The First Circular of Oberlin College, March 8, 1834," in *Father Shipherd's Magna Charta,* by Frances J. Hosford (Boston, 1937), 5; Gilbert Barnes, *The Antislavery Impulse, 1830–1844* (New York, 1964), 12–77; Robert S. Fletcher, *A History of Oberlin from Its Foundation through the Civil War,* 2 vols. (Oberlin, OH, 1942), 1:236–53; Charles G. Finney, *Memoirs of Charles G. Finney* (New York, 1876), 337–51; Godbold, *Church College of the Old South,* 29, 75, 89–90, 166.

68. Kilby, *Minority of One,* 36, 118–20, 171–74, 187, 196, 207, 217–18; Earnest, *Academic Procession,* 128.

69. Schmidt, *Old Time College President,* 78–80; Kilby, *Minority of One,* 152; Earnest, *Academic Procession,* 42–43.

70. Floyd B. Streeter, "History of Prohibition Legislation in Michigan," *Michigan History* (April 1918): 299.

71. James C. Olson, *J. Sterling Morton* (Lincoln, NE, 1942), 16; Godbold, *Church College of the Old South,* 102–3; Wertenbaker, *Princeton, 1746–1896,* 242–43; Sheldon, *Student Life,* 95–101, 106–10; Earnest, *Academic Procession,* 44–45.

72. Sheldon, *Student Life,* 113; Earnest, *Academic Procession,* 46.

73. Herbst, "American College Governance," 276–77; John T. Wahlquist and James W. Thornton, *State Colleges and Universities* (Washington, DC, 1964), 4–5.

74. Kent Sagendorph, *Michigan, the Story of the University* (New York, 1948), 64, 72, 74; Erastus O. Haven, *Autobiography* (New York, 1883), 144; *University of Michigan Regent's Proceedings, 1837–1864* (Ann Arbor, MI, 1915), 183–84, 720–22, 919; *University of Michigan Catalog, 1843–44,* 12–13; Wilfred B. Shaw, *History of the University of Michigan* (New York, 1920), 42.

75. E. Merton Coulter, *College Life in the Old South* (New York, 1951), 151; Godbold, *Church College of the Old South,* 179–80.

76. Naylor, "Antebellum College Movement," 269.

77. Ibid., 269; Coulter, *College Life in the Old South,* 47; Earle D. Ross, "Religious Influences in the Development of State Colleges and Universities," *Indiana Magazine of History* (December 1950): 354; Godbold, *Church College of the Old South,* 184.

78. Ross, "Religious Influences in the Development of State Colleges and Universities," 348–49, 353; Roger Ebert, *An Illinois Century: One Hundred Years of Campus Life* (Urbana, IL, 1967), 35–36; Sherman B. Barnes, "Learning and Piety in Ohio Colleges, 1865–1900," *Ohio Historical Quarterly* (October 1960): 331.

79. *University of Michigan Catalog, 1852–53*, 25; *University of Michigan Regent's Proceedings*, 720–22; Haven, *Autobiography*, 150; Christian Library Association of the University of Michigan, "Constitution and Minutes of the 1 May 1858 Meeting," Michigan Historical Collection, University of Michigan; Madison Kuhn, *Michigan State: The First Hundred Years* (East Lansing, MI, 1955), 91.

80. Thomas N. Hoover, *The History of Ohio University* (Athens, OH, 1954), 26; Godbold, *Church College of the Old South*, 172–77.

81. Wahlquist and Thornton, *State Colleges and Universities*, 4–5; R. P. Thomson, "Colleges in the Revolutionary South: The Shaping of a Tradition," *Higher Education Quarterly* (winter 1970): 404–7; Curti, *Growth of American Thought*, 226; Ross, "Religious Influences in the Development of State Colleges and Universities," 348–49.

82. Hofstadter and Metzger, *Development of Academic Freedom*, 298–99; Wahlquist and Thornton, *State Colleges and Universities*, 4–5.

83. Havighurst, *Miami Years, 1809–1959*, 46.

84. Godbold, *Church College of the Old South*, 52–53, 149–53; Andrew Ten Brook, *American State Universities: Their Origin and Progress* (Cincinnati, 1875), 223–24; Howard H. Peckham, *The Making of the University of Michigan* (Ann Arbor, MI, 1967), 64.

85. Godbold, *Church College of the Old South*, 148; Ringenberg, "Protestant College on the Michigan Frontier," 181.

86. Ten Brook, *American State Universities*, 356, 372–74.

87. See especially the writings of Richard Hofstadter.

88. McLachlan, "American College in the Nineteenth Century," 298–300; Naylor, "Antebellum College Movement," 261–70; Sloan, "American College Curriculum," 224–26; Potts, "College Enthusiasm," 28–30; James Axtell, "The Death of the Liberal Arts College," *History of Education Quarterly* (winter 1971): 341, 346; Potts, "American Colleges in the Nineteenth Century," 366.

Chapter 3

1. Frank H. Bowles and Frank A. Decosta, *Between Two Worlds, a Profile of Negro Higher Education* (New York, 1971), 25; H. M. Bond, "Origin and Development of the Negro Church-Related College," *Journal of Negro Education* (summer 1960): 219; Carter G. Woodson, *The Education of the Negro Prior to 1861* (New York, 1928), 265–72.

2. Woodson, *Education of the Negro Prior to 1861*, 265–78; Earnest, *Academic Procession*, 63.

3. Bowles and Decosta, *Between Two Worlds*, 12–13.

4. Bowles and Decosta, *Between Two Worlds*, 20–21; Woodson, *Education of the Negro Prior to 1861*, 256–64.

5. Stephen J. Wright, "The Negro College in America," *Harvard Educational Review* (summer 1960): 272–73; Frederick A. McGinnis, *A History and an Interpretation of Wilberforce University* (Wilberforce, OH, 1941), 37.

6. Dwight O. W. Holmes, *The Evolution of the Negro College* (New York, 1969), 79–83.

7. Holmes, *Evolution of the Negro College*, 79–83; *Berea College Catalog, 1977–79*, 9.

8. Henry A. Bullock, *A History of Negro Education in the South* (Cambridge, 1967), 18–24; Bowles and Decosta, *Between Two Worlds*, 27; Daniel C. Thompson, *Private Black Colleges at the Crossroads* (Westport, CT, 1973), 9–10.

9. Bowles and Decosta, *Between Two Worlds,* 30; Rayford W. Logan, "Evolution of Private Colleges for Negroes," *Journal of Negro Education* (summer 1958): 213–16; Bond, "Origin and Development of the Negro Church-Related College," 222–24; August Meier and Elliott M. Rudwick, *From Plantation to Ghetto* (New York, 1966), 146–47; Holmes, *Evolution of the Negro College,* 12.

10. Bowles and Decosta, *Between Two Worlds,* 33.

11. Richard I. McKinney, *Religion in Higher Education among Negroes* (New York, 1972), ix, 3; Bond, "Origin and Development of the Negro Church-Related College," 220–21; Francis G. Peabody, *Education for Life: The Story of Hampton Institute* (New York, 1919), xii.

12. Wilmot Carter, *Shaw's Universe* (Raleigh, NC, 1973), iv, 1–3; Elizabeth Geen, "Morehouse College," in Keeton and Hilberry, *Struggle and Promise,* 370–71.

13. Woodson, *Education of the Negro Prior to 1861,* 256; Bond, "Origin and Development of the Negro Church-Related College," 219–20, 223–24.

14. Bullock, *History of Negro Education in the South,* 175.

15. For a shocking description of the persecution faced by teachers from the North, see Henry Lee Swint, *The Northern Teacher in the South, 1862–1870* (Nashville, 1941), 96–109.

16. Holmes, *Evolution of the Negro College,* 11–12; Bullock, *History of Negro Education in the South,* 24; Meier and Rudwick, *From Plantation to Ghetto,* 146–47; Curti and Nash, *Philanthropy in the Shaping of American Higher Education,* 177; also see Jacqueline Jones, "Women Who Were More Than Men: Sex and Status in Freedman's Teaching," *History of Education Quarterly* (spring 1979): 48–49.

17. Logan, "Evolution of Private Colleges for Negroes," 217–18; Bowles and Decosta, *Between Two Worlds,* 29.

18. One study conducted in the 1960s stated that the black schools which then attracted the best quality students included Fisk, Hampton, Howard, Lincoln, Morehouse, and Xavier. See A. J. Jaffe, Walter Adams, and Sandra G. Meyers, *Negro Higher Education in the 1960s* (New York, 1968), 242.

19. Geen, "Morehouse College," 376–77.

20. Ibid., 370; Curti and Nash, *Philanthropy in the Shaping of American Higher Education,* 168; James P. Browley, *Two Centuries of Methodist Concern: Bondage, Freedom, and Education of Black People* (New York, 1974), 433.

21. Curti and Nash, *Philanthropy in the Shaping of American Higher Education,* 168–81; Holmes, *Evolution of the Negro College,* 163–78.

22. Curti and Nash, *Philanthropy in the Shaping of American Higher Education,* 171; Joe M. Richardson, *A History of Fisk University, 1865–1946* (University, AL, 1980), 24–32.

23. Curti and Nash, *Philanthropy in the Shaping of American Higher Education,* 175.

24. Most of the United Negro College Fund colleges are at least somewhat church-related. See Thompson, *Private Black Colleges at the Crossroads,* 275–76.

25. Curti and Nash, *Philanthropy in the Shaping of American Higher Education,* 183; Bond, "Origin and Development of the Negro Church-Related College," 226.

26. Earnest, *Academic Procession,* 183–202, 259; Schmidt, *Liberal Arts College,* 143; Liva Baker, *I'm Radcliffe; Fly Me* (New York, 1976), 173–77; Arthur C. Cole, *A Hundred Years of Mount Holyoke College* (New York, 1940), 103ff.; Thomas Woody, *A History of Women's Education in the United States,* 2 vols. (New York, 1974), 2:198.

27. Mabel Newcomer, *A Century of Higher Education for American Women* (New York, 1959), 6–9.

28. Ibid., 9; Anne Firor Scott, "The Ever Widening Circle: The Diffusion of Feminist Values from the Troy Female Seminary, 1822–72," *History of Education Quarterly* (spring 1979): 3, 7; Elizabeth A. Green, *Mary Lyon and Mount Holyoke* (Hanover, NH, 1979), xiii–xvi; Woody, *History of Women's Education in the United States,* 1:361.

29. Earnest, *Academic Procession,* 169–92.

30. Woody, *History of Women's Education in the United States,* 2:151–55; Newcomer, *Century of Higher Education for American Women,* 25–32.

31. Earnest, *Academic Procession,* 176.

32. Earnest, *Academic Procession,* 174–75; Woody, *History of Women's Education in the United States,* 2:144, 149.

33. Jeanne L. Noble, *The Negro Woman's College Education* (New York, 1956), 17–22.

34. Woody, *History of Women's Education in the United States,* 2:148–49; Earnest, *Academic Procession,* 180–82; Baker, *I'm Radcliffe; Fly Me,* 175–76.

35. Elaine Kendall, *Peculiar Institution: An Informal History of the Seven Sisters Colleges* (New York, 1976), 30; Earnest, *Academic Procession,* 192; Jean Glasscock, ed., *Wellesley College, 1875–1975* (Wellesley, CT, 1975), 132.

36. Woody, *History of Women's Education in the United States,* 1:361; Earnest, *Academic Procession,* 192; Newcomer, *Century of Higher Education for American Women,* 171–72.

37. Woody, *History of Women's Education in the United States,* 2:368–69; Page Smith, *Daughters of the Promised Land* (Boston, 1970), 181–82.

38. Smith, *Daughters of the Promised Land,* 189.

39. Earnest, *Academic Procession,* 192.

40. Ibid., 197; Woody, *History of Women's Education in the United States,* 2:231–33.

41. Earnest, *Academic Procession,* 197; Godbold, *Church College of the Old South,* 103, 171; *Texas Christian University Catalog, 1978–79,* 14–15.

42. Earnest, *Academic Procession,* 198; Woody, *History of Women's Education in the United States,* 2:3–4, 16.

43. Edwin Mims, *History of Vanderbilt University* (Nashville, 1946), 13, 84; Curti and Nash, *Philanthropy in the Shaping of American Higher Education,* 124.

44. Nora C. Chaffin, *Trinity College, 1839–1892: The Beginnings of Duke University* (Durham, NC, 1950), 492–98; Curti and Nash, *Philanthropy in the Shaping of American Higher Education,* 125.

45. Curti and Nash, *Philanthropy in the Shaping of American Higher Education,* 126–27.

46. Ibid., 127, 147; *Wake Forest College Catalog, 1926–27,* 10.

47. Richard J. Storr, *Harper's University* (Chicago, 1966), 3–105; Thomas W. Goodspeed, *A History of the University of Chicago* (Chicago, 1916), 10–11, 69, 292–93; Curti and Nash, *Philanthropy in the Shaping of American Higher Education,* 116–17, 124.

48. Orrin L. Elliott, *Stanford University: The First Twenty-five Years* (Stanford, CA, 1937), 106, 137–41.

49. John C. French, *A History of the University Founded by Johns Hopkins* (Baltimore, 1946), 64–71, 324–32; Hugh Hawkins, *Pioneer: A History of Johns Hopkins University, 1874–1889* (Ithaca, NY, 1960), 214–15.

50. Curti and Nash, *Philanthropy in the Shaping of American Higher Education,* 158–59.

51. Ibid., 212–37.

52. James H. Lehman, *Beyond Anything Foreseen: A Study of the History of Higher Education in the Church of the Brethren* (n.p., n.d.), 2, 6–8; Hubert R. Pellman, *Eastern Mennonite College, 1917–1967* (Harrisonburg, VA, 1967), 16; C. Henry Smith and E. J. Hirschler, eds., *The Story of Bluffton College* (Bluffton, OH, 1925), 109.

53. David T. Nelson, *Luther College, 1861–1961* (Decorah, IA, 1961), 18–20, 343; Emory Lindquist, *Bethany in Kansas* (Lindsborg, KS, 1945), 2; Leland H. Carlson, *A History of North Park College* (Chicago, 1941), 45–46; Walter C. Schnackenberg, *The Lamp and the Cross: Pacific Lutheran University* (n.p., 1965), 2; Nicholas P. Wolterstorff, ed., *Christian Liberal Arts Education: Calvin College Curriculum Study* (Grand Rapids, 1970), 22; Willis F. Dunbar, *The Michigan Record in Higher Education* (Detroit, 1963), 170; Harold H. Lentz, *A History of Wittenberg College* (Wittenberg, OH, 1946), 13; Wynand Wichers, *A Century of Hope, 1866–1966* (Grand Rapids, 1968), 65–73.

54. Nelson, *Luther*, 34; also see Lehman, *Beyond Anything Foreseen*, 37.

55. Conrad Bergendoff, *Augustana . . . a Profession of Faith* (Rock Island, IL, 1969), 78, 97, 104–6; Lindquist, *Bethany in Kansas*, 282.

56. Wichers, *Century of Hope*, 78–79.

57. Lehman, *Beyond Anything Foreseen*, 37; John S. Umble, *Goshen College: 1894–1954* (Goshen, IN, 1955), 7.

58. Morison, *Three Centuries of Harvard, 1636–1936*, 341–46; Hislop, *Eliphalet Nott*, 231–32.

59. Hofstadter and Metzger, *Development of Academic Freedom*, 360; Rudolph, *American College and University*, 246; Morison, *Three Centuries of Harvard, 1636–1936*, 262.

60. Lehman, *Beyond Anything Foreseen*, 36–37, 43, 50; Glasscock, *Wellesley College, 1875–1975*, 132; Leal A. Headley and Merrill E. Jarchow, *Carleton: The Final Century* (Northfield, MN, 1966), 164; *Franklin College Catalog, 1896*, 16; Hershey, *Colorado College, 1874–1949*, 192–93; Merrimon Cuninggim, *The College Seeks Religion* (New Haven, 1947), 143–44; James B. Sellers, *History of the University of Alabama* (Tuscaloosa, AL, 1953), 463; Alice D. Miller and Susan Myers, *Barnard College: The First Fifty Years* (New York, 1939), 72–73; Barnes, "Learning and Piety in Ohio Colleges," 333–34; Martha Frances Montague, *Lewis and Clark College, 1867–1967* (Portland, OR, 1968), 59, 77–78; Lawrence E. Nelson, *Redlands: Biography of a College* (Redlands, CA, 1958), 181.

61. Morison, *Three Centuries of Harvard, 1636–1936*, 384–87, 446.

62. Curti, *Growth of American Thought*, 580–86. For a discussion of how the rising middle class encouraged the development of professional expertise and authority in the universities, see Burton J. Bledstein, *The Culture of Professionalism: The Middle Class and the Development of Higher Education in America* (New York, 1976), x–xi, 287–90; also see Alexandra Oleson and John Voss, *The Organization of Knowledge in America, 1860–1920* (Baltimore, 1979), and Bruce Leslie, "Between Piety and Expertise: Professionalization of College Faculty in the 'Age of the University,'" *Pennsylvania History* (July 1979): 245–65.

63. Barnard, *From Evangelicalism to Progressivism at Oberlin College*, 65–66; also see Wertenbaker, *Princeton, 1746–1896*, 229, 265, 310–11, 350.

64. Harold S. Wechsler, *The Qualified Student: A History of Selective College Admission in America* (New York, 1977), 40–50; William K. Selden, *Accreditation* (New York, 1960), 27–28.

65. Earnest, *Academic Procession*, 220; Wertenbaker, *Princeton, 1746–1896*, 162–63.

66. Sheldon, *Student Life*, 202–3; Carter, *Shaw*, 85–86; William C. Ringenberg, *Taylor University: The First 125 Years* (Grand Rapids, 1973), 116–18; John R. Betts, *America's Sporting Heritage, 1850–1950* (Reading, MA, 1974), 124, 129.

67. Earnest, *Academic Procession*, 137–38; Rudolph, *American College and University*, 154; Wells Twombly, *Two Hundred Years of Sport in America* (New York, 1976), 70–71, 74–78, 81–83; John A. Krout, *Annals of American Sport* (New Haven, 1929), 144.

68. Twombly, *Two Hundred Years of Sport in America*, 78–81; Manhart, *DePauw through the Years*, 1:142–43; Wertenbaker, *Princeton, 1746–1896*, 325.

69. Twombly, *Two Hundred Years of Sport in America*, 78; *Albion College Standard*, December 1868, 6.

70. Earnest, *Academic Procession*, 220–25; Betts, *America's Sporting Heritage, 1850–1950*, 124–29.

71. Earnest, *Academic Procession*, 220–21, 225.

72. Twombly, *Two Hundred Years of Sport in America*, 93; Oliphant, 235–36; Betts, *America's Sporting Heritage, 1850–1950*, 127.

73. Between 1883 and 1901, Yale fielded nine undefeated teams and three unscored-upon teams, including the 1888 squad, which outscored its opponents 700–0 (see Earnest, *Academic Procession*, 222).

74. Twombly, *Two Hundred Years of Sport in America*, 93–96; Krout, *Annals of American Sport*, 238.

75. James Naismith, *Basketball: Its Origin and Development* (New York, 1941), 18–60, 111–24.

76. John Robson, ed., *Baird's Manual of American College Fraternities* (Menasha, WI, 1968), 5; J. E. Morpurgo, *Their Majesties' Royall Colledge: William and Mary in the Seventeenth and Eighteenth Centuries* (Williamsburg, VA, 1976), 181–82.

77. Morpurgo, *Their Majesties' Royall Colledge*, 6–7; Hislop, *Eliphalet Nott*, 389; Havighurst, *Miami Years, 1809–1959*, 91.

78. Hislop, *Eliphalet Nott*, 390; Wertenbaker, *Princeton, 1746–1896*, 281, 322.

79. Walter Pilkington, *Hamilton College: 1812–1962* (Clinton, NY, 1962), 131–32; Lentz, *History of Wittenberg College*, 112–14.

80. Henry C. Hubbard, *Ohio Wesleyan's First Hundred Years* (Delaware, OH, 1943), 267; David D. Wallace, *History of Wofford College, 1854–1949* (Nashville, 1951), 79, 181–85.

81. Charles W. Cooper, *Whittier* (Los Angeles, 1967), 218.

82. Robson, *Baird's Manual of American College Fraternities*, 9; also see Charles S. Johnson, *Fraternities in Our Colleges* (New York, 1972), 14.

83. Johnson, *Fraternities in Our Colleges*, 13.

84. This, for example, was the experience of Baptist Colgate in the 1840s. See Harold D. Williams, *A History of Colgate University, 1819–1969* (New York, 1969), 90–91.

Chapter 4

1. Billy Graham, "Why I Believe in Christian Education," *Abundant Life*, June 1967, 17.

2. See Pattillo and Mackenzie, *Church Sponsored Higher Education*, 153; Phillip E. Jacob, *Changing Values in College* (New York, 1957), 204; Myron F. Wicke, *The*

Church Related College (Washington, DC, 1964), 7; and C. Robert Pace, *Education and Evangelism* (New York, 1972), 92–93. The higher-educational institutions in Canada have secularized even more completely than they have in the United States; see Masters, *Church Colleges in Canada*, v, 207–11.

3. Butts, *College Charts Its Course*, 395; Howard R. Bowen, *Investment in Learning: The Individual and Social Value of American Higher Education* (San Francisco, 1977), 125–30; Kenneth A. Feldman and Theodore M. Newcomb, *The Impact of College on Students* (San Francisco, 1969), 8, 10. Also see Dean R. Hoge, *Commitment on Campus: Changes in Religion and Values over Five Centuries* (Philadelphia, 1974), 186, 190.

4. Curti, *Growth of American Thought*, 531–32. For a lucid summary of the many rapid changes in American higher education in this period, see Mark A. Noll, "Christian Thinking and the Rise of the American University," *Christian Scholar's Review* (1979): 3–16. Also see Noll's introduction to this book.

5. Curti, *Growth of American Thought*, 542; Carl Diehl, *Americans and German Scholarship* (New Haven, 1978), 3–4; Gabriel, *Religion and Learning at Yale*, 197–98; also see Jerry W. Brown, *The Rise of Biblical Criticism in America, 1800–1870: The New England Scholars* (Middletown, CT, 1969), 7–9.

6. Gabriel, *Religion and Learning at Yale*, 183–84, 195; Lawrence R. Veysey, *The Emergence of the American University* (Chicago, 1965), 204.

7. William R. Hutchinson, *The Modernist Impulse in American Protestantism* (Cambridge, 1976), 76–115; Veysey, *Emergence of the American University*, 204; Barnard, *From Evangelicalism to Progressivism at Oberlin College*, 121–32; Ross, "Religious Influences in the Development of State Colleges and Universities," 356.

8. Schmidt, "Colleges in Ferment," 29–33.

9. Schmidt, "Colleges in Ferment," 29–33, 37; Hofstadter and Metzger, *Development of Academic Freedom*, 334–35.

10. Paul A. Carter, *The Spiritual Crisis of the Gilded Age* (DeKalb, IL, 1971), 28; Schmidt, *Liberal Arts College*, 161–66; A. Hunter Dupree, *Asa Gray* (Cambridge, 1959), 358–59; Barnard, *From Evangelicalism to Progressivism at Oberlin College*, 50–51.

11. Curti, *Growth of American Thought*, 549; Schmidt, "Colleges in Ferment," 34–35, 37; Gabriel, *Religion and Learning at Yale*, 152, 156–58.

12. Wertenbaker, *Princeton, 1746–1896*, 311–12; Curti, *Growth of American Thought*, 548–51; Glenn C. Altschuler, "From Religion to Ethics: Andrew D. White and the Dilemma of a Christian Rationalist," *Church History* (September 1978): 308–24.

13. Gabriel, *Religion and Learning at Yale*, 180, 191–94.

14. Kuhn, *Michigan State*, 91; Hofstadter and Metzger, *Development of Academic Freedom*, 326, 345–46; *Wake Forest University Catalog, 1978–79*, 15.

15. Hofstadter and Metzger, *Development of Academic Freedom*, 330–31; Wright, *Transylvania*, 240–41; Kenneth M. Plummer, *A History of West Virginia Wesleyan College* (Buckhannon, WV, 1965), 19–20.

16. Interview with D. Elton Trueblood, 21 August 1978; also see Earnest, *Academic Procession*, 126.

17. Veysey, *Emergence of the American University*, 48; Barnard, *From Evangelicalism to Progressivism at Oberlin College*, 112; Plummer, *History of West Virginia Wesleyan College*, 132; Wicke, *Church Related College*, 65; Richard Solberg and Merton P. Strommen, *How Church-Related Are Church-Related Colleges?* (New York, 1980), 55–64, 84.

18. Cuninggim, *College Seeks Religion,* 139; Pattillo and MacKenzie, *Church Sponsored Higher Education,* 147–48.

19. Cuninggim, *College Seeks Religion,* 168.

20. John H. Timmerman, *Promises to Keep: A Centennial History of Calvin College* (Grand Rapids, 1975), 131.

21. Schmidt, *Liberal Arts College,* 191–92; Cuninggim, *College Seeks Religion,* 135, 301.

22. Earl J. McGrath, "Future of the Protestant College," *Liberal Education* (March 1961): 47; Pattillo and MacKenzie, *Church Sponsored Higher Education,* 138–39; Interview with Milo A. Rediger, 26 October 1978.

23. Hofstadter and Metzger, *Development of Academic Freedom,* 352; Rudolph, *American College and University,* 419; E. Wilson Lyon, *The History of Pomona College, 1887–1969* (Claremont, CA, 1977), 289.

24. Butts, *College Charts Its Course,* 61; Morison, *Three Centuries of Harvard, 1636–1936,* 189–90, 195, 242–45, 257, 259.

25. Morison, *Three Centuries of Harvard, 1636–1936,* 218; Cunningham, *Timothy Dwight, 1752–1817,* 224–32; Brown, *Biblical Criticism,* 46.

26. Barrett Wendell, *A Literary History of American Criticism* (New York, 1931), 407–8, 421.

27. Bronson, *History of Brown University, 1764–1914,* 186–92; Louis Hatch, *The History of Bowdoin College* (Portland, ME, 1927), 289–90.

28. Harold Bolce, "Blasting at the Rock of Ages," in *Portraits of the American University, 1890–1910,* ed. James C. Stone and Donald P. DeNeve (San Francisco, 1971), 269–80.

29. Lee A. Dew, *A History of Arkansas State University, 1909–1967* (Jonesboro, AR, 1968), 113; Clifford S. Griffin, *The University of Kansas* (Lawrence, KS, 1974), 224–25. For an able and largely representative study of the role of religion in the state university in the transitional late nineteenth century, see Winton U. Solberg, "The Conflict between Religion and Secularism at the University of Illinois, 1867–1894," *American Quarterly* (summer 1966): 183–99.

30. Cedric Cummins, *The University of South Dakota, 1862–1966* (Vermillion, SD, 1975), 226; John K. Bettersworth, *People's College: A History of Mississippi State* (Birmingham, AL, 1953), 372; McKinney, *Religion in Higher Education among Negroes,* 46, 63–65.

31. Gabriel, *Religion and Learning at Yale,* 163–65.

32. *Geneva College Catalog, 1878–80,* 24; Barnes, "Learning and Piety in Ohio Colleges," 343–44; Kilby, *Minority of One,* 200.

33. Morris Bishop, *A History of Cornell* (Ithaca, NY, 1962), 190–94, 213–15; Hugh Hawkins, "The University-Builders Observe the Colleges," *History of Education Quarterly* (winter 1971): 353–58; C. Howard Hopkins, *John R. Mott, 1865–1955* (Grand Rapids, 1979), 220.

34. Henry D. Sheldon, *History of University of Oregon* (Portland, OR, 1940), 63, 115, 227.

35. Cuninggim, *College Seeks Religion,* 1, 14, 80–89, 298–300; Edgar M. Carlson, *Church Sponsored Higher Education and the Lutheran Church in America* (New York, 1967), 37.

36. William F. Buckley Jr., *God and Man at Yale* (Chicago, 1951), xiii, 4–5, 9–11, 14–16.

37. Potts, "American Colleges in the Nineteenth Century," 373; John D. Millett, *Strengthening Community in Higher Education* (New York, 1974), 1.

38. Cornelius H. Patton and Walter T. Field, *Eight O'Clock Chapel: A Study of New England College Life in the Eighties* (Boston, 1927), 199–212.

39. Potts, "American Colleges in the Nineteenth Century," 369–73.

40. Wicke, *Church Related College*, v; McGrath, "Future of the Protestant College," 45; George A. Buttrick, *Biblical Thought and the Secular University* (Baton Rouge, 1960), 4; Pattillo and MacKenzie, *Church Sponsored Higher Education*, 153; Pace, 92–93; Christopher Jencks and David Riesman, *The Academic Revolution* (Garden City, NY, 1969), 332.

41. Pattillo and Mackenzie, *Church Sponsored Higher Education*, 140–41.

42. *Christianity Today*, 29 June 1979, 45; Richard G. Hutcheson Jr., *Mainline Churches and the Evangelicals* (Atlanta, 1981), 15–17.

43. Barnard, *From Evangelicalism to Progressivism at Oberlin College*, 50–51, 67, 77, 110–13, 127; for another excellent study of the secularization process in a specific institution, Knox, see Thomas A. Askew, "The Liberal Arts College Encounters Intellectual Change: A Comparative Study of Education at Knox and Wheaton Colleges, 1837–1925" (Ph.D. diss., Northwestern, 1969).

44. *Franklin College Catalog, 1900–01*, 16, 40.

45. *Franklin College Catalog, 1921–22*, 25–26, 45, 50–52.

46. *Franklin College Catalog, 1950–51*, 27, 129–30.

47. *Franklin College Catalog, 1978*, 94, 119; interview with John Shelly, 17 October 1978; Byron E. Waterman, "A Study of the Purposes of a Private Liberal Arts College: Franklin College" (M.A. thesis, Indiana University, 1977), 4, 8.

48. *Ripon College Catalog, 1883*, 24; *Ripon College Catalog, 1904*, 35; *Ripon College Catalog, 1926*, 8–9, 77.

49. *Ripon College Catalog, 1950–51*, 18, 76.

50. *Ripon College Catalog, 1978–79*, 4–5, 11–12, 93, 108.

51. Kendall, *Peculiar Institution*, 178–79, 211; Thompson, *Private Black Colleges at the Crossroads*, 100, 249–50; McKinney, *Religion in Higher Education among Negroes*, 109–11.

52. Pattillo and Mackenzie, *Church Sponsored Higher Education*, 21.

53. For a discussion of the origins of the contemporary evangelical Friends movement, see Jones, *Haverford College*, 28.

54. Chitty, *Episcopal Church in Education*, 22–24; "Academies, Colleges, and Seminaries Related to the United Church of Christ," *Journal of Current Social Issues* (1976–77, supplement): 30–31; *Wake Forest College Catalog, 1978–79*, 18–19, 25, 122–23.

55. Wicke, *Church Related College*, 30, 41; W. A. Geier, "A New Trail in Methodist Higher Education," *School and Society*, 14 September 1957, 250.

56. Earnest C. Marriner, *The History of Colby College* (Waterville, ME, 1963), 578.

57. Pattillo and Mackenzie, *Church Sponsored Higher Education*, vii, 20–21, 248; Safara A. Witmer, *Bible College Story: Education with Dimension* (Wheaton, IL, 1970), 15, 44.

58. Pattillo and Mackenzie, *Church Sponsored Higher Education*, 27–29, 295; National Center for Education Statistics, *1980 Digest of Education Statistics* (Washington, DC, 1980), 82, 88.

59. Pattillo and Mackenzie, *Church Sponsored Higher Education*, 26–29, 102–10; Wicke, *Church Related College*, 98.

60. Alexander W. Astin and Calvin B. T. Lee, *The Invisible Colleges: A Profile of Small Private Colleges with Limited Resources* (New York, 1972), 99; S. A. Clark and R. F. Larson, "Mobility, Productivity, and Inbreeding at Small Colleges: A Comparative Study," *Sociology of Education* (fall 1972): 426, 432.

61. See Merrimon Cuninggim, "Categories of Church-Relatedness," in *Church-Related Higher Education*, ed. Robert Parsonage (Valley Forge, PA, 1978), ch. 2.

62. N. F. S. Ferre, "Place of the Chapel in a Christian College," *Journal of Higher Education* (April 1967): 155; Havighurst, *Miami Years, 1809–1959*, 252; *Miami University Catalog, 1980–81*, 68, 74.

63. *Pomona College Catalog, 1977–78*, 5, 23, 78, 199–202.

64. *Wellesley College Catalog, 1974–75*, 10, 30, 42, 166–69.

65. *Texas Christian University Catalog, 1978–79*, 5, 53, 66.

66. Commission of Higher Education, National Council of Churches, *What Is a Christian College?* (New York, 1958), 9–10, 14, 27, 33, 37, 39, 45.

67. Ferre, "Place of the Chapel in a Christian College," 177; G. A. Buttrick et al., "Toward a Philosophy of the Church-Related University," *Christian Scholar* (summer 1962): 95–96; L. A. King, "A Fable about a Slanted Education," *Eternity* (August 1978): 22–25, 37.

Chapter 5

1. Louis G. Geiger, *University of the Northern Plains: A History of the University of North Dakota* (Grand Forks, ND, 1958), 256; Harold F. Williamson and Payson S. Wild, *Northwestern University: A History, 1850–1975* (Evanston, IL, 1976), 90; Shedd, *Two Centuries of Student Christian Movements*, 9.

2. Shedd, *Two Centuries of Student Christian Movements*, 9.

3. See, for example, George H. Callcott, *A History of the University of Maryland* (Baltimore, 1966), 242; Smith and Hirschler, *Story of Bluffton College*, 246–50; *University of Wisconsin Catalog, 1920–21*, 87.

4. Shedd, *Two Centuries of Student Christian Movements*, 167; Robert N. Daniel, *Furman University: A History* (Greenville, SC, 1951), 130; Bettersworth, *People's College*, 371; James B. Sellers, *History of the University of Alabama* (Tuscaloosa, AL, 1953), 462; Dunaway, *Pennsylvania State*, 382–85.

5. McKinney, *Religion in Higher Education among Negroes*, 87–88.

6. Shedd, *Two Centuries of Student Christian Movements*, 92–94, 103–4, 118–20, 123–26, 152; C. Howard Hopkins, *A History of the YMCA in North America* (New York, 1951), 274; idem, *John R. Mott*, 53.

7. Shedd, *Two Centuries of Student Christian Movements*, 188–97, 206–10.

8. Ibid., 120, 167; Hopkins, *History of the YMCA*, 282–83, 625–27, 646, 655–56.

9. Hopkins, *History of the YMCA*, 625–27; Franklin H. Littell, *From State Church to Pluralism: A Protestant Interpretation of Religion in American History* (New York, 1971), 155–57; Hopkins, *John R. Mott*, 21, 24, 44, 210, 225.

10. Shedd, *Two Centuries of Student Christian Movements*, 92, 100–104, 119.

11. Sheldon, *Student Life*, 271–81; Sheldon, *Oregon*, 130.

12. Hopkins, *History of the YMCA*, 274, 284–86; Sheldon, *Student Life*, 281.

13. Shedd, *Two Centuries of Student Christian Movements*, 167–68.

14. Ibid., 166–67, 248; Hopkins, *History of the YMCA*, 282–86, 628; Sheldon, *Student Life*, 281.

15. Sheldon, *Student Life*, 271–74; Hopkins, *History of the YMCA*, 288–89.

16. Shedd, *Two Centuries of Student Christian Movements*, 238–67, 289, 405; Hopkins, *History of the YMCA*, 295; Watson A. Omulogoli, "The Student Volunteer Movement" (M.A. thesis, Wheaton College, 1967), 123–25.

17. Sheldon, *Student Life*, 283–85.

18. Omulogoli, "Student Volunteer Movement," 104; Hopkins, *History of the YMCA*, 282–83; Shedd, *Two Centuries of Student Christian Movements*, 381–93, 422.

19. Omulogoli, "Student Volunteer Movement," 108, 117.

20. Ibid., 125–26.

21. Hopkins, *History of the YMCA*, 646, 655–56.

22. Clarence P. Shedd, *The Church Follows Its Students* (New Haven, 1938), xiii–xviii, 9–32, 281–82; John Strietelmeier, *Valparaiso's First Century* (Valparaiso, IN, 1959), 78.

23. Charles E. Hummel, *Campus Christian Witness* (Chicago, 1958), 1–11.

24. Ibid., 191–94; also see David M. Howard, *Student Power in World Evangelism* (Downers Grove, IL, 1970), ch. 9.

25. Richard Quebedeaux, *I Found It: The Story of Bill Bright and Campus Crusade* (New York, 1979), 52–66, 125–29, 142–46.

26. Ringenberg, *Taylor*, 163–67; Quebedeaux, *I Found It*, 142.

27. Quebedeaux, *I Found It*, xii, 58.

28. Nomenclature is a problem in Bible college history. Later in this section I will discuss the evolution from Bible training schools and Bible institutes to Bible colleges; however, to minimize confusion and misunderstanding, throughout the text I will usually use the term "Bible college" and "Bible colleges" except when referring exclusively to the pre-1940 period. While this may be generous, it probably compares favorably with the generally accepted practice of using the term "college" to describe the many nineteenth-century liberal arts institutions that enrolled primarily preparatory students.

29. Virginia L. Brereton, "Education and Evangelism: Protestant Fundamentalist Bible Schools, 1880–1940," paper presented at the Conference on Urban Education, Columbia University, New York, 12 December 1980, 20ff.; Safara A. Witmer, "A New Form of American Education," in *Christian Education in a Democracy*, ed. Frank E. Gaebelein (New York, 1951), 165–67; H. Richard Niebuhr, Daniel D. Williams, and James Gustafson, *The Advancement of Theological Education* (New York, 1957), 5; Louis Gasper, *The Fundamentalist Movement* (Paris, 1963), 11–12; William S. McBirnie Jr., "A Study of the Bible Institute Movement" (Ph.D. diss., Southwestern Baptist Theological Seminary, 1952), 6; Harold W. Boon, "The Development of the Bible College or Institute in the United States and Canada since 1880" (Ph.D. diss., New York University, 1950), 2–3, 30–34, 41. Also see Virginia L. Brereton, "Protestant Fundamentalist Bible Schools" (Ph.D. diss., Columbia University, 1981).

30. Ernest Sandeen, *The Roots of Fundamentalism: British and American Millenarianism, 1800–1930* (Chicago, 1970), 183, 241–42; Gene A. Getz, *MBI: The Story of Moody Bible Institute* (Chicago, 1969), 22, 28, 48; Witmer, *Bible College Story*, 53–66; Don Gray, "A Critical Analysis of the Academic Evolutionary Development within the Assemblies of God Higher Education Movement, 1914–1975" (Ph.D. diss., Southwestern Baptist Theological Seminary, 1976), 57, 97–101; McBirnie, "Study of the Bible Institute Movement," 37; Johnson, *Higher Education of Southern Baptists*, 401–4. Also see Gerald C. Tiffin, "The Interaction between the Bible Col-

lege Movement and the Independent Disciples of Christ Denomination" (Ph.D. diss., Stanford University, 1968).

31. George Dollar, *A History of Fundamentalism in America* (Greenville, SC, 1973), 113–17, 199–200; William Bell Riley, *The Menace of Modernism* (New York, 1917), 115.

32. McBirnie, "Study of the Bible Institute Movement," 11–12, 16, 19–23; Witmer, *Bible College Story*, 33; Boon, "Development of the Bible College," 26–29.

33. Boon, "Development of the Bible College," 30–36, 40–41; James Findlay, "Moody, 'Gapmen,' and the Gospel: The Early Days of Moody Bible Institute," *Church History* (September 1962): 325–26; Stanley N. Gundry, *Love Them In: The Proclamation Theology of D. L. Moody* (Chicago, 1976), 55–56, 166–68.

34. Getz, *MBI*, 90–91; Findlay, "Moody, 'Gapmen,' and the Gospel," 323; Witmer, *Bible College Story*, 36.

35. Getz, *MBI*, 21, 24, 47–55, 346.

36. Nathan R. Wood, *A School of Christ: Gordon College* (Boston, 1953), 17–18; Witmer, *Bible College Story*, 38, 73; Charles B. Eavey, *History of Christian Education* (Chicago, 1964), 338–41.

37. Boon, "Development of the Bible College," 50–51; Wood, *School of Christ*, 10–20.

38. Witmer, *Bible College Story*, 35; Findlay, "Moody, 'Gapmen,' and the Gospel," 326.

39. Witmer, *Bible College Story*, 89; *Montana Institute of the Bible Catalog, 1980–82*, 24.

40. S. A. Witmer, "If J. E. Ramseyer Had Lived in Days Like These," *The Missionary Worker*, 15 June 1962, 6.

41. Getz, *MBI*, 45–46; *Fort Wayne Bible Training School Catalog, 1906–07*, 10; Harry M. Shuman et al., *After Fifty Years: A Record of God's Working through the Christian and Missionary Alliance* (Harrisburg, PA, 1939), 87–97.

42. Kenneth S. Latourette, *A History of Christianity*, 2 vols. (New York, 1975), 2:1046; Witmer, "New Form of Education," 164–65; Witmer, *Bible College Story*, 77–83, 111; *American Association of Bible Colleges Manual, 1975*, 7; Getz, *MBI*, 352–53; Kenneth Gangel, "The Bible College: Past, Present, and Future," *Christianity Today*, 7 November 1980, 35.

43. Byron O. Osborne, *The Malone Story* (Newton, KS, 1970), 233; Boon, "Development of the Bible College," 92; "Educational Experiences and Career Patterns of Bible College Graduates," survey conducted by the American Association of Bible Colleges, 1980, 5.

44. Witmer, "New Form of Education," 163–66; Boon, "Development of the Bible College," 66; Getz, *MBI*, 114–16; *Gordon Bible Institute Catalog, 1914*, 42.

45. *Liberty Baptist College Catalog, 1978–79*, 6, 37; Conrad Hilberry, "Wheaton College," in Hilberry and Keeton, *Struggle and Promise*, 35; Melton Wright, *Fortress of Faith: The Story of Bob Jones University* (Grand Rapids, 1960), 214.

46. McBirnie, "Study of the Bible Institute Movement," 82–83; Boon, "Development of the Bible College," 75–76; Witmer, *Bible College Story*, 42–44; Gangel, "Bible College," 35.

47. McBirnie, "Study of the Bible Institute Movement," 88; Witmer, *Bible College Story*, 44; Osborne, *Malone Story*, 206–7; Eavey, *History of Christian Education*, 344.

48. Witmer, "New Form of Education," 158–62, 176; S. A. Witmer, "Bible College Education," *School and Society*, 16 October 1954, 113–15.

49. Interview with Samuel D. Sutherland, 20 October 1978; Witmer, *Bible College Story*, 74; *Biola Catalog, 1978–79*, 25; *Northwestern College Catalog, 1979–81*, 37, 40–41.

50. Witmer, *Bible College Story*, 45; Lenice F. Redd, "The Bible Institute Movement in America" (M.A. thesis, Wheaton College, 1947), 55–57; Boon, "Development of the Bible College," 19–22; Robert W. Lynn and Elliott Wright, *The Big Little School: Two Hundred Years of the Sunday School* (Nashville, 1971), 40ff.

51. Interview with Samuel D. Sutherland, 20 October 1978; Witmer, *Bible College Story*, 45–47; McBirnie, "Study of the Bible Institute Movement," 115; *American Association of Bible Colleges Manual, 1975*, 7–8.

52. S. A. Witmer, "The Paradox in Bible College Education," in *S. A. Witmer: Beloved Educator*, ed. Timothy M. Warner (Wheaton, IL, 1970), 33–35; *The Missionary Worker*, 15 June 1962, 2; Warner, *S. A. Witmer*, 5.

53. Witmer, *Bible College Story*, 46; *American Association of Bible Colleges Manual, 1975*, 45–46, 75–76; *American Association of Bible Colleges Manual, 1979–80*, 3–17.

54. Witmer, *Bible College Story*, 44; Getz, *MBI*, 11–12, 21.

55. *American Association of Bible Colleges Directory, 1979–80*, 3–17.

56. Boon, "Development of the Bible College," 99–101; *Baptist Bible College Catalog, 1978–79*, 33–36.

57. Witmer, *Bible College Story*, 40, 55–56; McBirnie, "Study of the Bible Institute Movement," 2; *American Association of Bible Colleges Manual, 1975*, 22; *American Association of Bible Colleges Directory, 1979–80*, 3–17; Gangel, "Bible College," 35; Letter from R. E. Bell, 24 November 1980; *AABC Newsletter* (fall 1974): 7; *Fact Book on Theological Education, 1980–81*, 66.

58. Letter from R. E. Bell, 9 April 1981; *AABC Newsletter* (winter 1975): 1; *AABC Newsletter* (winter 1980): 6; R. E. Bell, ed., "Student Recruitment in the Bible College" (study conducted by the American Association of Bible Colleges, 1975), 8, 10, 15–16.

59. Hilberry, "Wheaton College," 35.

60. Askew, "Liberal Arts College Encounters Intellectual Change," 235–48.

61. If Redlands was reluctant to be known as "the Wheaton of the West," another California school, Westmont, gladly accepted that label following its beginning in Santa Barbara in 1940.

62. Lawrence E. Nelson, *Redlands: Biography of a College* (Redlands, CA, 1958), 247–48.

63. *Bryan College Catalog, 1977–79*, 7–8.

64. William Jennings Bryan, *Darwin's Confession* (Upland, IN, n.d.), 1–4.

65. Percival A. Wesche, *Henry Clay Morrison: Crusader and Saint* (n.p., n.d.), 72, 93–94, 169, 187.

66. See Ronald H. Nash, *The New Evangelicalism* (Grand Rapids, 1963); George M. Marsden, *Fundamentalism and American Culture* (New York, 1980), 228.

67. Dollar, *History of Fundamentalism in America*, 283–85.

68. Roger C. Ellison, "A Foundation Study of the Development of Tennessee Temple Schools" (Ph.D. diss., Bob Jones University, 1973), 13–15, 61–80, 163; Dollar, *History of Fundamentalism in America*, 195, 242–43.

69. Billy Vick Bartlett, *The History of Baptist Separatism* (Springfield, MO, 1972), 2–7, 32–33, 50–51, 60–65, 79; Dollar, *History of Fundamentalism in America*, 197–98, 271–72; *Baptist Bible College Catalog, 1978–79*, 9, 14, 16.

70. "Man with Vision," *Christian Life* (March 1978): 20–21, 59–63; "A Tide of Born-Again Politics," *Newsweek*, 15 September 1980, 28–35.

71. Wright, *Bob Jones University*, 24–51; Dollar, *History of Fundamentalism in America*, 270–71.

72. *Bob Jones University Catalog, 1978–79*, 184, 189; "Tax Troubles," *Christianity Today*, 7 June 1974, 50; Larry King, "The Buckle on the Bible Belt," *Harper's Magazine*, June 1966, 55; R. Behen, "Ars Sacra in the Peruna Belt," *National Review*, 20 July 1973, 792; R. G. Sherrill, "Bob Jones University, New Curricula for Bigotry," *The Nation*, 29 March 1965, 326–27.

73. *Bob Jones University Catalog, 1978–79*, 2, 8, 190, 197–204.

74. See, for example, Gasper, *Fundamentalist Movement*, 105–6.

75. Dollar, *History of Fundamentalism in America*, 270; "World's Most Unusual," *Time*, 16 June 1952, 74; *Bob Jones University Catalog, 1978–79*, 5, 45; *Liberty Baptist College Catalog, 1978–79*, 3, 37.

76. Wright, *Bob Jones University*, 213.

77. Ellison, "Foundation Study of the Development of Tennessee Temple Schools," 51, 198; *Baptist Bible College Catalog, 1978–79*, 5, 45; *Liberty Baptist College Catalog, 1978–79*, 3, 37.

78. Dollar, *History of Fundamentalism in America*, 259; Ellison, "Foundation Study of the Development of Tennessee Temple Schools," 199; *Liberty Baptist College Catalog, 1978–79*, 55; Wolterstorff, *Christian Liberal Arts Education*, 25–26; Gasper, *Fundamentalist Movement*, 114; B. Drummond Ayres, "Private Schools Provoking Church-State Conflict," *New York Times*, 28 April 1978, 1, 23.

79. Ellison, "Foundation Study of the Development of Tennessee Temple Schools," 92; King, "Buckle on the Bible Belt," 53, 56; "The Sins of Billy James," *Time*, 16 February 1976, 52; "Personalia," *Christianity Today*, 5 September 1980, 79.

80. "Sunday Schools of the Decade," *Christian Life*, October 1977, 30–34.

81. Sherrill, "Bob Jones University," 328; John Pollack, *Billy Graham: The Authorized Biography* (New York, 1966), 11; Ellison, "Foundation Study of the Development of Tennessee Temple Schools," 174.

82. Ellison, "Foundation Study of the Development of Tennessee Temple Schools," 44–46; Sherrill, "Bob Jones University," 327–28; Bartlett, *History of Baptist Separatism*, 62–69; Wright, *Bob Jones University*, 73.

83. Sherrill, "Bob Jones University," 327–29; "Born-Again Politics," 28–32.

84. Adlai S. Croom, *The Early History of Harding College* (n.p., 1954), 128–31; also see Marsden, *Fundamentalism and American Culture*, 206–7.

85. By contrast, before the Civil War a significant number of evangelical colleges and leaders promoted a radical brand of social activism. See Donald W. Dayton, *Discovering an Evangelical Heritage* (New York, 1976); and David R. Huebner, "Reform and the Pre–Civil War American College" (Ph.D. diss., University of Illinois, 1972).

86. Hilberry, "Wheaton College," 37.

Chapter 6

1. Young, *History of Colleges of the Churches of Christ*, 186; Mary A. Tenney, *Still Abides the Memory* (Greenville, IL, 1942), 282–83; Stanley High, "Pity the Poor Collegian," *Saturday Evening Post*, 3 June 1939, 71.

2. Brigham Young University with its 28,000 students is the largest of the seri-

ously religious colleges, but few Mormons or non-Mormons would wish to classify it as Protestant.

3. Bernard Cochran, "Southern Baptist Dilemma in Higher Education," *Christian Century,* 28 December 1966, 1600; Earl J. McGrath et al., *Study of Southern Baptist Colleges and Universities, 1976–77* (Nashville, 1977), 18–20, 63; *Baylor University Catalog, 1978–79,* i, 15, 22, 126–32.

4. Carlson, *Church Sponsored Higher Education,* 12–13; *Lutheran Higher Education Directory, 1980–82,* 10–59; interview with Gary Greinke, 29 June 1981. For a helpful explanation of the complex denominational genealogy from which the Lutheran colleges developed, see Arthur L. Olsen, "Unpacking Luther's Heritage — American Style," in *Lutheran Higher Education in the 1980s: Heritage and Challenge,* ed. J. Victor Ham (Washington, DC, 1980).

5. Pattillo and Mackenzie, *Church Sponsored Higher Education,* 253–54, 256–60; interview with Gary Greinke, 29 June 1981; McGrath, *Southern Baptist Colleges,* 84, 96; Education Commission of the Southern Baptist Convention, *Baptist Education Study Task* (Nashville, 1978), 62; letter from Charles J. Miller, 18 September 1978.

6. Pattillo and MacKenzie, *Church Sponsored Higher Education,* 15–16.

7. Some of the more aggressively separatist of these were discussed in the section on fundamentalist higher education in chapter 5.

8. Vinson Synan, *The Holiness-Pentecostal Movement in the United States* (Grand Rapids, 1971), 51, 209; William W. Menzies, *Anointed to Serve: The Story of the Assemblies of God* (Springfield, MO, 1971), 362–64; also see Klaude Kendrick, *The Promise Fulfilled: A History of the Modern Pentecostal Movement* (Springfield, MO, 1961), and Timothy L. Smith, *Called Unto Holiness: The Story of the Nazarenes* (Kansas City, MO, 1962). Synan and Kendrick emphasize the similar origins of the Holiness and Pentecostal movements.

9. Oral Roberts, *The Call* (New York, 1971), 198–99; "Oral Roberts College Has Grown in Seven Years," *New York Times,* 13 June 1972, sec. 2, 1; *ORU News Bulletin,* September 1976; *Oral Roberts University Catalog, 1978–79,* 16.

10. Roberts, *The Call,* ch. 10; *ORU News Bulletin,* September 1976; "Oral Roberts College," 1; *Oral Roberts University School of Medicine Catalog, 1980–81,* 45; "When God Talks, Oral Listens," *Time,* 16 November 1981, 64.

11. "Oral Roberts College," 1; *Oral Roberts University Student Handbook, 1978–79,* 46–47, 50; *ORU News Bulletin,* September 1976.

12. *ORU News Bulletin,* September 1976.

13. Ibid.

14. Roberts, *The Call,* 177–96; Pollack, *Billy Graham,* 41–46; Philip Yancey, "The Ironies and Impact of PTL," *Christianity Today,* 21 September 1979, 30.

15. Donald F. Ackland, *Moving Heaven and Earth: R. G. LeTourneau* (New York, 1949), 155–56; *LeTourneau College Catalog, 1979–80,* 7–8, 14–15.

16. *The Story of America's Most Unique College: The School of the Ozarks* (n.p., n.d.); *School of the Ozarks Catalog, 1981–83,* 10–12, 22–26.

17. John W. Snyder, "Why Not a Christian College on a University Campus?" *Christianity Today,* 17 February 1967, 14–17; Frank C. Nelsen, "Evangelical Living and Learning Centers: A Proposal," *Christianity Today,* 26 May 1972, 7–8; Ron Sider, "Christian Cluster Colleges Off to a Good Start," *Christianity Today,* 24 May 1974, 12–16; *Conrad Grebel College Catalog, 1981–82,* 8–12, 30, 33–34; Shedd, *Church Follows Its Students,* 21; Geiger, *University of the Northern Plains,* 144, 163–65, 336;

Johnson, *Higher Education of Southern Baptists,* 405–6; *Northwest Christian College Catalog, 1978–80,* 12–13, 36–37.

18. A similar enrollment pattern occurred in seminary education, where the conservative Protestant institutions — especially the Southern Baptist and independent ones — experienced the sharpest growth. A clear majority of the following twenty-five largest seminaries (fall 1980) were evangelical or orthodox in nature:

1. Southwestern (Southern Baptist), 3,684
2. Fuller, 2,394
3. Southern (Southern Baptist), 2,068
4. New Orleans (Southern Baptist), 1,242
5. Southeastern (Southern Baptist), 1,055
6. San Francisco (United Presbyterian), 962
7. Trinity (Evangelical Free), 833
8. Princeton, 810
9. Dallas, 777
10. Asbury, 742
11. Concordia of St. Louis (Lutheran Church Missouri Synod), 724
12. Talbot, 720
13. Drew (United Methodist), 705
14. Gordon-Conwell, 693
15. Luther (American Lutheran Church), 643
16. McCormick (United Presbyterian), 618
17. Candler (United Methodist), 608
18. Golden Gate Baptist (Southern Baptist), 587
19. Concordia of Ft. Wayne (Lutheran Church Missouri Synod), 571
20. Nazarene, 499
21. Boston (United Methodist), 486
22. Yale, 473
23. Andover-Newton, 463
24. Bethel (Baptist General Conference), 443
25. Perkins (United Methodist), 438

This enrollment data appears in the January 1981 *Bulletin of the Association of Theological Schools* and the 1980–81 *Yearbook of Higher Education.* Also see Kenneth S. Kantzer, "Documenting the Dramatic Shift in Seminaries from Liberal to Conservative," *Christianity Today,* 4 February 1983, 10–11.

19. Kenneth Briggs, "Evangelical Colleges Reborn," *New York Times Magazine,* 14 December 1980, 140–44; Pace, *Education and Evangelism,* xii, 2; Carl Henry, *Evangelicals in Search of Identity* (Waco, 1976), 62; *Christian College News,* 8 August 1980, 3; David Riesman, "The Evangelical College: Untouched by the Academic Revolution," *Change* (January/February 1981): 15; Pattillo and MacKenzie, *Church Sponsored Higher Education,* 114.

20. For the philosophy and history of CASC in its early years, see Alfred T. Hill, *The Small College Meets the Challenge: The Story of CASC* (New York, 1959).

21. "Dean's List Top Ten," *Christianity Today,* 30 January 1970, 36; "Evaluating Christian Colleges," *Christianity Today,* 27 March 1970, 23; Conrad Hilberry, "Wheaton College," in Keeton and Hilberry, *Struggle and Promise,* 21, 40, 73; "All That and Billy Graham, Too," *Time,* 22 September 1980, 83.

22. "Graham Center," *Christianity Today*, 10 October 1980, 74–75; interview with William Shoemaker, 3 July 1980.

23. Askew, "Liberal Arts College Encounters Intellectual Change," 231; Harold W. Berk, "The Christian College Consortium in Social Context" (Ph.D. diss., University of Toledo, 1974), 64–74.

24. Paul Ramsay and John F. Wilson, eds., *The Study of Religion in Colleges and Universities* (Princeton, NJ, 1970), 11; Jack Haas and Richard Wright, "What Christian Colleges Teach about Creation," *Christianity Today*, 17 June 1977, 8–11; Hilberry, "Wheaton College," 33; James O. Buswell III, "Creationist Views on Human Origin," *Christianity Today*, 8 August 1975, 4–6.

25. Bernard M. Loomer, "Religion and the Mind of the University," in *Liberal Learning and Religion*, ed. Amos N. Wilder (New York, 1951), 159–63; Ernest L. Boyer and Martin Kaplan, *Education for Survival* (Washington, DC, 1977), 11.

26. Nicholas P. Wolterstorff, *Christian Liberal Arts Education*, 23–26; Bernard Ramm, *The Christian College in the Twentieth Century* (Grand Rapids, 1963), 76–80.

27. *Christian College News*, 31 October 1980, pp. 2a–4a; 14 November 1980, pp. 1a, 5; 28 November 1980, p. 2a; 26 December 1980, p. 8; 30 January 1981, p. 6; 13 February 1981, p. 8; *Goshen College Catalog, 1980–82*, 45–46, 75–78; Kenneth A. Briggs, "Evangelical Institute Preaches Ecology," *New York Times*, 29 June 1981, B12. For an excellent institutional self-study promoting the integration idea, see St. Olaf's Henry Hong, ed., *Integration in the Christian Liberal Arts College* (Northfield, MN, 1956). Also note Frank E. Gaebelein, *The Pattern of God's Truth* (New York, 1954), and the very influential writings of Arthur F. Holmes, especially *The Idea of a Christian College* (Grand Rapids, 1975), ch. 4; and *All Truth Is God's Truth* (Grand Rapids, 1977).

28. James R. Cameron, *Eastern Nazarene College: The First Fifty Years, 1900–1950* (Kansas City, MO, 1968), 287.

29. Jay B. Kenyon, *Ten College Generations* (New York, 1956), 125.

30. Kenyon, *Ten College Generations*, 130–31; "42 Hours of Repentance," *Time*, 20 February 1950, 56, 58; "Wheaton Repents," *Newsweek*, 20 February 1950, 82–83; "College Revival Becomes Confession Marathon," *Life*, 20 February 1950, 40–41.

31. "Asbury Revival Blazes Cross-Country Trail," *Christianity Today*, 13 March 1970, 46–50.

32. Kenyon, *Ten College Generations*, 124–25; Pattillo and MacKenzie, *Church Sponsored Higher Education*, 111–13.

33. Pace, *Education and Evangelism*, xii; John H. Furbay, "Undergraduates in a Group of Evangelical Christian Colleges" (Ph.D. diss., Yale University, 1931), 141, 184; Hilberry, "Wheaton College," 36.

34. *ORU News Bulletin, 1972.*

35. Part of this section originally appeared in the essay "Why Did Christian Colleges Remain Calm?" *Taylor University Magazine*, fall 1972.

36. *Houghton College Catalog, 1926–27*, 13.

37. "Evangelical Colleges Plan Consortium," *Christianity Today*, 9 April 1971, 44–45; Berk, "Christian College Consortium in Social Context," 1, 79, 289; Christian College Consortium Articles of Incorporation, 24 June 1971.

38. Gordon R. Werkema, "Description of the Christian College Consortium," unpublished letter, 4 February 1976. Also, see *A Guide to Christian Colleges* (Grand Rapids, 1982).

39. Carnegie Foundation for the Advancement of Teaching, *The States and Higher Education* (San Francisco, 1976), 41.

40. George N. Rainsford, *Congress and Higher Education in the Nineteenth Century* (Knoxville, 1972), 96, 130–31, 135.

41. Carnegie Foundation, *States and Higher Education*, 28; Richard G. Axt, *The Federal Government and Financing Higher Education* (New York, 1952), 79–81, 122–43, 156–57; Alice M. Rivlin, *The Role of the Federal Government in Financing Higher Education* (Washington, DC, 1961), 61–97.

42. W. H. McFarlane, "Patterns of State Aid to Private Higher Education," *College and University Journal* (May 1972): 19–20; Carnegie Foundation, *States and Higher Education*, 80–81; Paul Hardin et al., *Endangered Service: Independent Colleges, Public Policy, and the First Amendment* (Nashville, 1976), 83–84.

43. C. Stanley Lowell, "Will Churches Give Up Their Colleges?" *Church and State* (July–August 1971): 10–11; "Public Aid to Church-Related Colleges and Universities," *School and Society*, 30 October 1965, 404–5; Frank J. Sorauf, *The Wall of Separation* (Princeton, NJ, 1976), 52–53; H. I. Hester, *Southern Baptists in Christian Education* (n.p., 1968), 58, 86; *Baptist Education Study Task Report*, 63; Luther J. Carter, "Facilities Grants Forbidden to Baptist Colleges," *Science*, 29 April 1966, 626–29; Cochran, "Southern Baptist Dilemma in Higher Education," 1600; "Baptists in a Bind," *Christian Century*, 8 December 1965, 1502.

44. Carnegie Council on Policy Studies in Higher Education, *The Federal Role in Postsecondary Education* (San Francisco, 1975), 36–39; Peggy Heim et al., *A National Policy for Private Higher Education* (Washington, DC, 1974), 19; Hardin et al., *Endangered Service*, 30, 82; "Packwood-Moynihan Parochial Bill Introduced," *Church and State* (April 1981): 3; "Senate Holds Parochial Hearings," *Church and State* (July–August 1981): 5–10; interview with John Dellenback, 24 December 1980.

45. "Church Colleges and the Scramble for Public Funds," *Christian Century*, 20 October 1976, 883–85.

46. *Baptist Bible College Catalog, 1978–79*, 41.

47. Sorauf, *Wall of Separation*, 361–69; Edward N. Leavy and Eric A. Raps, "The Judicial Double Standard for State Aid to Church-Affiliated Educational Institutions," *Journal of Church and State* (spring 1979): 209–22; Hardin et al., *Endangered Service*, 93ff.

48. Hardin et al., *Endangered Service*, 93ff.; *Christian College News*, 19 October 1979, 3.

49. "Grove City in Legal Thicket," *Christianity Today*, 16 November 1979, 45–46; *Christian College News*, 11 July 1980, 2; and 8 August 1980, 3–4; "ORU Takes Offensive over Law School Accreditation," *Christianity Today*, 4 September 1981, 73–74; "The Bar Association Does Accreditation About-Face," *Christianity Today*, 18 September 1981, 47.

50. For an interesting explanation of the reasons for these mixed results, see Walfred H. Peterson, "The Thwarted Opportunity for Judicial Activism in Church-State Relations: Separation and Accommodation in Precarious Balance," *Journal of Church and State* (fall 1980): 437–58.

Chapter 7

1. The Bloom book was published by Simon and Schuster of New York.

2. The Smith book was published by Viking of New York.

3. Edward Ericson Jr. of Calvin College speaks of "the recent explosion of articles criticizing the academy" in his recent essay "The University under the Microscope," *Books and Culture* (May/June 2005): 13.

4. Andrew Delbanco, "The Endangered University," *New York Review of Books,* 24 March 2005, 20.

5. Rebecca Winters, "Higher Learning," *Time,* 2 February 2004, 58–60; Alan Wolfe, "The Opening of the Evangelical Mind," *Atlantic Monthly,* October 2000, 55–71; "Evangelical Colleges Make Marks in a Secular World," *Los Angeles Times,* 30 November 2003, A-1; www.cccu.org; http://spirituality.ucla.edu/research/.

6. See the chart by Robert Andringa entitled "Profile of U.S. Postsecondary Education," which appears as appendix A of this book.

7. Robert Benne, *Quality with Soul: How Six Premier Colleges and Universities Keep Faith with Their Religious Traditions* (Grand Rapids, 2001), ch. 3.

8. See James A. Patterson, *Shining Lights: A History of the Council for Christian Colleges and Universities* (Grand Rapids, 2001); and also Patterson's supplement, *Shining Lights and Widening Horizons: A History of the Council for Christian Colleges and Universities, 2001–2006* (Washington, D.C., 2006).

9. Patterson, *Shining Lights,* 44, 54, and chs. 4, 6; Newsletter, Council for Christian Colleges and Universities Profile, fall 2004.

10. Interview with Robert Andringa, 29 September 2004; http://www.cccu.org/about/members.asp?q=3. For a description of how one denomination works closely and harmoniously with its colleges, see Jerry D. Lambert, Al Truesdale, and Michael W. Vail, "Emerging Models in the Church of the Nazarene," in *The Future of Religious Colleges,* ed. Paul J. Dovre (Grand Rapids, 2002), 141–59.

11. http://hirr.hartsem.edu/org/faith_congregations_nondenom_FACT.html.

12. http://abhe.gospelcom.net/accredited.htm; http://abhe.gospelcom.net/affiliates.htm; http://abhe.gospelcom.net/news-release.htm; Larry J. McKinney, *Equipping for Service: A Historical Account of the Bible College Movement in North America* (Fayetteville, AR, 1997), 203–7, 215–36; Joseph L. Castleberry, "Bible Colleges and Institutes," in *The Encyclopedia of Protestantism,* ed. Hans J. Hillerbrand, 4 vols. (New York, 2004), 1:237–38; interviews with Philip Dearborn and Bruce McCracken, 1 June 2005. Also see Timothy Millard, "From Bible School to Christian College: A Study of the Evolution of Christian Mission," *Research on Christian Higher Education* 4 (1997): 13–27.

13. For the list of institutional sponsors of the *Christian Scholars Review,* see the inside front cover of any issue.

14. Interviews with Melvin Piehl, Margaret Franson, Marcia Bunge, and Thomas Kennedy, 22–23 July 2004; interview with Mark Schwehn, 25 March 2005; interview with Craig Dykstra and Christopher Coble, 4 November 2004; "Lilly Fellows Program Directory," 2004, 1, 5; Lilly Endowment, Inc., "Programs for the Theological Exploration of Vocation," 2002.

15. Interview with Craig Dykstra, 4 November 2004; letter from Christopher Coble, 3 January 2005; interview with Christopher Coble, 27 September 2005; interview with Ruth Kath, 17 May 2005; interview with Harvey Stalwick, 5 May 2005; letter from Mark D. Travik, 20 May 2005; interview with Peg Falls-Corbitt, 23 May 2005; interview with Bernard Richardson, 8 June 2005; interview with Judith Cebula, 18 May 2005; interview with Bobby Fong, 21 May 2005; interview with Betsy Taylor, 9 May 2005; interview with Timothy Beach-Verhey, 7 April 2005; interview with Karen Wood, 25 May 2005; http://www.ptev.org/school_contacts.aspx?iid=26; http://www.ptev.org/school_contacts.aspx?iid=44; "Programs for the Theological Exploration of Vocation," 2002.

16. Interview with George Marsden, 11 July 2004; Randy Frame, "Christian

Colleges: Graduating Excellence," *Christianity Today*, March 2005, 88; Ronald Kirkemo, *For Zion's Sake: A History of Pasadena/Point Loma College* (San Diego, 1992); Rick Ostrander, *Head, Heart, and Hand: John Brown University and Modern Evangelical Higher Education* (Fayetteville, AR, 2003); interview with Larry Eskridge, 1 April 2005.

17. Harry Lee Poe, *Christianity and the Academy* (Grand Rapids, 2004), 185ff.; the core curriculum sections of the catalogs of the member institutions of the Council for Christian Colleges and Universities.

18. Mark R. Schwehn, *Exiles from Eden: Religion and the Academic Vocation in America* (New York, 1993); interview with Melvin Piehl, 22 July 2004; interview with Mark Schwehn, 25 March 2005; "Lilly Fellows Program Directory," 2004, 1.

19. Douglas Jacobson and Rhonda Hustedt Jacobsen, *Scholarship and Christian Faith: Enlarging the Conversation* (New York, 2004), 16–23, 47, 54, 59–60; Parker J. Palmer, *To Know as We Are Known: Education as Spiritual Journey* (San Francisco, 1993); Ernest L. Boyer, *Scholarship Reconsidered: Priorities of the Professoriate* (New York, 1990), ch. 2; "Ernest L. Boyer: A Leader of Educators, an Educator of Leaders: 1928–1995," reprinted from the ninety-first Annual Report of the Carnegie Foundation for the Advancement of Teaching, 30 June 1996, 15–29.

20. Mark A. Noll, *The Scandal of the Evangelical Mind* (Grand Rapids, 1994); Mark Noll, "The Evangelical Mind Today," *First Things* (October 2004): 34–39.

21. Michael S. Hamilton and Johanna G. Yngvason, "Patrons of the Evangelical Mind," *Christianity Today*, 8 July 2002, 42–47; "Evangelical Institutions," report prepared for the Pew Foundation, October 1988 (Wheaton College Archives).

22. Interview with Robert Andringa, 29 September 2004; interview with Coein Trudeau, 4 April 2005.

23. The early fall "Best Colleges" issues of the *U.S. News and World Report* have appeared since 1983 and annually with a relatively consistent format since 1990. For an analysis of the limitations of these ratings, see Marguerite Clark, "Weighing Things Up: A Closer Look at the *U.S. News and World Report*'s Ranking Formulas," *College and University Journal* (winter 2004): 3–9.

24. "Almanac Issue," *Chronicle of Higher Education*, 27 August 2004, 14, 32, 36; "Baccalaureate Origins of Doctoral Recipients," 8th ed. (Lancaster, PA, 1998), 31, 65, 81; *America's Best Colleges*, 2005 ed. (*U.S. News and World Report*), 82–113.

25. Interview with Robert Andringa, 29 September 2004; CCCU Enrollment Reports, 2003; interview with Bayard Baylis, 16 September 2004.

26. "Fact Book on Theological Education," 2002–03, Association of Theological Schools, 5, 18–19, 24–32; Stanley H. Skreslet, "Doctoral Dissertations on Mission," 1992–2001, *International Bulletin of Missionary Research*, July 2003, 97–103.

27. http://www.baylor.edu/graduate/index.php?id=2843; "Pepperdine University," in *Choosing the Right College*, ed. Winfield J. C. Myers (Grand Rapids, 2001), 538–39; http://www.pepperdine.edu/welcome/about/schools.htm; *America's Best Graduate Schools*, 2005 ed. (*U.S. News and World Report*), 22–33; http://www.llu.edu/llu/grad/programguide.html.

28. Interview with Robert Andringa, 8 June 2005; interview with Dennis Sheridan, 19 April 2005; Larry J. McKinney, "Evangelical Theological Education: Past Commitments, Present Realities, and Future Considerations," *Christian Higher Education* (April–June 2004): 150; http://abhe.gospelcom.net/faqs.htm; interview with Philip Dearborn, 1 June 2005.

29. Interview with David Gyertson, 11 February 2005; letter from Baxter Ennis, 15 February 2005.

30. Diane Winston, "Adult Programs Challenge Christian Colleges' Mission," *Chronicle of Higher Education*, 10 November 2000, B12–13; interview with Mark Smith, 25 July 2005.

31. Winston, "Adult Programs," B12–13; http://www.cahea.org/html/questions .htm. Also see Richard W. Flory, "Intentional Change and the Maintenance of Mission: The Impact of Adult Education Programs on School Mission at Two Evangelical Colleges," *Review of Religious Research* 43, no. 4 (2002): 349–68.

32. "Christian Colleges Graduating Excellence," *Christianity Today*, March 2005, 106; interview with Bayard Baylis, 16 September 2004; "IWU Names Barnes as First Chancellor," *Marion Chronicle Tribune*, 4 April 2005, 1; interview with Mark Smith, 25 July 2005; http://www.indwes.edu/about/iwu_profile.htm.

33. Gene Maeroff, *A Classroom of One: How On-Line Learning Is Changing Our Schools and Colleges* (New York, 2003), ix–xiv, 212–13; Richard Detweiler, "At Last We Can Replace Lectures," *Chronicle of Higher Education*, July 2004, B8; Mary Cagney, "Distance Learning to the Rescue?" *Christianity Today*, 17 November 1997, 68; Richard Vedder, *Going Broke by Degree* (Washington, DC, 2004), 162–63; interview with Gary Friesen, 18 February 2005.

34. Robert Zemsky and William F. Massey, "Why the E-Learning Boom Went Bust," *Chronicle of Higher Education*, 9 July 2004, B6–8; Linda Drake Gobbo et al., "Virtual Limits: Multicultural Dimensions of Online Education," *International Educator* (summer 2004): 30–39.

35. http://www.liberty.edu/index.cfm?PID=6916; letter from Baxter Ennis, 15 February 2005; interview with Gary Friesen, 18 February 2005; Bob Smietana, "Christian Ed That Pays Off," *Christianity Today*, February 2005, 24.

36. Burton Bollag, "For the Love of God (and Money)," *Chronicle of Higher Education*, 3 September 2004, A29–31.

37. David D. Kirkpatrick, "College for the Home-Schooled Is Shaping Leaders for the Right," *New York Times*, 8 March 2004, A1; *Pensacola Christian College Catalog, 2005–06*, 6–7. Also see James C. Carper and Brian D. Ray, "Religion, Schooling, and Home Education," in *Religion, Education, and the American Experience*, ed. Edith L. Blumhofer (Tuscaloosa, AL, 2002), 223–42.

38. Interview with Robert Andringa, 8 June 2005; http://www.jointcenter.org/ databank/educationfinal/1997%20Educational%20Digest/Enrol/-HiEd/reference1 .htm; http://nces.ed.gov/programs/coe/2005/section5/indicator31.asp; "1991 Enrollment by Race at 81 Institutions within the Christian College Coalition," manuscript, Wheaton College Archives.

39. Interview with Robert Andringa, 8 June 2005; *America's Best Colleges*, 2005 ed. (*U.S. News and World Report*), 51–52; http://www.oakwood.edu/admissions/ default.asp?ID=7; http://www.concordiaselma.edu/general.htm; http://www.swcc .edu/our_history.htm.

40. Interview with Robert Andringa, 8 June 2005; interview with James Earl Massey, 16 January 2005; interview with Bernard L. Richardson, 8 June 2005; Samuel Dubois Cook, "The United Methodist Church and Its Predominately Black Colleges," in *The Future of Religious Colleges*, ed. Paul J. Dovre (Grand Rapids, 2002), 261–62; interview with Jerry Cain, 19 August 2005.

41. *Open Doors 2002: Annual Report on International Educational Exchange* (Insti-

tute of International Education, 2002), 15–18; *Open Doors 2003: Annual Report on International Educational Exchange* (Institute of International Education, 2003), 18, 65–68; Megan Rooney, "Keeping the Study in Study Abroad," *Chronicle of Higher Education*, 22 November 2002, A64; David M. Carson, *Pro Christo et Patria: A History of Geneva College* (Virginia Beach, VA, 1997), 157.

42. http://www.bestsemester.com/; Robert A. Hess, ed., *Internationalizing the Curriculum* (St. Paul, MN, 1987); newsletter, CCCU Advance, spring 2004, 8; Calvin College Off-Campus Study Programs Brochure (n.p., n.d.); William C. Ringenberg, *Taylor University: The First 150 Years* (Grand Rapids, 1996), 166–67, 192, 253.

43. Ellen G. White, *Education* (Boise, ID, 1903), 30; Statistical Report of the Seventh-day Adventist General Conference, 2002, 6, 36, 52–57; interviews with Erich Baumgartner, Gary Land, Russell Staples, and Charles Tidwell, 24 March 2005; http://www.andrews.edu/visitors/about_au/.

44. Interview with Oystein S. LaBianca, 24 March 2005; letter from Beth Birmingham, 24 May 2005; interview with Linwood Geiger, 9 May 2005; David Black, "A Message from the President," *The Economic Development Program of Eastern University: A Commemorative Magazine*, 2004, 2.

45. David Cohen, "The Worldwide Rise of Private Colleges," *Chronicle of Higher Education*, 9 March 2001, A47–49.

46. Joel Carpenter, "New Evangelical Universities," pt. 1, *International Journal of Frontier Missions* (summer 2003): 55–65; interview with Robert Andringa, 8 July 2004. Also see Paul F. Scotchmer, "Christian Universities as a Mission Strategy," *Journal of Frontier Missions* (summer 2003): 66–71.

47. Interview with Rich Gathro, 9 June 2005; interview with Steven G. W. Moore, 24 August 2004; interview with Dwight Jessup, 18 May 2004; interview with Kimberly Spragg, 3 June 2005; http://www.cccu.org/about/affiliates.asp?9=3; http://www.wocati.org/about.html.

48. Paul Bowers, "International Council for Evangelical Theological Education," in *Evangelical Dictionary of World Missions*, ed. A. Scott Moreau (Grand Rapids, 2000), 497; http://www.icete-edu.org/; interviews with Jason Ferenczi, 19 May 2005 and 15 June 2005; interview with Nancy Merrill, 17 June 2005.

49. Comprehensive bibliographies of mostly recent, church-related higher-education literature include those compiled by Michael Beaty for the Baylor Institute for Faith and Learning (http://www3.baylor.edu/IFL/bib.htm) and Stephen Haynes as part 1 of his edited work, *Professing in the Modern Academy: Faculty and the Future of Church-Related Colleges* (Waco, 2002).

50. John Schmalzbauer has identified 130 religious-study centers and institutes with Lilly connections, while Philip Goff of the Center for the Study of Religion and American Culture at Indiana-Purdue Indianapolis has charted many others, including those based in public institutions (letter from John Schmalzbauer, 14 July 2004; "Centers and Institutes Project, 2003," Center for the Study of Religion and American Culture, IUPUI).

51. With Dykstra the key figure in Lilly's sponsorship of so many projects since 1990, it is useful to note his own philosophy. A Christian educator by background, Dykstra emphasizes that one should not focus so much on making wise decisions as on becoming a wise person whose decisions develop naturally from a transformed personhood. "We should understand moral education," he states, "as having to do with the formation of character, which means most fundamentally to be-

come persons who see deeply into the reality of things and who love that reality —
over time and across circumstances." See his *Growing in the Life of Faith: Education
and Christian Practices* (Louisville, 1999), 132; and also *Vision and Character* (New
York, 1981).

52. Interview with Craig Dykstra, 4 November 2004; Kathleen Mahoney, John
Schmalzbauer, and James Youniss, *Revitalizing Religion in the Academy: Summary of
the Evaluation of Lilly Endowment's Initiative on Religion and Higher Education* (Chest-
nut Hill, MA, 2000), 5, 7. Also see Paul J. Dovre, "Re-examination and Renaissance:
Lilly-Sponsored Studies at the Turn of the Century" (http://www.resourcing
christianity.org).

53. David A. Roozen and C. Kirk Hadaway, *Church and Denominational Growth*
(Nashville, 1993), 393–95; Michael S. Hamilton and Jennifer McKinley, "Turning
the Mainline Around," *Christianity Today*, August 2003, 37; Charles H. Bayer, *The
Babylonian Captivity of the Mainline Church* (St. Louis, 1996), 1.

54. Dean R. Hoge, Benton Johnson, and Donald A. Luidens, *Vanishing Boundaries: The Religion of Mainline Protestant Baby Boomers* (Louisville, 1994), 7–8, 21, 178,
181; Robert Wuthnow, *The Reconstruction of American Religion* (Princeton, NJ, 1988),
330; also see Dean M. Kelley, *Why Conservative Churches Are Growing* (New York,
1972), and Christopher Lee Coble, "Where Have All the Young People Gone? The
Christian Endeavor Movement and the Training of Protestant Youth, 1881–1918"
(Ph.D. diss., Harvard University, 2001).

55. Dorothy C. Bass, "The Context and Challenge of Church-Related Higher
Education," *A Point of View* (fall 1996): 4–5.

56. Hamilton and McKinley, "Turning the Mainline Around," 34, 36, 40;
Thomas C. Oden, *The Rebirth of Orthodoxy: Signs of New Life in Christianity* (San
Francisco, 2003), ix, 139ff.

57. Kathleen A. Mahoney, "Religion: A Comeback on Campus," *Liberal Education* (fall 2001): 38.

58. James Nuechterlein, "Faith and Learning in the Christian University," *The
Cresset* (December 1986): 9–16.

59. Interviews with Mel Piehl, Marcia Bunge, and Thomas Kennedy, 22 July
2004; letter from Robert Benne, 12 July 2004; Robert Benne, "A College Recovers Its
Christian Identity," *Christian Century*, 18–25 April 2001, 12–15; interview with
Mary Todd, 4 May 2005; interview with Mark Tranvik, 20 May 2005; interview
with Ruth Kath, 17 May 2005; interview with Harvey Stalwick, 5 May 2005; letter
from Mark D. Travik, 20 May 2005; *Yearbook of American and Canadian Churches,
2004* (Nashville, 2004), 365–79.

60. Patrick J. Reilly, "Are Catholic Colleges Leading Students Astray?" *The
Catholic World Report*, March 2003, 38–39, 42; Alice Gallin, *Negotiating Identity:
Catholic Higher Education since 1960* (Notre Dame, IN, 2000), 56ff., 151ff., 183; James
Burtchaell, *The Dying of the Light* (Grand Rapids, 1998); interview with Mel Piehl, 22
July 2004; interview with Kathleen Cummings, 27 July 2004; interview with Larry
Braskamp, 12 May 2004; letter from John Schmalzbauer, 14 July 2004; James L. Heft
and Fred P. Pestello, "Hiring Practices in Catholic Colleges and Universities," *Cur-
rent Issues in Catholic Higher Education* (fall 1999): 89–97; Colleen Carroll, *The New
Faithful: Why Young Adults Are Embracing Christian Orthodoxy* (Chicago, 2002), 164;
Joseph M. Herlihy, "Reflections on Ex Corde Ecclesiae," in Dovre, *Future of Religious
Colleges*, 284–89.

61. Bradley Longfield and George M. Marsden, "Presbyterian Colleges in Twentieth Century America," in *The Pluralistic Vision: Presbyterians and Mainstream Protestant Education and Leadership,* ed. Milton J. Coalter, John M. Mulder, and Louis B. Weeks (Louisville, 1992), 99–100; Paul C. Kemeny, "Princeton University, Secularization Theories, and Revisionist History: A Review Essay," *Journal of Presbyterian History* (summer 1997): 71–72; Leslie Scanlon, ". . . Church-Related Higher Education Debate," *The Presbyterian Outlook,* 7 July 2004, 1–5.

62. Interview with Timothy Beach-Verhey, 7 April 2005; interview with John Kuykendall, 19 April 2005; interview with Timothy Thyreen, 11 June 2005; Michael S. Hamilton, "A Higher Education," *Christianity Today,* June 2005, 35; Allen Fisher, "Religious and Moral Education at Three Kinds of Liberal Arts Colleges," *Religious Education,* 1 January 1995, 36, 45; http://www.eckerd.edu/academics/index.php?f=gened; http://www.eckerd.edu/csl/goals.shtml.

63. Interview with James Heidinger, 9 August 2004; F. Thomas Trotter, "The College as the Church's Gift," *Christian Century,* 20 November 1988, 1098–1101; letter from Will Willimon, 9 April 2005; http://archives.umc.org/interior.asp?ptid=2&mid=5063.

64. Interview with Michael G. Cartwright, 26 May 2005; Michael G. Cartwright, "Moving beyond Muddled Missions and Misleading Metaphors," in *The Church-Based University in a Liberal Democratic Society,* ed. Michael Budde and John Wright (Grand Rapids, 2004), 185ff. Also see Michael G. Cartwright, *Ecumenical and Interfaith* (n.p., n.d.); and Jerry Israel, "Above All and through All," presidential address, University of Indianapolis, 5 September 2002.

65. Interview with Nancy Lee, 28 June 2005; interview with Bryant Cureton, 21 July 2005; interview with Jerry Cain, 19 August 2005; interview with David Eller, 31 May 2005; David Eller, "The Soul of a Brethren College," *Brethren Life and Thought* (summer/fall 2004): 191, 198.

66. Interview with Greg Wills, 6 August 2004; Michael D. Beaty, "Baptist Models: Past, Present, and Future," in Dovre, *Future of Religious Colleges,* 117; http://www.cccu.org/about/members.asp?q=3.

67. Beaty, "Baptist Models," 116; interview with Greg Wills, 6 August 2004; interview with Jason Fowler, 6 August 2004; Tammi Reed Ledbetter, "Conservative Resurgence at 25," *Southern Baptist Texan,* 31 May 2004, 6–10; R. Albert Mohler, "A Conflict of Visions: The Theological Roots of the Southern Baptist Controversy," *The Southern Baptist Journal of Theology* (spring 2003): 4–10; R. Alan Culpepper, "The Relationship between the University and the Church," *Southern Baptist Educator* (winter 1997–98): 3–7.

68. William E. Hull, "Southern Baptist Higher Education Prospect," *Southern Baptist Educator,* September 1996, 3; interview with Betsy Taylor, 9 May 2005; http://www.wfu.edu/president-elect/; Hamilton, "Higher Education," 35.

69. http://www.cccu.org/about/members.asp?q=3; interview with Coein Trudeau, 11 April 2005; "IFACS Dissolves," *Newsletter of the Conference on Faith and History,* fall 2003, 9; Donald D. Schmeltekopf, "A Christian University in the Baptist Tradition: History of a Vision," in *The Baptist and Christian Character of Baylor,* ed. Donald P. Schmeltekopf, Dianna M. Vitanza, and Bradley J. B. Toben (Waco, 2003), 11–12. Also see Barry Hankins, "Moving Off the Plantation: Southern Baptist Conservatives Become American Evangelicals," ch. 2 in *Uneasy in Babylon: Southern Baptist Conservatives and American Culture* (Tuscaloosa, AL, 2002).

70. See Schmeltekopf et al., *Christian University*, the many essays in *Christianity Today*, and the many scholarly articles by Michael Beaty and his colleagues. Letter from Michael Beatty, 20 November 2005.

71. http://www.cccu.org/about/members.asp?q=3; Lilly Fellows Program Directory; http://www.ptev.org/schools.aspx.

72. General overviews of the relationship between the federal and state governments and the Christian colleges and universities include the earlier Philip R. Moots and Edward McGlynn Gaffney Jr., *Church and Campus: Legal Issues in Religiously Affiliated Higher Education* (Notre Dame, IN, 1979); and idem, *Government and Campus: Federal Regulation of Religiously Affiliated Higher Education* (Notre Dame, IN, 1984). Also see the more recent William A. Kaplan and Barbara A. Lee, *The Law of Higher Education* (San Francisco, 1995); Ralph D. Mawdsley, "Government Aid to and Regulation of Religious Colleges and Universities," ch. 1 of *Religious Higher Education in the United States: A Source Book,* ed. Thomas C. Hunt and James C. Carper (New York, 1996); Kent Weeks, "State and Local Issues," in Dovre, *Future of Religious Colleges*, 332–51; and the First Amendment Center of the Freedom Forum website at http://www.firstamendmentcenter.org.

73. For example, the CCCU colleges receive 10 to 25 percent of their revenues from federal student aid (http://www.Christianpost.com/article/education/890/section/interview.president.of.the.council.for.christian.colleges.and.universities/1.htm).

74. "Falwell's College Alters Mission to Keep it Alive," *The New York Times*, 19 August 1992, B7; R. D. Mawdsley, "Government Aid and Regulation," 6–7; "Notes on Church-State Affairs," *Journal of Church and State* (winter 2001): 180.

75. Herlihy, "Reflections on Ex Corde Ecclesiae," 300–301; http://www.freedom forum.org/templates/document.asp?documentID=9070; "Notes on Church-State Affairs," *Journal of Church and State* (summer 2001): 655; http://www.cir-usa.org/cases/columbia_v_clarke.html.

76. Linda Greenhouse, "Court Says States Need Not Finance Divinity Studies," *The New York Times*, 26 February 2004, A1, A20; http://traylight.law.cornell.edu/supct/html/02-1315.ZS.html; http://pewforum.org/school-vouchers/locke/; "Notes on Church-State Affairs," *Journal of Church and State* (summer 2003): 636–37, and August 2003, 851–53.

77. Kaplan and Lee, *Law of Higher Education*, 58–59, 728–30; Mawdsley, "Government Aid and Regulation," 21.

78. Interview with Dwight Jessup, 18 May 2004; interview with Robert Andringa, 29 September 2004; Gregory S. Baylor, "Christ-Centered Higher Education and the Law of Church and State," address to the Union University Board of Trustees meeting, 16 April 2004.

79. Fernand N. Dutile, "God and Gays at Georgetown," *Journal of College and University Law* (summer 1988): 1–2; Mawdsley, "Government Aid and Regulation," 21; Justice Souter, "Excerpts from Court Opinion Barring Homosexuals from Boston Parade," *The New York Times*, 20 June 1995, B6; http://www.firstamendmentcenter.org/faclibrary/casesummary.aspx?case-Hurley_v_Irish._American_Gay_Group; Linda Greenhouse, "Supreme Court Backs Boy Scouts in Ban of Gays from Membership," *The New York Times*, 29 June 2000, A1, A28; http://www.theinterim.com/2001/june/01trinitywestern.html.

80. Michael W. McConnell, "Academic Freedom in Religious Colleges and Uni-

versities," *Law and Contemporary Problems* (summer 1990): 303–24; George M. Marsden, "Liberating Academic Freedom," *First Things* (December 1998): 11–14; http://www.aaup.org/statements/Redbook/1940stat.htm; Anthony J. Diekema, *Academic Freedom and Christian Scholarship* (Grand Rapids, 2000), 23, 86.

81. Marsden, "Liberating Academic Freedom," 12; http://www.acenet.edu/AM/Template.cfm?section=statements_and_testimony; http://www.aaup.org/newsroom/Newsitems/JointStatementon%20AF.htm; interview with Dwight Jessup, 18 May 2004.

82. James D. Gordon III, "Individual and Institutional Freedom at Religious Colleges and Universities," *The Journal of College and University Law* 30, no. 1 (2003): 1–19.

83. See Marsden, "Liberating Academic Freedom," 11–14; George Marsden, "The Ambiguities of Academic Freedom," *Church History* (June 1993): 221–36; Nicholas Wolterstorff, "Academic Freedom in Religiously Based Colleges and Universities," in *Educating for Shalom: Essays on Christian Higher Education by Nicholas Wolterstorff*, ed. Clarence W. Joldersma and Gloria Goris Stronks (Grand Rapids, 2004), 241ff.; and Diekema, *Academic Freedom and Christian Scholarship*. Also note Barry L. Callen, "Faculty Academic Freedom in Member Institutions of the Christian College Coalition" (Ph.D. diss., Indiana University, 1983), and the academic freedom articles by Samuel Logan Sr., Eugene Habecker, and Edward Ericson in the December 1991 issue of *Christian Scholar's Review*.

84. Candace DeRussy, "Rule by Those of Little Faith," *The Chronicle of Higher Education*, 22 February 2002, B11–13; http://catholiceducation.org/articles/persecution/pch0061.html; David A. French, *Fire's Guide to Religious Liberty on Campus* (Philadelphia, 2002), 2; Diekema, *Academic Freedom and Christian Scholarship*, 16. Also see Alan Charles Kors and Harvey A. Silvergate, *The Shadow University: The Betrayal of Liberty on America's Campuses* (New York, 1998), and the many cases identified on the FIRE website.

85. *Engel v. Vitale* (1962), *Abington v. Schempp* (1963), and *Murray v. Curlett* (1963).

86. An objective summary of major Supreme Court decisions on religion appears on the Rutherford Institute website (http://www.rutherford.org/pdf/SupremeCourtReligionFinal.pdf).

Epilogue

1. Duane Litfin uses the phrase "the Voluntary Principle" to describe the orthodox-college effort to balance the individual professor's right of academic freedom and the college's right of institutional definition. See Litfin's *Conceiving the Christian College* (Grand Rapids, 2004), ch. 10.

2. Evangelical Protestantism focuses less upon defending specific branches of orthodoxy than was the case a generation ago. Also, while evangelicals still tend to associate the gospel with a specific political tradition too easily, this is less the case than is generally portrayed in the media and even less true of orthodox-college educators. For example, Robert Andringa estimates that in political identification the CCCU college professors are about evenly divided among Republicans, Democrats, and Independents. See Christian Smith, *Christian America? What Evangelicals Really Want* (Berkeley, 2000).

3. Bradley J. Longfield and George M. Marsden, "Presbyterian Colleges in

Twentieth Century America," in Coalter, Mulder, and Weeks, *Pluralistic Vision,* 113; Robert McAfee Brown, "The Reformed Tradition and Higher Education," *The Christian Scholar* (March 1958): 30–32.

4. See, for example, Richard John Neuhaus, "The Christian University: Eleven Theses," *First Things* (January 1996): 20–22; and Mark Schwehn, "A Christian University: Defining the Difference," *First Things* (May 1999): 25–29.

5. See Warren A. Nord, *Religion and Rethinking American Education: A National Dilemma* (Chapel Hill, NC, 1995).

6. http://www.ptev.org/school_contacts.aspx?iid=61.

7. Interview with Robert Andringa, 29 September 2004; Vedder, *Going Broke by Degree*; Hull, "Southern Baptist Higher Education Prospect," 4–9.

8. Litfin, *Conceiving the Christian College,* 246–50.

INDEX

303